THE STORY OF
OPERA

THE STORY OF
OPERA

RICHARD SOMERSET-WARD

FOREWORD BY KIRI TE KANAWA

HARRY N. ABRAMS, INC., PUBLISHERS

EDITOR: JAMES LEGGIO
DESIGNER: ANA ROGERS
PHOTO EDITOR: JOHN K. CROWLEY

LIBRARY OF CONGRESS CATALOGING-IN-PUBLICATION DATA

Somerset-Ward, Richard.
The story of opera / Richard Somerset-Ward ;
foreword by Kiri Te Kanawa.
p.   cm.
Includes bibliographical references and index.
ISBN 0—8109—4193—7 (clothbound)
I. Opera.   I. Title.
ML 1700.S7   1998

782.1'09—dc21   97-42488

Printed and bound in Japan

 Harry N. Abrams, Inc.
100 Fifth Avenue
New York, N.Y. 10011
www.abramsbooks.com

PAGE 1: *Gluck's* ARMIDE *at La Scala, Milan, 1996. Directed and designed by Pier Luigi Pizzi.
With Anna Caterina Antonacci in the title role.*

PAGES 2–3: *Puccini's* TURANDOT *at the Arena di Verona, 1988. Designed by Serge Creuz.*

PAGE 5: *Mozart's* LE NOZZE DI FIGARO *at the Glyndebourne Festival, 1997. Directed by Stephen Medcalf,
designed by John Gunter. Norah Amsellem as the Countess (disguised as Susanna in Act IV).*

PAGES 6–7: *Shostakovich's* THE LADY MACBETH OF MTSENSK *at the Metropolitan Opera, New York, 1994.
Directed by Graham Vick, designed by Paul Brown. With Vladimir Ognovenko as the Police Chief.*

CONTENTS

FOREWORD

At the end of Richard Strauss's opera *Capriccio*, alone on the stage and lit only by the light of the moon, the Countess has to make a decision: Which of her two suitors—the poet or the composer—will she accept? Together, they are writing an opera for her. Only she can decide how the opera will end. But she cannot make the decision—because she realizes that, in the creation of an opera, the words of the poet and the music of the composer must be bound together inextricably. To favor one over the other would be to trivialize the whole enterprise.

Yet every time I go on stage to sing that scene, I rejoice (very privately) in the knowledge that Strauss did know the answer to his conundrum. He knew that music was supreme—and he said so, eloquently and very beautifully, in the music he composed for the Countess. Words alone could not portray the intensity, or the conflict, of that moment.

Is that treason? I don't think so. Opera was invented in Florence four hundred years ago because some wise men wanted to increase the drama of the stage play, and they saw music as the way to do that: *il dramma per musica* they called it—drama expressed through music. It's what we've been doing ever since, experimenting with the idea that music is uniquely able to express the inner emotions, and, by doing so, to create drama more powerful and more revealing than words alone can.

It seems funny, after four centuries, to say that opera is still experimental, but that's what makes it so exciting and alive. Every time I arrive in an opera house to take part in a new production—no matter what continent it's on, no matter how old the opera is—I feel that excitement all over again. Singers, orchestra, conductor, director, designers—all of us have come together to create drama out of the raw materials we have been given. I freely admit that there are a few productions I would rather forget (and generally because the director has taken the "license to experiment" to mean that he or she can impose a load of personal obsessions or insecurities on the rest of us), but, for the most part, it has been a joyful experience, and one that I would not willingly swap for anything else.

It is also the reason why the story of opera—the history of this four-hundred-year experiment— is so important. Turning the pages of this book, you will read about many remarkable people, and many weird and wonderful happenings, but you will also discover, I think, why opera is, and always has been, such an exciting phenomenon. Its story is, in its own right, a wonderful and enthralling drama.

KIRI TE KANAWA

Opposite: *"First the music, then the words?" Or "First the words, then the music?" The Countess's dilemma in Richard Strauss's* Capriccio. *Kiri Te Kanawa as the Countess at the Metropolitan Opera, New York, 1998. Costume by Peter J. Hall.*

PREFACE

OPERA COMBINES MANY DIFFERENT ART FORMS—MUSIC AND DRAMA, ACTING and singing, design and stage direction. Take away any one of these components and the whole effect can be nullified, or at any rate diminished. It is a matter of argument as to which of them is paramount. Music and singing are clearly of the essence (otherwise it would not be opera), but drama is equally essential, and that is the element that has been missing for too much of opera's four-hundred-year history.

Only during the last fifty years has drama been given its rightful role as an equal of the music. We live, therefore, in the first truly great age of opera—the first era in which all the components are regularly brought together on the stage. That is not to say that we always like the results: as with any creative process, opera is frequently controversial and manifestly capable of failure. But any modern opera house worthy of the name can now be expected to put almost as much time, effort, and resources into the dramatic aspects of a production as it does into the purely musical.

This is indeed a very recent development. For the better part of three centuries the term *stage director* (or *régisseur*) was virtually unknown in opera. It came to be used quite commonly in the first half of the twentieth century, but then it generally meant a "house producer"—a resident director responsible for getting all the theater's productions on stage. Distinguished directors of individual productions, such as Max Reinhardt for the 1911 premiere of *Der Rosenkavalier,* were rare. The change dates from the years immediately following World War II, when Walter Felsenstein (in Berlin) and Wieland Wagner (at Bayreuth) became the first great stage directors to devote themselves almost exclusively to opera. Luchino Visconti, Giorgio Strehler, Franco Zeffirelli, and Peter Brook were their young contemporaries. Even more recently, in the last quarter of the century, stage directors have come to dominate the opera scene. We speak of "Chéreau's *Ring*" or "Jonathan Miller's *Rigoletto*" where, not so long ago, we defined productions by their conductors. We will argue forever about which aspect should have priority, music or drama, but at least there is a general recognition that the two must work together if a production is to succeed.

No one has been more greatly affected by this development than the singer. Extravagant waistlines and statuesque poses are no longer acceptable: the singer must be able to act, and to act as part of an ensemble. Ah! (says the critic), so that explains why we no longer have any really great singers! I do not think so. We *do* have great singers, but much more is required of them than ever was in the 1830s, or at the turn of the century, or in the 1950s (to take three of the greatest eras of singing). They must convince on stage (and very often on camera, too); they must meld into what are generally very subtle and complex productions; and, always, they must take part in the drama. It is no longer permissible just to sing.

Nor do audiences come just to listen. For most of three centuries, operagoers sat in lighted auditoriums and followed the action in roughly printed librettos or translations. When electric lighting arrived in the 1880s, with the consequence that house lights were lowered during a performance, this privilege was withdrawn. Those who failed to do their homework were doomed to sit, or doze, in ignorance. The arrival of supertitles in the 1980s restored the privilege. Whatever the shortcomings of supertitles, they once again enable audiences to become intimately involved in the drama. That is a very positive development, especially for the performers.

So is it true that they don't sing as well? Every generation tends to believe that the singers of its youth were vastly superior to those it hears in later years. Memory is not always a reliable agent—but CDs and videos enable us to make more objective judgments. To see Rosa Ponselle (on ancient film) in the "Habañera" from *Carmen* is to know that her reputation as one of the truly great singers of the century is justified: it is also to know that she was not a great actress. The same might be said of Renata Tebaldi, with Jussi Björling in a 1956 televised excerpt from *La bohème*. We cannot know what judgment we would make of singers before the age of recording—of Giovanni Battista Rubini or Giuditta Pasta or María Malibran—but I doubt if it would be much different. Maria Callas, on the other hand, in her mature years, was a remarkable actress: she was also prepared to sacrifice a little of the purity and beauty of her singing in the interest of greater drama. That, I am sure, is also true of Plácido Domingo's Otello, yet it does not in any way detract from that performance as one of the great operatic impersonations in recent history. On the contrary: it is one of the reasons why it is so great.

It is strange, and rather sad, that the vast majority of all the operas we see today were written for a different century and a different audience. Yet opera is more vital and healthy at the end of its fourth century than it has ever been before. Expensive, certainly; but elitist? The National Endowment for the Arts recently published figures showing that the number of eighteen-to-twenty-four-year-old operagoers in America increased by eighteen percent between 1982 and 1992.

Opera is a multimedia entertainment; its ingredients include myth and spectacle, message and music. It is an experience larger than life. And that may be why the twenty-first century will embrace it.

This book sets out to tell the story of the first four centuries of opera. It does so by concentrating on the personalities who created and shaped it. It does not pretend to original scholarship, and it is certainly not a musicological study. It hopes only to show how an entertainment thought up by some rather obscure "amateurs of the arts" in Florence in the 1590s has become an obsession, an industry, and (most important) a creative hothouse in the 1990s.

Opera was one of the delightful discoveries of my adult life, one that I plunged into in the early 1960s and from which I hope never to emerge. As a television executive and producer, I have had the good fortune to be involved with opera professionally for almost twenty years, but the idea of writing about it took more nerve than I would have had on my own. I have therefore relied heavily on the encouragement and advice of a number of wise friends, among whom Lena Tabori and Gene Fairly rank very high. It was they who took me in hand and marched me down Fifth Avenue to the places where publishers do their work, and it was Gene who happily delivered me to the door of Harry N. Abrams, Inc.

At Abrams, I have been indebted to two professionals: James Leggio, who edited the text with the necessary astringency and integrity; and John Crowley, who found, and cleared for reproduction, the book's illustrations, which have come from an astonishing number of unlikely sources.

At a very early stage, when the book was no more than a pipe dream, Harold Schonberg gave me much-needed advice, and Richard Hutton provided equally necessary encouragement. To them, and all the other friends and family members who have been so supportive, I am truly grateful. Whatever faults may remain in the book are entirely my own responsibility.

R. S.-W.

"Il dramma per musica"

Opera didn't just happen. Its evolution can be traced back to many different sources — literary, dramatic, and musical. But the story of how the first "operas" came into being is well documented and clear enough.

It happened in Italy four hundred years ago, and it was no coincidence that it happened in the last years of the Renaissance, at a time when Italian arts and literature were being revived and "reborn" under the influence of classical models. It was one such model — ancient Greek drama — that inspired the first operas. The idea caught on surprisingly quickly — partly because there was a ready-made route through the Renaissance courts of northern Italy, but mainly because it became a commercial success in less than fifty years.

Its inspiration was not primarily musical. It was conceived as a literary device, as a method of improving the performance of drama. Many

ABOVE: *Engraving by Epifano d'Alfiano for "The Descent of Rhythm and Harmony" in the sixth and final* intermedio.

RIGHT: *Jacopo Peri as Arion. Costume design by Bernardo Buontalenti. Well before he composed* DAFNE *and* EURIDICE, *the first "operas," Peri was famous as a virtuoso singer. For the 1589 intermedi, he composed and performed Arion's song* con gli echi *(with double echo), one of the great successes of the production.*

PRECEDING PAGES: *The Teatro Olimpico, Vicenza. The oldest opera theater still standing, it actually predates the earliest operas. It was designed by Andrea Palladio (completed by Vincenzo Scamozzi) and opened in 1585.*

of the early librettos were described as *dramma per musica* (drama expressed through music), and that is still the phrase that best describes the idea of opera.

The very first "opera" was performed in Florence in 1598. How and why it happened can best be explained by beginning the story a few years earlier, in 1589.

THE CAMERATA

In that year, Ferdinand de' Medici, grand duke of Tuscany, was married. He was not a very pleasant gentleman. Two years earlier, he had almost certainly poisoned his predecessor, who happened to be his older brother. Now he had to surrender his cardinal hat in order to get married. But marry he must—and marry well—if he was to strengthen

his position in the turbulent world of Italian politics. He found himself a worthy bride. She was a French princess, Christine of Lorraine, and the marriage once again united the Medici family of Florence with the powerful throne of France.

Because it was a dynastic marriage, and because it was essential that all the movers and shakers of Europe take note of it, the wedding celebrations of Ferdinand and Christine were of unparalleled magnificence. The Medici possessed ample means to achieve this. They had presided over the city of Florence for a hundred and fifty years, and the greatest of the Medici rulers—Cosimo the Elder and Lorenzo the Magnificent—had made Florence one of the workshops of the Renaissance. Leonardo da Vinci, Raphael, and Michelangelo had done some of their finest work in the city, and the Medici had paid for much of it. Ferdinand's wedding celebration lived up to expectations, not least because he was able to call on the services of a very talented group of poets, musicians, and artists who enjoyed his patronage. The most spectacular entertainment they devised were known as *intermedi*. As their name implied, *intermedi* took place "in the middle" of another entertainment—during a tournament perhaps, or a stage play, or sometimes just a feast. In 1589, the main event was a new play by Girolamo Bargagli—*La pellegrina* (The Pilgrim). It was in five acts, so a total of six *intermedi* were needed—one before the play and one after, with the other four, somewhat shorter, being given between acts.

The play was meant to be the chief attraction, but it was the *intermedi* that caused the sensation. Ferdinand was so pleased with them that he had them repeated several times during the following days, and he took the unusual step of having the music and texts published—which is why we know what they sounded like, and (more or less) what they looked like.

By any standard, they were magnificent. They were tableaux rather than dramas, each of them based on a mythological subject and telling its story in a static, rather leisurely fashion. But the music was full of wonderful things—catchy dances, big choral numbers, florid solos, and occasional pyrotechnics for virtuoso singers—all of them perfectly designed to hold the attention of an audience that was probably moving about and stretching after sitting through a long act of Bargagli's play. And if the music did not hold every member of the audience, then the spectacle certainly did. Bernardo Buontalenti, one of Florence's leading artists, had spent eight months creating costumes and scenery, and adapting the Uffizi Theater to house the astonishingly sophisticated battery of platforms, flying machines, ropes, and pulleys that enabled him to amaze the audience with storms, wrecks, dragons, and all manner of theatrical effects. Engravings of the sets have survived to tell the tale.

These *intermedi* were not opera. They lacked the dramatic content that would be opera's defining quality. But the men who created them—the poets, intellectuals, and musicians—were the very same men who were already in the process of articulating the idea of opera. They were members of a Florentine society that had been formed in 1569. It was called the Accademia degli Alterati and it existed for the "alteration," or improvement, of its members "through the cultivation of elegant speech, good conduct, and a knowledge of all the arts and sciences."[1] One of the arts that intrigued them was the performance of ancient Greek drama. They had read the recent works of Girolamo Mei, a classical scholar who lived in Rome, and they had taken note of his opinion (stated as fact) that the great Greek tragedies of antiquity had been written to be sung, not to be spoken.[2] This was the art form they sought to rediscover.

Their premise—that Greek drama had been sung—was probably only partly true. There had certainly been some musical content. The word *orchestra* is derived from a Greek expression denoting the semicircular space in front of the stage where the chorus danced and sang. But there was no real evidence that the tragedies had been entirely sung. Nevertheless, these Florentine gentlemen were discussing the subject as early as 1576 in a group (a sort of subgroup of the Alterati) presided over by Count Giovanni de' Bardi. Bardi was a well-known patron of music and the arts, and acted as superintendent of court entertainments at Florence. But it was in 1592 that the discussions took a more practical turn. In that year, Count Bardi moved to Rome. In his absence, the meetings took place at the home of Jacopo Corsi. Corsi was a wealthy merchant with interests in wool, silk, and banking, but he was also a good musician—a harpsichordist and a composer. His colleagues included the best musicians in Florence—Jacopo Peri and Giulio Caccini, as well as the best-known poet, Ottavio Rinuccini. A club

or society such as Bardi's original group or Corsi's later one (there was a considerable overlap in membership) was known as a *camerata*—from the word *camera*, meaning a chamber or private room, which was presumably where they met.[3]

What these Florentine men were chiefly concerned about was drama. They wanted to make use of music, and thus to create *dramma per musica*, because they believed that, however good the text and however good the acting, the straightforward recitation of words was incapable, by itself, of rendering the emotions of great drama. But they had a problem. The prevailing style of music at the end of the sixteenth century was polyphonic—music of "many sounds" in which several simultaneous melodies were blended to produce an overall effect, as in madrigals (or, very often, in *intermedi*). It was a style that had been supreme in Italy since the thirteenth century, but its days were almost over. Two of its greatest masters, Giovanni Palestrina and the Flemish composer Roland de Lassus, died in 1594. In any case, it was not the solution for which the *camerata* members were looking. They wanted something much simpler, something that would complement and underline the words, not overwhelm them. Writing more than thirty years later, Count Bardi's son, Pietro, stated categorically that his father and his friends had been motivated by the "wretched state" of modern music.[4] (How many more people, in different countries and different contexts, would make that same complaint during the next four hundred years!)

The man who is generally credited with solving the problem was Vincenzo Galilei. He was a music theorist and a composer for the lute, but he was also the *camerata* member most familiar with Greek and Latin music, and with Girolamo Mei's researches on the subject. It was Galilei, according to Pietro de' Bardi, who first articulated the new style of music with which opera was launched.[5] This was monodic, rather than polyphonic, music. It was just a single line—a series of notes to which the actor-singer declaimed the text, with improvised accompaniment consisting of no more than occasional chords on a harpsichord or a lute. In a word, it was recitative—a "reciting line" designed to give the words extra impact and greater drama.

Galilei did not live to see the first "opera." He died in 1591 (by which time his son, Galileo Galilei, was already on his way to becoming the greatest astronomer of the day). But Vincenzo

Galilei's ideas were not lost on his colleagues, and when Jacopo Peri set *Dafne*, a dramatic poem by Ottavio Rinuccini, the musical convention he used was recitative. What he was attempting, he wrote, was "a kind of music more advanced than ordinary speech but less than the melody of singing, thus taking a middle position between the two."[6]

Dafne, which was the first "opera," was performed in Jacopo Corsi's house in Florence in February 1598. Afterward, the librettist, Rinuccini, wondered why it had taken so many hundreds of years to revive the glories of ancient Greek drama:

> I used to believe that this was due to the imperfections of modern music, by far inferior to the ancient. But the opinion thus formed was wholly driven from my mind by . . . Jacopo Peri, who . . . set to music with so much grace the fable of *Dafne* (which I had written solely to make a simple test of what the music of our age could do) that it gave pleasure beyond belief to the few who heard it.[7]

Very little of the music of *Dafne* has survived, but it seems safe to say that several hours of recitative, occasionally punctuated by a song or a chorus, must have been hard going. Nevertheless, news of the experiment quickly got around intellectual circles in Italy, and when the Medici staged their next big wedding celebration, in 1600, the *camerata* was able to use it as a showcase for its latest offering. The wedding was the biggest yet. Maria de' Medici was marrying no less a personage than the king of France himself, Henri IV. Ottavio Rinuccini wrote a brand-new libretto, *Euridice*, and both Peri and Caccini provided settings for it. Peri's was performed at the wedding. He sang the role of Orpheus himself, distinguished, as always, by his long golden hair, which was responsible for his popular nickname, "Il Zazzerino" (the long-haired one). But *Euridice* was, at best, a qualified success. The next time the Medici staged a wedding, in 1608, they commissioned *intermedi* rather than an "opera."

Nevertheless, the 1600 performance of *Euridice* had one very important consequence. In the audience was the ruler of Mantua, Duke Vincenzo Gonzaga, and it is likely, though we do not

know for certain, that he was accompanied by the most promising musician on his payroll at Mantua: Claudio Monteverdi.

For all their pioneering spirit, the members of the *camerata* did not have the talent to translate their ideas into a popular art form. It took the genius of Monteverdi to do that. Nevertheless, Count Bardi, Jacopo Corsi, and their colleagues had laid the groundwork for what became a four-hundred-year odyssey—a never-ending search for ways and means of creating *dramma per musica*. Within forty years, it had become an art form in its own right, and had acquired a name that became universal: *opera in musica*, quickly shortened to *opera*.

But the original description, *il dramma per musica*, was always a better definition, because what made opera unique, and gave it its peculiar quality, was the tension it generated between words and music, on the one hand, and between music and dramatic values, on the other. The story of opera is the story of how, in the course of four centuries, creative people in many countries have taken the *camerata*'s original idea and developed it in many different directions in order to produce their own variations of *dramma per musica*. Composers, singers, and conductors; poets, dramatists, and librettists; stage directors, designers, and impresarios; and audiences, too—all of them have played a vital part.

Could they see it in retrospect, those Florentine gentlemen of the *camerata* would find it very hard to connect their original "invention" with some (indeed, most) of the things that have since transpired. They did not anticipate the use of an orchestra—and certainly not the hundred-strong orchestras of Wagnerian opera. They always gave primacy to the words: they would be deeply shocked by the carefree way in which so many of their successors have allowed the words to be drowned out. They believed that the addition of music was simply a way of emphasizing the drama: they would be amazed (but not necessarily horrified) if they could see how much of opera's drama is actually created by, and carried in, the music.

The basic idea of *dramma per musica*, the combination of words and music to produce drama, is intrinsically powerful. It enables artists from different disciplines to combine their talents to create a uniquely powerful form of drama, one that is capable of affecting audiences at many dif-

ferent levels simultaneously—musically, poetically, emotionally, dramatically. At its best, when all these elements come together in a creative whole, opera is capable of being the supreme dramatic art form, the one that is peculiarly able to move the spirit and to touch the soul.

MONTEVERDI

Several members of the Florentine *camerata* lived to see the beginnings of this dream come true. In February 1607, they traveled to Mantua for the premiere of Monteverdi's first opera, *La favola d'Orfeo* (The Legend of Orpheus). The first thing they heard—the great trumpet toccata with which Monteverdi began the opera—must have startled them, and deeply impressed them. It announced a score for thirty-eight instruments, chorus, ballet, and eleven principal singers led by the tenor Francesco Rasi in the title role. The Prologue and two female parts were taken by *castrati*. It was a far cry from Peri's *Dafne* and *Euridice* of just a few years previously. It was also the moment when opera became a composer's medium.

The members of the *camerata* were not entirely unprepared for this development. They had had their own arguments about the role of music in *dramma per musica*, and one of them, Giulio Caccini, had already moved some distance from the original idea of an austere recitative by adding ornaments and trills to show off the singers' voices. Caccini was doubtless motivated by the fact that his two daughters, Francesca and Settimia, were among the leading singers of Florence. But Monteverdi had now taken the role of the music, and therefore of the composer, a giant step forward.

Claudio Monteverdi was nearly forty years old when he wrote *Orfeo*. A supremely gifted musician from Cremona (a century before the Stradivari and Guarneri families made the town famous for the manufacture of violins and stringed instruments), Monteverdi published a set of madrigals when he was fifteen. In his early twenties, he found employment as a musician at the Gonzaga court in Mantua, rising eventually, but not without difficulty, to become *maestro di cappella*, the official in charge of all musical activities at the court. He was a popular and well-known composer of both sacred and secular music. His fifth book of madrigals was a phenomenal bestseller in 1605. To the Gonzaga family, however, he was just a musician. In the custom of the time, he was therefore treated as a servant.

The Gonzagas, like the Medici of Florence, were one of the great princely families of Italy, but less established than the Medici and consequently more ambitious. The duke who employed Monteverdi, Vincenzo Gonzaga, sought to ingratiate himself in the complex European balance of power by marching his small army from one side of the continent to the other—from Hungary in the east to Flanders in the west—to assist whatever causes he thought might win him powerful allies. Because he was genuinely a lover and patron of music, he sometimes took his *maestro di cappella* with him on these martial expeditions. Back home, the Gonzaga court, where Peter Paul Rubens was one of the painters in Monteverdi's time, was generally admired for its magnificence and its cultural sophistication. Not least, it was admired for its *maestro di cappella*. The duke showed his gratitude by paying Monteverdi a pittance, and frequently forgetting to pay it on time.

Florence and Mantua were about a hundred and fifty miles apart. The artistic elements of the two courts kept in touch with each other, and Monteverdi, whether or not he attended the 1600 performance of *Euridice* with Duke Vincenzo, was certainly well informed about developments in Florence. One of the people who kept him in touch was Alessandro Striggio the Younger. He was chancellor of the Mantuan court, and therefore Monteverdi's immediate employer. Striggio came from Florence. He had played an instrument in the 1589 *intermedi* alongside his better-known

Claudio Monteverdi (1567–1643). Portrait on the title page of Giovan Battista Marinoni's FIORI POETICI, *published in Venice in 1644 to commemorate the composer's death the previous year. The musical instruments are all ones for which Monteverdi composed.*

The hall of the Palazzo Ducale, Mantua, where Monteverdi served the Gonzaga family, and where ORFEO *was first performed. This maquette, which can be seen at the Musée de la Musique in La Villette, Paris, shows how the hall would have looked when lit for an evening performance in Monteverdi's time. The palace had been partly designed by Raphael's chief assistant, Giulio Romano, about 1531. Most of it survived the siege and fire of 1630.*

father, and he had certainly been present at the 1600 performance of *Euridice* in Florence. Now he was Monteverdi's librettist for *Orfeo*.

There is no doubt that Monteverdi used the Florentine blueprint as his model, but he developed it beyond recognition. He made use of recitative in *Orfeo*, but only in moderation. He was the greatest madrigalist of the age, a composer of beautiful and intricate choral music, and a considerable expert on dance music. All this was evident in *Orfeo*, as was his mastery of what was for those times a large orchestra, and a wind band besides. There was nothing we would recognize as an "aria," but there was much that was tuneful. It clearly delighted its audience. Unfortunately, no firsthand description of the production has survived, so we cannot know what it looked like. But the score and libretto were both printed, and *Orfeo* remains the oldest opera still regularly in production.

Monteverdi's greatest ally in getting *Orfeo* produced at the Mantuan court was the duke's son, Francesco, and the following year, 1608, Monteverdi was commissioned to write another opera, this time to celebrate Francesco's wedding. Once again, the librettist was a Florentine, Ottavio

Rinuccini. The new work, *Arianna*, was an even greater success than *Orfeo*, but, for Monteverdi himself, it was surrounded by tragedy. First, he had to write it in the immediate aftermath of the death of his young wife, whom he clearly adored. Then, only days before the premiere, twenty-year-old Caterina Martinelli, who had lived with the Monteverdis for seven years, and who was to have created the title role, died in a smallpox outbreak and had to be replaced by Virginia Ramponi.

Only one piece of music survives: "Arianna's Lament." It was the first "hit tune" in opera, touchingly performed by Signora Ramponi. "No one hearing it was left unmoved," wrote the court archivist, "nor among the ladies was there one who did not shed a few tears at [Arianna's] plaint."[8] For Monteverdi, it must have been one of the most truly heartfelt pieces of music he ever wrote.

Arianna was the centerpiece of Prince Francesco's wedding celebration, but it was only a part of it. In the course of eight days between May 28 and June 5 in that summer of 1608, the Mantuan court staged five musical-dramatic works, all of them specially commissioned, all of them premieres. It was probably the first "opera festival" ever held—and one that would tax the resources of any modern festival. As *maestro di cappella*, and regardless of whatever personal problems he might have had, Monteverdi was responsible for all the music—its rehearsal and performance, as well as much of its composition. In addition to *Arianna*, he wrote music for a play by Giovanni Battista Guarini, and he composed an opera-ballet to a text by Rinuccini (it was called *Il ballo della ingrate*—The Prudes' Ball, as it might loosely be translated). The other major composer on display was Marco da Gagliano. He was a Florentine, but too young to have been a member of the *camerata*. Nevertheless, by 1608, at the age of twenty-six, he was one of the foremost practitioners of the *stile rappresentativo* (the new device of recitative developed by the *camerata*), and the setting of *Dafne* that he created for the Mantuan festival was much admired by Peri. It was important for another reason: Gagliano wrote a preface to the score in which he advised singers (and directors, had they existed) on how best to perform the work. It was, in fact, a production manual—the earliest one to survive in the history of opera, and probably the first to have been written in such detail before *livrets de mise-en-scène* were compiled for the Paris Opéra in the 1840s. Already, a century and a half before Gluck, Gagliano was advocating dramatic reality as being more important than the showing off of a singer's voice.

As for Monteverdi, he was left with two young sons to bring up, and an inadequate and often unpaid salary. He was a proud man, reduced to writing begging letters to his employer. But when Duke Vincenzo died in 1612 and was succeeded by his son Francesco, patron of *Orfeo* and *Arianna*, it seemed that Monteverdi would finally get the recognition he deserved. Instead, within weeks, he was dismissed. With his two sons and all his worldly possessions, he went wearily home to Cremona.

Three decades later, in the last year of his life, Monteverdi returned to Mantua—whether out of nostalgia or bitterness is not known. He found much of the city in ruins, and the rest of it still recovering from the ravages of the imperial troops who had sacked the city in 1630 after Francesco and his brother had failed to provide a male heir to ensure the Gonzaga succession. Somewhere amid the rubble (Monteverdi must have known) were the remnants of twenty years of his life—the unpublished manuscripts of much of the music he had written for the ungrateful Gonzagas, reduced to ashes and lost to posterity.

Luckily for us, however, Monteverdi's parting with the Gonzagas turned out to be a godsend. In 1613, within months of being dismissed by Duke Franscesco, he was selected to fill the most important and influential post in Italian music—*maestro di cappella* at San Marco in Venice. That was where he spent the last thirty years of his life. But it was not until 1640, when he was seventy-three years old, that he once again became passionately involved in opera.

FLORENCE AND ROME
In the meantime, news of the *camerata*'s experiments in Florence, and of Monteverdi's spectacular demonstrations in Mantua, had spread through northern Italy. The intellectual ferment of the Renaissance was still alive, if somewhat muted, and wealthy patrons were keen to show their neighbors that they were on the cutting edge. But none of them could boast a composer like Monteverdi. Moreover, court entertainments were meant to glorify the princes, dukes, and noblemen who were their patrons: *il dramma per musica* was not the ideal medium for this, and certainly not as effective as *intermedi*. So the experience of "opera" in the first forty years of the seventeenth century was at best erratic. Court extravaganzas in places like Parma, Padua, Turin, and Ferrara were as sumptuous as ever, and several cities without courts (Bologna was the most important) joined in by commissioning works that were undoubtedly inspired by events in Florence and Mantua. Examples of recitative began to appear in pageants and *intermedi* and semidramatic musical works. But there were only two cities—Florence and Rome —where the experiment with *dramma per musica* was generally sustained.

In Florence it continued to depend on the Medici. Their power and prestige meant that they did a lot of entertaining, but large-scale musical-dramatic works were commissioned only for major state occasions. One such occasion was in 1625. The prince of Poland was the visitor, and one of the productions with which the Medici entertained him was an opera-ballet called *La liberazione di Ruggerio dall'isola d'Alcina*. The composer was Francesca Caccini—the same Francesca for whom her father, Giulio, had written the trills and ornaments that had so annoyed some of his colleagues in the *camerata*. It is thought to be the first opera written by a woman.

Not even Florence, however, could match Rome's enthusiasm for *dramma per musica*. In this, as in so much else, Rome owed its primacy to the Church. It began its love affair with the new art form in earnest in 1623, when a member of the powerful Barberini family was elected as Pope Urban VIII. The Barberini established their ascendancy in a number of very visible ways, with grand new buildings and opulent entertainments, and none more so than the 1632 inauguration of the Great Hall of the Palazzo Barberini. It was probably for that occasion that Stefano Landi composed a *dramma per musica* on the suitably sacred subject of Alexis, a fifth-century saint. A description of the stunning production has been pieced together by the modern critic and scholar Rodolfo Celletti:

> The designs for *Sant'Alessio* included forests, gardens, scenes of Hell, angels who flew while singing and an immense great cloud that opened at the finale to reveal the splendors of Paradise. It was a triumph of both theatrical mechanics and lighting. Illumination was provided by wax and tallow candles and movable oil lamps; smoke was drawn off by ventilation holes onstage. Lighting depended largely on reflecting materials used in the scenery. These included mirrors, pieces of glass and metal and phosphorescent powders.[9]

CLEMENS IX, Iulius Rospigliosius.
Piſtoriens. creat'die 20.Iunij an.1667.
Sedit an 2.mens.5. dies 20.Ob. die 9.
Decemb. an.1669. Vac.Sed.mens 4.d20

Giulio Rospigliosi (1600–1669), one of opera's early librettists, subsequently became Pope Clement IX (1667–69).

Landi's librettist for *Sant'Alessio* was a young priest called Giulio Rospigliosi. History knows him as Pope Clement IX, but his progress to the Throne of Peter was marked by singular contributions to the development of opera—not least the introduction of comic characters to lighten the mood from time to time. This must have provided welcome relief, most notably in Rospigliosi's own librettos, which erred on the side of length. His 1642 opera *Il palazzo incantato*, written with the composer Luigi Rossi, was reputed to have a running time of seven hours. Nevertheless, Rospigliosi saw the potential of *dramma per musica* earlier than most. He peopled his plots with large numbers of characters, many of them with their own subplots, and it was he, a leading churchman, who led the way toward more secular subject matter and less dependence on mythology. A composer of Monteverdi's genius might have turned them into great opera. As it was, Rospigliosi's texts were generally set to fast-paced recitative, occasionally interrupted by a chorus, and even more occasionally by a melody for a solo voice.

Roman opera had one other notable peculiarity. It was generally a male affair. In deference to the Vatican, women were strongly discouraged from appearing on the stage, so female parts, as well as the customary male leads, were normally sung by *castrati*.

Venice had no such inhibitions. The city in which Claudio Monteverdi lived the last three decades of his life was unique. Nowhere else could opera so quickly have escaped the elitism of court patronage and become a public phenomenon.

VENICE

Venice was known as "La Serenissima"—the Most Serene Republic. Its serenity derived not so much from its fabled beauty as from the stability of its government. It was not a princely state dominated by a single family; it was a republic—a constitutional oligarchy in which the wealthy, the aristocratic, and the commercial classes all had a stake. Its character was essentially cosmopolitan, for it was the center of a great commercial empire. It stood at the crossroads of the world, a meeting point for East and West. In the previous century it had extended its influence aggressively, conquering parts of Turkey, Greece, and the Greek islands, including Crete. Not for nothing had its ruler, the doge, traditionally taken the title "Lord of a Quarter and Half a Quarter of the Roman

Empire." The popular myth about Venice was that it was, indeed, the "new Rome," and it was no coincidence that many of the operas written in seventeenth-century Venice (including some of Monteverdi's contributions) were designed to bolster that myth.

By 1600 Venice was at the height of its commercial prosperity, and famously independent. It began the new century by getting itself excommunicated by the Roman Catholic Church for, among other things, banning the Jesuits from operating within its territories. It was the Vatican, not Venice, that eventually backed down. As the century progressed, with much of Europe submerged in the Thirty Years' War, Venice reveled in its freedom and stability. There was a succession of wars against the Ottoman Empire, and there were disasters on the home front, too: in 1630, almost fifty thousand people, a third of the population, died in a plague. But it was also a time when La Serenissima flourished as a center for the performing arts and when opera became a public entertainment.

Monteverdi was *maestro di cappella* at San Marco from 1613 until his death in 1643. He composed a stream of innovative madrigals and a huge corpus of sacred music, but he also received occasional commissions from Parma and Mantua for dramatic works, so he never ceased to experiment

with *dramma per musica*. Aside from a "dramatic cantata" of 1624, *Il combattimento di Tancredi e Clorinda*, most of the stage works he wrote in Venice prior to 1637 have been lost. We know about them through his correspondence with the librettists—letters that reveal him as a dramatist as well as a musician, a man whose attitude to the creation of opera was almost as obsessive as Verdi's, Wagner's, and Richard Strauss's in later generations. Among Monteverdi's lost manuscripts of this period is one that was almost certainly the first comic opera, *La finta pazza Licori* (Licori, Who Feigned Madness) (1627).

Until 1637, despite Monteverdi's presence, opera in Venice was not much more than an occasional pastime staged in private theaters and the homes of the wealthy. Two things combined to change it. One was the ever-increasing success of Venice's annual Carnival season—the six- to eight-week period immediately preceding Lent. By the seventeenth century, Carnival in Venice was one of the great tourist attractions of Europe—a night-after-night display of masquerades, fireworks, bull runs, dances, and theatrical performances. For those few weeks each year the population of the city was more or less doubled, and in Venice, where the Jesuits had no standing, the dampening influence of the Church was not much in evidence.

VIEW OF THE PIAZZA SAN MARCO, VENICE, *painting by Josef Heintz the Younger, mid-seventeenth century. On the left, a music drama of some sort is taking place on the open-air stage; on the right, commedia dell'arte performers are apparently preparing for a performance; in the center of the piazza, a bullbaiting game appears to have gone spectacularly wrong.*

The second factor was the spirit of commerce that drove Venice. No one had a greater interest in this than the patrician families—the Tron, the Grimani, the Contarini, the Vendramin, and many other illustrious names. They applied to Carnival the same principles they applied to their commercial activities: they invested money in order to make money. It was the Tron family who made the first sizeable investment in opera. They owned the Teatro San Cassiano and used it for the staging of private performances commissioned by members of the family. But in the 1630s, having rebuilt the theater after a fire, the Tron decided to take advantage of Carnival by transforming it into a public place of entertainment on a strictly commercial basis. In 1637, they leased it to two traveling musicians from Rome, Benedetto Ferarri and Francesco Manelli. Entirely dependent on box office, Ferrari and Manelli put together a company (it included Manelli's wife and son) and presented a season of opera for the public—for Venetians, tourists, and anyone who would buy a ticket. They quickly discovered that they could sell a great many tickets.

San Cassiano, which is reputed to have had a capacity greater than that of the modern Metropolitan Opera House in New York,[10] thus became the first public opera house in the world. It began with performances of *Andromeda* (score by Manelli, libretto by Ferrari; with Manelli, who was also a famous bass, singing two of the leading roles). And it clearly succeeded, because within a very short time, public opera houses were springing up all over Venice. The statistics alone were extraordinary. By the end of the century, there were sixteen or seventeen parish theaters doing business, of which nine were opera houses. It was estimated that 385 different operas were given in the city during the course of the century, most of them between 1640 and 1680. Precious few have survived, and it is one of the tragedies of opera that this first flowering of the art form was wiped from memory in an incredibly short time. Neither Mozart nor Beethoven had ever heard of Claudio Monteverdi. It would take twentieth-century scholarship to resurrect his reputation and the reputations of a few—a very few—of his contemporaries. Yet in their own time, these men did something few opera people have ever succeeded in doing: they made money for their backers.

Even more important, perhaps, they brought Monteverdi back into the field. He was in his seventies by this time, the greatly venerated *maestro di cappella* of San Marco, and, since 1632, a priest as well. He saw what Manelli and Ferrari were doing at the San Cassiano, and in 1640 he was prevailed upon to revive *Arianna* for the opening of another public opera house, the Teatro San Moisè. Then, in the last three years of his life, he wrote three completely new works. Two of them were based on mythical stories of the Trojan War—always good for boosting the idea of Venice as the "new Rome" (had not Troy given birth to Rome?); *Il ritorno d'Ulisse in patria* (The Return of Ulysses to His Country) has survived in various forms; the other, *Le nozze d'Enea e Lavinia* (The Marriage of Aeneas and Lavinia), has disappeared. But it was the third work, *L'incoronazione di Poppea* (The Coronation of Poppea), that turned the nascent world of opera upside down and set a standard for posterity—even though, for almost three hundred years, it remained a secret from posterity.

Poppea was the first great operatic masterpiece. Musically and dramatically, it occupied a different world from the one the *camerata* had outlined less than fifty years before. Its subject matter alone would have horrified them. It was not about mythical characters; it was about actual historical figures—the Emperor Nero (written for *castrato*) and his wife Poppea. Above all, it was about the triumph of evil. Poppea schemes her way from Nero's bed to the imperial throne itself, causing any number of innocents to be killed along the way. And Nero (that same Nero who murdered his mother) shares the final triumphal scene of the opera with Poppea at her coronation. The fact that these two historical characters eventually got their comeuppance may have been known to the audience, but it has no part in the opera. "Pur ti miro" (I behold thee) they sing to each other in the ecstatic duet that ends the work. It was deeply offensive—and tremendously effective.

Monteverdi's collaborator in *Poppea* was the librettist Gian Francesco Busenello. He was a lawyer and a former Venetian ambassador to the court of Mantua—a man who lived and breathed real-life politics. He provided Monteverdi with what was certainly the most powerful and credible text yet devised for *dramma per musica*. But it would have been nothing without Monteverdi's genius for dramatic composition. *Poppea* was written for much smaller forces than *Orfeo* had been thirty-five years earlier. The public theaters of Venice did not possess the resources available to

the wealthy court of Mantua. Orchestras normally consisted of no more than a nucleus of stringed instruments, with the possibility of adding trumpets, recorders, and drums when necessary. But that was all Monteverdi needed to dramatize Busenello's text through music. It was *dramma per musica* for real—certainly the best example of it written in the seventeenth century, and arguably the best example before the time of Gluck and Mozart.

Monteverdi died in 1643, just over a year after the first performance of *Poppea*. For the next thirty years, Venetian opera was dominated by Pier Francesco Cavalli. As a boy he had sung in the choir of San Marco under Monteverdi, and eventually, in 1668, he would himself become *maestro di cappella* there. He wrote no fewer than forty operas, and there can be no doubt that his immediate influence (as opposed to Monteverdi's much longer-term, and more distant, influence) was greater than that of anyone else in the seventeenth century. His operas dominated the public theaters of Venice between 1640 and 1670; they were often used to introduce the art form to other Italian cities (such as Naples); and they eventually spearheaded the export of opera to other countries, most notably France.

Cavalli had no shortage of talented collaborators. He wrote three operas with Busenello, the librettist of *Poppea*, and nine with the outstanding young poet Giovanni Faustini (whose death at the age of thirty-one was a major setback). Many of their subjects were mythological, and fairly repetitive, but Cavalli was not afraid, on occasion, to follow Monteverdi's example by tackling real historical situations—*Xerse* and *Scipione Affricano* were two of his greatest successes. Cavalli may not have had Monteverdi's skill as a musical dramatist, but he possessed a facility for melody that clearly pleased his audiences. By the late 1660s, however, as singers and audiences began to demand the inclusion of more and more arias, he faltered. It was a taste to which he was unwilling to cater (though he was very capable of it—Xerxes' great aria "Ombra mai fu" was as fine an example as any written in the seventeenth century). Cavalli eventually suffered the indignity of having two of his last three operas rejected by theater managements

Monteverdi's L'INCORONAZIONE DI POPPEA *at the Glyndebourne Festival, 1984. Directed by Peter Hall, designed by John Bury. With Maria Ewing as Poppea.*

Cavalli's L'Ormindo *at the Glynde-bourne Festival, 1967. Directed by Günther Rennert, designed by Erich Kondrak. With Anne Howells as Erisbe and John Wakefield as Ormindo.*

because they lacked the showstopping set pieces that now became the sine qua non of opera.

Other composers had come and gone. Francesco Sacrati was one. In a much shorter career (he died in 1650, aged only forty-five) Sacrati developed one facet of opera in particular—the insertion of comic characters with scenes of their own. Monteverdi did it in *Il ritorno d'Ulisse* and in *Poppea*, and the librettos of the future pope, Rospigliosi, did it in Rome, but Sacrati used comedy to even greater effect. His opera *La finta pazza* (The One Who Feigned Madness), written in 1641, was probably the most popular work ever staged in seventeenth-century Venice. It was an antecedent of what, in the next century, would become *opera buffa*—a speciality of Naples.

Pietro Antonio Cesti was another Venetian contemporary of Cavalli—and another with an abbreviated career. He died in 1669, aged forty-six, but not before he had become one of the first ambassadors of opera, when he was appointed *maestro di cappella* to the Archduke Ferdinand of Austria.

It is impossible to make judgments about these early Venetian operas because so little remains of them. Librettos were published almost as a matter of course, but music scores were not. Cavalli, apparently anxious to be known to posterity, had most of his operas hand-copied, and they became part of the collection of 113 opera scores put together by Marco Contarini, one of the principal patrons of opera in Venice. Monteverdi's *Poppea* was part of that collection—in a version that appears to have been written out by Maria Cavalli (she was her husband's chief copyist until her death in 1652), with annotations in the hand of Cavalli himself. Parts of this score are not by Monteverdi—the prologues, for instance, were evidently added by Cavalli, and there is even doubt about the authorship of the final duet: some attribute it to Cavalli, others to Sacrati; it may even have been written by Monteverdi himself.

At all events, none of these surviving scores

Design by Giacomo Torelli for Act I of Sacrati's La finta pazza, *Paris, c. 1645. Within a few years of its Venetian premiere in 1641,* La finta pazza *was being performed in towns throughout northern Italy. It was Cardinal Mazarin who commissioned the Paris production of 1645 and brought Torelli to France to design sets and stage effects more spectacular than those that could be afforded by Venice's commercial theaters. French reaction was, at best, mixed.*

give much idea of what the composers intended, or what Venetian audiences actually heard. They are, at best, skeletons, rarely indicating what instruments should play what lines, and often with very incomplete vocal parts. The versions performed today are mostly reconstructions by music scholars.

The sparseness of the vocal scoring was a constant invitation to singers to make their own contributions. As early as 1600, Jacopo Peri had praised Vittoria Archilei, who sang the title role in *Euridice,* for her ornamentation of his score ("those charms and graces that cannot be notated and, if notated, cannot be deciphered"[11]). Ornamentation of a Peri score was desirable, one might even say necessary, but the sort of liberties singers were taking half a century later were altogether more questionable, and one must assume that that was at least one reason why Cavalli was so loath to cater to them.

The power of the singers was a direct result of opera's dependence on the box office. It was not long before the more popular singers (or those who thought themselves more popular) began giving instructions to composers. Parts had to be rewritten for them, preferably with set-piece vocal solos—a lament, a love song, a mad scene. Mad scenes were particularly esteemed. As early as 1643, Cavalli and his librettist, Giovanni Faustini, were forced to add a mad scene to *Egisto* in order to keep the leading singer happy.[12] It quickly became the most successful scene in the opera.

Gradually, the role of recitative was lessened, and more of the emotional content was expressed in structured arias, which gave singers the opportunity to show off their talent. And when singers felt a composer was not doing justice to their talents, they increasingly felt free to interpolate their own decorations, ornamentations, trills—even whole passages from other operas by other composers. The age of the prima donna (and the primo uomo, too) was just beginning.

No one understood the importance of singers better than the theater managers. They measured it by ticket sales at the box office, and there was little they would not do to keep popular singers happy. In 1658, Signora Girolama, appearing in an opera by Cavalli, Venice's highest-paid composer, received twice Cavalli's fee. Eleven years later, Signora Masotti was being paid six times the composer's fee and was clearly enjoying the adulation of her audiences.[13] A French diplomat, Saint-Disdier, reported that such adulation often took the form of curtain calls in which the prima donna was showered with poems written in her honor. "The partisans of these admirable singers have quantities of sonnets printed in their honor, and . . . shower thousands of them from the heights of Paradise, filling the loges and parterre."[14] And it was not only female singers who could command such treatment. In 1665 Antonio Cavagna, a famous male soprano, or *castrato,* who clearly felt secure in his audiences' affections, wrote to the impresario Marco Faustini. He complained about an aria that had been written for him: "Unless you get him [the composer] to write new music for it I won't sing it at all."[15]

Twenty-five years earlier, the issuing of such an ultimatum would not have occurred to a singer. Certainly, from all the surviving descriptions of her, it would not have occurred to Anna Renzi,

Intima si cantum simulat præcordia mulcet,
Ipsam animam sensim si canit Anna rapit.
Iacobus Ploinus Venetus incidebat Veni.

Anna Renzi (c. 1620—after 1660), the first diva of Italian opera. Already well established in Rome, she was only twenty-one when she was brought to Venice by Francesco Sacrati to create the role of Deidamia in LA FINTA PAZZA, *and thus became the protagonist of the first great mad scene in opera. A virtuoso singer and a fine actress, she had stamina, too: "It has befallen her to have to bear the full weight of an opera no fewer than twenty-six times, repeating it virtually every evening, without losing even a single carat of her theatrical and most perfect voice." So wrote Giulio Strozzi in his introduction to* LE GLORIE DELLA SIGNORA ANNA RENZI ROMANA, *from which this portrait is reproduced.*

who was probably the outstanding female singer in the first years of public opera. Sacrati brought her to Venice from Rome in 1640 to sing in one of his productions, and Monteverdi thought so highly of her that he wrote the role of Ottavia for her in *Poppea.* She certainly had a fine voice, but it was her acting, and the dramatic intensity she was able to sustain throughout a performance, that endeared her to composers, librettists, and audiences. Few singers have ever had a better press than Renzi had in Venice—much of it preserved in a magnificent volume produced by her admirers and entitled *Le glorie della signora Anna Renzi romana* (she was still only twenty-one at the time of publication).

In a system dependent on box office, star singers were obviously important. But so was the spectacle of opera—the magnificence of its productions. Visitors arriving in Venice for Carnival tended to make a beeline for the opera (it was still a genuine novelty) and then to report at length to their diaries. One such was the Englishman John Evelyn. He arrived in Venice for Carnival in 1645 and saw an opera called *Ercole in Lidia* (Hercules in Lydia) by Giovanni Rovetta. It was the sets and costumes that impressed him:

> [a] variety of scenes painted and contrived with no less art of perspective, and machines for flying in the air, and other wonderful motions: taken together, it is one of the most magnificent and expensive diversions the wit of man can expect.... The scene changed thirteen times. This held us by the eyes and the ears until two o'clock in the morning.[16]

The most famous set designer in Venice was Giacomo Torelli. If Monteverdi was the first great genius of opera, then Torelli was probably the second. He normally took the credit "represented and invented by"—part designer, part stage director. A wonderful record exists of his work, and that of his peers, in an illustrated book by Niccola Sabbatini: *A Manual for Constructing Theatrical Scenes and Machines.*[17] It was published in 1638, at the very beginning of the era of public opera houses, so it is mainly concerned with designs for private (and therefore more lavish) productions, but its descriptions and drawings give an idea of the sophisticated sets designed by Torelli and his colleagues. Worked by ropes, pulleys, flying plat-

forms, and wheels, they created memorable effects—cloud machines descending with full orchestras aboard; whole corps de ballets making their entrances from above; flats and backdrops arranged and painted in such a way that stage pictures had convincing perspective. The designers of these early operas were "Renaissance men." Their representations of mythology were as grand, and often as striking, as those of the painters and sculptors on whose art they had been brought up.

Lighting was rudimentary, but nonetheless ingenious. It was provided by chandeliers with either candles or oil lamps (candles tended to drip, but oil lamps had the even worse habit of smoking and spreading the nastiest smells throughout the auditorium). The so-called "drop" curtain went out of fashion in the 1630s. It came down from above at the end of each scene, often with a crash; Sabbatini pointed out that it was frightening for the audience and often damaged the scenery. Its replacement was known as the "rising" curtain because it was raised at the beginning of a performance and generally stayed up until the end. Scene changes took place in full view of the audience, often at very high speed, with flats sliding out and new ones sliding in. It was all part of the spectacle. So were the pyrotechnic effects that often accompanied the entrance of dragons, gods, or other supernatural creatures. Fire was a constant hazard, and the average production must have been an insurance company's nightmare.

In both their design and their organization, the new opera houses of Venice were remarkably similar to their modern-day equivalents, and often just as large. A contemporary plan of the Teatro Santi Giovanni e Paolo, where *Poppea* was given its premiere in 1642, shows a horseshoe-shaped auditorium, completely surrounded by boxes, all of them angled toward the stage. The patrician families and wealthy entrepreneurs leased the boxes for a season, while down below, in the pit, seats or benches were available to anyone willing to pay four lire—not cheap, but neither was it prohibitive. And all these paying customers watched the opera (and each other) in a fully lighted auditorium where conversation and social intercourse competed with the singers and musicians for attention. It was hard work for singers, and even harder for orchestra players, who sat on the main floor beside the stage. It was no wonder that impresarios relied so heavily on spectacular stage effects to sell tickets.

✷

So, in the course of barely half a century, *dramma per musica*, now occasionally known as "opera," was established as an art form. A private experiment dreamed up in the chambers of a few Florentine noblemen developed into a popular and commercially successful form of entertainment in republican Venice. It had spread to cities all over Italy—sometimes as a fashionable entertainment at the princely courts, where it existed alongside *intermedi* and the traditional court extravaganzas; sometimes as a commercial entertainment in public theaters, where it was introduced by traveling companies like the one led by Ferrari and Manelli. Monteverdi's *Il ritorno d'Ulisse* was actually given in Bologna by a touring company in 1640, the same year as its premiere in Venice.

One of the Italian cities to which opera came late, but with great effect, was Naples. So far as is known, no opera was performed there at all until 1650, when Cavalli's *Didone* (Dido) was reported to have been staged. The following year a private performance of Monteverdi's *Poppea* was given. But opera quickly took root in Naples and became, just as it had in Venice, a public and commercial success. By the end of the century, Naples had supplanted Venice as the leading opera city of Italy.

And by that time it had already begun to take hold in other European countries—notably in Austria and Germany, but most of all in France.

THE SINGERS TAKE THE STAGE

Barrôco IS A PORTUGUESE WORD. LITERALLY, IT MEANS A ROUGH OR IRREGULARLY SHAPED PEARL. IT IS A DEROGATORY TERM. SO WHEN *BAROQUE* WAS APPLIED (RETROSPECTIVELY) TO AN ENTIRE PERIOD IN THE HISTORY OF EUROPEAN ART, IT WAS NOT THE POLITEST WAY OF DESCRIBING IT.

THE BAROQUE PERIOD IS GENERALLY DEFINED AS COVERING MOST OF THE SEVENTEENTH CENTURY AND THE FIRST HALF OF THE EIGHTEENTH — EXACTLY THE TIME WHEN OPERA WAS ESTABLISH-ING ITSELF. IN THE POST-RENAISSANCE ATMOSPHERE OF EUROPE (AND OF ITALY, TO BEGIN WITH), ARCHITECTS, SCULPTORS, PAINTERS, MUSICIANS, AND EVEN WRIT-ERS DRESSED UP THE OLD CLASSICAL FORMS IN VERY UNCLASSICAL CLOTHING. THE SIMPLE BEAUTY OF THE PEARL WAS COMPROMISED, SO TO SPEAK, IN ORDER TO ADD NEW QUALITIES — ORNATE DECORA-TION, EXTRAVAGANT HYPERBOLE, GRAN-DIOSE REPETITION. NOWHERE WAS THIS BETTER ILLUSTRATED THAN IN THE ARCHITECTURE OF THE PERIOD, AND ST. PETER'S BASILICA IN ROME MAY BE ITS MOST VISIBLE MEMORIAL.

Artists wanted their work to be admired, but they wanted more than that. Whether they were creating a building, a painting, or a piece of music, they wanted people to be emotionally involved with it. So they designed their art to convey an experience—an experience of the fantastic, a feeling of wonder. In a popular phrase, it was called the "poetics of the marvelous." And nowhere was it better exhibited than in opera.

This was certainly not what opera's founders had intended. They had started out with a very austere and classical art form in mind, but now, in less than half a century, the simple use of what was called "dry" recitative—long declamatory passages to underline the drama of the text, accompanied by occasional chords on the lute or harpsichord—had been overtaken by the need, at quite regular intervals (certainly at the end of each scene), to stop the narrative altogether while one or more of the characters expressed the emotions of the moment in an aria.

The trend had been apparent as early as 1608, when Monteverdi wrote his famous "Lament" for *Arianna,* but by the 1650s the singers were taking control. They needed set-piece arias to hold the attention of the audience in fully lighted theaters where a lot was going on besides the performance on the stage. The more brilliant and decorative those arias were, the better for the singers, and since composers could not always be relied upon to write such showstoppers, singers were in the habit of improvising on the material at hand—adding their own decorations and variations, and even their own cadenzas. This undisciplined behavior would remain a characteristic of Italian opera, wherever it was performed, until Gluck, on behalf of all composers everywhere, took his stand against it near the end of the eighteenth century.

THE CASTRATI

There was real virtuosity. Nowadays, when the art of improvisation has almost disappeared (to the great relief of composers, conductors, and directors), it is hard to imagine the vocal demands singers made on themselves. It is even harder to imagine the sound of the most virtuosic of the singers, the male *castrati.* It contained all the elements most essential to the Baroque style—bravura, artificiality, and an otherworldly quality that could only be marveled at.

Quite simply, it was the practice of the time for a young boy with a fine treble voice to be castrated in order to preserve his voice unchanged into maturity. It was generally illegal, but little boys had no one to stand up for their rights against greedy and ambitious parents. The Church publicly frowned upon the practice—but the Church was also partly responsible. Saint Paul, in his First Epistle to the Corinthians, had stated categorically, "Let your women keep silence in the churches" (I Corinthians 14:34), so even the Vatican employed *castrati* in its choirs to substitute for female soprano and alto voices, the pope having formally authorized their employment in 1589.

The greatest of the *castrati* are generally recognized as the most accomplished singers there have ever been. Their range and their power set them apart: "female" vocal cords powered by male lungs—a formidable combination, and totally distinct from the male contraltos and countertenors with whom we are familiar today. Very little evidence exists of the sound of the true *castrato* voice, but there are recordings made by the last known professional *castrato,* an Italian called Alessandro Moreschi,[1] who sang for thirty years in the choir of the Sistine Chapel in Rome. Moreschi was certainly not a singer to compare with the greatest of the *castrati,* and his recordings, made at the very beginning of the gramophone era in 1902–3, are technically inferior. Nevertheless, they give an impression of an awesome range—and a sound that we, in our day, may find ugly, and even embarrassing.

The best-known *castrati,* and probably the most famous singers of the eighteenth century, were Francesco Bernardi, known as Senesino (because he came from Siena), and Carlo Broschi, known as Farinelli. Their contemporary, Caffarelli, was almost as well known, but in his case infamy was mixed with fame: he twice served prison sentences for assaulting fellow singers and once fought a duel with a French poet, whom he wounded, over the respective merits of French and Italian music. He nevertheless accumulated a large enough fortune to buy himself a dukedom and two palaces for his retirement (which would have pleased his long-dead grandmother, who had started him on his musical career by giving him the income from two vineyards to pay for the costs of his education and his operation).

Senesino, whose voice was quite low for a *castrato* (some described it as mezzo-soprano, some as contralto), became Handel's muse in London

GREAT CASTRATI

and created many of his greatest roles. Farinelli, on the other hand, was a high *castrato*—a soprano—and it was his legendary feats of vocal acrobatics that (depending on your point of view) either raised singing to a level it has never before or since attained, or gave singing a bad name. Dr. Charles Burney, an Englishman who traveled through Europe in the 1770s collecting material for his *General History of Music*, heard a number of firsthand accounts of Farinelli's singing, and subsequently visited him in his retirement outside

Bologna. One of the stories he had heard concerned Farinelli's debut engagement in Rome in 1722, when he was only seventeen. Performance after performance, it was said, Farinelli waged a musical battle with a trumpet player in the orchestra. One night, the battle reached a fearful climax, transfixing the audience, as Farinelli and the trumpeter competed to outshine and outlast each other. Finally, Dr. Burney's informants reported,

> both seemed to be exhausted: and, in fact, the trumpeter, wholly spent, gave it up, thinking, however, his antagonist as much tired as himself, and that it would be a drawn battle: when Farinelli, with a smile on his countenance, showing he had only been sporting with him all that time, broke out all at once in the same breath, with fresh vigor, and not only swelled and shook the note, but ran the most rapid and difficult divisions, and was at last silenced only by the acclamation of the audience.[2]

It was the Holy Roman Emperor Charles VI who later advised Farinelli that it was not necessary always to amaze his listeners, and that he should also try to engage their emotions.[3] Farinelli took the advice to heart—to his great profit, because the listener whose emotions he engaged more than any

agant Baroque style, which dominated all forms of art; whereas Metastasio, as a product of the so-called Arcadian academy in Rome, was the embodiment of a countermovement that sought to restore discipline and classicism to the arts—to poetry, literature, and drama, most of all. Ironically, but very conveniently, these two movements, which appeared to be so much at odds, found they could exist side by side within the operatic mold known as *opera seria* (literally, serious opera).

It would be hard to find a more off-putting title for a form of entertainment, but *opera seria*, for all its rigidity and repetitiveness of subject matter, was a marvelous vehicle for singers. Its very seriousness spurred the development of *opera buffa* (comic opera) as a counterattraction, and together they provided Italian opera, wherever it was performed, with a rich diet throughout the eighteenth century and beyond. In the works of Mozart and Rossini, the two forms, *seria* and *buffa*, would reach their zenith.

Much of the musical framework for *opera seria* was provided by Alessandro Scarlatti. Like Metastasio thirty years later, he was greatly influenced by the Arcadian academy in Rome. It had been founded by Queen Christina of Sweden, a remarkable and flamboyant lady who abdicated the crown of Sweden in her late twenties and moved to Rome (she actually entered the city on horseback, dressed as an Amazon). There, between abortive attempts to win back the crown of Sweden and capture the crown of Poland, she founded her academy, dedicated to the ancient ideals of Arcadia. What these were, in essence, were the "purification" and "elevation" of poetry and drama by simplifying the forms in which they were written and by concentrating on pastoral subjects.

The operas of Alessandro Scarlatti (he wrote 115 of them between 1679 and his death in 1725) were full of Arcadian pastoral allusions. Aria after aria invoked the beauties of nature and the importance of relating to the natural world. Even the greatest military heroes found time to sing paeans to the rays of the sun or the wings of the honeybee. But Scarlatti's very real importance in the story of opera had little to do with his narrative subject matter and a great deal to do with the musical formulations in which he set it. First in Rome, then in Florence, but most of all in Naples, he refined the principal musical features of *opera seria*—the introductory overture; the use of recitative (both in the form of simple accompaniment

Interior of the Teatro Regio, Turin, during a performance of Francesco Feo's Arsace, *1740. Painting by Pietro Domenico Olivero. Feo, a Neapolitan composer and teacher, was described by Dr. Charles Burney as "one of the greatest Neapolitan masters." Olivero's painting depicts* opera seria *in its prime. Onstage, the tragedy of Arsace is enacted in the splendid setting of Persepolis. The pit is too small for the thirty-two-piece orchestra. In the audience, drinks are being served, a soldier maintains order, and several people are evidently following the opera in printed librettos.*

other was King Philip V of Spain. That aging melancholic paid Farinelli a considerable sum of money to sing to him every evening for the last nine years of his life—the same four songs each evening, according to Dr. Burney. And when Philip died, his successor, Ferdinand VI, retained Farinelli in the royal service as a powerful counselor and adviser. By the time Farinelli retired to Italy, in 1759, he was a very rich man.

Opera Seria

Farinelli had a "twin"—not a real twin, but a boyhood friend he always referred to as his *gemello* (twin brother)—Pietro Antonio Domenico Bonaventura Trapassi. His friend chose, like Farinelli, to be known by a "professional" name: Metastasio. And if Farinelli and his fellow *castrati* defined the age for singers, then Metastasio defined it for the writers of opera, both the librettists and the composers.

But these "twins" represented different and contrasting trends in the development of opera. Farinelli and the *castrati* were symbols of the extrav-

of a singer by one instrument, normally a harpsichord, and in the form of much more sumptuous accompaniment when extra dramatic effect was called for); and, most of all, he developed what was known as the *da capo* aria.

Nothing could have been better designed to keep the singers happy than the *da capo* aria. It was a vocal showpiece, written within a fairly rigid formula, but one that allowed the singers to add their own ornamentation and cadenzas. It was normally in three parts, the third of which was a reprise of the first "from the top" or "from the beginning" (that was the literal meaning of *da capo*). Rodolfo Celletti, one of the most authoritative modern writers on the history of Italian singing, describes it thus:

> The orchestra opened the first section (A), which was very long and concluded with vocalises invented by the singers themselves, called cadenzas. Then a new instrumental passage paved the way for the second section (B), which usually was in a minor key; it, too, ended with a cadenza by the singer. Finally, the orchestra returned to the original key, and the repetition of the first section (A) followed, with the singer's variations and a cadenza that was customarily quite ornate.[4]

What could be better designed to show off a singer's skills? And when you consider the theater in which the singer performed—a fully lighted auditorium, buzzing with conversation and movement; surrounded by boxes in which wealthy socialites entertained each other; and with noise filtering in from the lobbies, where gaming tables often provided a rival attraction—it is no wonder that singers welcomed the opportunity to claim the full attention of the house with a brilliant *da capo* aria. Most often, it would be an "exit" aria—a chance for a character to savor the emotions of the moment before leaving the stage—and principal singers frequently had as many as five of them in a single opera. *Opera seria* was extremely class-conscious, and such arias would normally be given only to high-born or noble characters (sung by the best-known singers, of course), while the lower ranks would have to make do with a much briefer, less showy number, known as an *arietta*. Worst of all, a singer of little consequence might be allocated what the Italians called an *aria del sorbetto* (a "sorbet" aria, during which members of the audience might retreat to the lobbies for an ice). Not surprisingly, leading singers liked to insure themselves against a composer's "inadequacies" by commissioning an *aria di baule* ("suitcase" aria). This, quite literally, traveled with the singer and was inserted into operas (with or without the composer's permission) if the singer felt that he or she had been given insufficient opportunity to dazzle.

THE METASTASIAN LIBRETTO

Opera seria depended as much on words as it did on music, and the name most frequently connected with it was that of Farinelli's "twin," Metastasio. In the last half of the eighteenth century, a libretto for an *opera seria* was almost certain to be "Metastasian." But Metastasio had a predecessor, Apostolo Zeno, who deserved almost as much of the credit. Zeno was a Venetian, a historian and critic by profession, who would probably not have been involved in writing opera librettos had he not been appointed court poet to Emperor Charles VI in 1718. The post required the holder to provide librettos for operas performed at the imperial court in Vienna. It said much for the importance of the Italian language that Europe's leading German-speaking court employed an Italian as its official poet. Zeno was nothing like so good a poet as Metastasio—nor was he in the slightest bit musical—but he supplied composers, including Scarlatti, with texts well suited to both the cultural and operatic requirements of the time. His texts, generally based on historical sources, featured the great and the good caught up in nasty situations not of their own making, and invariably had happy endings. There was a certain amount of action, one or two central confrontations, and a succession of exit arias in which the principal characters reflected on their moral predicaments and their closeness to nature.

Metastasio, who succeeded Zeno as imperial court poet in 1729, was in a different league—perhaps the greatest poet of his day. He was a grocer's son from Rome, a literary prodigy adopted and educated by a rich man who later left him a fortune. Like Scarlatti before him (but thirty years after Queen Christina's death), Metastasio came under the influence of the Aracadian academy and adopted its reverence for classicism and for things pastoral. In the course of more than sixty years, most of them spent in Vienna, he wrote about thirty opera librettos. That may not seem a great number, but those same librettos were used again and again by different composers, some of them as many as sixty times, so that by the end of the eighteenth century there may have been eight hundred Metastasian operas in existence. Every great composer of the age made use of them—with the notable exception of French composers, who set only French texts. The German composer Johann Adolf Hasse, who became a close friend of Metastasio's, was reputed to have set every one of his texts. Handel, Gluck, and Mozart all made use of them, and even Meyerbeer did so in the nineteenth century (before he settled in France).

Metastasio's plots were convoluted enough, but they were also predictable—classical, class-conscious stories in which gods and aristocrats presided over the world, forever upholding the status quo and glorifying their own social order. It was all very graceful, but it was one-dimensional: comedy was outlawed, along with pageantry, and the massive stage machinery of earlier times was no longer needed. Metastasio's texts were ideally constructed to allow singers to do what they did best—show off. At frequent intervals, the action stopped altogether while a singer performed a *da capo* aria of great brilliance—most often set to verses in which the character compared his or her feelings to those of such well-known creatures of nature as a raging lion, a lovesick turtledove, or a simple shepherd boy. It was the imagery of these verses, often striking and always elegant, that inspired so many composers to make use of Metastasio's librettos.

NAPLES AND OPERA BUFFA

Nevertheless, it was a rigid formula and there was, inevitably, a reaction. Audiences needed relief from the artificial and conformist sentiments of gods and heroes, and it came in the form of *intermezzi*—lighthearted and often comic pieces performed during the intermissions of full-length operas. *Intermezzi* had been in evidence as early as 1623 in Bologna, and by the early eighteenth century there were literally hundreds of them in existence. But it was the reaction to an overdose of *opera seria* that transformed *intermezzi* into an operatic genre of their own: *opera buffa*. Here, the principal characters were no longer gods and kings and noble heroes (or if they were, they were being made fun of). More often, the characters were real people—housewives, cuckolded husbands, jilted lovers—characters the audience could recognize and respond to directly (the more so because the texts were often written in the local Italian dialect).

Not surprisingly, the librettists of these comic *intermezzi* were not normally the librettists of *opera seria*, but their composers were generally the same. Scarlatti was one of the pioneers, and Neapolitan composers as distinguished as Giovanni Battista Pergolesi and Leonardo Vinci were at least as well known for comic *intermezzi* as they were for their full-length "serious" works.

Pergolesi wrote the most popular of them all: *La serva padrona* (The Maid Turned Mistress). It was originally an *intermezzo* for one of his own *opere serie*, but it was so successful that it eventually assumed a life of its own. Indeed, twenty years after its first performance in Naples it would set off a terrible row in France—the so-called *guerre des bouffons*.

Pergolesi may have been one of music's greatest geniuses. Because he died at only twenty-six we shall never know, but in those few short years he produced a stream of wonderful music, both sacred and secular, that marked him as an original—someone who could compose comic operas as earthy as *La serva padrona* and religious music as ethereal as the *Stabat Mater*, his last completed work.

Vinci, like Pergolesi, died very young, so it was left to Nicola Porpora, a less gifted composer than either, but a singing teacher and musical technician of great importance, to play the principal role. In Naples, in the early 1720s, Porpora taught singing to Farinelli and techniques of composition to Metastasio; in the 1730s, he established an opera company in London to rival Handel's—an undertaking he eventually abandoned in the face of Handel's much greater success; in the 1750s, he settled in Vienna and numbered Joseph Haydn among his pupils.

This "Neapolitan School" of opera composers spread its influence far and wide across Europe, and continued to do so until well into the nineteenth century. Scarlatti, Pergolesi, Vinci, and Porpora were succeeded by Jommelli, Piccinni, Paisiello, Cimarosa, and Spontini, all of whom would play a distinguished part in the story of opera—and they, in turn, would give way to the young Rossini. With all this talent on hand, it was hardly surprising that so many of the outstanding Italian singers of the period trained in Naples.

Pergolesi's LA SERVA PADRONA *at La Scala, Milan, 1961. Directed by Corrado Pavolini, designed by Orlando Collalto. With Paolo Montarsolo as Uberto, Mariella Adani as Serpina, and Ferruccio Soleri as Vespone (a non-singing part). Pergolesi's opera buffa (it has only two singing roles) was enormously successful in Naples, in 1733—and much farther afield. Its production in Paris in 1752 precipitated the* guerre des bouffons *between supporters of France's traditional Italian opera and those (like Rousseau) who believed that the simplicity and naturalness of Italian* opera buffa *should be a model for the development of French opera.*

There was another reason for Naples's preeminence. Eighteenth-century Italy was little more than a geographical idea. It was made up of a number of individual kingdoms, fiefdoms, provinces, city-states, and islands, all of which, at various times, fell prey to the ambitions of larger European states. These larger states, bound up in their Continental conflicts, had always considered Naples especially valuable: it was a warm seaport and one of the most important strategic strongholds in southern Europe. Whatever the discomforts of occupation, and they were many, Neapolitans at least benefited from the conquerors' willingness to turn Naples into a showpiece. In the 1730s, the Spanish Bourbons were the ruling power, and they spent lavishly to rebuild the city.

One of the first fruits of the rebuilding program was a magnificent new opera house, the San Carlo. Like the building it replaced, the San Bartolomeo, it quickly became the most important social club in Naples. A visitor to the theater in its early years described "the amazing noisiness of the audience during the whole performance of the opera"[5] (except, interestingly enough, when dances were being performed). Successful operas were repeated night after night, and it was not unusual for people to see each of them several times. But it was not always a single opera they saw. A lengthy *opera seria* would often share the bill with a comic *intermezzo*; and there were frequent evenings of what was called *pasticcio*, when excerpts from a number of different operas were glued together to make a composite entertainment, carefully tailored to show off the theater's principal singers.

Naples was not alone. The level of operatic activity throughout Italy was amazing. Most of the major cities, led by Rome, Bologna, and Venice, had several opera houses; even quite small towns often had one. Theater owners and impresarios were hard-pressed to meet the demand. The best-known composers wrote at a rate that would be unthinkable in modern times, and much of the output was, understandably, second-rate and soon forgotten. Audiences wanted new operas—with rare exceptions, they did not welcome new productions of old operas—so there were a lot of journeyman composers who traveled from theater to theater, took whatever libretto they were given, and made an opera out of it in a matter of days, being careful only to ensure that there were suitable parts for the local singers. The results were not always bad; this was, after all, more or less what Rossini was doing when he composed *Il barbiere di Siviglia* in Rome in 1815.

The eighteenth century was not so kind to the city where opera had first thrived, the Most Serene Republic of Venice. Its Mediterranean empire wilted and disappeared, and at the very end of the century it capitulated timidly to Napoleon's conquering army. But it never ceased to be a center for gracious living—the principal objective for all those monied Europeans who made the Grand Tour. It was the city immortalized in the paintings of Canaletto and Tiepolo, in the comedies of Carlo Goldoni, and in the music of its great composer, Antonio Vivaldi.

As surely as Monteverdi had done a century earlier, Vivaldi wrote the music of his age—and just like Monteverdi, he had to await the twentieth century to be recognized for what he was. "Il Prete Rosso" (the redheaded priest) spent most of his life teaching at the Ospedale della

Antonio Vivaldi (1678–1741). Caricature by Pier Leone Ghezzi—the only authenticated likeness of the composer.

Pietà, one of Venice's four orphanages for girls. In this unlikely setting, he wrote much of the instrumental music for which he is best remembered, as well as the forty-five operas for which he is remembered hardly at all. *Orlando furioso* is one of the few that is ever performed today. Yet, in his time, Vivaldi was best known to the Venetian public as a theatrical composer — and one who staged his own works, complete with the spectacular effects for which the public theaters had become known.

By the time Vivaldi died in 1741, Carlo Goldoni was already Venice's leading playwright and librettist. His satirical comedies, most of them written in dialect, were ideal material for the new vogue in comic opera, and it was actually in Venice, rather than Naples, that *opera buffa* became established as a distinctive form of Italian opera. For fifteen years, Goldoni collaborated with the composer Baldassare Galuppi, writing a series of three-

act comic operas that were no longer *intermezzi:* they were, in every sense, the "main attraction." Not the least of the innovations Goldoni and Galuppi pioneered was a uniquely operatic one, the finale, in which several strands of the plot and the musical development would come together in a large-scale ensemble. In works like their 1750 "hit," *Il mondo della luna,* finales provided exciting and often very dramatic climaxes. It was a convention that Mozart and Rossini, the greatest exponents of *opera buffa,* would develop to enormous effect.

So, by the middle of the eighteenth century, the essential ingredients of Italian opera, *seria* and *buffa,* were in place. But Italian opera was by no means an Italian monopoly. It was a European phenomenon. Singers and composers from Naples, Rome, Venice, and many other Italian cities rode the dangerous stagecoaches across Europe to fulfill lucrative engagements in cities as far afield as Dublin in the west and St. Petersburg in the east—but not, on the whole, in Paris, because France, alone among European countries, had nurtured an opera of its own, an opera that was not Italian.

OPERA IN FRANCE

France was the first country outside Italy to catch the opera bug. Opera traveled to Paris in the person of Maria de' Medici. At her wedding to Henri IV of France in Florence in 1600, Jacopo Peri's *Euridice* had first been showcased for an international audience, and the new queen lost little time in inviting Ottavio Rinuccini, the librettist of *Euridice*, to visit Paris. The French court was interested, but not smitten. Dynastic marriages were a necessity of international politics, but the French had a culture of their own; they saw little reason for importing a foreign culture as part of the deal.

The equation became more complicated when Cardinal Mazarin became first minister of France in 1642. Mazarin was an Italian by birth; he had been a naturalized French citizen only since 1639. He was not popular. What was worse, he continued to believe that France might benefit from the importation of Italian culture. Between 1645 and 1647, while Louis XIV was still in the first decade of his life and too young to rule, Mazarin caused a number of Italian operas to be staged in Paris. Some of these were established Italian successes, like Sacrati's *La finta pazza* and Cavalli's *Egisto,* both of them spectacularly restaged for Paris by the Venetian designer Giacomo Torelli. But Mazarin's greatest service to Italian opera was the commission he gave to Luigi Rossi, the Roman composer of *Il palazzo incantato*. Rossi traveled to Paris in 1646 and wrote *Orfeo* for Mazarin. It was a large and complex version of the familiar story, with a running time of more than six hours. Mazarin saw to it that the French court paid for a lavish production. The citizens of Paris were not amused by this extravagance, and by the time Rossi was invited back, in 1648, the court had been forced to take refuge outside Paris; not even Mazarin could find funding for another commission.

Nevertheless, Rossi's *Orfeo* was almost as important a landmark in the story of opera as Monteverdi's *Orfeo* had been, forty years before. It was infinitely more complex than Monteverdi's relatively simple telling of the tale. There were dances and big vocal ensembles; the plot twisted and turned with intricate subplots and downright absurdities; it frequently relied on elaborate scenic effects; and there was a profusion of arias for solo voices, giving welcome and melodic relief from what (with most of Rossi's contemporaries) was an overreliance on dry recitative for storytelling. In many ways, Rossi's *Orfeo* might be called Baroque. It had a powerful effect on future opera composers, both Italian and French.

Mazarin soft-pedaled his promotion of Italian opera in the 1650s, but he had one final and spectacular use for it when the time came for his master, Louis XIV, to be married. The Bourbon dynasty of France needed to establish a claim to the Spanish throne, and it was France's good fortune that Louis was single, available, and extremely eligible. In 1660, Mazarin negotiated the young king's betrothal to the Infanta María Teresa of Spain. It was important to France, and to Mazarin in particular, that the marriage should be celebrated with great pomp and splendor so that all the world could see that France and Spain were allies, and that their thrones should logically be united when the ruling family of Spain died out (as it was shortly expected to do) for want of a male heir. What better way to entertain and impress the wedding guests than by exposing them to the most elaborate and expensive of artistic enterprises—an opera?

Once more Mazarin turned to Cavalli and Torelli. He commissioned a new opera, *Ercole amante*. In the event, it was not ready in time (it was eventually staged in Paris in 1662 and got a lukewarm reception, despite its massive size and spectacular staging), so the wedding celebration centered instead around a new production of one of Cavalli's earlier Venetian successes, *Xerse*. Torelli staged it, and additional dance music was written by another Italian resident in France, Giovanni Battista Lulli.

This thoroughly Italian celebration of a Franco-Spanish wedding was not a great success either. Mazarin himself died the following year, having done the cause of Italian opera in France a good deal of harm. But he had planted a seed. Within the space of barely two decades, opera was thriving in France—not Italian opera, but French opera. The ultimate irony was that Lully (to give him his French name) became its founding father.

The king himself was responsible for the change. When Mazarin died in 1661, Louis (he was only twenty-three) immediately took over the reins of government and set about establishing his pure and absolute monarchy. He was the Sun

ABOVE: *Lully's* ARMIDE, *performed at the Palais Royal, Paris, 1686. Drawing by Jean Berain of the destruction of Armide's palace at the end of the opera. This was the last opera in Lully's fifteen-year collaboration with the librettist Philippe Quinault. It remained in the repertoire of the Académie Royale de Musique until 1764.*

RIGHT: *Lully's* ALCESTE, *performed in the Marble Courtyard at Versailles, July 4, 1674. Engraving by Jean Le Pastre, 1676.* ALCESTE, *a* tragédie *in a prologue and five acts, was Lully's second opera and a particular favorite of Louis XIV's. It remained in the repertoire of the Académie Royale de Musique (later the Paris Opéra) for eighty-three years.*

King, the most splendid ruler of the age, whose power was symbolized by the great Palace of Versailles, to which, on its completion in 1682, he moved his court.

The court was the center of power, and it reflected Louis's concept of kingship—*la gloire*, the glory that was the king himself. All court entertainments, and especially those involving Louis's special enthusiasm, dance, revolved around it. When he was fourteen, he took part in a court

The fourteen-year-old Louis XIV as Apollo in LE BALLET DE LA NUIT *(1653)*. *Gouache by the workshop of Henri Gissey. The original, and magnificent, designs were by Giacomo Torelli, the Venetian designer, who was by this time based in Paris. The ballet depicted the events of the night in terms of both ordinary people and mythology, culminating in the arrival of Dawn and the Rising Sun (played by Louis himself). It was this ballet that led to Louis's being called the Sun King.*

extravaganza called *Le ballet de la nuit.* It took thirteen hours, and when he made his final entrance, it was as the Rising Sun, surrounded by the Graces and Virtues. That was the way Louis saw himself, and it was the way he intended that France and the world should see him, too.

Dance had been a feature of the very earliest Italian operas—Jacopo Peri had written a ballet for the ending of *Euridice* in 1600; so had Monteverdi for *Orfeo* in 1607—but Italian opera had subsequently developed as a singers' medium. Dance, when included, was of secondary importance. In France, however, opera and dance were intimately linked, and would continue to be so right up to the end of the nineteenth century.

No one better represented that link than Jean-Baptiste Lully. Although he was born and brought up in Florence, his prodigious promise as a musician and singer earned him the patronage of a Frenchman, the Chevalier de Guise, who took the fourteen-year-old boy to Paris and placed him as a page in the household of Mademoiselle d'Orléans, a cousin of the young king. Despite a stubborn Italian accent that plagued him all his life, Lully quickly became more French than the French. At the age of twenty he entered the service of Louis himself; ten years later, he became court composer and *maître de la musique* to the royal family. Given Louis's enthusiasm for things musical, it was a powerful position, and Lully used it for all it was worth.

His first success was as a dancer, performing in court entertainments, often alongside Louis himself. Soon, he was composing pieces for those entertainments, and developing forms which united the court's two great enthusiasms—dance and theater. He joined forces with Molière, greatest of French playwrights, to create a number of comic ballets with spoken dialogue; *Le bourgeois gentilhomme* (The Would-Be Gentleman) was the best known. From there it was but a short step to the beginnings of French opera, signaled in 1672 by the first of Lully's many collaborations with the poet and dramatist Philippe Quinault. By the time he died in 1687, Lully had written some twenty operas, most of them to texts by Quinault. And there was virtually no competition.

The explanation for the lack of competition was simple: Lully had a monopoly. He possessed a patent from the king, which authorized him, and him alone, to commission and perform operas in the French language, and to stage them at the Académie Royale de Musique (an institution that long outlasted Lully; it was later known as the Paris Opéra). The patent carefully defined the word *opera* as "a play in verse, set to music and sung, accompanied by dances, machines and decorations."

Lully was not the first owner of that patent. In fact, he and Quinault owed a considerable debt to a man who is less remembered but who had more right than either of them to be considered the founder of French opera. He was the Abbé Pierre Perrin, a dramatist and librettist who staged a form of French opera as early as 1659 (the year

before Louis's wedding). It was Perrin, much more than Lully, who convinced the young king that there should be such a thing as French opera, and it was to Perrin that Louis granted the original monopoly in 1669. The abbé's first and only production for the Académie was an opera called *Pomone*, with music by Robert Cambert. It was successful, but the backers ran off with the profits and the wretched Perrin was imprisoned for debt. In an effort to pay his creditors, he surrendered the patent to Lully, who thus became the sole proprietor of the first state-subsidized opera house in the world.

He made good use of it. Arch courtier and brilliant intriguer that he was, he devised a form of opera that was certain to win royal approval. Its label, given it by Lully himself, was *tragédie lyrique* or, more generally, *tragédie en musique*, and it was very different from the form of Italian opera that had become so popular in Venice and Naples. To begin with, it was in French, and every word was intended to be heard. It could even be said (as Quinault did) that words took priority over music, with one note assigned to each syllable. "No embellishments," said Lully; "my recitative is made only for speaking."[6] And it could hardly fail to win royal approval since each opera was preceded by a prologue addressed directly to the king and his court. Whatever the subject matter of the operas (most of them were adaptations of mythology or, in a few cases, stories from the age of chivalry), the prologue began the entertainment by glorifying Louis and his concept of kingship. Only when that was done would the overture to the first of the five acts commence.

Having been suitably glorified, Louis would have enjoyed the ballets and dances that cropped up at frequent intervals. He would have appreciated the sense of theater, too, since Lully and Quinault were careful to give their operas a much more dramatic character than was usually the case with Italian opera. The spectacle was important; scenic "machines" were much used in France at a time when they were disappearing in Italy. And the emphasis on words was akin to the straight theater, with recitatives and arias (or *airs*) melding into each other—not at all like the Italian method of presenting arias as set-piece events designed mainly to show off the singer's technique. *Castrati* were unpopular in France, and few roles were written for them. The chorus, on the other hand, played a large part in Lully's operas. So did the orchestra, which not only accompanied some of the recitative but also had its own set pieces—grand overtures and occasional *symphonies* within the opera.

This was the *tragédie lyrique* that became the classic form of French opera—partly for want of an alternative, partly by virtue of its strengths. Lully himself remained in fashion long after his death, and his ghost hovered obstinately over his successors. Some of them were originals in their own right—Marc-Antoine Charpentier, for instance, and Jean-Philippe Rameau most of all—but none of them could escape the formal, ornate style that Lully had established under the protection of King Louis's monopoly. Six years after Lully's death, his disciples were able (in his name) to derogate Charpentier's *Médée*—a *tragédie lyrique* as brilliant as anything Lully had written—and to have it taken off after very few performances (it would not be seen again until 1984). Charpentier's "sins" were that he had studied in Italy and (even worse) he had become Molière's collaborator when Lully had fallen out with the playwright.

There were other forms of French opera beside the *tragédie lyrique*. They included another Lullian invention, the *opéra-ballet*. It was a combination of dance, singing (mainly choral), and spectacular scenic effects, and it remained popular in Paris well into the nineteenth century. *Les Indes galantes* by Rameau was probably the most famous example. Altogether different—and much disapproved of by Lully—was *opéra-comique*. Its roots

Jean-Philippe Rameau (1683–1764). Portrait after Chardin.

own theater in Paris. Despite continuing efforts by the Comédie-Française to have it outlawed, the Théâtre de l'Opéra-Comique flourished, and it continued to do so for more than two hundred fifty years.

The popularity of *opéra-comique* was hardly surprising. For most audiences, especially those outside the immediate circle of the court, it compared very favorably with the rigid formality of Lully's operas. Despite its name, it was by no means confined to comedy. The principal meaning of *comédie* is "play"; a *comédien* is an actor. So *opéra-comique* included all forms of musical theater in which there was spoken dialogue (including, for instance, Bizet's *Carmen* in 1875). In this much looser format there was more room for Italian influences than there ever had been in the Lullian model, so when Neapolitan *opera buffa* (which really was comic) began to take hold in the eighteenth century, it had its supporters in France. In 1752, they came out of their corner fighting.

GUERRE DES BOUFFONS

The *guerre des bouffons*, as it was called, was a war of pamphlets, but nonetheless brutal for that. It divided Paris, and worse still, it divided the court. Louis XV, true to the spirit of his great-grandfather and predecessor, the Sun King, was on the side of French opera: he had the energetic support of his mistress, Madame de Pompadour. The queen lined up against her husband in the pro-Italian camp, and allied herself with the leading intellectuals of the Enlightenment, Denis Diderot and Jean-Jacques Rousseau. Unwillingly caught in the middle was the greatest French composer of the day, Rameau, master of harmony. He had no option but to campaign for French opera in the Lullian mode. He was easily its finest exponent and in many ways developed the art much further than Lully, but he had studied in Italy, he had written a number of successful *opéras-comiques* at the beginning of his career, and he understood better than most the virtues as well as the vices of Italian opera.

The "war" was precipitated by performances in Paris of Pergolesi's stunning little *opera buffa*, *La serva padrona*. Its success encouraged the pro-Italian camp to argue that French opera was moribund; what it needed was to be brought down to earth, to be made less artificial and put more in touch with the real world, and that would mean abandoning the rigid formalities enforced by Lully and

went back well beyond Louis's time, to the public entertainments that were part of France's medieval agricultural fairs. They were boisterous, often raunchy, affairs, and they included genuinely popular musical plays. Louis and his courtiers thought of them as vulgar, rabble-rousing events that frequently poked fun at the authorities. But even an absolute monarch found it impossible to put them out of business altogether. A succession of ordinances laid harsh restrictions on them, and royal monopolies granted to Lully's Académie for opera, and to another company for the performance of theatrical comedies, made life even more difficult for their producers. Yet they prospered. Eventually, in 1715, the year Louis died, *opéra-comique* was legitimized and allowed to establish its

his successors. Rousseau weighed in with a famous pamphlet, *Lettre sur la musique française*, in which he berated the court, the establishment, and the unenlightened attitude of French musicians for the parlous state of opera in Paris. Rousseau could afford to be outspoken. In 1752, the year before he published his pamphlet, he had written a one-act opera (he called it an *intermède*). *Le devin du village* (The Village Soothsayer) was in French all right, but it appeared to have little connection with any known tradition of French opera. Its model was clearly Italian *opera buffa*. Its success (and it remained popular for many years) seemed to be proof that French opera really did have something to learn from Italy.

The Lullistes and the Rameauistes fought back, of course, but the *guerre* had given *opéra-comique* the boost, and the legitimacy, it needed. Ironically, it was once again an Italian immigrant, rather than a Frenchman, who led the way. Egidio Duni had made his reputation in Parma as a composer of *opere serie*, but when he arrived in Paris in 1755 he quickly established himself as the leading composer at the Opéra-Comique—and became all the more so when it was merged with the Comédie-Italienne in 1762. He had competition from French composers—Pierre-Alexandre Monsigny and François-André Philidor, in particular—but the French opera tradition that Lully and the Sun King had founded had been released from its century-old corset.

The last years of the Ancien Régime witnessed a much more cosmopolitan attitude toward opera in France. Its language remained rigidly French, but Italian and German influences were no longer proscribed. Gluck and Antonio Salieri were two of Paris's most popular composers, and André Grétry, a Belgian who had trained in Rome, was the most successful of them all. Unlike Rameau, he was not a great harmonist. Nor did he possess a fraction of the musical genius of Gluck or even Salieri. But he had a splendid dramatic imagination, and two fine librettists in Jean-François Marmontel and Michel-Jean Sedaine. It was with Sedaine that he enlarged the bounds of French opera to include a genuine form of music drama. *Richard Cœur-de-Lion*, *Raoul Barbe-bleue*, and *Guillaume Tell* were precursors of a genre that was to dominate the Paris Opéra for much of the nineteenth century—larger-than-life drama, spectac-

ular effects, and a fine sense of melody. Not for nothing would it become known as *grand opéra*.

The *tragédie lyrique* of Lully and his disciples did not fade away easily. It was too well dug in for that. But reform was on its way. In 1762, ten years after the outbreak of the *guerre des bouffons*, Gluck gave the first performance of *Orfeo ed Euridice* in Vienna, and another twelve years after that he brought his reforming program to Paris. "Serious opera" would never be the same again. As for Rameau, who had been attacked by the pro-Italians in much the same way that Richard Wagner would be attacked a century later (for supposedly having too many discords, not enough melody, and noisy instrumentation), he emerged from the *guerre* bruised but unbowed, though he lived only until 1764. Gluck once praised one of Rameau's operas as "*puzza di musica*" ("reeking of music").[7]

French Baroque opera never died: it merely disappeared for the best part of a century and a half. One of the happier developments of the last two decades of the twentieth century was its rediscovery. A number of musicians (not all French) put together performing editions of works by Lully, Charpentier, Rameau, Grétry, and others; several of them were staged; a great many more were released on CD. Together, these events recreated for a skeptical generation some of the glories of the French Baroque, and proved that it deserved a great deal more than just a footnote in the story of opera.

A footnote (quite literally) of some interest, but less importance, was the manner of Lully's death. He was, so far as can be determined, the only great musician to be killed by his own conducting baton. In fact, it was a staff rather than a baton; Lully used it to beat time on the floor. Rude, arrogant, irascible, and unpleasant man that he was, he had the misfortune in a moment of more than usual agitation to bring down the staff on his own foot instead of the floor. An abscess developed, it turned septic, and Lully died of the poison.

OPERA IN ENGLAND

While French opera ruled in Paris, Italian opera was supreme almost everywhere else. Nowhere more so than in London, where it was brought to its zenith by a German composer, Georg Friedrich Händel (he became a British citizen in 1727 and changed his name to George Frideric Handel).

The English tradition of court entertainment was the masque—a lavish combination of

Purcell's Dido and Aeneas *in a video performance for the BBC, 1995. Directed by Peter Maniura, designed by Niek Korte-kaas. With Karl Daymond as Aeneas.*

music, dance, and mime, championed by Queen Elizabeth and continued by her Stuart successors, until, in 1649, Charles I was beheaded and court activities came to an involuntary stop. Thus, at exactly the time that opera was blooming in Venice and reaching out to Paris, the brief, austere, and puritanical despotism of Oliver Cromwell banned spoken theater in England and did little to encourage music. But it had one very healthy result. The Stuart court, exiled on the European mainland, returned to England in 1660 with a much more cosmopolitan outlook on things cultural. As a result, Italian and French developments were closely watched at the Restoration court.

Henry Purcell was a youthful member of that court. His principal responsibilities were for church music. He was organist at Westminster Abbey and spent most of his life (from boy treble to principal composer) in the service of the Chapel Royal. But he was also drawn into the

Restoration's love of theater. This was the age of John Dryden, John Vanbrugh, William Congreve, and William Wycherley—some of the greatest playwrights of the English theater. Purcell was their admirer and sometimes their collaborator. He began to fashion a genuinely English form of musical theater. "He was especially admired for the *Vocal*," one of his contemporaries wrote, "having a peculiar Genius to express the Energy of *English* Words, whereby he mov'd the Passions of all his Auditors."[8]

Purcell collaborated with Dryden, among others, on a series of works best described as "semi-opera"—part masque, part pageant, part opera. *King Arthur* and *The Fairy-Queen* are the best known. He also composed one genuine opera, *Dido and Aeneas*. It was written (like so many of the works of his contemporary, Vivaldi) for a girls' school—Mr. Josias Priest's School for Young Gentlewomen at Chelsea. It was brief and compact—three acts and an overture in not much more than an hour. Purcell could say in a few bars what it took French and Italian composers whole arias to say. There were certainly foreign influences, most noticeably Lully's, but the language of the opera—both words and music—was unmistakably English. Among many delights, it included dances (doubtless for the young ladies of Mr. Priest's academy), a very racy chorus for the sailors, and one of the most sublime laments ever written, Dido's "When I am laid in earth."

The tragedy of English opera was that Henry Purcell died, in 1695, when he was only thirty-six. It would take more than two hundred years for a comparable successor to emerge. In the long interim, opera in England did flourish—but it was Italian, and later French and German, opera that flourished, not English opera. Handel began this process when he arrived in London only sixteen years after Purcell's death.

The two greatest masters of the Baroque, Handel and Johann Sebastian Bach, were born in the same year, 1685, less than a hundred miles apart. They never met. Bach, the organist and teacher, spent almost all his life in his native Thuringia, quietly writing the textbooks of music for all the ages. Handel, on the other hand, was an international celebrity, an impresario, and a man of the theater, who devoted his life to having his works performed in public. Bach's life was private and inconspicuous; he was a deeply religious fam-

ily man, father of twenty children, ten of whom survived infancy. Handel, too, was religious, but he was celibate, and his professional life was played out on center stage.

Handel was writing operas before he was twenty. His first efforts were written in Hamburg and were therefore in German (Hamburg was an isolated center of German-speaking opera). But in 1706, he began a four-year stay in Italy. There he got to know both Vivaldi and Alessandro Scarlatti, and it was during this period that he began writing in the Italian language and the Italian style, an art from which he rarely deviated in his long operatic career. On his return to Germany, at the age of twenty-five, he was appointed *Kapellmeister* to the elector of Hanover.

Within weeks, he obtained leave of absence to visit London. There, he composed and directed the first Italian opera ever written for the London stage, *Rinaldo*. It was a great success for Handel, though, with his recent experience of superior Italian production, he must have been as surprised as the correspondent of *The Spectator*, Richard Steele, to see on the stage in the middle of the performance "a well-dressed young Fellow, in a full-bottom'd Wigg, appear in the midst of the Sea, and without any visible Concern taking Snuff."[9] English production standards were abysmal. But, as Handel's first biographer, John Mainwaring, wrote, "the arrival of Handel put an end to this reign of nonsense."[10]

MASQUERADES AND OPERAS, *engraving by William Hogarth. In this satire of the fashion for foreign operas in London, the banner entitled "Opera" shows aristocratic impresarios offering two* castrati *and a prima donna the huge sum of £8,000 to perform in one of their theaters. The plays of Shakespeare and Ben Johnson are consigned to "waste paper for shops."*

George Frideric Handel (1685–1759). Portrait attributed to Balthazar Denner, 1726–28.

lar at this time (*The Beggar's Opera*, the most famous of them, was first performed in 1728), but even they were something of a compliment to Handel, since they sought to poke fun at his success.

In forty years Handel wrote thirty-six operas and almost as many dramatic oratorios, many of which could be (and are) staged. He was not a revolutionary in opera, but it could certainly be said of him, as it could of Mozart a few decades later, that he took the art form he inherited and ennobled it with his genius. In Italy, *opera seria* was largely dependent on the singers' ability to energize and beautify the composers' scores. In London, by contrast, Handel's scores made demands on singers and musicians that they had never contemplated before, and that often scared them. Unlike Italian composers, he was writing his operas for an audience that did not know the language: he was setting Italian texts, mostly sung by Italian singers, for an English audience. The success of his operas therefore depended on the ability of the music to describe the action, and the ability of the music and the singers to captivate the audience. Handel's orchestration was rich and expressive, but he relied chiefly on the frequent use of the *da capo* aria. There were few ensembles and even fewer choruses.

Handel was like a magnet to singers. He journeyed through Italy himself on more than one occasion to find suitable talent, and he was able to make use of a few native English singers as well. *Giulio Cesare* in 1724 was a good example. Senesino, the Italian *castrato* whose fame rivaled that of Farinelli, sang the title role; another popular *castrato*, Gaetano Berenstadt, created the role of Ptolemy; and the principal female roles, Cleopatra and Cornelia, were sung respectively by the Italian Francesca Cuzzoni and the Englishwoman Anastasia Robinson.

DIVAS

The age of the prima donna had arrived. While the *castrati* attracted much of the attention in Italian opera, and would continue to do so throughout the eighteenth century, female sopranos were almost as important, to both composers and the box office. But it was not easy for them. It was a male-dominated world, unrepentant in its chauvinism. A woman wishing to take up a profession that involved performing in public was frequently, sometimes automatically, referred to as a courtesan; it was generally assumed that she must have a

Handel liked London, and he clearly had it in mind that he might settle there. But he had a job back in Hanover to which he had to return. In less than a year he once again obtained the elector's permission to visit London, on condition that he return "within a reasonable time." But he did not return. Instead, the elector joined him in London—that is, the elector became King George I of England, the unlikely and bemused successor to the throne, and the first in a long line of England's Hanoverian monarchs.

Handel thrived on London's rich and varied theater life, and he made the era just as glorious for its music. As a composer, he stood head and shoulders above all others. Invasions of his territory by rival composers from Italy were repulsed—Giovanni Buononcini with difficulty, the more talented Porpora with relative ease. The only competition he could not shake off came from the ballad operas, which were hugely popu-

LEFT: *Handel's* GIULIO CESARE. *Design by Thomas Lediard for last act of the 1727 production in Hamburg. Julius Caesar and Cleopatra welcome Cornelia and Sesto (Pompey's wife and son) and celebrate their own undying love with a display of fireworks. The scene is set in the port of Alexandria, but the background in this particular production was apparently provided by a magic-lantern projection of the city of London.*

BELOW: *Handel's* XERXES *at the New York City Opera, 1997. Directed by Stephen Wadsworth, designed by Thomas Lynch. With (from left) Lorraine Hunt as Xerxes, Jennifer Lane as Amastre, David Daniels as Arsamene, Amy Burton as Romilda, and Jan Opalach as Ariodate.*

"protector." Very often this was true—female public performers *needed* protection—and their private lives tended to be the stuff of gossip and of scandal. Not even a woman as sanctified as Anna Renzi in Venice in the 1640s was free from these suspicions. Anyone prepared to take the time to trawl through the records of eighteenth-century police proceedings in cities like Venice, Rome, Bologna, and Naples will find hundreds of examples[11]—and further afield, for the prima donna had quickly become an international phenomenon.

In France, for example, not long after Lully's death, a certain Mademoiselle de Maupin electrified the theater by her feats both on and off the stage. She made her debut as a twenty-two-year-old in one of Lully's operas at the Académie, but by then she had (in no particular order) married, run away with a fencing master, taken vows as a nun in order to get into a nunnery to seduce a girl with whom she had fallen in love, and been condemned by a court in Avignon to be burned alive (a fate from which she escaped unscathed). None of this, we are told by Dr. Burney, who investigated her story at the same time he was researching Farinelli's, should be allowed to obscure the fact that she was a fine singer. But as her fame in the opera house increased, so did her notoriety. Insulted by a famous male singer, she waylaid him in the street and thrashed him. Dressed as a man at a ball given by Louis XIV's brother, she was

ABOVE: *Faustina Bordoni (1700–1781). Portrait by Rosalba Carriera, c. 1739.*

RIGHT: *Handel's* ORLANDO, *performed by Les Arts Florissants at the Brooklyn Academy of Music, New York, 1996. Directed by Robert Carsen, designed by Anthony McDonald. With Rosa Mannion as Dorina and Rosemary Joshua as Angelica.*

challenged to duels by three different men for being impertinent to a countess. She killed all three men, then walked back into the ballroom and obtained an immediate pardon from the king himself. She became mistress to the elector of Bavaria, and was eventually reunited with her original husband. In her latter years, we are told, still a great star on the Paris stage, she became very devout. But she was only thirty-four when she died.[12] More than a century later, Théophile Gautier immortalized her in a famous novella.[13]

Few prima donnas had careers as sensational as Mademoiselle de Maupin's. Nevertheless, Handel had his hands full in London. The cast of *Giulio Cesare* was not a happy group. Female English singers, whether they were married or not, were customarily billed as "Mrs." Anastasia Robinson was, in fact, secretly married to Lord Peterborough, an army general more famous for marching his troops than for leading them in battle, and even more renowned as a cook. Mrs. Robinson complained about "unseemly familiarities" from the male soprano Senesino and summoned Lord Peterborough to be her champion. The mighty hero appeared backstage, where he beat the *castrato* into submission and forced him "to confess upon his knees that Anastasia was a non-pareil of virtue and beauty."[14]

Handel had even more trouble with his other leading lady, Francesca Cuzzoni. She had been engaged the previous year, at Handel's behest, for his opera *Ottone* (also with Senesino and Mrs. Robinson), but from the first she exhibited all the worst characteristics of divas, including a refusal to sing arias she did not particularly like. Handel finally lost his temper. "Madam," he is supposed to have shouted at her, "I know that you are a veritable devil, but I want you to know that I am Beelzebub, the chief of the devils—and I intend to throw you through that open window."[15] The threatened defenestration did not take place, but Cuzzoni was sufficiently terrified to sing the prescribed arias, and to score a great success with them. Her submission, however, was only temporary. The greater the music Handel wrote for her, the greater her success with the audience, and the greater her capacity for outrageous behavior. Handel solved his problem in the way countless operatic impresarios have sought to imitate.

In 1726, he brought to London the one Italian soprano whose talents were as great as Cuzzoni's—and, in one respect, greater, because

Faustina Bordoni was petite and very beautiful, whereas Cuzzoni was (in the words of the diarist Horace Walpole) "short and squat with a doughy, cross face, dressed badly, and was silly and fantastical."

The Cuzzoni/Bordoni rivalry, while brief, was truly the stuff of legend. It came to a stupendous climax in June 1727, when the two ladies appeared together in an opera by Buononcini. In the middle of the performance, they completely lost control of themselves and went at each other, spitting, scratching, and screeching; it took the rest of the cast, as well as the stagehands, to separate them. This all took place in front of a goggle-eyed Princess of Wales and was immortalized a few months later, to the great delight of Londoners, in *The Beggar's Opera*—the scene in Newgate Prison where Polly Peachum and Lucy Lockitt go at each other hammer and tongs.

The following year Handel and his fellow directors ended the rivalry by offering the beauteous Bordoni a higher fee than Cuzzoni, causing Madame Cuzzoni to make an angry departure for Vienna. She returned in 1734 to sing in Porpora's company, which had been established to compete with Handel's, but she stayed only two seasons. She found herself billed beneath Farinelli, and Cuzzoni did not accept playing second fiddle to a *castrato*. A few years later, a London newspaper reported from Italy that Cuzzoni was "under sentence of death to be beheaded for poisoning her husband."[16] Whether or not the report was true, she survived, though she eventually died a pauper in Bologna.

Between them, Madame Cuzzoni and Mademoiselle de Maupin laid a firm foundation for the belief that prima donnas were generally capable of getting away with murder.

Faustina Bordoni, in the meantime, married Johann Hasse—who was, after Handel, the greatest German-born opera composer of the day—and departed to play a major role in the development of Italian opera in Germany. And Handel himself, moving to the new theater at Covent Garden, finally found a prima donna who was both talented and loyal. Anna Strada del Po sang ten seasons for him, without the fireworks (on or off stage) of Cuzzoni and Bordoni, but nevertheless with great success.

Handel died in London in 1759, in his seventy-fifth year. He was far and away the greatest operatic composer of the Baroque era, and an exponent of *opera seria* who would be equaled only by Mozart and Rossini. The irony was that this important composer of Italian operas was so little known in Italy. Most of his productive life was spent in the operatic boondocks, in England. And there, because of his dominance (and despite the presence of an English contemporary as talented as Thomas Arne), it could be argued that he set back the cause of opera in English by more than a century. Certainly, London would have a "Royal Italian Opera" before it ever had a "Royal Opera."

Handel's achievement was the more remarkable because he had neither a public theater for which to compose, as he might have had in Italy; nor a state-subsidized theater, as he might have had in France; nor even a court theater, as he certainly would have had in almost any other European country. Instead, he had to put up with running theaters for aristocratic English investors who, for personal as well as commercial reasons, thought that the importing of star singers was the most vital part of the job.

Handel's operas did not die with him, but they remained in abeyance for the best part of two centuries. The style in which he wrote—the Italian *opera seria*—and the singers for whom he wrote—particularly the *castrati*—went out of fashion. The revival, when it came, began in Germany in the 1920s and was enthusiastically taken up in Britain. It presented great problems to both musicologists and stage directors. Should *castrato* parts be reassigned to baritones and basses, as twentieth-century notions of dramatic verisimilitude seemed to demand, or should they be given to female mezzos and contraltos, as musical integrity seemed to dictate? Either method has drawbacks, as does the alternative use of tenors—a vocal category little used in *opera seria* except for minor, and usually villainous, roles. By and large, musical considerations have won the day: Handel's operas are usually performed in editions that retain the vocal pitches for which Handel originally wrote, regardless of whether they are sung by male or female singers. At the same time, modern production techniques have done something (though there is a limit) to bring the operas to life on the stage—sufficient, at least, to have made Handel once again a major operatic composer.

Even Handel, master of the Italian style that he was, found the rigid format of *opera seria* too constricting. During the last eighteen years of his life, he composed not one single opera: he concentrated instead on writing oratorios in English.

Freed from the obligation to run theaters and opera companies, released from the need to cater to the demands of Italian prima donnas and *castrati*, and liberated by the flexibility of the oratorio format, Handel was finally able to communicate with his English audience in words they understood, as well as in music.

OPERA IN CENTRAL EUROPE

As in England, so in the German-speaking world: Italian opera was supreme. But there were stirrings of German opera—a premonition of what was to come.

Germany, as such, did not exist. Like Italy, it was a mass of independent kingdoms, principalities, electorates, bishoprics, and city-states. Prussia, looming on the northern horizon, was always the state most likely to dominate the others, and during the reign of Frederick the Great, between 1740 and 1786, its claims became apparent. To the south, in the imperial capital of Vienna, the Habsburg family ruled the vast territory that was still known as the Holy Roman Empire (it included a substantial part of northern Italy around the city of Milan). And in almost all these lands, whatever their native language, Italian was the dominant language of opera.

The first significant demonstration of opera in Vienna took place in 1666. The occasion was yet another royal marriage, and this one, like Louis XIV's six years earlier, was intended to stake a claim to the Spanish throne. Louis of France thought he had staked a pretty good claim by marrying María Teresa, but the Habsburgs intended to trump that claim by arranging their own dynastic alliance. Their candidate was the emperor himself, Leopold I. He was two years younger than Louis, and every bit as eligible on paper. But Leopold was not the Sun King. He was slow and phlegmatic. His advisers, too, were slower than Louis's. Where Mazarin was able to snap up the Infanta María Teresa for Louis, Leopold had to settle for the much younger Infanta Margarita. She happened to be Leopold's niece, but that was not considered a problem. More of a problem was that, even by the standards of the day, Margarita was rather too young for marriage. So for six years, while Louis and María Teresa were playing the young marrieds in Paris, Leopold had to make do with postcards from Madrid—a stunning series of portraits he commissioned from Velázquez as the little princess grew up. Finally, in 1666, when

Cesti's IL POMO D'ORO, *Hoftheater auf der Cortina, Vienna, July 12 and 14, 1668. Engraving by Matthäus Küsel after the design by Ludovico Burnacini. Adrasto and his soldiers approach the Fortress of Mars, watched from above by the goddess Athena.*

she was fifteen, Margarita and Leopold celebrated their marriage in tremendous pomp in Vienna (Margarita ultimately bore him five children before she died in childbirth at the age of twenty-two).

The highlight of the wedding celebration was a new opera written by the assistant *Kapellmeister* at Leopold's court, Antonio Cesti. Like Cavalli, the composer Mazarin commissioned in Paris, Cesti was Italian and had learned his art in Venice. The work he composed for the wedding, *Il pomo d'oro* (The Golden Apple), may be the most ambitious extravaganza ever staged in the name of opera. It contained sixty-two scenes, involved twenty-four separate sets, and was mounted on a stage capable of bearing two elephants (for the assault on the fortress of Mars). Leopold himself, a genuinely gifted musician, wrote at least one of the arias. And all this was housed in a two-thousand-seat theater specially built on the palace grounds by Lodovico Burnacini. Everything about it was ornate, grandiose, extravagant—and Italian.

Louis XIV saw the potential of opera as an art form he could develop in his own image, as a mirror of his distinctively French kingship. Leopold saw no such thing. He loved opera, and did much to promote it in Vienna, but he always accepted it as an Italian art and one that should be performed in the Italian language. So Cesti's successor as *Kapellmeister* was another Venetian, Antonio Draghi. During his forty years at the imperial court, he was said to have produced sixty-seven operas, one hundred thirteen "festival plays," and thirty-two oratorios. The Italian influence was strengthened yet further when first Zeno and then

Metastasio became court poets to the emperor, virtually dictating the composition of Italian *opere serie* by German and Austrian musicians. But in one respect the German model generally outdid its Italian original: more effort, and a great deal more money, was expended on production. The staging of *Constanza e fortezza* (Constancy and Fortitude) by the Austrian composer Johann Joseph Fux for the coronation of the emperor Charles VI in Prague in 1723 was said to have used one hundred musicians and two hundred singers in a magnificent outdoor auditorium that seated four thousand spectators.

Most of the other German-speaking lands followed the emperor's example and adopted Italian as the language of opera. But opera in German was by no means out of the question. As early as 1609, a promising young musician, Heinrich Schütz, had been sent by his employer, the landgrave of Hesse, to study in Venice. Schütz's teacher was Giovanni Gabrieli, the leading Venetian composer of the day and an organist at San Marco. Monteverdi was still in Mantua at that time, but Schütz must have heard a great deal about the new art form, *il dramma per musica*. Back home in Germany, in 1627, he had Rinuccini's original libretto of *Dafne*—the one Jacopo Peri had set in 1598—translated into German so that he could set it to his own score. It was the first German opera: Italian in style and inspiration, but German at least in its language. It had few imitators. Most German composers were happy to stick with Italian.

The only significant German city to buck the trend was Hamburg. Like Venice, Hamburg was a polyglot maritime city; it had grown rich on the Baltic trade. And like Venice, though forty years later, it had its own public opera house, the Theater auf dem Gänsemarkt (The Goose Market). Opera was performed there in German—because that was the language of the ticket buyers, and without them there was no opera. The composer who presided over the Gänsemarkt for the best part of four decades at the beginning of the eighteenth century was Reinhard Keiser; he wrote more than a hundred operas. In contrast to Italian opera of the time, Keiser wrote virtuoso parts for instrumentalists as well as for singers. Handel, at the age of eighteen, had been one of his violinists at the Gänsemarkt, and he never forgot the debt he owed him. Handel's operas, like Keiser's, always featured the instruments of the orchestra as well as the voices of the singers. It was during his two years in Hamburg that Handel composed his first four operas, all of them in German.

But Handel soon departed for Italy, and Keiser's talents alone were not sufficient to create a tradition of German opera. No more were those of his successor, the largely self-taught Georg Philipp Telemann, though it was Telemann's talent for comic opera that signaled the beginnings of the *Singspiel* tradition—a tradition that would be as important for German opera as *opera buffa* was in Italy and *opéra-comique* in France.

Literally, *Singspiel* means "song-play." In many ways, it is the equivalent of the French *opéra-comique*—an operetta or musical play, generally but not always comic, in German, with spoken dialogue. It developed naturally from the medieval mystery plays and the comedies performed by itinerant troupes of traveling players. It was certainly influenced by French *opéra-comique*, which became quite popular in Vienna in Maria Theresa's time, and also by the English fashion for ballad operas, many of which were translated into German. What became known as *Singspiel* found its first home in Vienna about 1710, when a company moved into the newly built theater on the Kärntnertor and began performing popular musical comedies.

In Vienna, with its grand tradition of court entertainments and royal theaters, *Singspiel* was little more than a sop to the public until Joseph II founded the German National Theater in 1778, but in northern Germany, particularly in Leipzig, Hamburg, and Weimar, it became immensely popular. Its greatest exponent was Johann Adam Hiller. He wrote a stream of tuneful and entertaining *Singspiele* with plots that reflected the turbulent times in the German states immediately after the Seven Years' War—marching armies, draft dodgers, overmighty aristocrats, and simple but downtrodden heroes and heroines. Mozart and Goethe, in their separate ways, were both great admirers of Hiller, and would both contribute to the art of *Singspiel*.

There were other isolated examples of opera in German. One of them, *Alceste* by Anton Schweitzer, was a glorious anomaly. It was a German *opera seria*, complete with massive *da capo* arias. First performed in Weimar in 1773, it made the rounds of German court and public theaters, though it was a notoriously unpleasant experience when the singers were not up to the very severe demands Schweitzer made on them. Much more popular, and much more influential, were the "operas" of Gotha's resident composer, Georg Anton Benda. Attracted by the talents of Charlotte Brandes, an actress in a theater company that performed in Gotha during the 1770s, he wrote two melodramas, *Ariadne auf Naxos* and *Medea*. They consisted of dramatic scenes with purely spoken dialogue (by Brandes's husband), but the scenes were connected by vividly descriptive orchestral interludes—the whole effect being magnified by Brandes's dramatic appearance in costumes of the classical period (in itself an innovation for the German stage). Benda's music for these productions was widely performed, and the idea of melodrama as an ingredient of German opera was successfully planted.

For the most part, however, opera in Germany in the eighteenth century was an Italian experience. In Stuttgart, the Neapolitan composer Niccolò Jommelli dominated the city's music. In the Saxon court at Dresden it was Johann Hasse, German by nationality but Italian by training. At Frederick the Great's court at Berlin, Carl Heinrich Graun wrote a series of Italian operas in the strict *opera seria* format, some of them to librettos supplied by Frederick himself. All these courts were wealthy, and the noble patrons expected their operas to be opulently and spectacularly staged, generally in theaters of great magnificence. The Rezidenztheater in Munich (reconstructed in 1958) and the margrave's theater in Bayreuth, both of them built in the mid-eighteenth century, are two splendid survivors of the period, testaments to the power of Baroque music in Baroque architecture.

END OF AN ERA

If it is possible to sum up the story of eighteenth-century opera in a single career, then it has to be that of Johann Adolf Hasse, whose life spanned the first eighty-three years of the century. As a young man he was enagaged by Reinhard Keiser to sing tenor parts in German at the Gänsemarkt in Hamburg. He went on to Naples, where he studied composition with Porpora and Scarlatti, and composed serenades for Farinelli. Then, in Venice, he met and married Faustina Bordoni, the Venetian prima donna who had just returned from her successful war with Cuzzoni in Handel's London. In 1731, Hasse was appointed director of the Dresden Opera (with Bordoni as prima donna), and during the next thirty years he, more than any other composer, imposed the conventions of *opera seria* on German opera—all of it written in Italian, mostly to the librettos of Metastasio, who was busy turning them out in Vienna almost as fast as Hasse set them in Dresden. It was not always clear sailing. In 1747, his erstwhile teacher Porpora sought to establish himself and his singing pupil Regina Mingotti in Dresden. After a brief and brutal confrontation, the Hasses won the day, and the invaders departed.

Europe, as ever, was a battlefield, and in 1760, at the height of the Seven Years' War, Hasse's house was set alight by gunfire during the siege of Dresden; almost all his manuscripts were lost. He and Bordoni moved to Vienna. There, together with their contemporary Metastasio, they watched as Gluck began the revolution which would over-turn the operatic formula they had known and relied on all their lives. From that time on, Hasse and Bordoni had outlived their epoch. They ended their days in Venice, the city where Bordoni had been born and where they had first met half a century before.

They had one final glimpse into the future. Hasse wrote his last opera in 1771. It was called *Il Ruggiero* (to a text by Metastasio—who else?), and it had been commissioned for the celebrations surrounding the wedding in Milan of the archduke Ferdinand, son of Empress Maria Theresa. Hasse and Bordoni traveled to Milan to supervise the staging. While they were there, they saw another work that had been commissioned for the same wedding. It was called *Ascanio in Alba,* and it was written by a sixteen-year-old Austrian boy.

"This boy," Johann Hasse said, "will cause us all to be forgotten."[17] He was right. The boy's name was Wolfgang Amadeus Mozart.

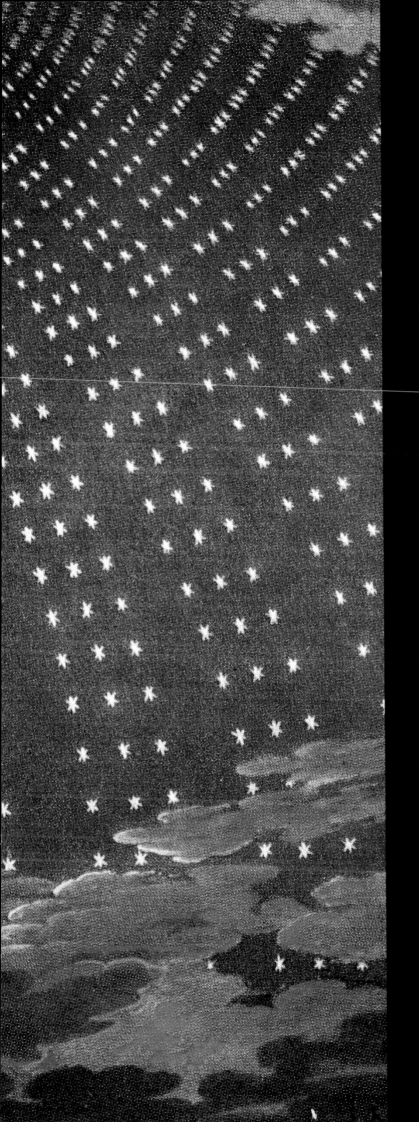

FROM GLUCK TO MOZART

BY THE MIDDLE OF THE EIGH-
TEENTH CENTURY, THE BAROQUE WORLD
OF EUROPEAN CULTURE WAS BEGINNING
TO CRUMBLE. WRITERS, DRAMATISTS, AND
ARTISTS OF ALL KINDS, INCLUDING MUSI-
CIANS, WERE CONFRONTED BY IDEAS THAT
WERE SPREADING ACROSS THE CONTI-
NENT AND THAT WERE SUMMED UP IN
THE TERM THE *ENLIGHTENMENT*. OPERA,
ONE OF THE CHOSEN ENTERTAINMENTS
OF THE RULING CLASSES, WAS SWEPT UP IN
THIS MOVEMENT AND PLAYED A MODEST
PART IN ITS EVOLUTION.

THE ENLIGHTENMENT WAS DEFINED
BY ITS NAME: IT SOUGHT TO THROW LIGHT
INTO AREAS THAT HAD BEEN DARK. IT
WISHED TO REPLACE SUPERSTITION WITH
REASON. IT QUESTIONED ALMOST EVERY-
THING, FROM THE ORIGIN OF THE WORLD
TO THE AUTHORITY OF GOVERNMENTS. IT
RECOMMENDED CRITICAL EXAMINATION
RATHER THAN AUTOMATIC ACCEPTANCE.

IT WAS A DANGEROUS DOCTRINE —
AS DANGEROUS FOR THE ENTRENCHED
AUTHORITIES OF COURTS AND GOVERN-
MENTS AS IT WAS FOR THE CLASS-CON-
SCIOUS ORDER OF EUROPEAN SOCIETY.

And it was very successful. In the last half of the eighteenth century, the social and political infrastructure of Europe (and the American colonies, too) was changed forever. Often, as in France, the change was accompanied by great violence. Elsewhere, as in Austria under Joseph II, the revolution was more peaceful and the results less radical. But everywhere, the ideas of the Enlightenment caused turbulence and social change.

The driving force came from France. French was generally accepted as the international language of ideas, and it was the writings of the French *philosophes*—Voltaire, Rousseau, Diderot, d'Alembert, and many others—that ignited the Enlightenment. These men were *philosophes* in the widest meaning of that term: they were writers, poets, dramatists, and in some cases musicians, who applied their thinking as much to the arts as they did to the rights of man.

Italian *opera seria* and French *tragédie lyrique* were obvious targets. Both were fundamentally artificial. In composition and performance, they were rigidly formal. Their plots were repetitive and frequently reused. At best they were undramatic, at worst, antidramatic. Stage directors were an unknown species. There were choreographers, "machinists," fencing masters, costumers, and set designers, but a librettist who wanted his stage directions observed would either have to attend rehearsals himself or live in hope. Arias were sung from the front of the stage, where lighting was best, and the singers gave physical expression to their emotions in a series of poses that were, by turns, statuesque and histrionic, and were generally quite fantastic. In Italian opera, the singers were thought to be out of control, while French opera, its critics maintained, was moribund.

The *philosophes'* general prescription for opera (for "serious opera," at any rate) was that it should return to its roots, and go back even earlier. They believed that the simple, disciplined example of Greek drama should be the model for librettists and composers. It was no longer good enough, they said, for the drama to be just an excuse for the singers. It was time music and singers got back to serving the drama, just as they were beginning to do in the best of Italian *opera buffa*.

REFORM

This was the scene that confronted Raniero de' Calzabigi when he arrived in Paris in 1750, in time to witness the *guerre des bouffons*. He was an Italian poet and playwright who tended to keep on the move, since his propensities for adventure and intrigue invariably got him into trouble. He was a notable rake. He was eventually expelled from Paris as a result of certain irregularities in a lottery he ran with his friend the notorious Casanova under the protection of the king's mistress, Madame de Pompadour. But his time in Paris was important for other reasons, not least because it led directly to the radical reform of opera that is normally associated, somewhat unfairly, with Gluck's name rather than Calzabigi's. It was when these two men came together in Vienna in the 1760s that they began to change the face of opera.

Calzabigi was familiar with the writings of the *philosophes,* and he subscribed to many of their opinions about opera. In the *guerre* he sided with Rousseau and the anti-Rameau clique, but his true feelings were much more traditionalist. He had corresponded with Metastasio, and in 1755, as part of a published collection of Metastasio's works, Calzabigi wrote an admiring dissertation on the Metastasian libretto.[1] He was somewhat more critical of the French form of *tragédie lyrique*, noting that it allowed very little in the way of characterization, but he found much to praise in the work of Philippe Quinault, Lully's long-dead librettist. Nevertheless, he believed passionately that "serious opera" had lost its way: it had been hijacked by singers, imprisoned within its own too-strict format, and had allowed drama to become a secondary (sometimes a nonexistent) priority.

Fleeing from Paris in 1760 in the wake of the lottery scandal, Calzabigi went to Vienna. There he met the like-minded Gluck, and together they engineered the first great reform of opera in its one and a half centuries of existence. It was probably no coincidence that the libretto Calzabigi prepared for Gluck to launch this reform went right back to opera's roots. It dealt with the familiar story of Orpheus.

Christoph Willibald Gluck was forty-seven years old when he set Calzabigi's Orpheus libretto. He was a coarse, self-centered man, and famously rude—especially to musicians, of whom he required the highest standards. German by birth, he had spent eight years in Italy absorbing the art of Italian music and composing his first Italian operas, just as Handel had done thirty years before him. By the time the two men met in London in 1745, Handel had already given up composing operas in favor of oratorios, and he doubtless told Gluck why. But there is little in the early works of Gluck, many of them written to librettos by Metastasio, to suggest that he was destined to be anything more than just another composer of rather predictable *opere serie*. He was not even a very good technician, his critics said. It was when he settled in Vienna in 1749 that things began to change.

To begin with, he married the daughter of a wealthy merchant. From that time on, Gluck was financially independent—a most unusual circumstance for an eighteenth-century musician, and one that was ideally suited to his temperament. He could afford to speak frankly, and he did so with alarming regularity. He was the first significant opera composer outside France who was able to call singers and musicians to account and to insist that what the composer wrote was what should be performed. This usually meant supervising his own productions, which he hated, but it was a necessary evil. In addition to *opere serie*, he began writing French-style *opéras-comiques* with lively, interesting characters and spoken dialogue. But he was distressed by the abuses of the Italian style. To do something about them, he needed a libretto very far removed from those of Metastasio, who was still the court poet in Vienna, and would be for another twenty years.

Calzabigi brought him the libretto, and Gluck, arrogant man though he was, never forgot the debt: "If my music has had some success, I think it is my duty to recognize that I am beholden for it to [Calzabigi], since it was he who enabled me to develop the resources of my art"[2] *Orfeo ed Euridice*, which was produced in Vienna in 1762, ignored most of the conventions of *opera seria*, and in doing so it made a conscious effort to return opera to its original description of *dramma per musica*. The libretto concentrated entirely on the story of Orpheus and Eurydice—no subplots, no excursions—so Gluck was able to write a score that very precisely complemented and emphasized the unfolding drama. There were no *da capo* arias at all, and therefore no prolonged artificial pauses in the action. The musical numbers connected with each other relatively seamlessly. There were short arias, orchestral recitatives, choruses, and ballets—with the dance sequences (especially those for the Furies) playing an important part in the narrative. The choreographer, Gaspare Angiolini, was an essential part of the collaboration. Indeed,

it was for Angiolini's ballet *Don Juan* that Count Durazzo, the pioneering head of Vienna's imperial theaters, had first brought together the team of Gluck and Calzabigi the previous year.

During the next eight years, Gluck and Calzabigi wrote two more operas in Vienna in the same style as *Orfeo*—first *Alceste*, then *Paride ed Elena*. In the published version of *Alceste* (1767), Gluck wrote a prologue that became the manifesto of opera's first great reform:

> I resolved to divest it entirely of all those abuses, introduced into it either by the mistaken vanity of the singers or by the too great complaisance of composers, which have so long disfigured Italian opera and made of the most splendid and most beautiful of spectacles the most ridiculous and wearisome. . . . I did not wish to arrest

Christoph Willibald Gluck (1714–1787). Portrait by Joseph-Siffred Duplessis, 1775.

an actor in the greatest heat of dialogue in order to wait for a tiresome
ritornello, nor to hold him up in the
middle of a word on a vowel favorable to his voice, nor to make display
of the agility of his fine voice in some
long-drawn passage, nor to wait
while the orchestra gives him time to
recover his breath for a cadenza. . . .[3]

It was not only against the singers' abuses that
Gluck waged his battles. Another distinguishing
mark of *Orfeo ed Euridice* was that it contained none
of the old-fashioned simple (or "dry") recitatives—the long declamatory passages invented by
Vincenzo Galilei and Jacopo Peri at the very
beginning of the story of opera, which were
accompanied only by occasional chords from a
lute or a harpsichord. All the recitatives in Gluck's
Orfeo had orchestral accompaniment, so they were
virtually absorbed into the musical texture of the
piece. Others had done this before, but none so
completely or so successfully as Gluck.

In this and much else, Gluck was the
prophet of what was to come, but his operas were
still essentially of the eighteenth century. The role
of Orfeo was written for a *castrato*—Gaetano
Guadagni, whose low, contralto voice was one of
the wonders of the age. Guadagni was also a fine
actor, and the success of *Orfeo* in Vienna owed not
a little to his presence, but when Gluck revised the
opera for Paris in 1774, in French, he reset the title
role for a tenor (*castrati* had always been unpopular in France). Today, it is as often sung by a female
contralto, so that Orfeo's famous lament, "Che
farò senza Euridice" (I have lost my Euridice),
knows no bounds of gender.

However important the reform operas of
Gluck and Calzabigi can be seen to be in retrospect, it would be a mistake to think they were
hugely popular at the time. *Orfeo ed Euridice* was
certainly a great success in 1762. Empress Maria
Theresa attended almost every performance, which
was good for the box office, and audiences were
undoubtedly entranced by the decor (by Giovanni
Maria Quaglio) and by the dancing, as well as by
the singing of Guadagni. But *Alceste* was at best a
moderate success, and *Paride ed Elena* was a complete failure. There were other composers active
in Vienna whose works were more familiar and
often as intriguing. Johann Hasse belonged to the
familiar category, busily setting every word Meta-

stasio wrote in the traditional *opera seria* format.
Tommaso Traetta was probably more intriguing,
and he certainly had a good deal of influence on
Gluck. He was a Neapolitan composer, com-
fortably employed at the notably culture-minded
court of Parma. He arrived in Vienna in 1761 and
had great success with his opera *Armida*. The following year, only a few months after the premiere
of Gluck's *Orfeo*, Traetta staged his *Ifigenia in Tauride*, an opera that had almost as much right as
Orfeo to be thought of as a "reform" opera. Gluck
conducted it himself, and it must have been a
considerable influence on him when he came to
set the same subject a few years later in Paris.
Traetta, however, was an itinerant with no real
roots. From Vienna he went to Venice, then to St.
Petersburg, where he spent seven cold and unproductive winters as Catherine the Great's resident
composer.

In 1773, Gluck was lured to Paris by
François du Roullet, a member of the French
embassy in Vienna, and it was du Roullet who
provided him with the text to his first French
opera, *Iphigénie en Aulide*. It was also du Roullet,
with a lot of help from Gluck himself, who pro-
voked a fierce debate in the French press about the
superiority (or otherwise) of Gluck's "reformed"
opera style over the "unreformed" and traditional
Italian style against which he had revolted. Between
1773 and 1779, Gluck wrote four French operas and
rearranged both *Orfeo* and *Alceste* in French—to
the intense delight of the queen, Marie-Antoinette,
to whom Gluck was both singing and harpsichord
teacher. He had great success in Paris, but he was
also, not unwillingly, a controversial figure. The
unfortunate representative of the traditional Italian school against whom he was arrayed by the
Parisian press was Niccolò Piccinni, a talented and
prolific Italian composer who was then living in
Paris. It became quite common to demand of
someone whether he was a "Gluckist" or a "Pic-
cinnist," and the rival camps even took to the
streets. At the end of 1776, Benjamin Franklin,
the commissioner to the French court from what
would soon become the United States of America, having recently arrived following certain
momentous events in Philadelphia, looked on in
disbelief: "Happy people! thought I, you live certainly under a wise, just and mild government,
since you have no public grievance to complain of,
nor any subject of contention *but the perfections and
imperfections of foreign music!*"[4] Franklin lived until

1790, long enough to know that the French people did, in fact, have more fundamental grievances to express.

On a personal level, Gluck and Piccinni had no quarrel, but it was Piccinni's misfortune that he should have found himself at the center of the controversy. In Naples, he had made his reputation as a composer of *opere buffe*. *La buona figliuola* (The Good Daughter) was probably the most famous opera of that genre since Pergolesi's *La serva padrona* thirty years before, but it did not necessarily equip him to be the champion of either Italian *opera seria* or French *tragédie lyrique*. The unfortunate confrontation came to a head when Gluck announced he was composing *Iphigénie en Tauride*, a sequel to his first Paris opera. Piccinni was already embarked on the identical subject. Graciously (and wisely), he postponed completion of

his version until Gluck's had had its triumphant premiere in 1779; it may have been the finest thing Gluck ever wrote. Piccinni's opera, brought to the same stage two years later, was an inferior version, to be sure, but it was hardly helped on opening night when the leading lady appeared to be intoxicated. "*C'est Iphigénie en Champagne!*" one member of the audience was reported to have shouted.[5]

By this time, Gluck, suffering from apoplexy and partial paralysis, was back in Vienna, where he held the mostly honorary position of *Kammermusicus* (chamber musician) at the imperial court until his death in 1787. The gospel he preached—simplification, at all costs—was not necessarily one his peers wanted to hear. It was more profitable for them to go on churning out the old recipes. That, after all, was what their patrons expected, and, almost without exception,

Gluck's Armide *at La Scala, Milan, 1996. Directed and designed by Pier Luigi Pizzi.* Armide *was written for the Paris Opéra in 1777 and was based, almost verbatim, on a libretto that Philippe Quinault had written for Lully ninety-one years earlier. The magnificent, and somewhat controversial, production illustrated here opened the 1996—97 season at La Scala.*

eighteenth-century composers were dependent on patrons—wealthy aristocrats or princes who would either employ them, or, failing that, commission new music from them. Gluck was the exception. Financially insulated by his marriage, he was nobody's servant. In the nineteenth century, he would be recognized for what he was, a prophet, by musicians as important as Hector Berlioz and Richard Wagner.

Gluck's immediate successors, already at the peak of their careers by the time he died, were composers of much greater genius. But both Joseph Haydn and Wolfgang Amadeus Mozart were dependent on patronage. Haydn found it and thrived on it: Mozart's short life was an endless search for it.

In 1787, the year of Gluck's death, Haydn was celebrating his twenty-first year as *Kapellmeister* to the Esterházy family. He was fifty-five years old, universally admired, and perfectly secure. He was, by his own description, a servant of the Esterházys, and very glad to be. Mozart, on the other

hand, was thirty-one years old, living in Vienna, and dependent for his living on taking in pupils, arranging public concerts of his own works, and obtaining commissions for new works wherever he could. The first and only post he held at the imperial court was the one Gluck vacated when he died—*Kammermusicus*—and Mozart was given it at less than half the salary Gluck had been paid. "It enrages me," wrote Haydn, the most generous of men, "to think that this incomparable Mozart is not yet engaged by some imperial or royal court! Forgive me if I lose my head but I love the man so dearly."[6]

At the time he wrote that letter, in December 1787, Haydn still had more than twenty years to live. Mozart had exactly four.

HAYDN

The castle of Esterháza was the scene of Joseph Haydn's great good fortune. When Prince Paul Anton of Esterházy first employed him as *Vice-Kapellmeister* in 1761, when he was still less than thirty years of age, the castle had not yet been built. But when Paul Anton died the following year and was succeeded by his brother, Prince Nicolaus, plans were quickly drawn up for the building of a fairy-tale palace almost as magnificent as Versailles itself. The Esterházys were an ancient Hungarian family, hugely wealthy landowners and famous servants of the Empire, whose patronage of music and the arts was renowned throughout Europe. The new castle reflected their interests. The second floor was dominated by a magnificent music room. A four-hundred-seat opera house was built on the grounds, with a separate marionette theater adjacent to it. There was accommodation for musicians, singers, and visiting troupes, though Haydn himself preferred to live in the nearby town of Eisenstadt. By 1766, when he became *Kapellmeister* in his own right, Haydn was spending most of his time at Esterháza, and as the years went by it became the focus of all his work.

We think of him for his symphonies, his masses, his chamber music—a vast corpus of work—but we think of him very little as an opera composer. Yet the major part of the three decades he spent at Esterháza was devoted to opera—

composing his own operas and performing them, as well as those of other composers. It was the empress Maria Theresa, visiting Prince Nicolaus in 1773 and being entertained with a performance of Haydn's *L'infedeltà delusa*, who later declared: "If I want to hear good opera, I go to Esterháza."

But not many people could go to Esterháza. It was a remote and private place. "I was cut off from the world," Haydn wrote; "there was no one in my neighborhood to make me unsure of myself or to persecute me; and so I had to become original."[7] Original he certainly was in his music, but his isolation at Esterháza militated against him as a dramatic composer. The librettos he set were generally undistinguished, but that could be said of many lesser composers who were much more successful with opera. Unlike them, and unlike his great contemporaries, Haydn had no experience of Italian opera in Italy. His apprenticeship had taken place in Vienna. There, it is true, he had worked for the greatest Italian singing teacher of the day, Nicola Porpora, and he had learned the Italian language from no less an expert than Metastasio himself. But he had no prolonged exposure to Italian opera in Italy—in the way that

Haydn's LA FEDELTÀ PREMIATA *at the Glyndebourne Festival, 1979. Directed by John Cox, designed by Sir Hugh Casson. With Thomas Allen as Perrucchetto and Kathleen Battle as Nerina.*

Handel, Hasse, Gluck, and even the young Mozart enjoyed. Nevertheless, given a good plot, such as Goldoni's *Il mondo della luna* (The World on the Moon), Haydn was capable of writing first-rate *opera buffa* that has endured into the modern repertoire.

Reflecting Prince Nicolaus's own preference, most of Haydn's early works were comic. So were many of the other operas performed at Esterháza—works by Cimarosa, Salieri, Piccinni, Dittersdorf, Paisiello, and Mozart, among others. There was serious opera, too. Haydn was familiar with Gluck's work, and a great admirer of it: he conducted *Orfeo ed Euridice* at Esterháza in 1776, and he several times tried his own hand at *opera seria*. But he was always conscious of his limitations. Writing to the director of the Prague Opera in 1787 (in the same letter in which he railed against Mozart's inability to find a proper patron), he said:

> You ask me for an *opera buffa*. Most willingly, if you want to have one of my vocal compositions for yourself alone. But if you intend to produce it on the stage at Prague, in that case I cannot comply with your wish, because all my operas are far too closely connected with our personal circle (Esterház, in Hungary), and moreover they would not produce the proper effect, which I calculated in accordance with the locality.[8]

Haydn was very modest, but in terms of his operas he was realistic as well. Better than anyone, he knew he would suffer by comparison with Mozart, who was just then in the midst of his great collaboration with Lorenzo Da Ponte. In any case, Haydn was busy enough at Esterháza. In 1786 alone, he prepared and conducted 125 performances of seventeen different operas, eight of them entirely new to the Esterháza repertoire. It is a wonder that he found time to compose any other kind of music.

In all this activity, Haydn was working directly to the dictates of his employer. His contract with Prince Nicolaus is a source of amazement to a modern reader, but it was by no means extraordinary at the time. As *Kapellmeister*, Haydn was required to wear his master's livery; he must eat at what was called the "officers' table" (which was certainly better than the servants' table); he must report daily to the prince to find out what music was required for that evening; he must take care of all the musical instruments; he must teach both singing and "instruments with which he is acquainted" to members of the household; and he must, of course, fulfill all the prince's musical requirements—composing, rehearsing, conducting, and overseeing performances to the highest artistic standards.[9] Haydn had no trouble with signing this contract, and being extremely grateful for it. "I have had converse with emperors, kings, and great princes," he wrote, "and have heard many flattering remarks from them, but I do not wish to live on a familiar footing with such persons, and I prefer people of my own class."[10]

After several misadventures with fire, the opera house at Esterháza was finally demolished in the nineteenth century. We know it had a large central box for the prince and two somewhat smaller boxes on either side for his guests. By the mid-1780s, there were three opera performances a week whenever the prince was in residence at the castle. The general public could attend for free except when the prince was entertaining his own guests. Haydn had a resident orchestra of twenty-four players (large for a private theater in those days); a resident scenographer, who was responsible for the staging and decor; and a theater manager, who looked after everything else. Prince Nicolaus himself seems to have acted as executive producer, especially where casting was concerned. To judge by contemporary prints, costume and design budgets were fairly lavish. Nevertheless, it was a small stage in a small auditorium; Haydn was well aware that he was not composing for one of the great Viennese theaters.

At the beginning of 1790, on a visit to Vienna, Haydn heard *Le nozze di Figaro* for the first time and attended rehearsals for *Così fan tutte* as Mozart's guest. Nine months later, back at Esterháza, he conducted two performances of *Figaro*. They were the last two performances ever attended by Prince Nicolaus, who died in Vienna the following week. That was the end of Haydn's fairy-tale at Esterháza. The new prince promptly closed down the music facilities at the castle, and Haydn, generously pensioned (he actually remained on the payroll until 1802), departed for Vienna, and then for London. Mozart, dining with him on his last day in Vienna, bade him farewell with the remark, "We are probably saying our last adieu in this life."[11] Neither of them could have guessed that

Mozart, rather than Haydn, would be dead within the year.

ROYAL PATRONS

By any standard, Prince Nicolaus Esterházy was an outstanding patron of music, and Haydn fully understood how fortunate he had been to enjoy his patronage for so long. But Esterháza was not unique. Only a few miles away, at Böhmisch Krumau, the Schwartzenberg family built a very similar opera house on their grounds (it still stands today), and all over Europe, especially in the courts of the German principalities, there were Baroque and Rococo theaters testifying to the importance of opera—almost always Italian opera.

The main exception to the Italian rule, of course, was France, but there were others. Sweden was one. Gustavus III had an inordinate love for things French, and he set out to emulate the culture of Versailles, more or less bankrupting his country in the process. At his summer palace at Drottningholm on the Stockholm archipelago, he built a court theater as magnificent as Esterháza's, and just as functional. At exactly the time that Prince Nicolaus and Joseph Haydn were celebrating Italian opera at Esterháza, Gustavus was importing French ballet and French opera (often in Swedish translation) to be performed in the summer months at Drottningholm. In Stockholm itself, at the Royal Opera House, he inaugurated a tradition of Swedish opera, with librettos often written by himself. But the principal influence was always French, and most notably that of Gluck. Stockholm actually staged the first performance of *Orphée et Euridice* (Gluck's French revision of his first "reform" opera) the year before it was seen in Paris. Eventually, it was Gustavus's scheme to send his Swedish army to support Louis XVI against the Paris revolutionaries that led to his own assassination in 1792 at a masked ball in the Stockholm Opera House—an event immortalized in opera by Scribe's libretto, set by both Daniel Auber and Giuseppe Verdi. For a hundred and twenty years after Gustavus's death, the theater at Drottningholm remained more or less in cobwebs—until in 1922 a royal archivist came across the actual stage machinery and thirty sets of original scenery, many of which are in use to this day at Drottningholm's modern summer festival.

Like Gustavus in Sweden (and Frederick in Prussia), Catherine the Great of Russia was a part-time librettist. Ever since Peter I had opened up Russia to Western influences at the beginning of the eighteenth century, successive czars and czarinas had sponsored a distinguished list of Italian composers, singers, and musicians who had come to Russia to head up the enterprise. In Catherine's time the list included Galuppi, Traetta, Paisiello, Sarti, Cimarosa, and the Spaniard Martin y Soler. Perhaps more than any other European monarch (she was actually German by birth), Catherine was influenced by the *philosophes* of the Enlightenment. Opera, in her view, should contain social commentary and should be used to indoctrinate audiences with political views. The language of opera was therefore Russian—set by Italian composers—and Catherine's own librettos concentrated on patriotic themes (including a notable tirade against her neighbor, Gustavus of Sweden). To the great relief of her court, she imposed on all operas, including her own, a maximum running time of two hours.

There was, then, a great deal of patronage available for talented musicians, especially those with expertise in Italian opera. So how was it that Mozart, the greatest expert of all, never found himself a regular, or a generous, patron?

MOZART

It was not for want of trying. As a seven-year-old boy, he was bucketed around Europe in stagecoaches by his ambitious father, Leopold. In Vienna, he played for the imperial court; at Versailles, he played for King Louis; in London, he played for King George; in the Palace of Schwetzingen, he played for the princes of Baden-Württemberg ("the orchestra is without contradiction the best in Germany," wrote Papa Leopold). All over Europe, the great and the famous applauded the child prodigy, but none of them offered him long-term patronage.

They were probably right. By the time he was a teenager, it was clear that Mozart had neither the temperament nor the temper to be patronized. Where Haydn had slogged his way through long years as a chorister at St. Stephen's Cathedral, and then faced up to the life of an unemployed, untrained musician on the streets of Vienna, Mozart's precocious talent opened doors to him at every turn throughout his boyhood. The nearest he got to a patron was the archduke Ferdinand, at whose wedding in Milan the composer Hasse and the singer Bordoni first came across the boy wonder. Ferdinand wished to employ him, but his mother, Empress Maria Theresa, warned him against employing these "useless people." On a visit to Paris a few years later, when he was twenty-two, Mozart's arrogance and rudeness insured him against French patronage. "I don't care about the Parisians' applause,"[12] he wrote. And when Leopold got him a job with his own patron, the prince archbishop of Salzburg, it turned into a dangerous, simmering relationship between an autocratic employer and a reluctant employee, ending in a spectacular bust-up. For the last ten years of his life, living in Vienna, Mozart had no regular patronage or employment. But they were prolific years.

It is one of the curious ironies of the story of opera that Mozart's massive intervention was largely posthumous. *Figaro*, first produced in Vienna five and half years before his death and arguably the most popular opera ever written, had only thirty-five performances in Vienna in his lifetime. Which is not to say that Mozart was not famous. He was, and well beyond the boundaries of the Empire, but when it came to Italian opera, he was low on the totem pole of popularity compared to some of his more established contemporaries. Sarti, Salieri, Paisiello, and Martín y Soler were the big names of the 1780s and 1790s in Vienna, along with Domenico Cimarosa, whose *Il matrimonio segreto* (The Secret Marriage) had a runaway success within a few weeks of Mozart's death. Part of the explanation lies in the obvious fact that Mozart did not live long enough to be widely recognized for what he was, but another part lies in the dominance of the Viennese court, of which Mozart was not a part, and its ability to keep an outsider outside. By contrast, Mozart was hugely popular in Prague, where his operas played to packed houses and where he himself was a genuine celebrity.

Even after his death—despite his manifest fame, despite the worldwide success of *Le nozze di Figaro, Don Giovanni*, and *Die Zauberflöte* (The Magic Flute), and despite the vigorous efforts of his friends and his wife, Constanze, who outlived him by more than fifty years—*Idomeneo* and *Così fan tutte*, two of the greatest operas ever written, remained practically unknown to the nineteenth century.

It is not as though Mozart was a revolutionary in opera. He took the established forms—Italian *opera seria* and *opera buffa*, and German *Singspiel*—and observed most of the conventions. But he did it better than anyone else had ever done

before (and, maybe, since). *Idomeneo* represented a dying breed, the *opera seria*, but it is doubtful if anyone ever produced a more perfect specimen of it. There were four central characters (one of them written for *castrato*) caught up in a tragic situation. The libretto contained all the potential problems of *opera seria*—static situations, predictable plotting, no real dramatic tension—but Mozart was able to take the text and, through his music, provide the drama so evidently missing when any other composer attempted the form. And if *Idomeneo* took *opera seria* to new heights, then *Die Zauberflöte* did the same for *Singspiel*—by using a combination of music and stagecraft to present a profoundly serious theme in a wrapping of pantomime, musical comedy, and dramatic imagery.

But no species of opera was better served by Mozart than *opera buffa*. The three operas he wrote with librettos by Lorenzo Da Ponte (*Figaro, Don Giovanni,* and *Così fan tutte*) were dramatic masterpieces—comedies, to be sure, but all of them containing strong dramatic material. For perhaps the first time on the operatic stage, music, drama, and stagecraft came together in a truly satisfying whole. If you look at the texts of any of those three operas, you will find literally hundreds of entrances and exits marked for the characters, and every one of them is precisely plotted as a part of the unfolding drama. They represent the sort of stagecraft previously only required of the straight theater (and not often, even then). Mozart and Da Ponte showed that it was possible in opera, too.

Even at its simplest, the task of writing an opera is immensely complicated. For a boy in his early teens to be able to do so—in German, Italian, and Latin (*Apollo et Hyacinthus* was a Latin stage play Mozart set when he was only eleven)—is staggering. Judged by his later creations, they were perhaps not much to write home about, but in the one-act *Singspiel* called *Bastien und Bastienne*, which he composed at age twelve, and the three-act *opera buffa* titled *La finta semplice* (The Feigned Fool), composed at age thirteen, his precociousness was clear to see. It became much more marked with his three operas for the archduke Ferdinand in Milan: *Lucio Silla*, composed at age sixteen, is an *opera seria* good enough to stand alongside the mature works of most eighteenth-century composers, other than Handel and Gluck.

For eleven years, from 1770 to 1781, Mozart was employed by Count Hieronymus Colloredo, the archbishop of Salzburg, as a *Konzertmeister*—

basically, just a violinist in the orchestra, though in 1778 he was also appointed organist. The last of Duke Ferdinand's commissions was in 1772, and there were few requests for operas after that. *La finta giardiniera* (The Feigned Garden Girl) was a charming three-act *opera buffa* written for the court theater in Munich in 1775, but otherwise Mozart had to be content with writing for Salzburg. *Il re pastore* (The Shepherd King) was given there as a festival play in 1775, to a text by Metastasio, with all the resulting limitations.

The great divide in Mozart's life came in 1778. In that year, he went to Paris with his mother—a disastrous trip during which his mother died and he was jilted by the woman he hoped to marry. He was away from Salzburg for sixteen months, but when he returned (in the words of one of his modern biographers, H. C. Robbins Landon), "he acquired the mantle of greatness."[13] He began to compose, at an unbelievable rate, the symphonies and sacred works of his maturity. They included the little-known incidental music for a play called *Thamos, König in Ägypten*, which prefigured the operatic music still to come. And it was during this period, in 1781, at the age of twenty-five, that Mozart finally received the commission

he most wanted, to write a full-length *opera seria* for Munich. The result was *Idomeneo*.

Idomeneo was a turning point in more ways than one. Musically and dramatically, it was probably the greatest opera ever written up to that

ABOVE: *Mozart's* IDOMENEO *at the Metropolitan Opera, New York, 1982. Directed and designed by Jean-Pierre Ponnelle. With Frederica von Stade as Idamante (back left), Luciano Pavarotti as Idomeneo, and Ileana Cotrubas as Ilia.*

LEFT: *Anton Raaff (1714–1797). Anonymous watercolor. Mozart (aged twenty-three) wrote the title role in* IDOMENEO *specially for Raaff, who was sixty-seven. This German tenor had studied with the* castrato *Bernacchi in Bologna and later sang with Farinelli in Madrid and Naples.*

moment—certainly the greatest *opera seria*. Of all its many wonders, which included an unprecedented amount of choral writing and superbly characterized arias for all the principal characters, it was the extraordinary power of the quartet in Act III that made the greatest impression, then and now. The opera was given half a dozen performances at the Residenztheater in Munich—and then forgotten. With the exception of a single amateur performance put on under Mozart's supervision in Vienna, it was never again performed in his lifetime and spent the best part of a hundred and fifty years in obscurity. But its production led directly to a fundamental change in Mozart's life. He overstayed his leave from Salzburg. When he returned to Archbishop Colloredo's service (the archbishop was on a visit to Vienna at the time), he found himself completely out of favor. After a few weeks, and with an awful inevitability, there was a blazing row in which Mozart was accused of being a "miserable brat," a "nasty rascal," and an "idiot." His employment was terminated.

From then until the end of his life—a period of just over ten years—Mozart lived in Vienna and made his living as a freelance musician and composer. At times, it was a very good living, but neither Mozart nor Constanze, whom he married in 1782, were good managers, so money was almost always a problem. But they were happy, and in Vienna Mozart quickly became famous. Up to that time his works had had very little dissemination, but from then on he performed for a cosmopolitan and sophisticated audience whose opinions bore weight throughout Europe.

This was "Josephine" Vienna. Since 1765, Joseph II had shared the imperial throne with his mother, Maria Theresa. She died in 1780, and for the next ten years, almost the span of Mozart's time in Vienna, Joseph ruled in his own right. He finally became the reforming monarch he had always wanted to be. He declared himself independent of the pope (quite a step for the Holy Roman Emperor); he slashed the number of clergy by more than half, and their power accordingly; he abolished serfdom in the Empire; he cut back the feudal privileges of the nobles; and he curtailed (but did not abolish) the government's powers of censorship. It was not as if Joseph believed in equality; rather, he saw his policies as a practical strategy for much-needed reform. And who was to say he was wrong? In the 1780s, France was already headed toward violent revolution, and England was losing its American colonies to the subversive doctrine of Democracy. Joseph's reforms were timely and benign—but he could not make them stick. Like so many of his predecessors, he got enmeshed in European wars, particularly against the Ottoman Turks, and he inevitably found himself raising taxes rather than lowering them. No ruler could remain popular while he was doing that.

Joseph also had an agenda on the cultural front. He wished to Germanize his subjects' entertainments, particularly those of the Viennese. This was something he was allowed to pursue during his mother's lifetime. It meant getting rid of, or at least cutting back, the French and Italian influences that had pervaded all forms of entertainment in Vienna for almost two centuries, and it explained why, when Mozart moved to Vienna in 1781, there was a dearth of Italian opera. Even French *opéra-comique* (a particular enthusiasm of Joseph's) was performed only in German translation. Joseph had no great difficulty in making these reforms since Vienna's two major theaters, the Burgtheater and the Kärntnertortheater, were owned and run by the court. In 1776, he established the German National Theater, followed two years later by the National-Singspiel at the Burgtheater. In addition, he had the Kärntnertortheater stage a succession of plays and *Singspiele* in German. They did well enough to begin with, but by the time Mozart arrived in the city, the German policy was beginning to pall on the Viennese. By 1782, Italian operas (by Gluck and Salieri, among others) were once again being performed at the imperial theaters.

There is a great deal of evidence that Mozart liked his emperor, and that the liking was to some degree reciprocated. They were hardly on intimate terms, and no place was found for Mozart at the court until Gluck's position as *Kammermusicus* became available in 1787, but Joseph was well aware of Mozart's presence in the city and had reason to be grateful for it—not least because Mozart's first contribution to the operatic life of Vienna was a *Singspiel*, an outstanding contribution to the ailing German National Theater.

Die Entführung aus dem Serail (The Abduction from the Seraglio) must have appealed to Joseph for another reason. Its ending, in which a magnanimous monarch (a Turkish one) forgave the lovers and set them free, was exactly the "enlightened" image of kingship he most wanted to project. Mozart's letter to his father in which he described the opening night has unfortunately been lost: a claque of hissers was apparently drowned by cheers, and legend has it that Mozart and the emperor had a famous exchange at the end of the performance: "Too beautiful for our ears, and far too many notes, my dear Mozart," said the emperor. "Exactly as many, Your Majesty, as are needed," replied the composer. At all events, *Die Entführung* made Mozart famous as an opera composer for the first time. It was acclaimed in Prague and all over the German-speaking world.

It was undoubtedly a *Singspiel*—a musical play with spoken dialogue—but *Die Entführung* also contained a number of magnificent arias that elevated it to the musical level of *opera seria* (most famously, "Martern aller Arten," sung by the heroine Constanze). It was music of a quality with which *Singspiel* had not previously been blessed.

It is clear from his letters that Mozart enormously enjoyed the challenge of writing opera, but his frenetic existence during those first years in Vienna gave him little time for it. Nor did he have the direct access to court theaters that was a perk of being on the imperial payroll. He had to watch while composers of lesser talent, but greater seniority, brought their works to the stage year after year. Joseph's *Kapellmeister* was the aging Giuseppe Bonno (an Austrian, despite his Italian name). He was an esteemed teacher but not much of a composer, and he tended to promote the works of his own pupils—men like Karl Ditters von Dittersdorf, whose forty operas were given undeserved currency by the regularity with which they were staged. The court composer, second only to the *Kapellmeister*, was Antonio Salieri. History, and very often fiction, has portrayed him as Mozart's enemy—and even his poisoner, which he was not.

Salieri was a genuinely talented composer. Italian by birth, he was taken to Vienna as a sixteen-year-old by Florian Gassmann, who was Bonno's predecessor as *Kapellmeister* and a great favorite of Joseph's. Under Gassmann's tutelage, Salieri became a successful composer of Italian operas and a powerful figure at court. At just about the time that Mozart arrived in Vienna, Salieri developed a close relationship with the aging Gluck, who recommended him to the Paris Opéra. Indeed, his first French opera, *Les danaïdes*, was originally billed as a collaboration with Gluck, until

Gluck, after the first performance, insisted it was all Salieri's work and had his own name removed. Salieri continued to prosper in Paris, most notably with *Tarare* in 1787. It had a libretto by Beaumarchais and remained a staple of Parisian opera for many years. But Salieri, much to Mozart's chagrin, never forsook his base in Vienna.

The truth about their relationship was that there was little love lost between them; Mozart's letters are evidence of that. The older man (by only six years) was probably jealous of the younger, and certainly protective of his own influence at court, where he was a master of intrigue. But the idea that Salieri conspired to have Mozart poisoned was pure fiction—a fiction that lived on long after his own death. Rossini and Wagner gossiped about it in Paris seventy years later, Pushkin wrote a poem about it, Rimsky-Korsakov an opera, and

Antonio Salieri (1750–1825). Salieri is best known to posterity for his intrigues against Mozart, but he was a fine composer in his own right, with major success in both Vienna and Paris. In 1778 he took over from Gluck the commission for the opening of La Scala, Milan (the opera was called L'Europa riconosciuta*). He gave much-needed help to Mozart's son after the composer's death, and he was greatly esteemed by his many pupils, most notably Beethoven.*

Wolfgang Amadeus Mozart (1756–1791). Unfinished portrait by Joseph Lange (his brother-in-law), 1789–90.

Lorenzo Da Ponte (1749–1838). Engraving by M. Pekenino, after N. Roger.

in the 1970s Peter Schaffer explored the story in his play *Amadeus.* As for Salieri, the renowned teacher of Beethoven and Schubert, he went to his grave thirty-four years after Mozart, still dogged by the rumors. On his deathbed he told one of his pupils that "there is no truth in the absurd reports." But that same pupil, Ignaz Moscheles, added his own opinion that Salieri had "no doubt by his intrigues poisoned many an hour of Mozart's existence."[14] And that, maybe, was close to the truth.

In one respect, Mozart owed a debt to Salieri, because it was Salieri who invited Da Ponte to Vienna in 1782 and was largely responsible for his appointment as official poet to the imperial theaters. Lorenzo Da Ponte was an extraordinary figure. An Italian Jew who became a Roman Catholic priest, he was dismissed from his job in Italy for insubordination and for expressing forbidden views on natural law; later, he was banished altogether for adultery. He moved, via Dresden, to Vienna and obtained his introduction to Salieri as one Italian to another. No composer who ever worked with him (and Mozart and Salieri were only two of the beneficiaries) doubted his enormous talent and his incredible energy. But he was always a dangerous influence—too dangerous for Joseph's successor, whose bureaucrats forced him to leave Vienna in 1790. He eventually wound up in New York, where he became a tobacco dealer, a grocer, and eventually professor of Italian at Columbia. He died in Manhattan in 1838, aged eighty-nine, having written some highly unreliable memoirs.

The three operas he wrote with Mozart are

unique in the story of opera, not just for their brilliance but because they are generally referred to by both names—the "Mozart/Da Ponte operas." There have been other great collaborations in opera—Strauss and Hofmannsthal, Verdi and Piave, Verdi and Boito, Meyerbeer and Scribe—but none of these were partnerships of even approximate equality: in every case, the composer was sovereign. In the case of Mozart and Da Ponte, it was a much more equal partnership of a supremely gifted playwright with a composer who understood the idea of *dramma per musica* better than anyone had ever done before, and who had the musical skills to complement and ennoble Da Ponte's stagecraft.

The subject of their first collaboration, *Le nozze di Figaro* (The Marriage of Figaro), was so daring as to be unthinkable for lesser souls. The Beaumarchais play on which it was based had had a runaway success at the Comédie-Française in Paris in 1784. Joseph banned it in Vienna. It was undoubtedly subversive: it lampooned the aristocracy, made fun of the class system, and celebrated the equality of all people, masters and servants alike. Yet, according to Da Ponte, it was Mozart's idea that they should make it into an opera. He was much influenced in this by the success Giovanni Paisiello had already had with the first part of Beaumarchais's trilogy about Figaro, *Il barbiere di Siviglia* (The Barber of Seville). Paisiello was an Italian composer, more itinerant than most, who wrote his *Il barbiere* in St. Petersburg in 1782, while he was employed by Catherine the Great. When it reached Vienna the following year, it had an astounding success—more than sixty performances, making it the most popular opera of the entire century—and it would go on to take Italy by storm as well. Only Rossini's intervention with a superior version in 1816 would slow down the bandwagon and ultimately bring it almost to a stop.

Paisiello's example was important in more ways than just subject matter. He was typical of a generation of talented Neapolitan composers who had cut their teeth on *opera seria*, only to discover that *opera buffa* offered more exciting opportunities. Writing fine arias was important (and diffi-

Mozart's Le nozze di Figaro *at the Glyndebourne Festival, 1994. Directed by Stephen Medcalf, designed by John Gunter. With Marie-Ange Todorovitch as Cherubino, Andreas Schmidt as the Count, and Alison Hagley as Susanna.*

Im kaiserl. königl. National-Hof-Theater
wird heute Montag den 1ten May 1786 aufgeführt:
(zum erstenmal)

LE NOZZE
DI FIGARO.
Die Hochzeit des Figaro.
Ein italiänisches Singspiel in vier Aufzügen.
Die Musik ist vom Herrn Kapellmeister Mozart.

Die Bücher sind italiänisch und deutsch jedes für 20 kr. beym Logenmeister zu haben.

Der Anfang ist um halb 7 Uhr.

Playbill for the premiere of Mozart's
Le nozze di Figaro *at the Burgtheater,*
Vienna, 1786. The playbill mentions neither
Beaumarchais nor Da Ponte.

cult), but how much more challenging was the construction of a great ensemble finale of the sort pioneered by Baldassare Galuppi in Venice in the 1750s. Galuppi had the advantage of working with a major dramatist, Carlo Goldoni, whereas most of the Neapolitans suffered from inferior librettos. Nevertheless, by the time Da Ponte and Mozart teamed up in 1785–86, the sophisticated Viennese audience was predisposed to think that an *opera buffa* would be much more interesting, much more dramatic, and much more fun than any other form of opera.

It was Da Ponte who persuaded the emperor that he and Mozart should be allowed to stage *Figaro* at the Burgtheater, even while Beaumarchais's play remained banned. According to Da Ponte's description of the encounter, Joseph was doubtful, but he succumbed—the more so when he had Mozart over to the palace to play through some of the music. Mozart was certainly in royal favor by this time (but not in its employ). A few months earlier, he had had the opportunity to show off his operatic prowess with a one-act *Singspiel* called *Der Schauspieldirektor* (The Impresario)—a hilarious comedy about the rivalry of competing prima donnas. Joseph had commissioned it for a winter entertainment at the Schönbrunn Palace, and although it had been somewhat overshadowed by a companion piece (in Italian) written for the same occasion by Salieri, it had had a subsequent and very well-received run at the Kärntnertortheater.

Joseph's judgment about *Figaro* turned out to be correct. It made few waves in Vienna. At best, it could be called a *succès d'estime*, and the first performance, led by the composer from the fortepiano, appears to have been somewhat chaotic. Writing twelve years after the event, Mozart's first biographer, Franz Xaver Niemetschek, gave an illuminating (but questionable) description of the sort of jealousies Mozart apparently aroused within his own profession:

> If it is really true, as has been definitely asserted—and it is difficult to disbelieve reliable eyewitnesses—that disgruntled singers, out of hate, envy and ill will, tried to spoil the opera by continually making mistakes at the first performance, the reader may gather how much the whole coterie of Italian singers and composers feared the superiority of Mozart's genius.[15]

Whether real or imagined, these problems did not last very long. By the fourth performance, the imperial bureaucracy had to issue a decree restricting the number of encores (no fewer than seven separate numbers had been repeated at the third performance, one of them three times), and a correspondent of the *Wiener Realzeitung* was able to report:

> One would have to side with the cabals or with tastelessness if one were to entertain a different opinion from that which admits the music of Herr Mozart to be a Masterpiece of the Art: it contains so many beauties and such richness of thoughts as can proceed only from the born genius.[16]

Niemetschek's suggestion that some of the singers may have attempted to sabotage the first performance seems very unlikely. By and large, the singers Mozart wrote for were his friends, and the roles were specifically tailored to their strengths. The Burgtheater had had a strong roster of Italian singers ever since the theater's director, Count Giacomo Durazzo, had staged Gluck's operas in the 1760s. Now, even allowing for the temporary vacuum caused by Joseph's experiment with his German National Theater, Vienna possessed ample resources for casting Italian operas. Not all the singers were Italian, but all of them were Italian-trained. And several of them were very good actors as well.

The first Figaro, Francesco Benucci, was a great favorite of the emperor's. He had a stentorian bass voice, which he used to great effect in his arias. The Irish tenor Michael Kelly, who created the roles of Basilio and Don Curzio, and who later wrote down his own reminiscences of the event, reported that Mozart kept repeating "Bravo! Bravo!" throughout Benucci's rendering of "Non più andrai" at the first performance.[17] One particularly intriguing question about the casting was left open for speculation: Who was the true prima donna? Was it the Countess, played by Luisa Laschi, the wife of one of Italy's leading tenors, Domenico Mombelli? Or was it the Englishwoman, Nancy Storace, who sang the part of the Countess's maid, Susanna? Tradition would have made it the Countess, but the evidence suggests that Mozart decided in favor of Susanna, giving her the top line in several ensembles. Storace, who was in her third Viennese season, was already an established favorite with audiences. For the 1789 revival in Vienna, when there were twenty-six performances, Mozart rewrote two of Susanna's arias in a somewhat more virtuoso style. On that occasion (Storace had returned to London) they were sung by Da Ponte's mistress, Adriana Gabrieli from Ferrara, who took second place to no one. The following year, in Così, she was the first Fiordiligi (one of the two sisters identified in Da Ponte's libretto as "women from Ferrara"— dame ferraresi).

Another of the female roles in the original Figaro must have aroused a good deal of interest. The small but important part of Barberina, complete with her own Act IV aria, was sung by Anna Gottlieb. She was twelve years old! Five years later, still only seventeen, she created the much larger role of Pamina in Die Zauberflöte.

The fact that so many of these singers were recalled by Mozart to create roles in his subsequent operas suggests that it was an unusually close-knit company. Further evidence can be deduced from the fact that the Figaro cast contained two married couples—Stefano Mandini (the Count) and his wife, Maria (Marcellina); and Francesco Bussani, who sang both Bartolo and Antonio, and his wife, Doretea, in the "trouser role" of Cherubino.

Nevertheless, whatever the critics said, Figaro was not a great hit with the Viennese. Maybe the aristocrats and wealthy burgers were uncomfortable with the subversive undertow of the plot; maybe they found too much in the piece that was new and hard to comprehend; maybe they just found it too long. At all events, it was taken off after only nine performances and replaced by a new opera by Martín y Soler, Una cosa rara, which had a wild success. The "rare thing" of the title was that the heroine was both beautiful and virtuous, a combination represented in the text as being most unusual. The librettist was once again Da Ponte.

If Vienna did not fully appreciate Mozart, then Prague did. The second city of the Empire and capital of the Kingdom of Bohemia, Prague was only three days' journey by stagecoach from Vienna. Mozart and Constanze went there early in 1787 at the invitation of the city's principal music society, for which Mozart had prepared a new symphony. He knew Figaro was being performed at the Nosticke Theater (now the Tyl Theater), and he knew it was a success, but he was unprepared for the extent of the success. Everywhere, he wrote, Figaro was being sung, whistled, and danced to, and he himself was a celebrity. Other than Mozart, no one was more excited by all this than Pasquale Bondini, who ran the Italian Opera in Prague. Beset by debts and lacking a regular audience, it had seemed that he would go out of business the previous autumn. But Figaro had saved him. Suddenly, the company was playing to sold-out houses, and it would continue to do so for two years. To the huge delight of the citizens of Prague, Mozart conducted a performance of Figaro; he gave the premiere of his Prague Symphony; and he accepted a commission from Bondini to write a new opera for the company.

In order to write the opera, Mozart had to have a libretto. Naturally, it would be by Lorenzo Da Ponte. But Da Ponte was by this time the busiest man in Vienna. In the spring of 1787 he found himself with three separate commissions, all due to be completed at the same time—immediately. He therefore organized his days in such a way that he could keep all three composers reasonably happy. In the mornings he worked on Martín y Soler's libretto; in the afternoons on Salieri's (it was an Italian adaptation of Tarare, the Salieri/Beaumarchais opera which had such a success in Paris); and in a succession of inspired evenings he wrote Don Giovanni for Mozart. Years

Design by Joseph Quaglio for the graveyard scene from Act II of Mozart's Don Giovanni, Mannheim, *1789.*

later, in his memoirs, Da Ponte recalled how he did it:

> I sat down at my table and did not leave it for twelve hours continuous—a bottle of Tokay to my right, a box of Seville [tobacco] to my left, and in the middle an inkwell. A beautiful girl of sixteen . . . was living in the house with her mother . . . and came to my room at the sound of a bell. To tell the truth, the bell rang rather frequently. . . .[18]

Da Ponte completed all three librettos on time. Mozart returned to Prague in October 1787 and conducted the first performance of *Don Giovanni* at the end of the month. Not surprisingly, there were many imperfections in the performance: this was a good, but nevertheless provincial, company tackling a work of great complexity. Even more than *Figaro*, it relied on music to portray the drama,

and it was the drama of terror. Don Giovanni's fate, prefigured in the overture and consummated in the final scene, when the statue came to life and dragged him down to Hell, had no precedent on the operatic stage. Between these bookends was a story that was comic, romantic, and terrifying in almost equal degrees, with set-piece arias of astonishing beauty, and ensembles to rival those of *Figaro*. It was a formidable undertaking for Bondini's company, and one in which (according to Mozart) it acquitted itself with honor. From Prague, he wrote wistfully to a friend at home, "Perhaps it will yet be performed in Vienna? I hope so."

His hopes were realized the following spring, but the cheers that had rung in his ears in Prague were missing in Vienna. It was well received, to be sure, but for the Viennese, in love with the more traditional music of Paisiello, Cimarosa, Salieri, and Martín y Soler, *Don Giovanni* was hard to comprehend. "Such music is not meat for the teeth of my Viennese," was the emperor Joseph's verdict, according to Da Ponte's memoirs (an unreliable source, as ever: the modern Mozart scholar H. C. Robbins Landon has shown that Joseph probably never saw *Don Giovanni*; he was too busy fighting the Turks [19]).

It was, however, Joseph himself who commissioned the final collaboration between Mozart and Da Ponte, and agreed to Mozart's being paid double the customary fee for it. It was the summer of 1789—a time of change. In Paris, the French Revolution was beginning in earnest: the Bastille was stormed in July. In New York, the first United States Congress was meeting; George Washington had been installed as president. And in Vienna—Emperor Joseph was dying. You did not need to be a doctor to work that out. You could hear it in his agonized coughing. It was clear that his lungs were giving out.

Mozart and Da Ponte knew it, and it scared them. Joseph's successor would be his brother Leopold, and neither Mozart nor Da Ponte knew quite where they would stand when he and his court advisers took over (there was good reason for concern in the case of Da Ponte, as it turned out). But their more immediate concern was that the emperor's death would entail a mandatory period of mourning during which the theaters would be closed for several months.

They made it with three weeks to spare. *Così fan tutte* had three performances before Joseph's death on February 20, 1790, and six more performances after the period of mourning. And that, more or less, was that. There were performances in Prague, Dresden, Leipzig, and Frankfurt, and it reached Paris and London eventually, but after about 1820 it was a rarity. The nineteenth century missed out on *Così* almost completely, and it was not until the 1920s and 1930s that it won recognition, and enormous popularity. Today, there is hardly an opera house in the world where it is not in the permanent repertoire.

Perhaps the nineteenth century found the story immoral. Niemetschek, Mozart's first biographer, found it "a miserable and trashy text,"[20] and the opera's subtitle—*La scuola degli amanti* (The School for Lovers)—suggested forbidden territory for respectable nineteenth-century operagoers (yet how much more so would Wagner's *Tannhäuser* or even Verdi's *La traviata?*). Constanze Mozart found it hard to defend the subject mat-

Mozart's Don Giovanni *in modern dress at the Glyndebourne Festival, 1994. Directed by Deborah Warner, designed by Hildegard Bechtler. With Sanford Sylvan as Leporello (foreground), Gilles Cachemaille as Don Giovanni, and Gudjon Oskarsson as the Commendatore.*

Mozart's Così fan tutte *at the Metropolitan Opera, New York, 1996. With Susanne Mentzer as Dorabella and Renée Fleming as Fiordiligi.*

ter after her husband's death, and there were all sorts of proposals to save the music by commissioning a new libretto. But Da Ponte's work endured, and the twentieth century has found very little wrong with it—except, perhaps, the title. The phrase "cosi fan tutte" is very hard to translate. In fact, Da Ponte was quoting himself. Four years earlier, in *Figaro*, he had put a popular catchphrase into the mouth of the cynical old music teacher, Don Basilio: "Così fan tutte le belle." It might be translated, "That's the way all beautiful women behave," or, more colloquially, "Women are all the same"—a sentiment more offensive to the twentieth century than ever it was to the nineteenth.

In any case, a synopsis of the story of *Così* would be unlikely to convince anyone that this is one of the great masterpieces of opera, yet that is what it undoubtedly is. The basic idea, that two young men should disguise themselves in order to test the fidelity of their lovers, is hardly compelling. But when you add in all the subtle symmetries of Da Ponte's ever-moving plot, its comedy and its heartbreak—and when you add to that the music of Mozart, with its unparalleled power to project the whole gamut of emotions and drama— then you have a work as funny and profound and moving as any that has ever been created. Together with *Figaro* and *Don Giovanni*, *Così* makes up a canon of creative genius that is unique in the story of opera—certainly a milestone in the development of *dramma per musica*.

Così was the end of the great partnership. Shortly after the death of Joseph, Da Ponte was forced to leave Vienna. For Mozart, 1790 was a difficult and unproductive year. He was deeply in debt and borrowing more all the time; he had no worthwhile commissions; and his family life was turbulent. Constanze was frequently ill, and three of their four children had died in infancy; one more, born in 1791, would survive into adulthood. The new emperor, Leopold II, confirmed Mozart in his existing position as *Kammermusicus,* with its derisory salary, but gave him no preferment.

The year 1791 was altogether different. It was prolific and exciting. From January (when he celebrated his thirty-fifth birthday) almost to the last day of his life on December 5 (when the *Requiem* was still incomplete), he never stopped composing. The year's work included two full-length operas, composed simultaneously and both performed in the last weeks of his life.

The first of them to be commissioned was *Die Zauberflöte* (The Magic Flute), but its composition was interrupted in July by an urgent request from Prague. Tradition demanded that the new emperor, having first received the imperial crown in Frankfurt, would then go to Prague for a second coronation, as king of Bohemia. Mozart had made the trip to Frankfurt the previous September in the rather forlorn hope that he might curry royal favor simply by being there, but now, at the second coronation, he was not only to be there: he was to be at the very center of the celebrations.

Salieri, the imperial *Kapellmeister,* was no friend of Mozart's, but he took no fewer than three Mozart masses to perform in Prague, as well as a number of other sacred pieces. *Don Giovanni* was scheduled to be given a special performance in front of the royal family, who would also be guests of honor (on the actual night of the coronation) at the premiere of the new opera that the Estates of Bohemia had commissioned—*La clemenza di Tito* (The Clemency of Tito).

Mozart had no choice in the subject matter. In fact, he would not have had the commission at all if Salieri had not rejected it for himself because he was too busy. The imperial bureaucrats in Prague, doubtless looking for a suitable and safe subject for an imperial coronation, had already decided that Metastasio's fifty-year-old libretto about the Roman emperor Titus would be the text (but in a shortened version). Salieri finally rejected the commission in mid-July, and it was immediately accepted by Mozart—in the full knowledge that it had to be delivered in time for a first performance on September 6. Mozart had the libretto shortened, and he must have begun writing at once, but he could not have written a great deal until mid-August, because the impresario responsible for staging the work in Prague had first to go to Italy to engage the singers: only when Mozart knew who they were, and the sort of voices they had, could he write the principal music. By the time he had this information, there were, at most, eighteen days before the premiere. Several of the arias were written (in his head) during the three-day journey to Prague at the end of August.

The new emperor was well versed in music and had a considerable knowledge of Italian opera (as archduke, he had lived in Milan). But he was not, apparently, an admirer of Mozart. He sat through *Don Giovanni* all right; he may not even have known who wrote the great coronation masses that accompanied the cathedral ceremonies; but *La clemenza di Tito* turned out to be a bit too much for him. He came, and he stayed, but he did not like it—any more than did his wife, Empress Maria Luisa. The empress delivered a verdict as succinct and as scurrilous as any in the history of musical invective: "una porcheria tedesca" was the phrase she is reported to have used to describe *Tito* (it might politely be translated as "German piggishness").

Maria Luisa was not alone in her dislike of the piece. The public performances that took place during the coronation celebrations were not well attended, and the critics were not kind. *Tito* was an old-fashioned *opera seria,* complete with a leading *castrato* part. It was not the sort of opera the citizens of Prague associated with their beloved Mozart. Few, if any, of them were familiar with *Idomeneo,* his last attempt at this genre, almost ten years before. Yet *Tito* was a superb example of *opera seria.* Despite all the disadvantages of a Metastasian libretto—static, predictable, and undramatic— the opera had music of great emotional power. Where Metastasio had littered the piece with his customary arias, Mozart replaced several of them with ensembles. The finale to Act I, with the capitol on fire in the background, was a hugely dramatic ensemble for the principals and chorus, in which the terror of the moment was as real as it had been in the final scene of *Don Giovanni. Tito* may have been written in a tremendous hurry; it may have been an example of an outmoded form of opera; and it may not have been the most entertaining story to put before a newly crowned emperor and his impatient court—but it was soon recognized as a fine opera, and it became extremely popular in Prague and throughout Germany (generally given in German translation). In 1806, it became the first Mozart opera to be performed in London.

For Mozart, however, it was no more than an interruption. Three weeks after the first performance of *Tito* in Prague, *Die Zauberflöte* was given its premiere in Vienna.

Even amid the hectic final days in Prague, when *Tito* was in rehearsal and not yet fully composed, there is evidence that Mozart was still living in the fantastical world of *Die Zauberflöte*, which had occupied him throughout the spring and early summer. One evening in Prague, after a game of pool, he sat down at the piano and played through a passage he had apparently composed during the game. It had nothing to do with *Tito*: it was the Act II quintet for Tamino, Papageno, and the Three Ladies in *Die Zauberflöte*. Whether true or not (and it is likely to be true, since the source is an 1828 biography of Mozart written by Georg Nikolaus Nissen, Constanze's second husband[21]),

Emanuel Schikaneder as Papageno. Engraving from the first published libretto of Die Zauberflöte, *1791.*

it illustrates the white heat of invention in Mozart's imagination during those last months—not just the two operas, but a number of other pieces, including the unfinished *Requiem*.

When Lorenzo Da Ponte lost his job as court poet and realized he would have to leave Vienna, he tried to persuade Mozart to go with him to London. But by that time, the spring of 1791, Mozart was already involved with Emanuel Schikaneder in the writing of *Die Zauberflöte*. He asked Da Ponte for six months to make up his mind, but Da Ponte could not wait and left alone.[22]

Schikaneder was an old acquaintance of Mozart's. They had met in Salzburg more than ten years earlier, when Schikaneder was an actor-manager with his own touring company. His itinerant life came to an end in 1789, when his wife inherited the directorship of a theater in the suburbs of Vienna. The Theater auf der Wieden was better known as the Freihaustheater because it was located in the Freihaus (literally, Free House—free of all taxes) on what had once been an island in the river Wien. Here Schikaneder's company was enjoying a considerable success. Its constituency was very different from that of the court theaters across the river, which relied on the wealthy, cosmopolitan Viennese of the aristocratic, commercial, and diplomatic classes. The audience at the Freihaus was more bourgeois, more middle-class, and much more down-to-earth—as were the plays and *Singspiele* Schikaneder and his colleagues devised for it.

Schikaneder was a man of great talent, not just as an actor but also as a playwright and librettist. His company was made up of actors who could also sing. Some of them, like Mozart's sister-in-law Josepha Hofer, could sing extraordinarily well; Mozart would hardly have written the role of the Queen of the Night, one of the most excruciatingly difficult *coloratura* roles ever written, for any ordinary soprano. The company had its own composers—Benedikt Schack (a good friend of Mozart's) and Franz Xaver Gerl—who wrote original music for many of the Freihaus productions. But for *Die Zauberflöte* Schikaneder wanted music of more than ordinary quality, so he turned to Mozart. There is evidence that Mozart had composed earlier music for Schikaneder's company, but never a full-length work.

It was nine years since *Die Entführung*, Mozart's previous full-length *Singspiel*. It had

brought him fame all over Germany and the Empire (much more so than his Italian operas), and he must have been keen to try his hand at it again. Moreover, he liked the subject matter very much. *Die Zauberflöte* is almost impossible to categorize: it is a comedy, a morality play, a fairy-tale, and an allegory—all of those things—but it is also profoundly based in the lore and imagery of the Masonic movement. Mozart was a Freemason—so was Schikaneder—and Freemasonry is a notoriously secretive form of association. Yet in *Die Zauberflöte*, Mozart and Schikaneder willfully broke the Masonic rules of secrecy in order to include parts of the rituals and symbols they had presumably sworn never to reveal.

There is circumstantial evidence that they did so with the concurrence of their Masonic lodges. By 1791, the movement was under great pressure in Vienna. By 1794–95, it had disappeared almost completely, a victim of its own secrecy and other people's suspicions of it. It may well be that there were leaders among the Viennese Masons in 1791 who felt that a certain amount of unveiling would do the movement

good rather than harm. At all events, it did the opera no harm.[23]

In the garden of the Mozarteum in Salzburg there is a little wooden pavilion. Legend has it that in Mozart's day it stood on the grounds of the Freihaus in Vienna, and it was in this pavilion that Mozart composed parts of *Die Zauberflöte* and rehearsed the individual singers. Anna Gottlieb, the twelve-year-old Barbarina of *Figaro*, was now seventeen: she was the first Pamina. The Freihaus composers, Benedikt Schack and Franz Xaver Gerl, were respectively Tamino and Sarastro. Constanze Mozart's sister, Josepha Hofer, was the Queen of the Night. And Emmanuel Schikaneder, librettist and company manager, was the irrepressible bird-catcher, Papageno, whose first song—"Der Vogelfänger bin ich ja" (I am the jolly bird-catcher)—was encored night after night during the first run, and has been ever since. In the two weeks between his return from Prague and the opening of *Die Zauberflöte*, Mozart worked at a furious pace in the little pavilion. His biographer Nissen, writing many years later and presumably quoting Constanze's recollections,

Design by Karl Friedrich Schinkel for the entrance to the Queen of the Night's palace in Mozart's Die Zauberflöte, *Berlin, 1816.*

Mozart's Die Zauberflöte *at the Metropolitan Opera, New York, 1991. Sets and costumes by David Hockney. Kurt Moll as Sarastro enters in his chariot.*

portrayed him as already being mortally ill: "He, to whom, when genius gripped him, day and night were interchangeable, often exhausted himself so much that he fainted and was unconscious for minutes on end."

From its very first performance, *Die Zauberflöte* thrilled and enchanted its audiences. It may also have mystified them—to some degree it was meant to—but most of all, it entertained them. The people of Vienna, high and low, flocked to the Freihaus night after night to hear this strange, beautiful, and wholly original piece of theater, with its score that seemed to span the whole firmament of music, from the ethereal to the downright earthy. It was simple and it was grand; it was mystical and it was funny. It was the ultimate creation of the German *Singspiel* tradition. Emperor Joseph would have reveled in it, had he still been alive.

Mozart's letters to Constanze (she had left immediately after the first night for treatment at the spa in Baden) were full of pride and delight at having such a palpable hit on his hands. One evening, he even took Salieri and his mistress to see it. Salieri evidently loved the opera and was unstinting in his praise for it. On the surface, everything seemed to be coming right for Mozart. Yet within nine weeks he was dead.

Mozart's death and its causes, so shrouded in mystery, are the subject of much research and many conflicting opinions. But in the story of opera, Mozart's influence was only just beginning. For all the impact he had within his lifetime (which was not inconsiderable), it was only after his death that the extent of his genius as an opera composer became apparent. His German operas, *Die Entführung* and *Die Zauberflöte*, had both had immediate success in the German-speaking world, but not one of his Italian operas was performed in Italy, France, Spain, or England while he was alive, and two of the greatest—*Idomeneo* and *Così fan tutte*—were virtually to disappear for almost a century. Even more extraordinary, perhaps, was the slowness with which his operas spread after his death. In London, although Italian opera was in vogue and all the greatest singers went there to perform, it was more than twenty years before either *Figaro* or *Don Giovanni* received so much as a performance.

Part of the explanation lies in the fact that Mozart was way ahead of his public. He had a vision of *dramma per musica* that was far more sophisticated than that of the merchants of *opera*

seria or even *opera buffa*. From *Idomeneo* onward, his operas were infused with a humanity that was new to the art form. It made no difference whether he was writing serious opera or comic opera, Italian opera or German opera; he wrote about life as he knew it. His audiences recognized this. Some of them (the people of Prague, for instance, and the

audiences at the Freihaus in Vienna) embraced it. But most operagoers were uncomfortable with it. They had an expectation of eighteenth-century opera—that it should stay within carefully defined conventions; tackle safe, predictable, and generally well-known, stories; and allow the singers to show off their virtuosity, regardless of the cost to the drama. Gluck had begun to change this, but he had lacked both the talent and the courage to go all the way. Mozart understood it instinctively—and he lacked neither talent nor courage.

There was another reason why Mozart's operas took time to become popular, and it helped to explain the discomfort of well-heeled audi-

ences in the last years of the eighteenth century.

"The World Turned Upside Down" was the title of a popular British song of the time. A British Army band played it at Yorktown in 1781 as their officers surrendered their swords to the American revolutionaries. Ten years later, at the time of Mozart's death, the world was truly turning upside down. The Age of Enlightenment had given birth to an age of revolutions. Everywhere, the old order was under threat—nowhere more so than in Paris, where the king was under house arrest and the advocates of *liberté, égalité, fraternité* were in power. Europeans were scared, and those who took the trouble to examine the social message writ large in *Le nozze di Figaro* must have hesitated before deciding to put on such an opera.

So Mozart, the child of his time, was during his lifetime and for some time thereafter considered secondary to lesser composers of opera—to Paisiello, Salieri, Martín y Soler, and Cimarosa, and later to Cherubini and Spontini. But Mozart's legacy could not be denied. At exactly the moment when the political and social world was being turned upside down, he turned the world of opera upside down, too—not by intent, but by sheer force of genius.

OPERA AT THE END OF THE EIGHTEENTH CENTURY

It was two hundred years since the Florentine gentlemen of the *camerata* had first outlined their vision of *dramma per musica*—a limited and myopic vision, at best, but there was no doubt that it had led to the establishing of opera as a popular art form, and one that had steadily enveloped all of Europe, and other lands besides. Huge advances had been made—in scenography and lighting; in the dramatic portrayal of emotions in music; and in the art of singing. But, until Mozart's time, the concept of *dramma per musica* had remained hardly more than a dream—an ideal that no one had been able to translate into the real thing. And that is not just hindsight: it was woefully apparent at the time. Opera was weighed down by its own baggage. It was enmeshed in conventions and structures that inhibited drama. It was held back by the need to please patrons, on the one hand, and generally conservative audiences, on the other. Opera houses were not the silent, attentive auditoriums we know today: they were talkative, fully lit social clubs in which much of the audience stood and there was

a great deal of coming and going throughout the performance.

But there had been some notable advances. The most obvious of these was in the staging and acting of opera. It was by no means universally true, but the advent of *opera buffa*, with its emphasis on familiar reality rather than the totally mythical, had encouraged theater managements, as well as composers and librettists, to insist on better stage management and more realistic forms of acting. Even in the high days of *opera seria,* there were composers willing to exert their influence to achieve these things. Lully and Handel were two of the foremost. There were even leading performers who were as famous for their acting as for their singing. Anna Renzi in Monteverdi's Venice and Marthe le Rochois in Lully's Paris were two fine examples. But few opera houses had stage directors before the end of the eighteenth century, and it was generally left to conductors (if they were interested) and librettists (if they were present) to enforce whatever artistic unity a performance might possess. Metastasio, whose librettos were ubiquitous, helpfully answered written enquiries about how best to stage his works, but he did so from his home in Vienna rather than from backstage at an opera house.

No one was more determined to change this state of affairs than Gluck. As his librettist Calzabigi pointed out, his music was "exactly fitted to what is happening on the stage." In Gaetano Guadagni, the *castrato* who created the role of Orfeo for them, they found a willing collaborator. He had trained with the great Shakespearian actor David Garrick, and even if (as Dr. Burney pointed out) some of his stage gestures were "studies for a statuary," there can be no doubt of the power of his performances and their ability to affect an audience. Nor can there be any doubt that it was his early experience in *opera buffa* that made him so keen to become a first-rate actor as well as singer. He was as famous for his performances in Piccinni's popular comedy *La buona figliuola* as he was for the grander roles of Gluck. The French soprano Sophie Arnould was similarly endowed as an actress. She was the Eurydice of Gluck's French *Orphée* as well as the original Iphigénie (*en Aulide*). And Caterina Gabrielli, perhaps the most acclaimed singing actress of the time, was another of Gluck's protégées in his earlier Italian operas.

Giuseppe Sarti (1729–1802) was one of the most popular composers of Mozart's day. The two of them met briefly in Vienna in 1784, and Mozart paid Sarti the compliment of parodying one of his most famous arias in the dinner scene of DON GIOVANNI. *The opera shown here,* GIULIO SABINA *(1781), was probably Sarti's most successful. The female singer is Katharina Cavalieri (1760–1801), a pupil of Salieri's and a great favorite of Mozart's, for whom he wrote Constanze in* DIE ENTFÜHRUNG *and Mlle Silberklang in* DER SCHAUSPIELDIREKTOR, *as well as Elvira's aria "Mi tradi" for the Vienna premiere of* DON GIOVANNI. *With Cavalieri in* GIULIO SABINA *is Luigi Marchesi (1754–1829), one of the finest male sopranos of the time.*

Mozart and Da Ponte were the beneficiaries of this change. They would hardly have written the complex stage dramas that they did unless they had known the singers and the stage staff were capable of realizing them. They were almost always writing to deadlines, so it was no surprise that there was more than an element of chaos about opening nights. Da Ponte tells us in his memoirs that he "stayed in Prague for a week in order to direct the actors" in *Don Giovanni*, a score that Mozart was still writing during rehearsals (an example of his first writing the ensembles and finales, leaving the arias to last, which was his favored way of working). There is precious little evidence of what these performances were really like, but what there is suggests a company of singers (very talented in Vienna, not so talented in Prague) who were all accomplished actors and, of necessity, "quick studies."

With or without Mozart, things were bound to change in the nineteenth century. Even as the Age of Enlightenment was ending catastrophically in violence and revolution, a reaction was beginning to set in within the cultural ethos of Europe. There was widespread revulsion against the rational self-interest of the Enlightenment, a growing refusal to believe that either reason or science could provide all the answers. The nineteenth century, rejecting its antecedents, fell back on a much more fundamental faith—a reliance on humankind's deepest instincts and emotions. It became fashionable to believe that what was natural (and therefore moral) was more likely to be superior to what was intellectualized (and therefore suspect).

Out of these burgeoning beliefs was born the Romantic movement. It dominated all forms of art, including literature and music, for most of the nineteenth century. With it came a loosening of opera's rigid formalities and, as a result, the most exciting and productive years in the entire story of opera. Gluck and Calzabigi to begin with—but Mozart and Da Ponte most of all—had made this possible by removing opera from eighteenth-century strictures, and by proving, in doing so, that *dramma per musica* could become a reality. The nineteenth century would begin to explore that reality in earnest.

In this exploration, German musicians and dramatists would play a very large part. So, to a lesser extent, would those of France, Russia, and Bohemia. But it was, as always, in Italy that the most popular, the most exciting, and the most tuneful opera was created.

Aloysia Lange as Zémire in André Grétry's popular opera ZÉMIRE ET AZOR. *Painting by Johann Nilson, c. 1784. Lange, who sang Donna Anna at the first performance of* DON GIOVANNI *in Vienna in 1788, was his wife Constanze's sister and Mozart's first love.*

THE GOLDEN AGE OF ITALIAN OPERA

IN 1868, SEVENTY-SIX YEARS OLD AND DYING, GIOACCHINO ROSSINI WROTE FROM HIS HOME IN PARIS TO THE DIRECTOR OF THE MILAN CONSERVATORY, LAURO ROSSI. HE ADDRESSED HIMSELF TO ALL ITALIAN MUSICIANS: "LET US NOT FORGET, ITALIANS . . . THAT DELIGHT MUST BE THE BASIS AND AIM OF THIS ART: SIMPLE MELODY, CLEAR RHYTHM." [1]

ROSSINI'S LIFE SPANNED A MIGHTY EPOCH IN THE STORY OF OPERA. HE WAS BORN JUST THREE MONTHS AFTER THE DEATH OF MOZART. AS A YOUNG MAN, HE VISITED BEETHOVEN AND CARL MARIA VON WEBER IN VIENNA. IN HIS MIDDLE YEARS, ALREADY RETIRED FROM OPERA COMPOSING, HE PRESIDED OVER THE THÉÂTRE-ITALIEN IN PARIS AND CHAMPIONED HIS TWO BRILLIANT COMPATRIOTS, VINCENZO BELLINI AND GAETANO DONIZETTI. AS AN OLD MAN, HE RECEIVED VERDI AND WAGNER AT HIS HOME IN THE FRENCH CAPITAL. NOW, AS HE LAY DYING, HE HARKED BACK TO THE RECIPE OF HIS OWN SUCCESS — "SIMPLE MELODY, CLEAR RHYTHM" — AND HE SOUNDED,

as he felt, like a man who had outlived his era.

Rossini is one of the seminal figures in the story of opera, but that was not always as obvious as it may seem today. In the first thirty-seven years of his life, when he composed all thirty-nine of his operas, he became hugely famous, not just in Italy and his adopted home of France, but far beyond. Yet in the fifty years that followed his death, up to the end of World War I, his reputation withered to the point where he was just another Italian composer whose operas were rarely performed. Yes, there was *Il barbiere di Siviglia* (The Barber of Seville), a favorite of almost everyone. But what of the other thirty-eight operas? Was it really possible that a critic of the eminence of George Bernard Shaw, writing on the centenary of Rossini's birth in 1892, could dismiss him as "one of the greatest masters of claptrap that ever lived"?[2]

Without knowing it, in his will Rossini laid the basis for his own renaissance. He left his autograph manuscripts to his second wife, Olympe Pélissier, to be passed at her death to the commune of Pesaro for the establishment of a Liceo Musicale.[3] The little town of Pesaro on the Adriatic Sea, not far from Urbino, was Rossini's birthplace. He lived there for only the first ten years of his life, but it always retained his affection and gratitude—qualities which it has, in recent years, returned a thousandfold. Many years later, one of the indirect results of Rossini's bequest was the establishment of the Fondazione Rossini di Pesaro. It was this foundation that eventually initiated much of the research and scholarship necessary to publish performing editions of some of the "forgotten" operas.[4] Since 1980, Pesaro has also been the home of the annual Rossini opera festival, where several of his operas have had their first modern performances, and where a new generation of outstanding Rossini singers have made their reputations in the *bel canto* repertoire.

The boy who grew up in Pesaro (he was christened Giaochino Antonio Rossini) certainly had a musical background. His father was the Pesaro town trumpeter, his mother was an accomplished local opera singer. And it was the human voice that would become the center of his musical world. As a fifteen-year-old, already in his second year at the Accademia Filarmonica at Bologna, he heard two of Europe's greatest singers perform. One was the last of the great *castrati*, Giovanni Battista Velluti; Rossini would later write a role specially for him.[5] For the other one, Rossini would write many roles. Her name was Isabella Colbran (Spanish by birth), and she was the rising star in the Italian firmament. She would play a large part in Rossini's life, professional and private. What Rossini had heard in those two performances in Bologna in 1807 was the past—the era of the *castrati*—and the future: the era of the great female singers with wonderfully developed coloratura techniques, which enabled them to perform amazing feats of vocal fireworks. Rossini never doubted that he belonged with the future— though there had been a heart-stopping moment a year or two earlier when one of his uncles, a barber, suggested that his fine treble voice might profitably be perpetuated if the necessary operation was speedily performed. "My brave mother would not consent at any price," Rossini later recalled.[6] It was just as well, because the "future" he had seen in Bologna, Isabella Colbran, would one day become Signora Rossini.

Opera was more popular than ever in Italy at the beginning of the nineteenth century. It was essentially a contemporary art form. Audiences expected to hear new operas every season rather than revivals of old ones, although the custom of putting on *pasticcio* evenings, in which highlights from a number of favorite operas were glued together to show off the voices of local singers, was still very common. It was automatically assumed that new operas would be in Italian and by Italians. Even Mozart was little known in most of Italy. What many might regard as the greatest Italian opera ever written, *Don Giovanni*, was not given its Italian premiere until 1811, twenty years after the composer's death.

In most cities the presentation of opera had fallen into the hands of impresarios. These were businessmen (very often aristocrats who aspired to be businessmen) who took over the management of a theater for a season, hired the company, commissioned the operas, and hoped to make a profit. Orchestras were normally made up of local amateurs. The principal expenditure was on singers. A lot of impresarios lost money consistently, especially the aristocrats, but they had the not inconsiderable recompense of being the center of local attention, and frequently having well-publicized romances with their leading female employees, both singers and ballerinas.

The position of the composer in all this was paradoxical. He was at once the most necessary ingredient, and the most undervalued. He was expected to work at incredible speed (four weeks was the customary deadline for delivery of a completed score), and he was required to accept whatever libretto the impresario gave him. Nevertheless, if he had the facility to compose quickly; the ability to write specifically for singers already hired by the impresario; and the humility to accept a one-time fee (no royalties) that was generally lower than a principal singer's fee for a single performance, then he would be in his element.

ROSSINI

And young Rossini *was* in his element. His breakthrough came in 1810, when he was eighteen. A composer failed to deliver a work commissioned by the Teatro San Moisè in Venice. Rossini, recommended by a singer who was a friend of his parents, hurried to Venice, was given the libretto of *La cambiale di matrimonio* (The Bill of Marriage), and wrote the score in a matter of days. The one-act comedy had a considerable success, and from that day on Rossini never lacked for commissions. He was recognized by impresarios as a reliable man, a composer who would deliver on time, and whose work was generally popular with singers.

One such singer was Maria Marcolini. The admiration was mutual (and probably went beyond admiration). Between 1811 and 1814 Rossini wrote five principal roles for her, including that of Clarice in *La pietra del paragone* (The Touchstone). It was the opera with which he made his debut at La Scala, and it ran for fifty-three performances in the 1812–13 season—a remarkable achievement. The next year, back in Venice, Rossini created two more roles for Marcolini. Since they were written for rival theaters, she was able to give the first performance of only one of them—Isabella in *L'italiana in Algeri* (The Italian Girl in Algiers). *L'italiana* was a masterwork of *opera buffa*, and is infrequently performed today only because Rossini's other contributions to that genre, *Il barbiere* and *La Cenerentola*, have overshadowed it. In any case, it was the second role that eventually made Marcolini most famous. *Tancredi* was an *opera seria* all right, but not quite as serious as that format had generally been in the past. Tancredi, a *travesti* role (a male character written for a female singer) composed

Domenico Barbaja (1778–1841).
Anonymous portrait, c. 1825–30.
Barbaja was the most important Italian
opera impresario between 1809, when he
became director of the royal opera houses in
Naples, and his death in 1841. At various
times, he also controlled La Scala, Milan,
and the Kärntnertortheater in Vienna. In
the background of this portrait can be seen
the figures of Rossini, Bellini, and Giuditta
Pasta, three of his most famous employees.

for Marcolini's mezzo-soprano range, sang his moving plea for forgiveness, "Di tanti palpiti," to a tune which quickly became a popular hit throughout Italy.[7] *Tancredi* was the first of Rossini's operas to be translated, and the first to make him famous beyond Italy.

After Marcolini, the next singer to inspire Rossini was Isabella Colbran. In point of fact, the contract he signed in 1815 with Domenico Barbaja, the impresario of the Teatro San Carlo in Naples, *required* him to be inspired by La Colbran. She was the local prima donna, probably the best known in Italy, and each of the operas Rossini wrote for Naples had to have a major role for her. Within three months of arriving there, he conjured up *Elisabetta, regina d'Inghilterra*, and thus began a long and fruitful partnership—a purely professional partnership to begin with, since Isabella was not only *favorita* to the king of Naples but was also

mistress to Rossini's new employer, Barbaja. It was not long before she abandoned both of these gentlemen for Rossini (though she did not actually marry him until they left Naples together in 1822), and he, in turn, created a series of glorious roles for her—from the Desdemona of *Otello* to the title role of *Semiramide* in 1823.

Domenico Barbaja was a hugely influential figure in nineteenth-century opera, and a most unlikely one. He had started out as a waiter and had acquired a modest amount of fame as the inventor of a concoction of whipped cream and coffee or chocolate, which became known as a *barbajata*. His financial fortune was derived partly from successful speculations in the French wars in Italy (the wars in which Napoleon made his military reputation) and partly from gambling—particularly roulette, which was a new and very popular game at the end of the eighteenth century. At this time, most opera houses had gaming tables in the lobbies; they were an alternative amusement for operagoers and a source of additional income to the house. Barbaja obtained the gaming concession at La Scala, Milan, and it was a logical step from owning the gaming concession to running the opera houses themselves. During the first forty years of the nineteenth century, Barbaja, at various times, ran La Scala, the San Carlo in Naples, and the Kärntnertortheater in Vienna.

From all accounts, including the evidence of his own letters, Barbaja was a foul-mouthed man and not very literate. Yet people seem to have liked him. The only picture that survives portrays him as a handsome, rather sleek man, very much in charge of his own destiny, but the interesting thing about the painting is the depiction, in the background, of three much smaller, rather distant figures. They are Rossini, Bellini, and "La Pasta" —Giuditta Pasta, who would succeed Isabella Colbran as Italy's leading prima donna. Add to them the missing man—Donizetti, who was also a friend and client of Barbaja's—and you have the most important people in Italian opera in the first part of the century. All of them owed their livelihoods, in some degree or another, to Barbaja.

In 1815, Barbaja was running the Teatro San Carlo in Naples. Along with La Scala in Milan and La Fenice in Venice, the San Carlo was in the very top league of Italian opera houses. Barbaja needed a regular source of new operas, and Rossini must have been the obvious man to go for. But why should Rossini, already established, successful, and in demand, want to tie himself to such a contract? He certainly did not think of it as a generous offer. "If he had been able to," Rossini later recalled, "Barbaja would have put me in charge of the kitchens as well."[8] But it was not a bad contract for a twenty-three-year-old composer at a time when there was little security for the average musician. The contract with Barbaja recognized that Rossini was *not* average. He was given charge of two opera houses in Naples—the San Carlo and the Fondo (the former promptly burned down, but Barbaja had it rebuilt within a year). He was required to write two new operas each year, and he was paid an annual salary of 8,000 francs. It represented a modicum of security in a world that was anything but secure. The year 1815 witnessed the Hundred Days and Napoleon's final defeat at Waterloo. The Congress of Vienna had only recently begun to sort out the mess that was post-Napoleonic Europe, and the biggest mess of all was in Italy, much of which was still under foreign occupation.

Perhaps the best part of Rossini's contract with Barbaja was that it was not exclusive. Provided he fulfilled its terms, he was able to take on as many guest engagements elsewhere as he could obtain. And he did. Whereas the operas he wrote for the two big theaters in Naples were invariably *opere serie*, his "outside" commissions were often *opere buffe*, and they included the works by which posterity has known him best. These guest contracts provide further evidence of how badly composers (and musicians in general) were treated at this time. In 1815, just a few months after arriving in Naples, Rossini was invited to Rome to compose an opera for the Teatro Argentina. The contract awarded him a single outright payment of 400 scudi (whereas the prima donna would receive 500 scudi per performance). He would have to accept whatever libretto the impresario gave him. He would have one month from the signing of the contract in which to compose the opera. He would supervise the staging and the rehearsals himself. He would attend the first three performances of the opera, leading the orchestra from the harpsichord. And he would have no copyright on the score (it would belong to the impresario) and therefore no royalties.

Rossini fulfilled that particular contract in fine style. He is said to have composed the opera in just thirteen days. It was *Il barbiere di Siviglia*.

The first night of *Il barbiere* at the beginning

Isabella Colbran (1785–1845). Portrait by Heinrich Schmidt, 1817. Colbran is shown in the title role of Giovanni Simone Mayr's opera SAFFO. *The year this portrait was painted, Colbran and Rossini were already lovers, but not yet married.*

of 1816 was one of the great fiascos in operatic history. It was no fault of Rossini's. The problem was the most familiar and ugly of operatic phenomena, the claque—in this case, two entirely separate claques. One came from a rival theater, determined at all costs to upset the performance. The other was made up of supporters of a rival composer. Giovanni Paisiello was hardly a true rival of Rossini. In 1816, he was seventy-five years old and would die later that year, but it was undeniable that in 1782, ten years before Rossini was born, he had composed an earlier version of *Il barbiere*, and it continued to enjoy great popularity. Rossini was very conscious of this, so much so that he used a different title for the first performance—*Almaviva, ossia L'inutile precauzione* (Almaviva, or the Use-

less Precaution). He also wrote a letter of explanation to Paisiello, and had a further explanation printed in the published libretto as "A Notice to the Public." In it, he emphasized his own "respect and veneration" for Paisiello. But nothing could save the first night. To add insult to injury, the impresario (who actually died in the middle of rehearsals) had ordered Rossini to wear a nut-brown jacket with gold buttons that he had had made especially for him. It was far too small, and Rossini had to endure much mockery and personal abuse throughout the performance.

Rossini pleaded sickness on the second night and absented himself from the theater. He need not have worried. There were no claques this time, and the opera was a triumph. The singers and musicians brought the good news to his hotel after midnight, and serenaded him with his own hit tunes.

Il barbiere has always been, and will always be, the popular favorite among Rossini's operas, with his adaptation of the Cinderella story, *La Cenerentola,* as the runner-up. In 1968, at the centenary of his death, most opera houses put on one or the other of those two operas, with the more adventurous perhaps adding *L'italiana in Algeri,* or *Le comte Ory,* or maybe even *La gazza ladra* (The Thieving Magpie). The extent of the renaissance is shown by what happened in the twenty-four years between 1968 and the bicentenary of Rossini's birth, in 1992, when practically the entire canon of his works was once again on display.

Almost a half of this canon was written during the prolific seven years that he was under contract to Barbaja. As required, the operas reflected the voices for which he was writing. In Naples, they were dominated by the soprano voice of Isabella Colbran and a group of male voices that was especially strong in the tenor range. Thus *Otello* was constructed very differently from Verdi's version seventy years later. Rossini wrote Desdemona as the dominant character—for Colbran, of course—and he gave all three of the leading male parts (Otello, Iago, and Rodrigo, who has a much greater part to play than in Verdi) to tenors. The conflict between them is at its most thrilling in their vocal duels, and in Naples Rossini had singers who could do them justice. The Otello was Andrea Nozzari. He refused to wear body makeup for the role, but his ringing baritonal tenor was, by all accounts, a highly dramatic antagonist for the Rodrigo of Giovanni David, who was reputed to have a range of three complete octaves. As drama, however, Rossini's *Otello* was badly let down by the aristocratic librettist, Marchese Francesco Berio di Salsa. He paid little attention to Shakespeare and had no great talent of his own. Indeed, this was generally the case with Rossini's *opere serie:* he was setting librettos in which he had almost no say. As he grew older and more experienced, however, he increasingly exerted his power. It is instructive, for instance, to compare the deplorable libretto for *Tancredi* (1813) with that of *Semiramide* just ten years later, both of them written by Gaetano Rossi and both of them using Voltaire as their source. In dramatic terms, *Semiramide* is a great leap ahead, reflecting Rossini's determination to make his librettists come to terms with *dramma per musica.*[9]

Italian opera was only slowly emerging from the straitjacket imposed on it by the eighteenth century's obsession with Metastasian texts and the formal rules of *opera seria.* It was no part of Rossini's contract with Barbaja that he should attempt to change the audience's expectations. On the contrary, he was required to feed those expectations. So most of the librettos he was asked to set dealt with tales of chivalry, or with historical events in the fairly distant past—safe enough territory, although Neapolitan audiences still preferred happy endings (Rossini eventually supplied an alternative, happy, ending to *Otello,* since the Shakespearian ending was not too well received). But even within this narrowly circumscribed range,

Romanticism was beginning to make itself felt.

During Rossini's lifetime, art, literature, and music were all affected by the Romantic movement. It rejected the rationalism of the previous century and prized instinct and emotion (the "egotistical sublime," as the poet John Keats described it). By the time Rossini was working for Barbaja in Naples, Romanticism had already taken a firm hold in England and Germany, and it reached southern Italy when Rossini became the first major opera composer to make use of one of Sir Walter Scott's stories—*La donna del lago* (The Lady of the Lake). In fact, Rossini was somewhat ahead of Scott: *Elisabetta, regina d'Inghilterra*, which is sometimes said to have been based on Scott's *Kenilworth*, actually predated *Kenilworth* by six years.

Away from Naples and the requirements of La Colbran, Rossini turned again to the type of female voice he had found so seductive in Maria Marcolini—the mezzo-soprano voice. Ten years earlier, in Bologna, he had had a childhood friend called Geltrude Righetti. She had become a popular singer in Bologna and Rome, but had quickly retired from the stage when she married a lawyer named Giorgi. Rossini persuaded Signora Righetti-Giorgi, as she now styled herself, to

come out of retirement, and he wrote both of his greatest female *opera buffa* roles for her—first Rosina in *Il barbiere*, and the next year Angelina (or Cinderella) in *La Cenerentola*. It is inconceivable that he could have written those two great coloratura roles for a less-than-great singer, and we have the testimony of the German composer Louis Spohr that Geltrude had "an extraordinary range of two and one-half octaves" and (Spohr offered this as criticism, though we might not) "that she contributes nothing of her own, but rather accepts what is drilled into her, with the result that her ornaments which are precisely the same, note for note, every night, soon become tiresome."[10] The fact that *Cenerentola* more or less disappeared from the stage for a hundred years after the mid-century was testimony, not to the lack of popularity of the opera, but to the lack of great coloratura mezzo-sopranos able to sing the part.

One of the miracles of *Il barbiere* and *La Cenerentola*, both of which were written for Rome, was that they worked so well as comic dramas (and in the case of *Cenerentola*, as highly emotional drama as well). Rossini had no Da Ponte with whom to collaborate, but in Rome he was indebted to the papal bureaucracy. Unknowingly, it provided the

Rossini's La Cenerentola *at the Glyndebourne Festival, 1983. Directed by John Cox, designed by Allen Charles Klein. With Kathleen Kuhlmann as Angelina and (behind her) Claudio Desderi as Don Magnifico.*

librettists for both operas—Cesare Sterbini for *Il barbiere* and Jacopo Ferretti for *Cenerentola*. Sterbini's adaptation of the Beaumarchais play, and Ferretti's of the various versions of the Cinderella story, were apparently written in very short order: Ferretti claimed in his memoirs to have written *Cenerentola* overnight, but that can surely be taken with a pinch of salt. At all events, the delivery of the librettos to Rossini, scene by scene, left him with hardly more time to compose the scores. Even by the standards of Mozart, who wrote *La clemenza di Tito* in eighteen days, Rossini's speed and facility were breathtaking.

And it never appeared to slacken. Just a few weeks after the opening of *Cenerentola* in Rome, Rossini was at La Scala, Milan, for the first performance of his next opera, *La gazza ladra* (The Thieving Magpie). This was what was called an *opera semiseria* (normally, a serious plot, with one comic character, and a happy ending). Once again it was written for a mezzo-soprano leading lady (Teresa Belloc-Giorgi—no relation to Geltrude Righetti-Giorgi), and it was extraordinary for its subject matter. The *verismo* (or realistic) school of Italian opera was still seventy years away, yet *La gazza ladra* prefigured it by taking a true and sensational case, in which a young serving girl in France had been hanged for a theft that was subsequently discovered to have been perpetrated by

a magpie, and turning it into an opera that was somewhere between *buffa* and *seria*. In Rossini's idiom, there was no danger of the audience's being overcome by the realism of the drama (and he gave it the compulsory happy ending by rescuing Ninetta before she could be executed), but it was nonetheless extraordinary to find Rossini, master of the Neapolitan *opera seria* and the Roman *opera buffa*, adapting his art to such a contemporary tale.

By 1823, when he was thirty-one, Rossini had written thirty-four operas. His contract with Barbaja at Naples was over. It had been a fruitful association (for both parties), and Rossini took with him his ultimate prize—the hand of Isabella Colbran, whom he married one week after leaving Naples. Her voice was well past its best, but he wrote one last opera for her, the last he was to write in Italy. It was *Semiramide*, a classic *opera seria*, written for the Carnival season in Venice. With that, the Rossinis departed for London, and eventually Paris. London was where he became rich, charging thousands of pounds for personal appearances at opera and concert performances, but it was Paris that became his home for much of the rest of his life. He had a contract with the Maison du Roi to write and produce new operas, and he was also to be director of the Théâtre-Italien, where his presence inspired a new generation

Set design by Alessandro Sanquirico for the original production of Rossini's La gazza ladra, *Milan, 1817. This is the courtroom scene. Sanquirico (1777–1849) was the leading Italian scenic designer of his day: his premieres also included Bellini's* Norma *and* Il pirata. *He was responsible for the redecoration of the interior of La Scala in 1829.*

of Italian composers led by Bellini and Donizetti.

Rossini himself wrote only one more opera in Italian, a magnificent pageant for the coronation of France's new king, Charles X (*Il viaggio a Reims*—The Journey to Reims). The other four operas he wrote in Paris were all for the Opéra, and had therefore to be written in French—a language Rossini knew only imperfectly when he arrived in 1824. Two of them were substantial reworkings of earlier Neapolitan operas. Another was a gem of an *opéra-comique*, *Le comte Ory* (Count Ory), which recycled some of the music from *Il viaggio*. Finally, in 1829, he wrote *Guillaume Tell* (William Tell), the largest and grandest of all his operas (see the chapter "Opera in Nineteenth-Century Paris").

Thereafter, for nearly forty years, Rossini wrote very little music, and not a note of opera. No one, including Rossini, was able to say with certainty why this was so. He was tired; he was bothered by the political eruptions that shook France in 1830; there was the death of his beloved mother; and he had what we would now call a manic-depressive illness. All these, no doubt, contributed. But, at any rate, he had done enough. As he himself put it much later, in a letter he wrote to his publisher, Tito Ricordi, urging him to encourage his son to study his operas: "He will see that I was not idle!"[11]

Rossini's genius for opera was at least comparable to Mozart's. He never found a librettist as good as Da Ponte, but he wrote for voices that were, in most cases, finer than those of Mozart's singers—even if the owners of the voices did not often know or care much about acting. Nevertheless, Rossini was essentially a dramatic composer. He had a conception of *dramma per musica* that enabled him to write, with equal facility, thundering melodrama, highly charged tragedy, and very funny comedy. The speed and wit of the comedies, their grand and intricate finales, and the musical characterization of their protagonists are remarkable enough. When you add in the superfluity of melody and the grace and subtlety of the orchestration, they become extraordinary theatrical experiences. The same was true in his serious operas, although here he was dealing with conventions and traditions that had already strangled lesser composers. In his earlier *opere serie* he often encouraged singers to make up their own ornamentations and decorations, as Italian singers had done for years, but later, as he developed his methods of

characterization, his style became so elaborate and unpredictable, and seemingly spontaneous, that further improvisation by the singers was virtually impossible (or ridiculous, if attempted). Increasingly, he did away with the old-fashioned "dry" recitative, accompanied only by the harpsichord, and developed orchestral string writing that accomplished the same thing but with far greater emotional impact. And always there were the tunes. As he so modestly proclaimed it at the end of his life, "Simple Melody, Clear Rhythm."

THE AGE OF BEL CANTO: BELLINI AND DONIZETTI

Rossini might no longer be composing new operas, but it was his presence in Paris (he was officially "Inspector-General of Singing at the Royal Theaters") that attracted many of the greatest singers and composers to come to the French capital. Where Rossini the composer had laid the foundations of what we know as the *bel canto* repertoire, it was Rossini the impresario who became

It is hard not to think of Bellini and Donizetti in the same breath. Bellini would have been outraged by such a sentiment, whereas Donizetti, an altogether calmer, milder, more generous man, would not have minded in the slightest. Neither of them was very much younger than Rossini—Donizetti by only five years, Bellini by nine—but by the time they had their first successes, Rossini's stunning career was all but over.

Bellini, the younger, had his first big hit at La Scala, Milan, in 1827 with *Il pirata*. It was only his third opera. Donizetti had to wait three more years before he scored a really significant success with *Anna Bolena* in 1830. It was his thirtieth opera.

They had known each other since the spring of 1822, when they were both in Naples—Bellini as a student at the conservatory, Donizetti as an aspiring composer whose work Bellini admired. Both of them, of course, were hugely influenced

Drawings after the original production of Bellini's Norma *at La Scala, Milan, 1831, with Giuditta Pasta as Norma. Pasta's creation of Norma, the Druid priestess, was, by all accounts, extraordinarily powerful. Here, she is seen in Act II: Norma contemplates killing her own children rather than allow them to be carried off to Rome as slaves.*

the link between the singers and a new group of younger composers. Together, they celebrated the high days of the art of *bel canto*.

The term *bel canto* has almost always been in the operatic vocabulary. It means nothing more or less than "beautiful singing," something all composers hope for, but it has come to have a special meaning when attached to the names of Rossini, Vincenzo Bellini, and Gaetano Donizetti. Anyone who has heard Maria Callas sing "Casta diva" from Bellini's *Norma*, or Joan Sutherland sing the Mad Scene from Donizetti's *Lucia di Lammermoor*, knows what *bel canto* is.

by Rossini, who was just completing his long stint as Barbaja's composer-in-residence. Barbaja was also leaving the city in that spring of 1822 to take up a new position at the Kärntnertortheater in Vienna, but it would not be long before he was back at the San Carlo—and at La Scala as well. The destinies of the four men—Barbaja, Rossini, Bellini, and Donizetti—would become ever more intertwined.

Bellini may have admired Donizetti's early work in Naples, but it was not long before there was competition between them. Yet it existed mostly in the mind of Bellini. Vincenzo Bellini was an ambitious man—convinced that the rest

Maria Callas in Bellini's Norma *at the Rome Opera House, 1958.*

of the world, led by Donizetti, was conspiring against him. In 1835, it would all come to a climax in Paris when Rossini had the idea of commissioning each of them to write a new opera for the Théâtre-Italien, using identical casts of principal singers. It was as close to a head-to-head joust as you could get, and it provided opera with one of its grandest moments—and one of its saddest.

By that time, there had already been several opportunities for audiences to make direct comparisons. Donizetti's *Anna Bolena* had preceded Bellini's *La sonnambula* (The Sleepwalker) by just a few weeks at the Teatro Carcano in Milan in the winter of 1830—31. In both cases, the libretto was by Felice Romani and the title role was sung by Giuditta Pasta. Both operas had great success. The following season the comparison took place at La Scala. This time, Bellini had a clearcut victory, though the opening night of his opera *Norma* was a fiasco to rival that of *Il barbiere*. As in the case of *Il barbiere*, however, it was only the first night that was disrupted. Thereafter it was a triumph for both Pasta (as Norma) and her soon-to-be successor Giulia Grisi, then only twenty years old, who sang Adalgisa in the original performances. Donizetti's contribution that season was a long-

forgotten work called *Ugo, conte di Parigi*. It fell foul of censors and audience alike.

Nevertheless, Donizetti was developing a style and a popularity of his own, and he was doing so on several different fronts. The earliest of his works to strike a spark with the audience had been a charming little comedy he wrote in Naples in 1824—*L'ajo nell'imbarazzo* (The Tutor Embarrassed). It was clearly Rossinian, and none the worse for that, but it also signaled some of the characteristics that were to make Donizetti stand

out among his peers, and that make his operas so appealing to this day. There was a humanity about them—Donizetti's own humanity. The emotions were genuine and therefore affecting, whether they were happiness or sadness, pathos or ecstasy— and that applied to the historical dramas he was increasingly drawn to, as well as the comedies. Soon after the success of *Anna Bolena*, he gave Bellini genuine cause for concern. *L'elisir d'amore* (The Elixir of Love) was, on the surface, a very slight pastoral comedy, but how many composers have ever given a tenor a more beautiful aria with which to win his soprano than Donizetti's "Una furtiva lagrima"? The next year, in an altogether different mode, he and Romani became the first opera writers to raid the works of Victor Hugo (who was not amused) and came up with a very popular Romantic melodrama, *Lucrezia Borgia.*

One of the obvious ironies of the competition between the two composers was that they were largely dependent on the same librettist. Felice Romani was a distinguished journalist and critic, and easily the most prolific Italian librettist of his day. Early on, he had written *Il turco in Italia* for Rossini. Now he wrote for both Bellini and Donizetti, and to both of them he was a valued friend. His very different relationships with them tell us much about the two composers. In a biography of Romani, his wife, Emilia, described the musical soirees in Milan at which Romani and the gregarious Donizetti were always stars: "Oh! Those beautiful and delicious evenings! Romani and Donizetti kept them more alive than any, because the two were the life of everything."[12]

And Emilia Romani had no doubts about the attractions of Donizetti: "He was a very handsome man: tall, a slender figure, he had a broad brow crowned with curly black hair. . . . He was likeable beyond all description, and the fair sex went mad for him."[13]

For Donizetti, Romani wrote *Anna Bolena, L'elisir d'amore, Lucrezia Borgia,* and several others. Yet his most famous collaboration was with the difficult, and often ungrateful, Bellini. He wrote the librettos for all Bellini's mature operas, with the single exception of the last, *I puritani.* And why did he work so hard for him? Romani himself supplied the answer: "I alone could comprehend that poetic spirit, that impassioned heart, that mind eager to soar beyond the sphere in which it had been confined. . . ."[14]

No one, not even Romani, could remain on good terms with Bellini for very long, and they eventually fell out over their opera *Beatrice di Tenda,* which was a terrible disaster in Venice in 1833. Bellini blamed the failure on the late arrival of Romani's libretto.

Bellini was still only thirty-two, but his health was beginning to fail. In his frenetic search for success, ever more conscious of the shadow of Donizetti at his back, he moved to Paris and became an habitué of the salons and drawing rooms where his looks (tall, blond, and handsome)

and his talents were admired. The cruelest and most oft-quoted description of Bellini in these years came from the German poet Heinrich Heine, who also lived in Paris. "A sigh in dancing pumps," he called him.

The climactic year was 1835. At Rossini's suggestion, Bellini and Donizetti would each write an opera for the season at the Théâtre-Italien. Bellini came first with the dazzling success of *I puritani* (The Puritans), his story of the English civil war. Not the least part of the dazzle was provided by the virtuoso parts he wrote for his four star singers—soprano Giulia Grisi, tenor Giovanni Rubini, baritone Antonio Tamburini, and bass Luigi Lablache. They quickly became known as the "Puritani Quartet." Moreover, in his determination to succeed, Bellini had gone to a great deal of trouble to consult with Rossini during the writing of the opera, so after its triumphant premiere he was able to write to his uncle in Italy: "Having won the friendship of Rossini, I said to myself: Let Donizetti come now!"[15]

Donizetti, in fact, was already in Paris and had witnessed Bellini's brilliant success. In his usual generous way, he wrote to the absent Romani: "Bellini's success has been very good. . . . Today I begin my own rehearsals, and I hope to give the first performance at the end of the month. I don't deserve anything like the success of *I puritani,* but I do want to please."[16]

And please he did. *Marino Faliero* was the name of his opera, now but seldom performed. Both public and reviewers gave it a good reception, not least, perhaps, because it was sung by that very same "Puritani Quartet" who had so recently triumphed for Bellini. There was, however, one savage critic in the audience, and it does not take much guesswork to know who it was:

> It is the worst Donizetti has composed so far, and his operas now have reached the number of forty-eight. . . . *Marino Faliero* had a mediocre effect. . . . The newspapers, influenced by his behavior, as he goes and acts the clown in all the houses of Paris and especially with the journalists, have tried to praise him.[17]

In the same letter, Bellini raged incoherently against what he alleged was a "Rossini-Donizetti plot" against him. He was apoplectic and, in truth,

Bellini's I PURITANI *at the Metropolitan Opera, New York, 1976. The modern quartet included Joan Sutherland, Luciano Pavarotti, Sherrill Milnes, and James Morris. Directed by Sandro Sequi, designed by Ming Cho Lee and Peter J. Hall.*

near mad. At the end of the season, he retired to his country lodgings at Puteaux, outside Paris—and at the end of September, aged thirty-three, he was dead.

No one knows what he died of, or how, except that he died alone. His hosts, an English couple, were mysteriously absent. There were rumors they had poisoned him. More likely, they mistook his illness for cholera (which it was not) and fled for fear of their own lives.

Like so many composers cut off in their prime (Pergolesi, Mozart, Weber), it is impossible to know what Bellini might have achieved for opera. He worked almost as fast as Rossini and Donizetti, but he worked less frequently: there were only eight operas in his mature (post-student) career, and very little other music. His detractors accused him of doing little more than

creating showpieces for virtuoso singers. It was an easy criticism to make because most of his operas were melodramas involving female heroines in extreme situations: women who went mad (*Il pirata* and *I puritani*), or made living sacrifices of themselves (*Norma*), or walked in their sleep (*La sonnambula*). They were roles that required genuine acting talent, as well as extraordinary vocal and musical skills. Yet even when this rare combination was present (in Pasta's Norma, perhaps—or, much more so, in Malibran's), the art of stage production was still very rudimentary, and a Bellini opera that was unconvincingly staged could easily deteriorate into fiasco. There was gas lighting in most theaters, but the sophisticated *spectacles d'optique* with which Pierre-Luc-Charles Cicéri was beginning to entrance audiences at the Paris Opéra were not yet available elsewhere. It was not until the second half of the twentieth century that gifted stage directors and *bel canto* sopranos finally came together and reestablished Bellini as one of the greatest of opera composers.

In the development of Italian opera, Bellini stood squarely between Rossini and Verdi. Like them, he rejoiced in melody, often much longer drawn-out melodies than either of them employed. Like Verdi (but often unlike Rossini), he had a great reverence for words. That was one of the reasons Richard Wagner so admired him. There was little attempt to characterize people in his music (that was something Donizetti was beginning to do, and Verdi would do to an even greater extent), but Bellini was a master of atmosphere. He could create violence or tenderness, melancholy or ecstasy, and always in music that was centered on those long, flowing melodies. It was an ideal prescription for Romantic melodrama.

Only three days after Bellini's lonely death in France, Donizetti scored the greatest triumph of his career, at the Teatro San Carlo in Naples. This was the brilliant premiere of *Lucia di Lammermoor*, perhaps the greatest Romantic melodrama of them all. Three months later, this time at La Scala, he had yet another success when María Malibran, the singer whose brief career was one of the most glorious phenomena of the *bel canto* era, created the title role in his *Maria Stuarda*.

For a decade now, with Rossini retired, Bellini dead, and Verdi only just embarking on his career, Gaetano Donizetti was king. And he displayed an astonishing versatility. He wrote in Italian and in French. He wrote *opere buffe* and *opéras-comiques* as well as *opere serie* (or, at any rate, *semi-serie*). He even wrote a *grand opéra* for Paris in the style then being trademarked by Giacomo Meyerbeer. He was adored by the singers for whom he wrote. Yet it was Bellini, not Donizetti, who was held in veneration by Berlioz and Liszt and Wagner, and only a handful of Donizetti's operas continued to be performed in the fifty years after his death.

There were some good reasons for this. Donizetti wrote sixty-five operas, many of them on very short notice. There was therefore a lot of recycling of material (even more than Rossini had done). Moreover, his real love was the human voice, and the orchestra generally played a very secondary role. As a result, a good deal of the drama of his Romantic plots was treated in a perfunctory manner, emerging with difficulty from the straitjacket of predictable formulas. But the vocal writing was stunning. Donizetti wrote for perhaps the greatest generation of singers there has ever been. He allowed them to dazzle and amaze (of course), but he was also one of the first Italian composers to make use of much more subtle compositional techniques to portray his characters in music. It was a skill much admired by Verdi, who would take it a great deal further.

Yet already, by 1837, only two years after Bellini's death, tragedy was stalking Donizetti as well. In that year, when *Roberto Devereux* gave him another great success, both his wife and his infant son died in Naples in a cholera epidemic. Rossini persuaded him to move to Paris, but Donizetti's own health was now beginning to decline.

You would never know it to look at the pictures of him at this time, debonair and confident, or when you listen to the music he composed in Paris, but during this period a terrible

Luigi Lablache and Henriette Sontag in Donizetti's Don Pasquale *at Her Majesty's Theatre, London 1851.*

Daguerreotype of Gaetano Donizetti (at right) and his nephew Andrea, 1847. At this time, Donizetti was in his final illness, and he died the following year.

illness set in. It was syphilis, or the effects of syphilis, and eventually the disease would affect his brain. In the meantime, he kept up a tremendous pace, turning out comedies and historical dramas with equal facility. In 1840, he wrote *La fille du régiment* for the Opéra-Comique and *La favorite* for the Opéra—the one a gentle and romantic comedy that made astonishing vocal demands on its singers, the other an almost Verdian drama set in Spain. In 1843 (to take another year), his comedy at the Théâtre-Italien, *Don Pasquale*, was followed within months by the massive and spectacular *Dom Sébastien* at the Opéra. His native Italy also made demands on him (new operas for Rome, Milan, and Naples), and Vienna gave him his crowning glory when he was appointed court composer to the emperor in 1842.

Finally, illness took possession of Donizetti. One day at a rehearsal for *Dom Sébastien,* he flew into a terrible rage, and from that time on he was more or less incapacitated. Less than fifty years of age, at the height of his musical genius, he was half-mad, and dying. He was put in an asylum outside Paris at Ivry, from where he wrote desperate, heartrending letters to his remaining family. "Rejoice, I am better," he wrote to his brother Giuseppe, but the almost illegible scrawl told another story entirely. There is a daguerreotype of him near the end, taken with his nephew Andrea, who helped look after him. The handsome, energetic man of a few years earlier is now slumped and despondent, clearly unable to tend to himself. It is one of the most pathetic pictures in the whole story of opera. Taken home to Italy by Andrea—to Bergamo, where he had been born—Donizetti died in April 1848.

And by that time, a new star had risen in

the Italian firmament. Giuseppe Verdi was fast becoming the great Italian composer of his generation. Rossini, Bellini and Donizetti had never been competitors to him, though they certainly influenced his early music a great deal. More to the point, they had provided him with fertile ground on which to work.

THE GREAT BEL CANTO SINGERS

Not the least fertile part of the ground was a generation of singers probably unsurpassed in the history of singing. We cannot know that for certain, of course, because the technology of sound recording was still half a century away, but the evidence is in the music. It is not the sort of music these composers could, or would, have written for mediocre talent.

Singers drove the box office. They always had, ever since the time of Anna Renzi in Monteverdi's Venice and Marthe Le Rochois in the Paris of Louis XIV. And the biggest box office of all had been for the *castrati*, from Farinelli onward. But the age of the *castrati* was just about over. Rossini and Meyerbeer were the last two major composers to write for that artificial and amazing kind of voice. They both wrote roles for Giovanni Battista Velluti, who had so impressed Rossini in Bologna in 1807 (and later infuriated him by the ornamentations he added to the music of Arsace in *Aureliano in Palmira*, though the two eventually became great friends). In 1825, at the end of his career, Velluti performed in London, where he was greeted by an editorial in the august London *Times*. "The manly British public," it thundered, "should have been spared the disgust of such an appearance as that of Velluti."[18]

Tastes and fashions had changed. The bass voice was beginning to win its proper recognition, with Filippo Galli and Luigi Lablache as its most distinguished exemplars. Galli had begun his career as a tenor and was reputed to have become a bass as a result of a serious illness. At all events, he quickly became the favorite bass of Rossini, who created a wonderful pantheon of roles for him—comic roles like the evil Mustafa in *L'italiana in Algeri*, and serious roles like Assur in *Semiramide*. His career overlapped with the era of Bellini and Donizetti (he created Enrico in Donizetti's *Anna Bolena*), but by then he had been overtaken by *their* favorite bass, who was Luigi Lablache. Lablache was half Irish, half French, but Neapolitan by birth. He was (and in contemporary prints he still is) instantly recognizable because of his great size, both in height and in girth. Onstage, he used it to advantage—as a remarkably lifelike Henry VIII in *Anna Bolena*, and as a comic Leporello in Mozart's *Don Giovanni* whose party trick was to carry off Masetto under his arm. For Donizetti he created no fewer than ten roles, including, most famously, the title role of *Don Pasquale*. Between engagements, he found time to teach the art of singing to Princess Victoria of England, among others.

These years also witnessed the development (or, at any rate, the recognition) of a new category of male voice: the baritone. Throughout the eighteenth century, composers had expected singers to transpose their parts (up or down a key, as necessary) to suit their individual voices—and that had applied to every vocal category. Thus, most of the parts we are used to hearing sung by baritones (Mozart's Figaro, for instance) were written for basses with a higher range than the true bass voice. Rossini was probably the first composer to formalize the new category, when he wrote the title role of *Il barbiere* for Luigi Zamboni. It included some passages that were unnaturally high for any normal bass,[19] and it began the tradition, so marked in the works of Bellini, Donizetti, and, most of all, Verdi, of writing entirely separate roles for basses and baritones.

Antonio Tamburini was the first to take full advantage of this, and the first baritone to become as famous and as popular as his colleagues. Like Lablache, he was a member of the "Puritani Quartet" in Paris in 1835, and he was on the same stage at the Théâtre-Italien eight years later when Lablache created the title role in *Don Pasquale* for Donizetti: Tamburini had the almost equally rewarding role of Dr. Malatesta. Like many of his successors, he appropriated the role of Don Giovanni from the bass repertoire and made it one of his most popular. Giorgio Ronconi, ten years younger than Tamburini, was another baritone for whom Donizetti wrote original parts, and he contributed greatly to the young Verdi's career by being the first Nabucco in the opera that established Verdi at La Scala in 1842. Again and again, Verdi would give leading roles, often title roles, to baritones, so that singers like Felice Varesi (the first Macbeth and Rigoletto) and later Victor Maurel (the first Iago and Falstaff) would become quite as famous as the tenors and sopranos.

Bel canto, so often associated with female singers, was just as applicable to men. The great female roles of Rossini, Bellini, and Donizetti were unthinkable without the male protagonists, and no one had more to gain from the demise of the *castrati* than the tenors. As we have seen, Rossini's Neapolitan operas were partly dictated by the need to write for several fine tenors on Barbaja's payroll. Andrea Nozzari, Giovanni David, and Manuel García were three of them, but there was a fourth, Giovanni Battista Rubini, whose fame would eventually outstrip that of all the others. Rubini arrived in Naples in 1815, the same year as Rossini. He was twenty-one years old, almost untried, and for several years he made very little impression, but he acquired an impressive repertoire—forty-four roles by the time he ended his contract at the San Carlo in 1829. And by that time he had transformed himself from a rather dumpy, unexciting singer into a blazing virtuoso with a stage presence to match. Wagner, who heard him sing in Paris at the height of his powers, likened him to a trapeze artist.

The Théâtre-Italien in Paris was the scene of Rubini's great success. He arrived there in 1825, invited by Rossini to sing Ramiro in the Paris production of *La Cenerentola*, and he had the good fortune to sing there as the *primo tenore* right through the Paris periods of Bellini and Donizetti. It was probably his friendship with Bellini that changed his life. At La Scala in 1827, during rehearsals for the premiere of *Il pirata*, which was Bellini's first significant success, the fiery composer somehow persuaded Rubini to throw off his calm, ever-so-professional stage manner and become the powerful, exciting singer that his voice and his technique equipped him to be. Rubini never looked back, and by the 1835 season Rossini would not have dreamed of engaging anyone else as the tenor in the "Puritani Quartet."

While Rubini was collecting bouquets at the Théâtre-Italien, the Frenchman Adolphe Nourrit was earning almost as much acclaim at the Paris Opéra. He was a genuine French hero—of the barricades as well as the opera stage—and he sang a repertoire that rarely trespassed on Rubini's. Nourrit was the tenor of Rossini's final large-scale operas in Paris, including *Guillaume Tell*, and of Meyerbeer's first *grands opéras*. He also had the rare distinction of being "professeur de déclamation" at the conservatoire even while he was a member of the Opéra's roster. But his place in the affections of French audiences was snatched from him, almost overnight, by Gilbert-Louis

Duprez. Duprez was only four years younger than Nourrit. He spent a good many years pursuing a not very distinguished career in Italy until, in 1835, three days after Bellini's death, he created the fiendishly difficult part of Edgardo in Donizetti's *Lucia di Lammermoor.* Duprez had a range to his voice that Nourrit could not match (nor could any other tenor, come to that), and on his return to Paris in 1837 he virtually took over Nourrit's repertoire at the Opéra.

The Frenchmen Nourrit and Duprez were not really rivals of Rubini. Nor was the Italian Domenico Donzelli, whose voice was much more baritonal and not really suited to the high-flying roles for which Rubini was famed. Donzelli created Pollione in *Norma* for Bellini, and he remained popular in Italy and Vienna for many years, but he lacked the range, and the good looks, of the man who eventually came to take Rubini's place. This was Giovanni Mario. Fifteen years younger than Rubini, Mario, having eloped with a ballerina, arrived in Paris the year after the "Puritani Quartet." He was an exceedingly handsome man, a fine actor, and a very good tenor, too. He quickly became the heartthrob of Paris and London. His ascent to Rubini's eminence was gauged by the premiere of *Don Pasquale* at the Théâtre-Italien in 1843. Donizetti's cast contained three from the "Puritani Quartet"—Giulia Grisi, Tamburini, and Lablache—but the tenor this time was Mario, not Rubini. The next year, Mario and Grisi began a personal relationship that would endure for the rest of their lives (they never got married because Grisi had not divorced her husband). The two of them made spectacular careers in Europe and America, singing well into the 1860s. Mario made his farewell appearance at Covent Garden in 1871, two years after Grisi's death.

All these great male singers were *virtuosi* in their own right. They created enormous excitement, they were feted and celebrated wherever they went, and they earned large fees. (Rubini was said to have collected the equivalent of twenty thousand pounds sterling for a single season in St. Petersburg at the end of his career.) Yet, for most of the time, they still had to play second fiddle to the greatest of the female singers. Bellini and Donizetti wrote first and foremost for tragic and dramatic heroines who captured the imagination of the Romantic age. And like Rossini before them, they delighted in the agility, the flexibility, and the range of the finest female voices—voices

which they challenged with their music, and from which they asked nothing less than beautiful singing, *bel canto.*

They did not always get it. There is a great deal of evidence from authoritative firsthand observers that the divas who were idolized by the public, and around whom legends were created by less knowledgeable but hugely enthusiastic writers like Stendahl, were not the models of vocal technique they are generally assumed to have been. One obvious reason was that these singers were required to do more than just sing. They had to present passable characterizations of Romantic heroines in the throes of emotional torment and/or ecstasy. Standing at the front of the stage and singing was no longer sufficient. Another reason (and it was a criticism frequently leveled at Rossini by both singers and audiences) was that the size of the orchestra and the volume of its accompaniment were increasing all the time. Mozart had shown the way in Vienna, but until Rossini's time it had been unusual for Italian opera orchestras to include many, if any, wind instruments. Flutes and clarinets had begun to make their presence felt, but Rossini brought heavier weapons to bear—the trombones of *Otello,* the horns of *Semiramide,* and eventually the cornets of *Guillaume Tell* (his father had, after all, been a town trumpeter). Where Italian recitatives had traditionally been accompanied only by a harpsichord or pianoforte, sometimes joined by a double bass, Rossini began to use orchestral accompaniment, and he began composing whole scenes as continuous pieces of music—nothing that had not already been done in Germany and France, but it put new burdens on Italian singers.[20]

The old and the new could be contrasted in the styles of the two most famous prima donnas in Italy during Rossini's Neapolitan years. Angelica Catalani and Isabella Colbran were born only five years apart. Catalani made her glittering career without ever finding it necessary to depart from the customs and practice of the eighteenth century, whereas Colbran, greatly influenced by Rossini, took up the new challenges and worked hard to meet them. Michael Scott, one of the finest modern historians of singing, sums up Catalani's method:

[She] was, perhaps, the greatest *virtuosa* who ever lived. In her day she was famous for her combination of talent, tastelessness and rapacity. . . . She had a passion for variations, even possessing herself of those written for the violin by Rode, which she would introduce into whatever opera she happened to be singing with a superb disregard for their dramatic relevance. . . . [Yet] in an age when we are grateful if a singer can trill at all—properly establish each note and clearly sustain it—we can only marvel at one whose art was such that she was able, at will, to execute a trill in either whole or half tones.[21]

Isabella Colbran was also a coloratura soprano—one who could decorate or ornament a melody with runs, trills, cadenzas, and roulades—but in her case she accepted and followed the written demands of Rossini's scores. Those demands were severe, and there can be little doubt that Colbran's voice suffered a great deal of wear and tear in the eight years she sang for him, from *Elisabetta* in 1815 to *Semiramide* in 1823. The German composer Louis Spohr, who heard her in Naples as early as 1816, commented unfavorably on "her strenuous high notes."[22] Very few sopranos who have ever sung those roles have been able to hide the strain of executing the acrobatic coloratura while also sustaining the dramatic recitatives against their

orchestral accompaniment. In this, and much else, Isabella Colbran was a pioneer—the instrument and the personality for which Rossini wrote.

As Colbran's career was ending, so Giuditta Pasta's was just beginning. The unknown painter of the portrait of Domenico Barbaja placed Pasta in the background of his picture, alongside Rossini and Bellini. It must have seemed perfectly proper that the first lady of opera should appear as an equal with her great patrons. They all adored La Pasta, as did Donizetti, and she was frequently the inspiration for their major roles. Her career took off in Paris in 1821 with performances of Rossini's *Otello* in which her Desdemona electrified the theater, but she did not meet Rossini in person until 1823 in Verona. By that time, she was already singing most of Colbran's roles, and it must have been clear that she was the true successor. Her voice was still young and relatively unused, and it would have made a welcome contrast to Colbran's (by then) somewhat worn instrument.

Nevertheless, there is little evidence to suggest that Pasta's voice was any better than those of Catalani or Colbran. By all accounts, she was an uneven singer who certainly accumulated her share of bad reviews. But her voice was very dramatic. It had a peculiar timbre, instantly recognizable, and she must have had a justified confidence in her technique, for this was the voice for which Bellini wrote Norma, the Druid priestess, and Amina, the sleepwalker, and for which Donizetti wrote Anna Bolena, the doomed wife of Henry VIII. The characters themselves provide what is probably the best clue to Pasta's success: she was the first great actress of the operatic stage—a vocal actress as well as a theatrical one. The contemporary prints depicting Act II of *Norma* are a vivid, and still moving, testimonial to her dramatic presence on the stage.

Pasta went on singing until as late as 1850, by which time her voice was well past its best. In the meantime, the one singer who may have surpassed her had come and gone in a wondrous, but all too brief, career. Her name was Maria Malibran, and it is one of the few names in the story of opera that should be spoken with reverence. She was dead by the age of twenty-nine, yet in those few short years she had created a legend. And she is a legend still.

She made her debut in London in 1825, aged seventeen. The role was Rosina in *Il barbiere*, and she stepped into it unexpectedly as the result

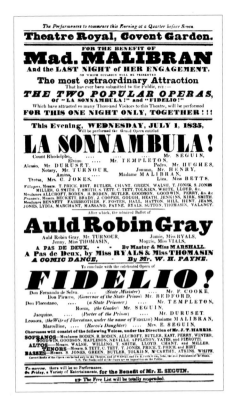

Poster for the final night of Malibran's engagement at Covent Garden in 1835, which included two full-length operas, plus a ballet. Malibran sang both Amina in Bellini's La Sonnambula *and Leonore in Beethoven's* Fidelio. *The tenor lead in both operas was John Templeton (1802–1886), a Scot who was Malibran's chosen tenor for most of her London appearances from 1833. Malibran made nineteen appearances at Covent Garden in the 1834–35 season, for which she was paid almost £4,000— a very large sum in those days. The management of Covent Garden, under Alfred Bunn, went into receivership at the end of the season. Bunn's two seasons at Covent Garden had included a number of interesting features—a performance of Act III of Rossini's* Otello *with the German soprano Wilhelmine Schröder-Devrient as Otello and Malibran as Desdemona, and Bellini's* Norma *"compressed into one act."*

of Pasta's late, and unexplained, cancellation. She died eleven years later, also in England, probably as a result of injuries received (but not admitted—she went on singing) in a riding accident while she was pregnant. If Rossini, Bellini, and Donizetti adored Pasta, then they worshiped Malibran, and the same could be said of audiences as far afield as New York, where she enchanted Americans in Mozart and Rossini operas only a few weeks after her London debut, and La Scala, Milan, where she unseated Pasta as the leading Norma during the 1834 season.

Malibran was the name of her first husband, whom she married during her New York visit and from whom she was quickly separated. She had been born María-Felicità García, eldest daughter of Manuel García. He was the Spanish tenor who had created Almaviva in *Il barbiere* and was a much-admired interpreter of Mozart and Rossini, but his ultimate fame was as a voice teacher and as the patriarch of the most prolific dynasty in nineteenth-century opera. María was his most famous daughter and pupil, but her sister Pauline was not far behind. She, too, was known by her married name—Pauline Viardot—and she became almost as celebrated in a much longer career. Their older brother was Manuel García, Jr., who truly spanned the century (he lived to be a hundred and one). Like his father, he was a voice teacher, but he was also a voice doctor, and the inventor of an important instrument for examining the throat: the laryngoscope.

María's voice was something of a curiosity. In category, it was a contralto voice, but her father, who was a very forceful man, helped her extend it at the top well into the soprano range. Between the natural voice and the extension, it was said that there was an interval of dead notes, which she had to be careful to avoid in performance. Whether this was so or not (and her brother's account in his 1847 book, *L'art du chant,* is probably the only authoritative account), there is no doubt that it was a very singular and very exciting voice, with great strength and agility. But it was clearly governed by María's volatile temperament—she was given to great emotion—and it was this which gave her performances so much power and rendered them so memorable to those who heard them.

Contemporary accounts agree that she possessed a special warmth, a special joy, which she seemed able to transmit across the footlights to the audience. Felix Mendelssohn and the pianist Ignaz Moscheles were among her closest friends. "Other singers may captivate by their art," wrote Moscheles, "but Malibran had magic power to lead us captives, body and soul."[23] And she did—as Rossini's Desdemona and Semiramide, as Bellini's Norma, Amina, and Romeo, as Donizetti's Maria Stuarda, as the *Figaro* Susanna and the *Fidelio* Leonore. Rossini thought the world of her. Near the end of his life, in his conversations with Edmond Michotte, a wealthy amateur musician from Belgium, Rossini gave a detailed portrait of her. Michotte reported him as saying:

> The greatest was Colbran, but unique was Malibran. Ah, that marvelous creature! She surpassed all her imitators by her truly disconcerting musical genius, and all the women I have known, by the superiority of her intelligence, the variety of her knowledge, of which it is impossible to give an idea. . . . She sketched, painted, embroidered, sometimes made her own costumes; above all, she wrote. Her letters are masterpieces of subtle intelligence, verve, of good humor, and they display unparalleled originality of expression.[24]

One of those to whom she often wrote was Bellini. On his cravat he sometimes wore a little gold locket, a gift from Maria; inside it were two miniature portraits she had painted—one of Bellini, one a self-portrait. On hearing the news of Bellini's tragic, lonely death, Maria burst into tears and said, "I feel I soon shall follow him."[25] She died exactly one year later, to the day.

The long shadows cast by Pasta and Malibran did not stop other sopranos from becoming great stars. The German-born Henriette Sontag was renowned for her showy technique and sureness of execution, and the French mezzo-soprano Rosine Stoltz, who created several of Donizetti's later and grander roles, dominated the Paris Opéra for a decade (and not just by her singing). Malibran's sister, Pauline Viardot, another mezzo-soprano, was also a tremendous star for more than three decades, right up to her retirement in 1870. Jenny Lind, the "Swedish Nightingale," might have outshone them all. In the 1840s, she amazed Berlin, Vienna, and London with her Amina (Bellini's sleepwalker) and

Marie (Donizetti's daughter of the regiment), and most of all with her Norma. Yet in 1849, not yet thirty, she renounced the opera stage forever. Thereafter, she sang only in oratorio and on the concert stage, most famously in her 1850–51 tour of the United States under the management of P. T. Barnum. The "Jenny Lind fever" that seized American cities was the nineteenth century's equivalent of a Beatles tour. It was perfectly summed up by the New York gentleman who vowed that if ever he had a daughter, he would name her Jenny. He did, and she grew up to be Jenny Jerome, Winston Churchill's mother.

But the true successor to Pasta and Malibran, with both of whom her career overlapped, was Giulia Grisi. At the age of twenty, she created the role of Adalgisa to Pasta's Norma at La Scala, but that was virtually the last time she ever sang in Italy. Dissatisfied with conditions at La Scala, she broke her contract and moved to Paris. There, she quickly joined the roster of Rossini's Théâtre-Italien, and her career took off. She was the Elvira of the "Puritani Quartet" and the Norina of the equally fabulous *Don Pasquale* team in 1843. Like Pasta and Malibran, she was a friend of all three of the great composers—Rossini, Bellini, and Donizetti—but unlike them, she went on to sing the much heavier dramatic roles of Meyerbeer and Verdi. As late as 1857, she was singing Leonora in *Il trovatore*. Her voice encompassed both the florid agility of the *bel canto* roles and the dramatic power of the Verdian soprano—a combination that would be increasingly necessary for sopranos of the next generation.

So this was the age of *bel canto*. All these singers were outstanding *virtuosi* in their own right, but the real wonder of the age was the ensemble they created when they came together. Though the "Puritani Quartet" was the most celebrated example, there were many others. Between 1825 and 1845, and especially in Paris, they could often be heard in what must have been thrilling performances of the operas that were being written around them and for them. One visitor to Paris at this time was Chopin. In awe, he wrote to a friend:

> I have never heard *Il barbiere* as I did last week with Lablache, Rubini and La Malibran. . . . You cannot imagine what Lablache is. . . . La Malibran subjugates with her marvelous voice. She dazzles like nobody else!

Wonder of wonders! Rubini, excellent tenor, sings full voice, never with the head voice. His roulades last at times two hours![26]

In the same letter, Chopin gave his correspondent a description of a practice that was still surprisingly popular—the appropriation of male roles, suitably transposed, by females. He described seeing María Malibran, "completely black," play the part of Otello opposite the Desdemona of another great singer, Wilhelmine Schröder-Devrient— "La Malibran petite and the German enormous!" Schröder-Devrient was as famous in the German repertoire as Malibran was in the Italian, and in different performances the two of them apparently alternated in the roles of Otello and Desdemona. What is interesting about their 1830 *Otello* is that it quite possibly took place in the presence of the composer—certainly in the theater of which he was a director—and presumably had his blessing. Beautiful singing was still more important than dramatic credibility, and it would continue to be for many years. As late as 1908, Mary Garden appropriated the tenor role of Jean in Massenet's *Le jongleur de Notre-Dame* and sang it successfully right up to her very last Chicago performance in 1931.

The Career of Verdi

By the end of his long life (he would live into the first years of the twentieth century), Giuseppe Verdi was the most widely known, and the most widely admired, musician in the world, but his beginnings had been much more modest.

He was born in the little village of Le Roncole, near Busseto in the old Duchy of Parma, in 1813—the same year that Richard Wagner was born in Leipzig. Verdi was the son of an innkeeper, but the real influence in his early life was a shopkeeper and amateur musician in Busseto, Antonio Barezzi. Barezzi became his patron, subsidized his early music studies, and even found him a wife—his own daughter, Margherita.

As an eighteen-year-old, Verdi applied for admission to the conservatory in Milan, and was turned down. That same conservatory now proudly bears his name, but the irony is not as great as it sounds. Verdi was three or four years older than was usual for entrants to the conservatory, and he lacked the expected instrumental skills (in his case, the piano). Instead, he studied privately in Milan for three years, paid for by Barezzi,

before returning to Busseto as the town's *maestro di musica*. It was while he was in that job that he wrote his first opera, *Oberto*. It opened the La Scala season in 1839 and scored a moderate success.

The impresario at La Scala at this time was Bartolomeo Merelli. Where Domenico Barbaja had once been the arbiter of operatic careers (he died in 1841), it was now Merelli to whom singers and composers were chiefly beholden. The comparison with Barbaja goes no further, however, because they were very different human beings. Where Barbaja was crude and uneducated, Merelli had trained as a musician and was something of a playwright. He had studied alongside Donizetti, and he had been a pupil of the distinguished teacher Simone Mayr at Bergamo; he had written librettos for several of Donizetti's early operas; he had commissioned Rossini's first opera for Paris, *Il viaggio a Reims* (and suggested the libretto for it,

too); and he had been responsible for giving both Bellini and Donizetti important commissions at Genoa in 1828.

Indirectly, Verdi owed Merelli another considerable debt. The performances of *Oberto* at La Scala came to the attention of the music publisher Giovanni Ricordi, and Ricordi bought the rights from Verdi for two thousand lire—a modest enough sum, in all conscience, but it was the beginning of a long and hugely profitable relationship for both of them. In his lifetime, Verdi would deal with three generations of Ricordis— Giovanni, the founder, whose first major client had been Rossini; Tito, his son; and finally Tito's son, Giulio, who would not be born until the year after *Oberto*, and who would play a crucial part in the long and brilliant evening of Verdi's career.

Right on the heels of this promising beginning came the low point of Verdi's life. In a period of less than eighteen months in 1838–39, both of his infant children died. And so, in June 1840, did his young wife, Margherita, daughter of his Busseto patron, Antonio Barezzi. Years later, recalling that terrible time, Verdi said: "I was alone! —alone! . . . I had no longer a family. And in the midst of this terrible anguish, to avoid breaking the engagement I had contracted, I was compelled to write and finish a comic opera!"[27] The opera, the first of three commissioned by Merelli for La Scala as a result of *Oberto*, was *Un giorno di regno* (King for a Day). It was a terrible disaster. Verdi himself was booed, and the opera was taken off after only a single performance. Verdi later recalled: "I persuaded myself that I should no longer find consolation in art, and formed the resolution to compose no more."[28]

Verdi wrote no autobiography and published no diaries, but in his mid-sixties he was persuaded to narrate the story of his life, up to that point, to his publisher, Giulio Ricordi. Ricordi wrote it down as accurately as he could. It is this narrative that tells us how Verdi was saved from the terrible misfortunes that had overwhelmed his life. He was twenty-eight; he was living in a garret in Milan; he was writing no music. One winter night, wandering through the streets, he had a chance meeting with Merelli. "It was snowing great flakes, and Merelli, drawing my arm in his, induced me to accompany him as far as his office at La Scala. We chatted on the way, and he told me he was in difficulties for a new opera which he had to bring out."[29] Arrived at the theater, Merelli showed Verdi a libretto by Temistocle Solera, who had been Verdi's librettist for *Oberto*. Verdi took it grudgingly and made his way home.

"I went into my room, and with an impatient gesture I threw the manuscript on the table, and remained standing before it. In falling on the table, it had opened by itself: without knowing how, my eyes fixed on the page which was before me, and on this verse: 'Va, pensiero, sull'ali dorate.'"[30]

"Va, pensiero" (Fly, thoughts, on wings of gold), the chorus of the Hebrew slaves in *Nabucco*, would become one of the most beloved choruses in all of opera—and for Italians almost a national anthem. Sixty years later, as Verdi's funeral cortege passed through the streets of Milan, it was the music chosen by Toscanini and the chorus of La Scala to pay their last respects to their greatest *maestro*.

Even though it was Merelli who had given

him the libretto of *Nabucco*, Verdi did not find it easy to persuade him to stage the opera.

> It was after I had dragged on in poverty and disappointment for a long time in Busseto, and had been laughed at by all the publishers, and shown the door by all the impresarios. I had lost all real confidence and courage, but through sheer obstinacy I succeeded in getting *Nabucco* rehearsed at La Scala, Milan. The artistes were singing as badly as they knew how, and the orchestra seemed bent only on drowning the noise of the workmen who were busy making alterations to the building. Presently, the chorus began to sing "Va, pensiero," but before they had got through half a dozen bars the theater was as still as a church. . . . When the number was finished, they broke out into the noisiest applause I have ever heard, crying "Bravo, bravo, viva il maestro!" and beating on the woodwork with their tools. Then I knew what the future had in store for me.[31]

One of the singers Verdi complained about at those first rehearsals of *Nabucco* was the leading lady, Giuseppina Strepponi. She was still a famous singer, but her voice was past its best, and she cer-

Design by Alessandro Sanquirico for the eruption of Vesuvius in Pacini's L'ULTIMO GIORNO DI POMPEI, *Milan, 1825.*

Verdi's ERNANI *at La Scala, Milan, 1982. Directed by Luca Ronconi, designed by Ezio Frigerio. In addition to Mirella Freni as Elvira and Renato Bruson as Don Carlo, seen here, this production featured Plácido Domingo as Ernani and Nicolai Ghiaurov as Silva. Verdi wrote of the 1844 premiere in Venice: "If I'd had singers — I will not say sublime singers, but just singers who would sing —* ERNANI *would have come off as well as* NABUCCO *and* LOMBARDI *in Milan."*

tainly did not do the role of Abigail justice, not even on the triumphant opening night. Four years later she retired from the stage and went to teach and live in Paris (she was still only thirty-one). In 1847, Verdi joined her there on a prolonged visit to stage his opera *Jérusalem* (the French version of *I lombardi* — The Lombards). She would be his partner, and ultimately his wife, for the remainder of her life.

The period that followed *Nabucco* was what Verdi called his "years in the galleys."[32] By the time he and Strepponi moved back to Italy in 1849 he had become very famous, and quite rich. Most of his operas, like *Nabucco*, had been associated with patriotic or nationalistic stories, and Verdi had come to be identified, as he undoubtedly wished to be, with the yearning for Italian sovereignty and independence. The Risorgimento, the movement to get rid of the foreign occupation and reunite the country, was moving slowly — frustratingly slowly — toward success. Verdi had written of other things as well (*Macbeth* and *Luisa Miller* were two of his recent operas), but it was with the big tunes and mighty choruses of *Ernani, I lombardi, Attila,* and *Giovanna d'Arco* (Joan of Arc) that he was chiefly associated during the years in the galleys.

Verdi's own nationalistic sympathies were very pronounced, and there is no doubt that many of his subjects must have been influenced by those feelings. *La battaglia di Legnano* (The Battle of Legnano), for instance, was based on the true story of the freeing of Italy in the twelfth century from the occupation of Frederick Barbarossa, the Holy Roman Emperor. The parallels with the modern French and Austrian occupations were hardly subtle. But Verdi was also developing a musical and dramatic style ideally suited to his subject matter. The strongest influences had to be Donizetti, who was very active during this period, and Rossini, whose operas still held sway in Italy. One has only to compare Rossini's *Mosè in Egitto* with *Nabucco* and *I lombardi* to see the extent of the influence. But Verdi was already reaching out for something more ambitious — something beyond the lyrical but rather artificial melodramas of Bellini and Donizetti, and something that would begin to approximate to genuine music drama.

He was certainly aware of this trend in the work of one his compatriots (someone he did not care for very much), Saverio Mercadante. Having begun his career as a throwback to the eighteenth century, setting Metastasian texts, Mercadante had

transformed himself into a reasonable imitation of Bellini and Donizetti, though not nearly so talented. Rossini invited him to write the third opera to be sung by the "Puritani Quartet" during the amazing 1835 season at the Théâtre-Italien, but even with that cast, Mercadante's *I briganti* did not succeed. While he was in Paris, however, Mercadante became thoroughly immersed in the newly fashionable genre of *grand opéra*, which Meyerbeer and his colleagues were pioneering at the Paris Opéra. *Les Huguenots*, which opened in February 1836, made a big impression on him. Returning to

Italy for his next commission at La Scala in 1837, Mercadante portentously announced a reform program. It was designed to give greater priority to the development of drama than had previously been the case in Italian opera—the sort of development that would work superbly in the big tunes and grand rhythmic surges of Verdi's vocabulary, but sounded overreached and nothing like so dramatic in Mercadante's less original invention. Nevertheless, Mercadante's *Il giuramento* (The Oath) was a revelation to the Scala audience (which included Verdi), as much for its scale and ambition as for its actual execution. Mercadante wrote several very similar operas in the following seasons, but they paled into insignificance when audiences heard what Verdi could do. Music drama depended, as always, on the quality of the music.

The early Verdian style of *dramma per musica* came more fully into focus with *Ernani* in 1844. The drama of Victor Hugo's story, in which three men pay court to the same woman, was conveyed in a series of huge vocal confrontations—intensely dramatic, emotional, and often explosive. Hugo had created memorable characters; Verdi gave them

Caricature of Francesco Maria Piave (1810–1876). Piave wrote the librettos for ten of Verdi's operas. In 1859, he moved from his native Venice to Milan and became resident stage director at La Scala until he was incapacitated by a stroke in 1869.

musical momentum of great power. The Venice cast, which was much the same as that of *Attila* two years later, was actually led by a German, the soprano Sophie Löwe. In a somewhat backhanded compliment after the premiere of *Attila*, Verdi said he "never would have believed that a German could display such patriotic fire."[33]

Verdi chose his own subjects, and he chose them carefully. After *Nabucco* there was no possibility of simply giving him a libretto and telling him to set it. He believed passionately in the idea of opera as drama, and he saw himself, the composer, as the presiding figure. First, he had to find a subject—not an easy matter. His letters were full of references to subjects later discarded, some because they were unsuitable to the singers at hand, some because he found the treatments lacking in drama, some (*King Lear* was a recurring example) because he simply could not come to terms with them. In 1853, the year of *La traviata*, he looked back over ten years and wrote: "Today I would refuse subjects of the kind of *Nabucco*. . . . They harp on one chord, elevated, if you like, but monotonous."[34] Patriotic themes remained a rich source right up to *Aida* in 1871, but there were elements in Verdi's makeup that attracted him to other, often more complex subjects. He was a highly literate man, well versed in the writings of the ancient Greeks, Shakespeare, and Friedrich von Schiller, as well as contemporary authors and playwrights. And he was a Romantic—no doubt about it. Schiller's *Die Räuber* (The Robbers), which became *I masnadieri* in Verdi's hands, was as Romantic as any German opera of the time. But perhaps the greatest attraction to Verdi was that of an individual character faced with a moral dilemma: Stiffelio, the Protestant minister, confronting his wife's adultery; Luisa Miller writing a false confession in order to save her lover; Violetta, the tragic heroine of *La traviata*, reflecting a dilemma like that faced by Giuseppina Strepponi and Verdi himself; and Rigoletto, the court jester, duped into betraying his own daughter. These were mighty subjects for a musician and dramatist of Verdi's stature.

Writing a libretto for Verdi was an exhausting process. As early as 1842, Solera, trying to fashion the text of *I lombardi* to Verdi's liking, referred to him as the "Tyrant,"[35] and the composer's voluminous correspondence with Francesco Maria Piave, who wrote ten librettos for Verdi from *Ernani* to *La forza del destino*, contains further evidence

of tyranny. Piave, however, talented poet and gentle human being that he was, took it all in his stride. He knew that Verdi was no less lavish with his friendship than he was with his criticism, and he eventually had reason to be certain of it. In 1869, just as he was about to embark on *Aida*, Piave suffered a stroke; Verdi gave him financial support for the remaining seven years of his life, and continued to support his family after his death. The *Aida* libretto was taken over by Antonio Ghislanzoni, a man with a colorful past that must have appealed to Verdi. He had been a singer (good enough to sing Don Carlo in *Ernani* in Paris) who earlier had been deported from Italy for revolutionary activities. His correspondence with Verdi on the *Aida* libretto is probably the most detailed case history of any operatic text.

"Stage director" was not a recognized profession at this time. There were stage managers, who controlled the prompt book and whose duties mainly consisted of ensuring that singers were on stage on cue, but if composers wanted their operas to have any sort of dramatic impact, then they would have to impose it on the staging themselves. And Verdi did. Each of his operas from *Les vêpres siciliennes* in 1855 to *Otello* in 1887 has its own production book. The books were compiled during rehearsals and performances supervised by Verdi himself, and they were then published so that they could be used by other theaters. They are immensely detailed, with instructions on everything from blocking to costuming.

The characteristics common to the early Verdi operas were big tunes and grand drama, but each work was different, each individually crafted. To each one Verdi ascribed what he called its *tinta*, its own unique musical coloring. Thus, *Macbeth* in 1847 had a dark and shadowy substance, *Attila* in 1846 a brassy triumphalism, and *Stiffelio* in 1850 a more complex and intimate theme. Verdi very rarely repeated himself.

Composer, dramatist, director—Verdi saw himself in all these roles, and he required that he be given the overall artistic, as well as musical, responsibility for the work. Richard Wagner would go even further: as well as being his own librettist, he would require a special theater to be built for his operas. That was something Verdi never wanted, though he was not above stipulating in his contracts with Ricordi where first performances of his operas could *not* take place —"except La Scala" was specified in every contract between 1845 and 1869: Verdi had fallen out with Merelli and La Scala over business matters, and for almost twenty years he did not set foot in Milan.

Verdi was a very good businessman when it came to representing his own interests. He sold publishing rights to Ricordi for increasingly large sums, and he once deserted Ricordi briefly for a rival publisher as a protest against some of Ricordi's methods. He charged additional fees for first productions under his own supervision, and yet more fees for all subsequent productions. He even included a clause requiring penalty payments in the event that any opera house should cut, transpose, or change the original score.

By 1848, the year of Donizetti's death, Verdi had become a rich man. He had bought a handsome house in Busseto, and soon afterward a country house, Sant'Agata, not far outside the town. As the years went by, he bought up additional plots so that the estate of Sant'Agata eventually stretched all the way to the river Po. From 1857 until his death in 1901, it was his permanent home.

To begin with, however, life in Busseto was not easy. His old patron and father-in-law, Barezzi (to whom he remained devoted), and Barezzi's friends in the town, had always felt possessive about him. He was, after all, their native son. But they reacted very differently to Giuseppina Strepponi when Verdi brought her home from Paris to live with him in 1849.

Strepponi had a notorious past. By the time she sang *Nabucco* at La Scala, her singing career, which had been a famous and very successful one,

was coming to its end. She was only twenty-six, but she had abused her talents. And she had had two, possibly three, illegitimate children, all of whom had gone to foster parents at birth. Yet the relationship with Verdi, apparently so upright and respectable, was a success from the beginning. It was as if both of them needed to start afresh and find stability together, which is just what they did. For reasons that remain obscure, however, they did not marry for ten more years. There is recent evidence that they may even have had an illegitimate child—also given to foster parents—but what is not in dispute is that the citizens of Busseto regarded her living out of wedlock with their beloved Verdi, and in the middle of their own town, as nothing short of scandalous. It was because of the hostility to Strepponi that she and Verdi moved from the town house to Sant'Agata in 1851, and even then, up until 1857 at least, they spent more time in Paris than they did in Italy.

Legend has it that they commemorated their first happy years together by planting three trees in the garden at Sant'Agata. Each tree represented a different opera: the plane tree was for *Rigoletto* (1851), the oak tree for *Il trovatore* (1853), and the willow tree for *La traviata* (1853). The operas were special to Verdi and Strepponi because they marked the beginning of their real happiness together, and they have been special to operagoers ever since.

The "years in the galleys" were over. The new operas were the mature works of a composer reaching out, closer and closer, toward his ideal of *dramma per musica*. The big tunes and mighty choruses of *Il trovatore* (The Troubadour) might be seen as a throwback to his earlier years, if a hugely successful one, but *Rigoletto* and *La traviata* were on a different level. For each of them, Verdi found not just a *tinta*, but a musical-dramatic style that ran right through each work, so that they were in a very real sense music dramas. Triboulet, the hunchbacked court jester of Victor Hugo's original play, *Le roi s'amuse*, became Verdi's Rigoletto, acting out his tragedy to music that vividly enhanced the contrasting sides of his character— warped comedian and adoring father. Monterone's great curse rang through the opera, first prophesying, then proclaiming, the tragedy. And in the astonishingly intricate quartet of the final act, Verdi enabled all four principal characters to express their very different emotions in a single, glorious, and highly dramatic, piece of music—

the Duke seducing, Maddalena resisting, Gilda despairing, Rigoletto swearing vengeance. Not even Mozart, not even Rossini, had written a more emotionally charged piece of musical drama.

Many would argue that two years later, in *La traviata* (The Fallen Woman), Verdi surpassed *Rigoletto*. But *La traviata* also showed up a problem that was endemic to opera—the gap between a composer's vision of *dramma per musica* and the singers' ability to achieve it on stage. Verdi's casts often included fine actors—Giorgio Ronconi, who created Nabucco and was later a celebrated Rigoletto, was said to be such a fine actor that audiences were rarely aware of the limitations of his singing—but they also included some very bad ones. *La traviata*, which was Piave's and Verdi's adaptation of Dumas's *La dame aux camélias*, demanded fine acting, most of all from the title character, Violetta. But at the premiere in 1853, when Violetta prepared to die in the final act, the audience's reaction was to laugh. The Violetta in question was Fanny Salvini-Donatelli. She was a large woman and quite obviously in the best of health, so the idea of her dying of consumption was altogether too much for the Venetian audience. There was a limit to how far its disbelief could be suspended. Verdi put the blame squarely on the singers. He wrote savagely about them in letters to friends, and it was an experience he never forgot. *La traviata*, slightly revised, was given again in Venice the following season—at a different theater and with an entirely different cast. As Verdi wrote to a friend: "Then it was a *fiasco*; now it is creating a *furore*. Draw your own conclusions!"[36]

Aside from singers, Verdi's most frequent expletives were reserved for censors. The Victor Hugo play that had been the source for *Rigoletto* was set in the court of the French king, François I. In an Italy still occupied by French and Austrian forces, that was too much for the censors. The action had to be moved to the imaginary court of a Duke of Mantua. Alexandre Dumas's *La dame aux camélias* did not present the same sort of problems for *La traviata*, but it had a contemporary setting, something that was still felt to be too difficult for opera audiences to accept. So it was "back-dated" to Louis XIV's time. The first "contemporary" production was not staged until 1906 in Milan. Nevertheless, the story—about a courtesan, a "fallen woman," who is begged by her lover's father not to marry the young man, not even to live with him, for fear of the family's reputa-

tion in society—must have had all sorts of uncomfortable echoes for Verdi and Strepponi. In their own case, however, there would be no unhappy ending. They were quietly married in 1859, and they lived on together into old age—Strepponi to eighty-two, Verdi to eighty-seven.

With his fame and fortune assured, Verdi was freer than he had ever been to pick and choose his subjects. He was in great demand, and not just in Italy. Ever since 1847, he had been a frequent visitor to Paris, sometimes for extended periods, and he was as well informed as anyone about the *grands opéras* that Meyerbeer and others were staging there. Verdi wanted to succeed in this genre, but his attempts to do so stretched his craft to its limits. *Les vêpres siciliennes* (The Sicilian Vespers), composed for the Paris Opéra during the great International Exhibition of 1855, tackled a subject that would have enraged Italian censors—the thirteenth-century revolt of Sicilians against their French occupiers—but Verdi's dramatic instincts failed him for once, and it ended up a rather long and listless piece. His instincts were even more at sea two years later when he wrote *Simon Boccanegra* for Venice—a story with a plot so complicated and contradictory that not even Piave, the librettist, appeared fully to understand it (*Boccanegra*, however, would be successfully revised later on). It was not until 1859 that Verdi finally wrote a "grand opera" he could be happy with. It was an adaptation of a libretto by Eugène Scribe that had already been used at the Paris Opéra sixteen years before—by Daniel Auber for *Gustave III*. In Verdi's hands it became *Un ballo in maschera* (A Masked Ball), the story of the assassination of King Gustavus III of Sweden in 1792. It was an event so recent and so regicidal that the Venetian censors could not be calmed down until the action had been removed altogether from Sweden and transplanted to colonial Boston, but it nevertheless inspired Verdi to write one of his loveliest scores—full of big tunes, but also full of intense drama, with repeated musical themes and motifs running through most of the opera.

The year of *Un ballo in maschera*, 1859, was also *the* year of the Risorgimento. Garibaldi landed in Sicily with only a thousand men, and the next year, with a famous handshake, he handed over all his conquests to Victor Emmanuel II of Sardinia, who became the first king of all Italy in 1861. The last two occupied territories were liberated during that decade—the Veneto in 1866, and Rome itself, which the French were forced to hand over in 1870. Italy was whole at last.

Verdi was very much a part of this story, not only because of his patriotic music, and not only because he was known to be a nationalist. It was also because of his name. "Viva Verdi!" was a popular cry in the streets of Italy during the French and Austrian occupations, and very often when Verdi was not within hundreds of miles. It was a code, an acronym. The letters V.E.R.D.I. stood for "Victor Emmanuel, Re D'Italia." Rather than shout Victor Emmanuel's name (which would have gotten them instantly locked up, or worse), Italians could freely shout the name of Italy's most celebrated composer. At the persuasion of Count Cavour, the true architect of Italian nationalism and a close personal friend of Verdi's, the composer took a seat in the new Italian parliament, though he attended infrequently after Cavour's early death. Much later, Verdi was made a senator as a mark of his country's esteem and affection for him.

The years of the Risorgimento's triumph were also Verdi's tourist years. Between 1861 and 1871, he wrote *La forza del destino* (The Force of Destiny) for St. Petersburg, *Don Carlos* for Paris, and *Aida* for Cairo. All of them could properly be described as *grands opéras*, but Verdi told his friend Cesare de Sanctis that what they really had in common was that they were "operas made with ideas."[37] The ideas were not particularly new for Verdi (patriotism, moral dilemmas, and anticlericalism being the most prominent), but he now wove them through the fabric of the operas in a much more insistent and dramatic way. Making operas with ideas rather than simply with arias, duets, and choruses, he told de Sanctis, was the "modern" way. This was not to say that Verdi had deserted the tunefulness that had always been his trademark, but he was now writing on larger canvases, and, as a consequence, spreading himself more.

La forza del destino suffered from the spreading, though Verdi later revised it successfully, adding the famous overture in which destiny is foreshadowed. *Don Carlos*, certainly the finest *grand opéra* ever composed for the Paris Opéra, was also the subject of later revisions. But it was *Aida* that caught the public imagination most fully, and obviously caught Verdi's imagination, too. From the moment he received the first synopsis of the plot, he knew it was good. The narrative was straightforward and easy to follow; there were only four principal characters, whose situations and emotions were intricately intertwined: and there were opportunities for a series of big set pieces, of which Verdi took full advantage.

Aida was commissioned for the new Cairo Opera House in 1870, the year after the opening of the Suez Canal, but it was not finally performed in Cairo until the end of 1871. Verdi was not there, but he supervised the opera's brilliant premiere at La Scala only three months later (La Scala was finally back in favor with Verdi). The delays to the original production had been unavoidable but frustrating. First, Piave, who should have been the librettist, was disabled by a stroke. Then, when the score had been written, the Franco-Prussian War of 1870–71 kept the sets and costumes in Paris, where they were being made. Finally, the intended conductor declined to go to Cairo.

The conductor was Angelo Mariani. He was one of the very few musicians Verdi trusted to prepare a performance of his work, and he had relied on him to be in Cairo. But Mariani refused, partly for reasons of health, partly for reasons of the heart. He was engaged to the soprano Teresa Stolz, who was to sing Aida at La Scala but not in Cairo. Mariani suspected Stolz of being romantically involved with Verdi—and she may have been: Strepponi certainly suspected as much, and it caused something of a rupture in their closeness. Happily, all trust restored, Teresa Stolz would eventually become the faithful companion of the Verdis in their old age. But poor Mariani, caught in between, and beginning to suffer the

The triumphal scene from Verdi's AIDA *at the Arena di Verona, 1997. This massive production, staged by Gianfranco de Bosio in 1982 and performed every season, is based on the Arena's very first* AIDA *production, in 1913. Since no trace of the 1913 costume designs could be found, however, the 1982 producers went back to the costume designs for the Cairo premiere, in 1871.*

effects of the cancer that finally killed him in 1873, did what was, for Verdi, the unforgivable: instead of going to Cairo to conduct *Aida*, he went to Bologna—to conduct the first performance ever of a Wagner opera in Italy.

The opera was *Lohengrin*, and in the event Verdi's own curiosity got the better of him. He, too, went to Bologna to hear it. It was Rossini, several years before, who had coined one of the great bons mots about Wagner: "Monsieur Wagner a de beaux moments—mais de mauvais quart

d'heures." Verdi, to judge by the notes he wrote on his score that night, was very much in agreement. He summarized his reactions at the end:

> Mediocre impression. Beautiful music; when it is clear, it is throughout. The action runs slowly, as do the words. From that, boredom. Beautiful effects in the instruments. Abuse of notes held too long, and that makes it heavy.[38]

Another interested observer in Bologna was Arrigo Boito. He had an opportunity to speak briefly with Verdi that day (probably about the upcoming *Aida* in Milan), and thus, in a circuitous way, began the final, and the greatest, chapter of Verdi's career. Verdi had encountered Boito before, and he had not formed a favorable impression.

Boito was a writer and composer, thirty years younger than Verdi. His opera *Mefistofele* had had a disastrous premiere at La Scala in 1868 (it was later revised and became a great success). More to the point, though, Boito had been a leading member of a group of young bohemian artists in Milan in the 1860s. They called themselves *il scapigliatura* (the disheveled, which was a fairly accurate description, by all accounts). They dreamed of, and preached, a new literature and a new music for Italy, shedding what they called its "decadent past." Boito, writing in 1863, characterized contemporary Italian music as "soiled like the wall of a brothel."[39] Verdi, Italy's most prominent musician, not unnaturally thought the remark was aimed at him.

who were to be of great importance to him in his final creations—the tenor Francesco Tamagno and the French baritone Victor Maurel.

Otello represented the culmination of all Verdi's art as a musician and a dramatist. It contained the usual profusion of melodies, but, more nearly than anything in the past, it was through-composed—almost symphonic in construction. Moreover, Verdi added the subtlest strokes of characterization and comment as he went along. The score was a hugely complex canvas of voices and instruments, yet its effect was to present the drama in the most direct and straightforward manner imaginable. In this sense, Verdi's *Otello* was every bit as much a masterwork as Shakespeare's *Othello*.

Of all the numberless nights in the theater that make up the story of opera, the opening night of *Otello* at La Scala on February 5, 1887, must have been one of the greatest and one of the most extraordinary. It had been fifteen years since *Aida*. The great *maestro* had come out of retirement for what must surely have seemed the last time. He had come to Milan to stage the opera himself. All the world's press was there to report the occasion. The opera opened with no prelude, no overture. The curtain came up, to the braying of the brass, on the greatest storm scene ever written for the stage.

From that unforgettable beginning, right through to Desdemona's "Willow Song" and "Ave Maria" in the final scene, with its tragic ending, *Otello* was an unmitigated triumph. The reception for Verdi, both inside the theater and outside in the streets of Milan, was astonishing. The writer for *The Musical Times* described the scene:

> Several times after each act two of the
> principal artistes would lead him on,
> and then, perhaps by way of sugges-
> tion that he had had enough of it,
> Verdi would step forward alone, hat
> in hand, with his frock coat tightly
> buttoned around him. For this the
> audience reserved their longest and
> loudest cheer. They became frantic
> with enthusiasm.[40]

In fact, nothing could have been further from the truth. Boito almost worshiped Verdi. Their meeting in Bologna may have begun to mend the rift, but the process was to take a long time, and it owed much to the patient diplomacy of Verdi's (and Boito's) publisher, Giulio Ricordi —the third generation of that family to deal with Verdi.

Without Boito, Verdi would have retired after *Aida*. In fact, with the exception of the great *Requiem* in honor of the poet Alessandro Manzoni, and some revisions and restagings of earlier operas, that is exactly what he did. He retired to Sant'Agata. But Ricordi and Boito (and Strepponi, too—she was their co-conspirator in this) had other plans for him. It was their long, patient campaign that finally made possible the sublime achievements of Verdi's old age—*Otello* when he was seventy-four, *Falstaff* when he was eighty. The librettist in both cases was Arrigo Boito.

The collaboration with Boito began with what might be termed a "dry run"—the revision of *Simon Boccanegra*. Piave's original libretto was hard to make sense of, but Boito's additions and amendments, including the magnificent scene in the council chamber as the finale to Act I, pleased Verdi and enabled him to give new life to the opera twenty-four years after its original premiere. It also enabled him to give major roles to two singers

In the orchestra on that opening night in 1887 was a young cellist, Arturo Toscanini. When he returned home to Parma a few days later, he arrived after dark and found his mother was already asleep. Shaking her awake, he shouted "*Otello* is a mas-

Verdi's OTELLO *at the Metropolitan Opera, New York, 1995. Directed by Elijah Moshinsky, designed by Michael Yeargan, costumes by Peter J. Hall. With Plácido Domingo as Otello and Renée Fleming as Desdemona.*

terpiece. Get on your knees, mother, and say 'Viva Verdi!' " She did as she was told.[41]

The age of recording was at hand. Edison's phonograph had been invented in 1877 and Berliner's gramophone would be patented the year after the *Otello* premiere. Tamagno made his only recordings in 1902, at the very end of his career, when he was fifty-two years old, but you can still hear, very distinctly, the magnificent trumpetlike voice that Verdi must have had in mind when he composed the role of Otello. Here was a voice that could project itself across a great orchestra at full volume—a thrilling sound that was quite new in Italian opera. Tamagno's model ensured that Otello would forever be a role in which only the most powerful of tenor voices could succeed.

Verdi had had a model in mind for Iago as well. Several times during the process of composition, he received letters from the French baritone Victor Maurel reminding him that he had promised the role to him. At one stage, in 1883, Verdi was alarmed to read a newspaper report: "Maurel has again told us that Verdi is preparing a huge surprise for the musical world and in his

description of Verdi taking his leave of the cast on the stage, and saying farewell to La Scala forever.

Once again, it was Boito who interrupted the quiet of Sant'Agata, and once again he used Shakespeare to perform the seduction. For years, Verdi had kept a libretto of *King Lear*, thinking that one day he might set it, but *Falstaff* was not a subject he had contemplated. For a start, it was a comic story, and Verdi's only previous excursion into comedy had been the ill-fated *Un giorno di regno*, at the time of his first wife's death. It was also a subject that had been successfully treated in the German repertoire as recently as 1849—*Die lustigen Weiber von Windsor* (The Merry Wives of Windsor) by the Prussian-born Otto Nicolai was immensely popular—and there had been other settings by composers as varied as Karl Ditters von Dittersdorf (1796), Antonio Salieri (1798), Michael Balfe (1838), and Adolphe Adam (1856).

It was in the winter of 1890, at a dinner party given for Verdi by Giulio Ricordi, that the project became public knowledge. Boito rose to propose a toast—presumably to the guest of honor. Instead, he proposed "Fat-paunch!" In the mystified silence that ensued, Ricordi banged the table and shouted, "Falstaff!"[43]

Fifty years of tragedies and heroic subjects, it turned out, had served only to disguise the genius of Verdi's comedic talents. *Falstaff* was, of course, a great success. It went further even than *Otello* in integrating the action and the drama with the music—there are few "set pieces" that can be lifted out—but it also contained a vivacity and gaiety that lit up the score from first to last. *Falstaff* is a technical and musical masterpiece. It is probably not as beloved by audiences as *Otello*, or even the great operas of the 1850s, but it is almost certainly the favorite among musicians.

Falstaff was truly the end of the road. Verdi lived for eight more years, the last three of them as a rather lonely widower after the death of Strepponi. One final work remained (Verdi said it was the finest of his whole career). It was the building of the Casa di Riposo per Musicisti, a home for aging singers and musicians in Milan—paid for and endowed, in his lifetime, by Verdi himself.

VERDI'S SINGERS

Verdi had begun his career during a golden age of Italian singing. The theaters for which he wrote, most of them in Italy, did not have rosters to compete with the "Puritani Quartet" or the starry casts

'Iago' will give the young 'musicians of the future' a very stiff lesson."[42]

The "musicians of the future" were the so-called *giovane scuola* (young school). They were the subject of much speculation to see which of them, if any, would follow in Verdi's mighty footsteps. Despite his indiscretions, Maurel remained in favor and became, indeed, the first Iago. Verdi, who had done so much for the baritone repertoire, must have had a great admiration for him, because Maurel would also be the first Falstaff.

At the time of *Otello*, however, no one (certainly not Verdi) thought there would be a successor. After the third performance, the Milanese newspaper *Corriere della serra* published a moving

of the Paris Opéra, but they had more than adequate singers. A tenor like Gaetano Fraschini was not exactly a household name outside Italy, but he was Verdi's favorite tenor for many years, and the six roles he wrote for him (roles like Arrigo in *La battaglia di Legnano* and Gustavus/Riccardo in *Ballo*) were clearly written for a singer of very considerable ability. They required a powerful voice, and the courage to expose it to huge climaxes, yet they also required ensemble singing of delicacy and subtlety. And he wrote music that often took singers into new territory. Baritones like Felice Varesi, Giorgio Ronconi, and even Antonio Tamburini (of "Puritani Quartet" fame) found his writing for them fearsomely high, and there were many who claimed that he was obsessed by the "upper fifth" of the voice.

As well as vocal demands, Verdi made dramatic demands on his singers. To Varesi, the first Macbeth and Rigoletto, he wrote: "I will never stop urging you to study the dramatic situation and the words; the music will come by itself."[44] Verdi had the same concern about female singers: Could they act? At opposite ends of the spectrum were Fanny Salvini-Donatelli, the Violetta who was almost laughed off the stage at the first night of *La traviata*, and Romilda Pantaleoni, who created Desdemona in *Otello* and who was sometimes likened to the greatest Italian actress of the late nineteenth century, Eleonora Duse.

Verdi wrote for many fine sopranos, from Strepponi when she was past her best, to Jenny Lind and Teresa Stolz in their prime. But who was the best? In a letter written at the end of 1877, Verdi supplied what may have been an answer to that question—a balance of singing and acting. He had just heard Adelina Patti sing in Genoa. She was Italian, though she had been brought up in New York, and Verdi had never had the opportunity to write a role especially for her. He had first heard her sing Mozart, Rossini, and Donizetti as long ago as 1861, when she was only eighteen ("What a marvelous actress-singer she was at eighteen," he told Ricordi). Now, having heard the mature Patti sing his own operas, he had no doubts about her place in the pantheon:

> [Her] artistic nature [is] so complete that perhaps there has never been anyone to equal her! Oh! Oh! And Malibran? Very, very great, but not always even! Sometimes sublime and sometimes exaggerated! Her singing style was not very pure, her acting was not always right, her voice shrill in the top notes! In spite of everything, a very great artist, marvelous. But Patti is more complete. A marvelous voice, an extremely pure singing style; stupendous actress with a charm and a naturalness that no one else has![45]

VERDI'S LEGACY

For every kind of singer, Verdi had added immeasurably to the repertoire (including some major dramatic roles for mezzo-sopranos and contraltos), yet singers of the first half of the twentieth century, in the fifty years after Verdi's death, got surprisingly few opportunities to sing them. The three last operas—*Aida, Otello,* and *Falstaff*—remained popular, as did the first three operas of his maturity—*Rigoletto, Il trovatore,* and *La traviata*—but few of the others were performed at all. It was not until the 1930s that scholars began to rediscover the earlier operas, and not until after World War II that they were performed at all regularly in Europe and America. In the fifty years since then, Verdi has been generally recognized for what he truly was—the greatest Italian exponent there has ever been of the art of *dramma per musica*.

The only one who has ever been able to cast any doubt on that verdict was a young man Verdi became aware of in the 1890s—a man who was perhaps not as great a musician as Verdi, but who certainly knew as much about music drama. His name was Giacomo Puccini.

Just eight days before *Falstaff* had its premiere at La Scala in 1893, Puccini had staged his own *Manon Lescaut* a few miles away in Turin—his first major success. In 1896 had come *La bohème,* and now, in the last months of the old century, Verdi had noticed that his friend Leopoldo Mugnone, the conductor, was making frequent visits to Pistoia. It turned out that these visits were to supervise the casting of the bells to be used in Puccini's next opera, *Tosca.* "How many bells does Puccini require?" asked Verdi. "Eleven," Mugnone told him. "Eleven bells!" exclaimed Verdi. "And to think that when I composed *Il trovatore* I hardly dared introduce *one* bell in the 'Miserere' for fear of the impresario's curses. . . . There's nothing more to say [Verdi added] except that the world has progressed—the operatic world, at least!"[46]

GERMAN
ROMANTIC
OPERA

BEETHOVEN WAS ONLY FIFTEEN YEARS YOUNGER THAN MOZART, YET IN THE HISTORY OF MUSIC THEY REPRESENT DIFFERENT ERAS AS WELL AS DIFFERENT CENTURIES. NEITHER OF THEM WAS VIENNESE, BUT VIENNA BECAME HOME TO BOTH OF THEM. AND IT WAS IN VIENNA, IN THE SPRING OF 1787, THAT THEY HAD THEIR ONE AND ONLY MEETING. SIXTEEN-YEAR-OLD BEETHOVEN HAD TRAVELED FROM HIS HOME IN BONN TO STUDY IN THE AUSTRIAN CAPITAL. AS THINGS TURNED OUT, HE DID NOT STAY LONG: HIS MOTHER TOOK ILL, AND HE HURRIED HOME TO BE THERE WHEN SHE DIED SEVEN WEEKS LATER. BUT BEFORE HE LEFT VIENNA, HE OBTAINED AN INTRODUCTION TO MOZART AND WENT TO HIS HOUSE TO PLAY FOR HIM. NOT OVER IMPRESSED TO BEGIN WITH, MOZART CHANGED HIS MIND WHEN HE HEARD THE YOUNG GERMAN IMPROVISE ON A THEME. "SOMEDAY HE WILL GIVE THE WORLD SOMETHING TO TALK ABOUT," HE IS REPORTED TO HAVE SAID.[1] BY THE TIME BEETHOVEN MOVED PERMANENTLY TO VIENNA, IN 1794, MOZART HAD ALREADY BEEN DEAD THREE YEARS.

PRECEDING PAGES: *Paul von Joukowsky's set for the Grail scene in Wagner's* PARSIFAL, *1882. Painting by Max Brückner, c. 1882. The set design for this scene continued to be used at Bayreuth until 1933.*

You could not be in Vienna at the end of the eighteenth century without knowing Mozart's music and hearing a great deal of it. In Beethoven's case, he not only knew the music, he also revered the memory of the man. So he was certainly not displeased when he gained a more direct link with his predecessor—in the irrepressible form of Emanuel Schikaneder.

Since his great collaboration with Mozart in *Die Zauberflöte* (The Magic Flute) during the last year of Mozart's life, Schikaneder's fortunes had fluctuated. The theater he had taken over with such panache in 1787, the Freihaus in the suburb of Wieden, had become a Viennese institution.

Die Zauberflöte continued to delight audiences there, and so, too, did a huge array of other plays and operas that Schikaneder staged. But even before he took over the Freihaus, Schikaneder had obtained a license from the emperor Joseph to build a new theater "in a suburb." He had never done anything about it, except to get the license renewed by Joseph's successors—first Leopold II, then Emperor Francis II—but in 1800 it suddenly became a practical possibility. Schikaneder had acquired a new partner, a rich merchant and a colleague in his Masonic lodge, Bartholomaus Zitterbarth. He paid off Schikaneder's debts and purchased a site only a few hundred yards from the Freihaus, on the other side of the river Wien.

The Theater an der Wien is still very much in business today. You can enter it through the "Papageno portal"—an impressive gateway between classical columns, topped by a stone sculpture of Papageno and lots of little Papagenos. The likeness, of course, is that of Schikaneder. This is the theater where Johann Strauss's *Die Fledermaus* would first see the light of day in 1874, and where the operettas of Franz Lehár and Emmerich Kálmán would mesmerize generations of Viennese. But before any of that, it was the theater in which Beethoven's *Fidelio* was first performed.

From the moment he deserted the Freihaus and built his new theater, Schikaneder's fortunes were never quite the same. He would eventually share the fate of Mozart—a pauper's grave—but for Schikaneder it would be worse: by the time of his death in 1812 he was not only destitute but insane.

In 1801, however, at the opening of the brave new theater on the Wien, no one could have forecast such an ending. It was a very grand theater, not at all like the shabby Freihaus from which the company had come. It could accommodate an audience of 2,200, although 1,400 of them had to stand. The auditorium was horseshoe-shaped and splendidly decorated, but the greatest glory of the new theater was its stage machinery. It had wings that could be let down from above or elevated from below, thus enabling scene changes to take place more frequently and much more quickly. The main stage was bigger and deeper than those of most other theaters, and there was even a stage extension that introduced sight lines and design possibilities not previously contemplated. For the audience, however, the greatest sensation was the new curtain machinery. For the first time, the curtain could be raised and lowered noiselessly and

gently on a set of pulleys—as opposed to the previous tradition of "jumping curtains," which relied on stagehands leaping from the rigging to act as the counterweights that pulled the curtain up and down, erratically and uncertainly.

Schikaneder was at the height of his popularity, He had a brand-new theater, no debts, and a wealthy partner. But he had a great deal of competition. In addition to three suburban theaters, Vienna boasted two court theaters—the Burgtheater and the Kärntnertortheater—and in 1801 they were both under the direction of Baron Peter von Braun. No holds were barred. Schikaneder scored a great success with Luigi Cherubini's *Lodoïska* (the Italian Cherubini, French by adoption, was probably the most popular opera composer of the day in France, Austria, and England). Braun riposted by announcing a production of Cherubini's next opera, *Les deux journées*. Schikaneder upstaged him by opening the same opera at the Theater an der Wien one day before Braun's opening at the Burgtheater. And so it continued. But keeping up with the competition was difficult and expensive. So Schikaneder sought to repeat the feat he had so famously brought off in 1791: he sought to ally himself with Vienna's leading composer in order to produce an entirely new and popular work. Thus he invited Beethoven to move into the Theater an der Wien and write an opera for him.

BEETHOVEN'S FIDELIO

Beethoven accepted the offer of accommodation, but he was too busy to write an opera. The libretto that had been submitted to him, *Vestas Feuer*, was eventually composed by Joseph Weigl, a pupil of Salieri who was also Haydn's godson. The opera was a very moderate success. Beethoven gave some important concerts at the Theater an der Wien, including the premiere of his Third Symphony, the *Eroica*, but by the time he was ready to write an opera, Schikaneder's fortunes had changed yet again. His partner Zitterbarth, seeing no commercial gain in the enterprise, had sold the Theater an der Wien to none other than Baron Peter von Braun. Schikaneder was dismissed, and the courting of Beethoven fell to his successor, Joseph von Sonnleithner. Since Sonnleithner was a close friend of Beethoven's, and since Sonnleithner himself supplied the libretto for the opera, the courting was successful—except for one thing: Beethoven distrusted Braun and was loath to sign a contract with him. So, to his surprise and disgust, Braun found himself doing the unthinkable: he reinstated Schikaneder, and Beethoven immediately started work on *Fidelio*.

Fidelio was written in the German *Singspiel* form, with spoken dialogue, but Beethoven's music far transcended the *Singspiel* tradition. Among many other glories, it included a succession of brilliantly characterized arias, a quartet written in the form of a canon ("Mir ist so wunderbar"), a chorus of emotional power that not even Verdi would equal (the "Prisoners' Chorus"), a pair of thrilling and passionate duets, and a noble finale that was really a cantata in itself. The whole opera was imbued with humanity, passion, and above all, drama. It was about freedom, and tyranny, and a wife's love for her husband. It was timeless and universal.

Unfortunately, it was Beethoven's only opera. It stood alone at the gateway to nineteenth-century German opera, a link with the past and a portent of the future. The quality of its music was purely Beethovenian and therefore inimitable, but its drama, its drive, and its tension were things that all composers would seek to emulate.

The principal role of *Fidelio* called for a singing actress of consummate ability, and in Anna Milder, the first Leonore, Beethoven found just that. She was only nineteen when she first sang the part in 1805, and she must already have acquired amazing power and technique for one so young ("Dear child," Haydn is reported to have said to her, "you have a voice like a house"[2]). But it was in her later performances, during the Congress of Vienna, that she achieved real fame and earned Beethoven's enduring gratitude.

The circumstances of *Fidelio*'s first production in 1805 were no less dramatic than the opera itself. As rehearsals got under way, Napoleon, at the head of his *grande armée*, was advancing on Vienna. On October 20, he crushed the Austrian army at Ulm. On November 12, he entered the city. Eight days later, the first of what would be only three performances of *Fidelio* was given at the Theater an der Wien before an audience of French officers (not many of whom understood German) and a few frightened Viennese. It was a fiasco. At the end of the month, Napoleon marched out of Vienna and decimated the Austrian and Russian armies at the Battle of Austerlitz.

For Beethoven it was a catastrophe, both personal and professional. This was the same Napoleon, after all, to whom he had originally dedicated the *Eroica* Symphony, only to tear out the dedication at the front of the score when he heard that the first consul had declared himself emperor. Now here was that same Napoleon

trampling across Europe, and through Vienna itself, in order to extend his empire, while Beethoven was trying to give the first performance of an opera that celebrated freedom from tyranny.

Truth to tell, the performances at the Theater an der Wien were probably not very good. Within a year, Beethoven had revised his original score into two acts rather than three, and with the French army gone (but with ignominious terms enforced on the Austrians), three further, and much more successful, performances were given—before Beethoven fell out with Braun and withdrew his score.

Fidelio did not reappear during the Napoleonic wars, but it was not forgotten. When Bonaparte was defeated in 1814 and exiled to the island of Elba (from where he would make one more dramatic comeback the following year in the Hundred Days, ending with the Battle of Waterloo), Vienna was finally able to celebrate freedom. To immense acclaim, Beethoven wrote the popular music of the restoration, *Wellington's Victory*, and it was only a matter of time before someone thought of reviving *Fidelio*. Schikaneder had already gone to his sad and lonely death, and it was a sign of the times in Vienna that the venue for the revival would be one of the court theaters rather than the suburban Theater an der Wien. Sonnleithner's libretto was adapted by Georg Friedrich Treitschke; Beethoven revised his score again; and the opera, in its final version, was given amid great enthusiasm on May 23, 1814.

Throughout that summer and autumn and winter, as the Congress of Vienna assembled and all the world's leaders took up residence in the city, *Fidelio* was given again and again. It was a time for optimism and rejoicing. Vienna's streets were lit by gaslight for the first time; the dance craze consumed the Viennese people as well as the Congress (the czar of Russia was said to have danced through forty consecutive nights); and at the Kärntnertortheater Anna Milder, now a mature twenty-eight-year-old, was the toast of the town. *Fidelio* was the signature music of what everyone hoped would be a new age.

For the leading musicians, at least, it was indeed a new age, and in many ways Beethoven epitomized it. He was not like Haydn, or even Mozart. He was nobody's servant. He had patrons, certainly, and he received money from them, but he saw no reason to bow to them, literally or metaphorically. The first biography of him after his death, written by his amanuensis, Anton Schindler, reproduced a letter Beethoven had written to a friend describing a meeting he had had with the greatest of all German poets and dramatists, Goethe.

Yesterday, as we were returning homewards, we met the Imperial family: we saw them coming at some distance, whereupon Goethe disengaged himself from my arm, in order that he might stand aside; in spite of all I could say, I could not bring him to stand forwards. I crushed my hat furiously on my head, buttoned up my top coat, and walked with my arms folded behind me, right through the thickest of the crowd. Princes and officials made a lane for me: Archduke Rudolph took off his hat. The Empress saluted me the first: these great people know me! It was the greatest fun in the world to me, to see the procession file past Goethe. He stood aside, with his hat off, bending his head down as low as possible. For this I afterwards hauled him over the coals properly and without mercy.[3]

Beethoven's high self-regard ("these great people know me") is symptomatic of a turning point in the attitudes of artists and musicians in Germany and Central Europe. Compared to Italy, where Rossini was bound to almost slavelike contracts at this very time (1816 was the year of *Il barbiere di Siviglia*), the German musicians—Beethoven, Weber, Wagner, and their contemporaries—would be beholden to no man, and would expect society (that is, the rich and the aristocratic) to provide them with money, and even luxuries. It was their due.

There was another good reason for this. Most of these composers were performers, too, highly paid performers. Beethoven was a virtuoso pianist until deafness overtook him. Weber and Wagner were two of the great conductors of the age, at a time when conducting was just beginning to be a recognized skill. As "box office," these men stood in the first rank, alongside the great singers (Pasta, Malibran, Henriette Sontag, Rubini, Duprez, Enrico Tamberlik) and the great instru-

mentalists (Niccolò Paganini, in a class of his own as both violinist and showman; and the virtuoso pianists of the century—Chopin, Liszt, Sigismond Thalberg, and Adolph von Henselt). The fame of these people was enormous; they were feted and lionized wherever they went. And if they had patrons, then they were the equals of these patrons, not their servants.

THE AGE OF ROMANTICISM

The philosophy that ran through this new age was Romanticism. It consisted of a very loose set of ideas (and a much larger set of attitudes) that glorified the emotional and the instinctive rather than the rational and the intellectual. Romanticism was about intuition, and feeling, and whatever was natural. It was opposed to the dictatorship of reason, which had been the watchword of the seventeenth and eighteenth centuries, and it provided for a sense of the infinite, a belief in the transcendental, and the central value of individual experiences.

The first Leonore, Pauline Anna Milder-Hauptmann (1785–1838). Portrait by Wilhelm von Schadow, c. 1818. Her success in FIDELIO was the prelude to a fine career during which she was most famous for her interpretations of Gluck's heroines. She married a rich jeweler, named Hauptmann, but this was not a success: Beethoven ungallantly observed that he, in any case, was her real Hauptmann (head man).

*Design by Eugen Quaglio for E. T. A.
Hoffmann's* Undine, *c. 1897. In six
generations from the seventeenth to the early
twentieth century, fifteen members of the
Quaglio family (German, but originating
in Italy) were active as stage designers for
the German theater. Eugen (1857–1942)
was the last of them.*

Those things were just as likely to illuminate a
man's soul and increase his understanding as were
the arid disciplines of the intellect.

So, in Romanticism the imagination was set
free to conjure up the best—and the worst. In literature it encompassed writers like Lord Byron,
Sir Walter Scott, and William Wordsworth in England; Victor Hugo, Théophile Gautier, and
Honoré de Balzac in France; Goethe in Germany;
and the ubiquitous E. T. A. Hoffmann. Their
musical equivalents were Franz Schubert and
Robert Schumann, Frédéric Chopin and Franz
Liszt, Hector Berlioz and Richard Wagner—and
Carl Maria von Weber in the vanguard. In a few
short years, the musical firmament shifted from the
serene, sure humanity of Mozart to the turbulent,
often violent, but always exciting world of the
Romantics—artists who celebrated the natural and
the supernatural, the emotional and the picturesque.

Weber was almost a caricature of the
Romantic artist—a restless genius, continually on
the move. He was thin, almost emaciated; he was
born with a diseased hip and walked with a limp
throughout his life; he was consumptive and died

when he was only forty. Not only a prolific writer
of music criticism, but a virtuoso pianist, guitar
player, and conductor, as well as a music administrator and composer, he was a driven man.

If it can be said that one work proclaimed
the beginning of Romanticism in opera, then it
must be Weber's *Der Freischütz* (The Freeshooter).
On the surface, it was a bucolic love story, but
underlying it was the sinister world of magic and
enchantment. In one scene—set in the Wolf's
Glen—all the elements of Romanticism seemed
to be concentrated: the beauty and grandeur of the
natural world coupled with the mysterious powers of evil. When Weber first discovered the story,
he wrote to his future wife: "This is super-extra,
for there's the Devil himself in it. He appears as
the Black Huntsman, the bullets are cast in a ravine
at midnight with ghostly apparitions all around.
Have I not made your flesh creep on your
bones?"[4]

Weber was not the first to explore this territory in opera. In 1816, E. T. A. Hoffmann, who
was a highly competent composer as well as a
famous writer of fantastic tales, produced his opera

Undine in Berlin. It dealt with a highly Romantic story about a knight's fatal love for a water sprite. The opera itself was not exactly epoch-making, though it is interesting in light of later events that Hoffmann marked the passage in which the lovers self-destructed "Liebestod." More important, Weber reviewed the opera enthusiastically and used his review to make a statement of Romantic ideals in opera. A German opera, he wrote, should be "a self-contained work of art in which all elements, contributed collaboratively by the related arts, merge into one another and are absorbed . . . so as to create a new world."[5]

In the same year, another German composer, Louis Spohr, wrote another Romantically inspired opera, *Faust*. Weber, who conducted the premiere, admired the way in which "a few melodies . . . weave through the whole work like delicate threads, holding it together intellectually."[6] The term used to describe these recurring melodies, or themes, was "reminiscence motifs." Mozart had used them in *Don Giovanni* to some extent. Spohr and Weber now developed them as a characteristic of Romantic opera. Wagner would eventually expand their use until they became leitmotifs that ran right through a work (even through a complete cycle of works, like the *Ring*) and acted as a vital element in the unfolding of the drama. Spohr continued to experiment with these musical devices in operas like *Jessonda* (which was set in India and became very popular, as did almost anything with an Eastern setting) and *Der Alchymist* (The Alchemist). He may not have been the most accomplished opera composer, but he was innovative. His operas were among the first to suggest (though not actually to achieve) the idea that an opera could be "through-composed"—in other words, that the score could be written as a continuous whole, like a symphonic score, with no obtrusive individual arias or set pieces to break up the continuity or stop the flow of the performance. In this and many other ways, Spohr influenced a generation of German composers, including Wagner.

Heinrich Marschner was also involved in these developments. Younger than Spohr and Weber, but older than Wagner, he earned himself considerable fame as a composer of operas that mined the popular Romantic seam. *Der Vampyr*, a work with characteristics very similar to *Der Freischütz*, had considerable success in 1828, two years after Weber's death, and several of Marschner's subsequent operas reflected the growing interest

MARSCHNER'S *DER VAMPYR*

LEFT: *Engraving by I. Axmann, 1830, after a drawing by Heinrich Romberg.*

BELOW: *BBC-TV production, 1992. With Omar Ebrahim in the title role and Fiona O'Neill. Adapted by Charles Hart (and relocated to the London of the 1980s), Nigel Finch's production was presented in the form of a television "soap opera," with brief episodes following each other night after night.*

in the epic sagas and legends of European literature. *Hans Heiling* and *Der Templer und die Jüdin* (The Templar and the Jewish Woman, a version of the *Ivanhoe* story) were both examples of this, as Weber's last opera, *Euryanthe*, had also been. Marschner had neither the musical nor the dramatic skills of his great contemporaries, and in Hanover, where he spent much of his career, he was frustrated by the elector's continuing passion for Italian opera. But Wagner, for one, noted with approval the way that Marschner steadily increased his use of "reminiscence motifs" as a part of the musical drama.

None of these composers achieved anything to equal the popularity of Albert Lortzing. He wrote comic operas—a series of tuneful, sentimental pieces of which *Zar und Zimmermann* (The Czar and the Carpenter) was the best known. It was based on the true story of Peter the Great working in a Dutch shipbuilding yard in order to learn the trade. The part of Peter was sung by the composer himself at the first performance. Lortzing was not one of the great Romantic composers, nor was he particularly important in the development of German opera, but it is salutary to discover that, in the years immediately after his impoverished death in 1851, Lortzing's operas were performed more often than those of any other German composer, with the exception of Mozart's.

The single most popular opera of those years, however, belonged neither to Mozart nor to Lortzing, but to Otto Nicolai. *Die lustigen Weiber von Windsor* (The Merry Wives of Windsor) was performed in Berlin in 1849, just two months before Nicolai's death at the age of thirty-eight. It was substantially the same Shakespearian story that Verdi later used for *Falstaff*, and it remains popular in Germany to this day.

WAGNER

Just as the development of Italian opera in the nineteenth century was closely bound up with the people's yearning for nationhood and reunification, so it was in Germany. In the 1820s, there were thirty-eight separate states in the German lands—kingdoms, princedoms, electorates, city-states, archbishoprics—all of them independent and self-governing. But one of these states, Prussia, with its capital in Berlin, was already a major force in the European balance of power. More than any other state, it had an interest in unifying Germany. In the 1870s, under Otto von Bismarck's leadership, it would do just that.

In the meantime, although there were many separate states, there was a common German language and a recognizably German culture. With them went a passionate longing, not simply for unification, but for the celebration, and even the hegemony, of what Wagner's character Hans Sachs would describe at the end of *Die Meistersinger von Nürnberg* as "die heil'ge deutsche Kunst" (holy German art). Romanticism was the perfect vehicle for such an ambition, and in music, above all

in opera, it found its ideal form of expression. In the works of Weber, Spohr, and Marschner, its characteristics were already apparent: the use of motifs, the beginnings of "through-composing," and an obsession with the supernatural and the legendary tales of the past. Wagner would take all these aspects a great deal further—to the *musikdrama*, and ultimately, he hoped, to the *Gesamtkunstwerk* (the total, unified work of art).

Wagner was the high priest of German Romanticism, and Dresden was its most important temple.

There is no simple reason why the city of Dresden should have played this role. Logically, one might think, it would have been Berlin. But the circumstances were right in Dresden—a city of seventy thousand people with a historic commitment to music and culture, and with the unusual combination of a Catholic ruling family (with close links to Italy) and a Protestant population. It was in Dresden that Weber was conductor and director of the German Opera; it was in Dresden that Wagner was *Kapellmeister* at the brand-new Royal Saxon Opera House, where he staged premieres of his first three major operas. And at the beginning of the next century, it would be in Dresden, now part of a united Germany, that Richard Strauss would shock the opera world with *Salome* and *Elektra*, and then bring Romantic opera to its brilliant conclusion with *Der Rosenkavalier* in 1911.

The State Opera House in Dresden is often known as the Semperoper—a tribute to its architect, Gottfried Semper. He had to build it twice—first in 1841 and again, after a fire, in 1878, both times to the same design. It was one of the first opera houses that we would describe as "modern," with the function of the interior dictating the shape of the exterior. Its importance to nineteenth-century Dresden is attested by its location—opposite the royal palace on the west side of the Theaterplatz. Like most of Dresden, it was destroyed by the Allied bombing of 1945, and although a temporary roof was put on it, nothing was done to rebuild it until the original architectural drawings were discovered in Vienna in 1975 (Semper had moved to Vienna in 1849 and had directed the first rebuilding from there). Finally, in 1985, splendidly restored, the house was reopened with a performance of Weber's quintessential German opera, *Der Freischütz*.

It was at the newly built original Semperoper that Wagner arrived in 1842. He was twenty-

nine years old—the same age as Verdi, who had had his first great success at La Scala that same year, with *Nabucco*. But success had so far eluded Wagner. His musicianship was not in doubt. He had already held brief appointments as music director in Magdeburg, Königsberg, and Riga, and several of his orchestral works had been performed, as well as one opera, *Das Liebesverbot* (after Shakespeare's *Measure for Measure*). But already he was afflicted by a disease from which he suffered all his life—a propensity to live beyond his means and to accumulate debts. He left Riga in 1839, and he and his young wife, Minna, spent the next three years in France. It was a frustrating time. The Paris Opéra showed no interest in staging his new works—neither *Rienzi* (written in Riga) nor *Der fliegende Holländer* (mainly written in France). He had, however, an admirer in Paris, and it was ironic in light of their subsequent antipathy that it should have been Giacomo Meyerbeer, the reigning king of the Paris Opéra, who recommended him to Dresden. Meyerbeer was German by birth, the son of a prosperous Jewish family, but it was in Paris that he had won permanent fame in the 1830s as the composer of *Robert le diable* and *Les Huguenots*—works that defined the newly fashionable term *grand opéra*.

Wagner was no stranger to Dresden. He had grown up there in the home of his stepfather, Ludwig Geyer, who was a member of the court theater and to whose home Carl Maria von Weber had been a frequent visitor. Wagner had been fourteen when he and his mother had left Dresden. Now he returned, and more or less took the place by storm. *Rienzi* was a tremendous success. Three months later, *Der fliegende Holländer* (The Flying Dutchman), though less spectacular and less memorable to Dresdeners, was nevertheless a *succès d'estime*. In February 1843, Wagner was awarded the lifetime appointment of Royal Saxon *Kapellmeister*.

Six years later, Wagner fled from Dresden, a political exile with a price on his head, and he was not to set foot in any German state for a full decade thereafter. But the achievements of his tenure in Dresden were remarkable by any standard. Many of his projects never came to fruition (among them a fifty-page sketch for a *musik-drama* about Jesus of Nazareth), but it is amazing how much of his work at Dresden would later translate into operatic history. In addition to *Rienzi* and *Der fliegende Holländer*, his *Tannhäuser* was composed and given its first performances in 1845—to a respectful, if

The Semperoper, Dresden. Hand-colored lithograph by Johann Richter. The brand-new Royal Opera House in Dresden, as completed by Gottfried Semper in 1841. Twice rebuilt since then, it has been the historic venue for the early works of Richard Wagner and for nine of Richard Strauss's operas.

The Dresden Opera was not a company of the first rank when Wagner took it over. One recent visitor, Hector Berlioz, had complained that the contrabassist in the orchestra was too old to support the weight of his own instrument.[7] However, in addition to the new theater, Wagner found in Dresden two major assets, without which the Dresden premieres could not have succeeded at all. They came in the form of two voices.

Joseph Tichatschek was a vain and simple-minded man, but he had a glorious *heldentenor*—a heroic tenor voice of clarion timbre. In his autobiography, *Mein Leben* (My Life), Wagner described "his childish limitations and superficial, but exceptionally brilliant, talents. He did not trouble to learn his parts by heart, as he was so musical he could sing the most difficult music at sight, and thought all further study needless."[8] Rienzi the Roman tribune suited Tichatschek to perfection, and he had a stunning success with it. Tannhäuser, the more famous part, which he created three years later, was, however, too difficult for him. He coped, but (according to Wagner) barely.

The second voice was one with which Wagner had fallen in love many years before. It belonged to Wilhelmine Schröder-Devrient, who was already well advanced in a storied career. As a sixteen-year-old, she had made her debut in Vienna as Pamina in *Die Zauberflöte*. The next year (1822), she had sung Agathe in *Der Freischütz* in performances conducted by Weber, and in the same season she had earned tributes from Beethoven himself for her performance of the *Fidelio* Leonore. Still only eighteen, she cannot fully have penetrated the part, but seven years later, when the young Wagner heard her sing the same role, it made an impression he was never to forget. In *Mein Leben* he wrote:

> When I review my entire life I can discover hardly another occurrence which affected me so profoundly. Whoever remembers that remarkable woman at that stage of her career will testify to the almost demoniacal warmth radiated by the human-ecstatic achievement of this incomparable artist. After the performance, I dashed to the home of a friend of mine to write her a letter in which I solemnly stated that, as of that day, my life had acquired its meaning, and

rather lukewarm, reception. *Lohengrin* was completed, though not performed, and the preliminary prose outline of what would ultimately become *Götterdämmerung* (Twilight of the Gods) was written. So was the prose sketch of *Die Meistersinger von Nürnberg*, right up to Hans Sachs's line in the final scene, "zerging in Dunst das heil'ge röm'sche Reich, uns bliebe gleich die heil'ge deutsche Kunst" (The Holy Roman Empire may fade away, but holy German art will be with us forever).

These were the great sagas with which Wagner lived during the Dresden years, and for the remainder of his life. And though they obsessed him, at the same time he had to run a busy opera house and conduct a fair amount of the repertoire himself.

that if she was ever to hear my name mentioned as of consequence in the world of art, she should remember that on this evening she had made me what I herewith vowed to become. I dropped the letter at her hotel and rushed off into the night.[9]

That was in 1829. Wagner was sixteen years old.

Half a century, and many adventures, later, when Wagner was settled at Bayreuth, he had a frieze constructed on the facade of his home, Haus Wahnfried. It depicted the figures of Tragedy, Music, and Ancient Myth. The features of the figure of Tragedy were those of Wilhelmine Schröder-Devrient, not forgotten after all those years and still revered by a composer who owed so much to her.

She had not at first wanted to sing the part of Adriano Colonna in *Rienzi*. It was a *travesti* role (what in English was charmingly known as a "breeches part," a female singer playing a male character), but she quickly fell in love with the music and the opera. Senta in *Der fliegende Holländer* was more to her liking, and it was Schröder-Devrient's performance in the Dresden premiere

that gave that opera its critical success. And for *Tannhäuser*, she created the role of Venus, clearly more suitable for her than the more central role of Elisabeth, which was sung by Wagner's nineteen-year-old niece, Johanna.[10]

Much of *Tannhäuser* was written in the Bohemian mountains above Teplitz. This was where Wagner and Minna loved to vacation, and it was here that Wagner found the inspiration for both his poetry and his music. The process of creating *dramma per musica* was thus unified in a single person: it could not have happened any other way for Richard Wagner. Nor was it sufficient just to create the words and the music; he must also stage the works himself—and to do that properly he would require a theater of his own, built to his own unique specifications.

But this would not happen in Dresden. Wagner, like many other members of the artistic community, including Wilhelmine Schröder-Devrient, got swept up in the whirlwind of political and revolutionary activity that shook all Europe in 1848–49. There is no doubt that Wagner played an active role in the events of 1849 in Dresden. He went to the barricades like a true revolutionary and several times risked his life. His

Decorative panel on the front wall of Haus Wahnfried, Wagner's home at Bayreuth. The panel was designed by Robert Krausse in 1874 to depict Tragedy, Ancient Myth, and Music. All the figures bear the features of people who played important parts in Wagner's own life.

motives were less obvious. Certainly, he was bitterly disappointed that his operas had hardly been performed outside Dresden, and never outside Germany (Louis Spohr in Kassel was one of the few conductors who dared to stage his works). He was furious at the cancellation of the proposed production of *Lohengrin* in 1848. And he was, once again, heavily in debt. Wagner had socialist friends in Dresden (August Röckel, a prominent manager of music events, was one of them), and he had acquaintances who were anarchists. Mikhail Bakunin, the most influential of all the Russian émigrés in Europe, was well known to Wagner during this period—which was the time of *The Communist Manifesto*, published by Marx and Engels in 1848. Wagner made speeches against capitalism in general; he advocated the abolition of money (a cunning ruse to wipe out his own debts at a stroke, perhaps); and he spoke against the Saxon monarchy.

By the time Prussian troops marched into Dresden to put down the uprising on behalf of the Saxon king, it was clear that Wagner had to flee. He was lucky. Had he stayed with Röckel, Bakunin, and his other colleagues, he would have been captured and might well have been sentenced to death. But he was separated from them and was able to get safely to Weimar, where Franz Liszt looked after him, and from there to Switzerland.

In 1851, safe in exile, Wagner issued an extraordinary prophecy of what was to come:

> The revolution alone will provide me
> with artists and audiences, for the
> coming revolution is bound to put
> an end to our muddled theatrical
> institutions. It is inevitable that they
> will all come crashing down. From
> these ruins, I shall reclaim what I
> need. Then I shall erect a theater by
> the Rhine and send out invitations
> to a great dramatic festival.[11]

A quarter of a century later, he did just that, though the invitations came from Bayreuth rather than the banks of the Rhine. The years between were not pleasant ones—most of them spent in exile, most of them heavily in debt—but they were prolific.

"From these ruins, I shall reclaim what I need." What he needed most urgently were financial sup-

porters. He found them erratically and infrequently, but he found them. At various times he treated them all with a stunning arrogance and boorishness, and he supplemented their generosity with his own earnings as one of the most distinguished conductors in Europe. For most of his years in exile, and for all the years thereafter, Wagner managed to live in the way to which he chose to be accustomed—extravagantly.

Ironically, had there been a proper system of fees and royalties at that time (the sort of system Verdi was busily establishing with the Ricordis in Italy), Wagner would not have needed patrons. For no sooner had he left Germany than his operas began to be performed there with a frequency that must have amazed him. It was Franz Liszt, patient and faithful friend to Wagner for more than thirty years, who made it possible. He was *Kapellmeister* at Weimar at this time, and in 1850, in quick succession, he staged productions of *Tannhäuser* and *Lohengrin* (the world premiere) that proved to other opera houses that Wagner's works were not too huge or too complex to be performed in normal theaters. During the next few years, performances took place in opera houses all over Germany, despite the fact that the composer had a price on his head. And for this, Wagner received a single outright fee from each opera house for the "use" of each opera. It was less than a quarter of the fee that Joseph Tichatschek commanded for each and every performance in which he sang.[12]

Not surprisingly, the operas found it harder to win acceptance outside Germany. When *Tannhäuser* was eventually staged at the Paris Opéra in 1861, Wagner must have wished most fervently that it had never happened. It ranks with Stravinsky's premiere of *Le sacre du printemps* (The Rite of Spring), half a century later, as one of the most shameful episodes in the history of Parisian theater.

The problem in 1861 concerned the traditions (or, at any rate, the prevailing fashions) of the Paris Opéra. At this time, it was dominated by the fashionable young bloods of the Jockey Club, about as philistine an organization as has ever dominated an opera house. Its members liked to dine late in Paris, so they would not normally arrive at the Opéra until the second act, and then they liked to see a ballet. So Wagner was asked by the management to restructure *Tannhäuser* to include a ballet in Act II. Not for Act II, said Wagner, but he was quite prepared to write a bal-

let around the Venusberg scene in Act I. He did so, but the Jockey Club was not to be so lightly appeased. On opening night (after no fewer than one hundred sixty-three rehearsals on which Wagner had absolutely insisted), the members of the Jockey Club turned up in force, armed with hunting horns and tin whistles, and disrupted the performance almost continuously from the second act onward. They did the same to the next two performances, after which Wagner withdrew the work. It was not to be staged again in Paris until the very end of the century, by which time the Jockey Club no longer controlled the Opéra.

Nothing, perhaps, better sums up Wagner's complicated creative and personal life than an event

that took place in Zurich four years before the ill-fated staging of the Paris *Tannhäuser*. In the spring of 1857, Minna and Richard Wagner had moved into a little house called the Asyl. It was the property of Otto Wesendonk, a wealthy silk merchant. It adjoined a magnificent new villa into which Otto and his wife, Mathilde, had recently moved, and in which they entertained the intelligentsia of Zurich. One week, late in the summer, Wagner read the whole of his poem *Tristan und Isolde* to an audience of three ladies and one man. The ladies represented the past, present, and future of his life. They were Minna, his wife of twenty years; Mathilde Wesendonk, his current muse; and Cosima von Bülow (the illegitimate daughter of Franz Liszt), who would become Wagner's second wife (but not before she had borne him three

Wagner's TANNHÄUSER *at the Metropolitan Opera, New York, 1992. Directed by Otto Schenk, designed by Günther Schneider-Siemssen. With William Johns as Tannhäuser (at left).*

by that time Cosima was already beginning to learn from her husband's example: she was learning to love Richard Wagner. For it was certainly no exaggeration to say that Hans von Bülow loved Wagner, indeed worshiped him. "I am willing to become your bootblack," he wrote, as he signed himself "your true vassal and servant."[13] Wagner treated him as such.

These tangled personal stories reached a stunning climax in Munich in 1864–65, at the time when all things became possible for Richard Wagner. What made them possible was something that not even Wagner, in his wildest dreams, could have predicted. It happened at the moment when he was most in need.

His affair (if that is what it was) with Mathilde Wesendonk was over. The patient Otto proceeded to treat him with breathtaking generosity. In order to help Wagner pay his debts, he purchased the publishing rights to the *Ring* operas. The money gave Wagner temporary relief, but he continued to spend far more than he earned. The failure of the Paris *Tannhäuser*, his inability to get *Tristan und Isolde* performed by any opera house (it actually went into rehearsal in Vienna, but was canceled before it reached the stage), and his lack of a secure home base, had driven him to the verge of desperation. *Die Meistersinger* was almost complete, as were the first two operas of the *Ring* cycle, but Wagner's only income came from his fees as a conductor, and that was nowhere near enough. At Vienna's Theater an der Wien, where the story of nineteenth-century German opera had begun sixty years before, he gave the first orchestral performances of excerpts from his new operas, including the "Ride of the Valkyries," to tremendous acclaim. But no one wanted to stage them. Wagner's only full-time activity was avoiding his creditors.

Into this sea of desperation rode the Dream King. Eighteen-year-old Ludwig II ascended the Wittelsbach throne of Bavaria on the death of his father, Maximilian II, early in 1864. Among his first acts was to send his cabinet secretary, Franz Seraph von Pfistermeister, to find Richard Wagner. He found him in Stuttgart (with difficulty: Wagner thought he was another debt collector and tried to take evasive action). Pfistermeister gave Wagner a picture of the king, a ring, and a message. In essence, the message was that Ludwig was his greatest admirer, that he wished to relieve him of all further material problems, and that Wagner was to come at once to Munich.

Ludwig II (1845–1886), king of Bavaria from 1864 to 1886. Portrait by Ferdinand Piloty, 1865, at the time when Wagner was living in Munich.

children out of wedlock). The man was Hans von Bülow, pianist and conductor, disciple and acolyte of Wagner. In that summer of 1857, he and Cosima were on their honeymoon.

This was the curious ménage that listened to the *Tristan* poem for the first time. Minna's turbulent life with Wagner was coming to an end: she would leave him five years later (she died in Dresden in 1866). Mathilde Wesendonk, in contrast, was about to be immortalized in the music of *Tristan*. As for Cosima, she would eventually play the biggest part of all in Wagner's life. They would all meet again at the Asyl in the summer of 1858, and

To understand how besotted with Wagner the young king was it is only necessary to visit his most visible memorials, the three castles he built in the countryside south of Munich. Herrenchiemsee was less than half finished at the time of Ludwig's death in 1886, but Linderhof, with its Grotto of Venus, and Neuschwanstein, most of all, remain monuments to his obsession. Everywhere are paintings and mock tapestries of scenes from Wagner's operas. The walls of the king's study at Neuschwanstein illustrate the *Tannhäuser* legend; the throne room is surrounded by murals of the *Parsifal* story and the legend of the Grail; the Minstrels Hall pays homage to the Wartburg of *Tannhäuser*. Ludwig's letters to Wagner speak even more eloquently:

> Unique One! Holy One! How glorious!—Perfect! So full of rapture! . . . To drown . . . to sink down . . . unconscious . . . supreme joy. Divine work.[14]

This was after a first hearing of *Tristan*. It has to be said that Wagner's written responses were no less disturbing.

The king paid off Wagner's debts. He bought him a magnificent house in Munich, and he formally commissioned the *Ring* cycle with a payment of thirty thousand gulden—a huge sum in those days (Wagner ungraciously demanded that Otto Wesendonk, who thought *he* had purchased the publishing rights to the *Ring*, return the original score of *Das Rheingold*).

The first great enterprise of this partnership (it was to be a partnership of equals, the king announced) was to make preparations for the first staging of *Tristan und Isolde*. This, finally, was the *Gesamtkunstwerk*, the unified work of art, a total synthesis of music, language and stage design. *Tristan* is a landmark, a defining moment in the story of opera. Like all Wagner's work, it was unified in his own person: he wrote the poem, he wrote the music, he wrote the stage directions, he even staged the first production himself. But it is the music of *Tristan* that makes it unique—virtually a new musical language in itself, massively orchestrated, wholly intense, utterly sensuous.

This was the miracle that happened at the Court Theater in Munich in 1865 in the presence of the ecstatic Ludwig. He was not the only person who made it possible. There had to be musicians

capable of playing the extraordinarily difficult score, a conductor with the vision to lead it, and singers with the dramatic and vocal ability to portray the title roles. They were all present in Munich.

The conductor, of course, was Hans von Bülow. He would later conduct the first performance of *Die Meistersinger von Nürnberg*, also in Munich. His position at this time was difficult—most would have said untenable. His wife of eight years, Cosima, by whom he had two daughters, gave birth to a third daughter, Isolde, in the midst of the *Tristan* rehearsals. Isolde was Wagner's child, not Bülow's, and although Bülow publicly accepted paternity of the child (and of the two subsequent children of Wagner and Cosima, both born while she was still legally married to the conductor), the actual facts were public knowledge. A cartoon of the time shows the situation as it really was. Yet Bülow was a genuinely great musician—a renowned disciplinarian with orchestras; a piano virtuoso (in Boston in 1875 he was the soloist at the premiere of Tchaikovsky's First Piano Concerto); and, among many other things, the man who would eventually give young Richard Strauss his first opportunities.

Richard Strauss was actually born in Munich in 1864, at the very moment that Ludwig was establishing Wagner in that city. Richard's father, Franz, was a *Kammermusiker* at the court theater—the first horn player in the orchestra—and he was certainly one of the people who made *Tristan* possible. If ever there was an exposed position in an orchestra, then it must have been that of first horn at the very first public performances of *Tristan*, *Die Meistersinger*, *Das Rheingold*, and *Die Walküre*, all of them played by the orchestra of the Royal Court Theater. Franz Strauss hated Wagner and disliked his music. He considered Wagner's horn parts to be technically clarinet parts and therefore unplayable on the horn. Yet he played them magnificently. Wagner, who reciprocated the dislike, admitted that Strauss was "intolerable, but when he plays you simply cannot be angry with him."[15] Young Richard Strauss was brought up to revile Wagner, yet when he died in 1949 at the venerable age of eighty-five, that same Richard Strauss could accurately be described as one of Wagner's greatest champions and interpreters—and, many would say, his legitimate successor.

The orchestra and the conductor were vitally important, but the people who really made *Tristan* possible were the first Tristan and Isolde.

Wagner escorts Cosima von Bülow along the Maximilianstrasse in Munich after a rehearsal of Tristan und Isolde, *with Hans von Bülow, her husband, following behind, dropping pages of the score (King Mark's monologue). Cartoon by M. Schultze, 1865.*

During the years in which Wagner had been trying unsuccessfully to get the opera performed in German and Austrian theaters, the greatest doubt expressed had always concerned the title roles. Was it possible to find singers capable of performing them? Clearly, there was one *heldentenor* in Germany capable of singing Tristan. He was not only Wagner's choice; he must also have been Ludwig's, because it was this singer who had come to Munich in 1861 to sing *Lohengrin* at a special performance commanded by Ludwig's father for his son, and who had had such an effect on the young prince. His name was as sonorous as his mighty voice—Ludwig Schnorr von Carolsfeld.

Schnorr was a massive man with a gigantic girth. He was only twenty-nine when he sang Tristan in Munich. He was a man of great intelligence, the son of a famous artist, and a genuine student of Wagner's music. Moreover, he came with his own Isolde—his wife Malvina, eleven years older than he was. Together, at the four performances of *Tristan* in Munich that summer of 1865, they proved that the roles were both singable and actable. The critics, predictably, were taken aback and cautious when they were not openly hostile, but everyone admired the Schnorrs. After the final performance, loaded with public tributes and the private thanks of Ludwig, Wagner, and von Bülow, they went home to Dresden. There,

three weeks later, Schnorr von Carolsfeld died— of typhus according to some reports, of rheumatic fever according to others. The news reached Munich like a thunderclap.

Every tenor who has ever attempted the role of Tristan has to be aware of the great legend that is Schnorr von Carolsfeld. Just as you cannot enter Haus Wahnfried at Bayreuth without looking up at the frieze above the doorway and seeing the features of Wilhelmine Schröder-Devrient on the face of Tragedy, so you must be aware that the features of Ancient Myth, the central figure looking down at you from the frieze, are those of Schnorr von Carolsfeld.

To the right of Ancient Myth on that frieze is the figure of Music. Her features, unmistakably, are those of Cosima, with her son Siegfried at her side. From the time of *Tristan* onward, Cosima was central to Wagner's life. They finally got married in 1870, just a few weeks after her divorce from Bülow. Their third child, Siegfried, was already a year old. Cosima was not just the daughter of Franz Liszt, and she was not just the wife of Richard Wagner. She would become, in her own right, a towering figure in the story of opera. She lived to be ninety-two, outlasting Wagner by forty-seven years, and acted as his trustee, his chief apostle, and (in terms of caring for and supervising his operas) his successor.

TRISTAN UND ISOLDE

TOP: *Herbert von Karajan's production at the Salzburg Easter Festival, 1972, designed by Günther Schneider-Siemssen. With Helga Dernesch as Isolde and Jon Vickers as Tristan.*

ABOVE: *Ludwig and Malvina Schnorr von Carolsfeld, the first Tristan and Isolde, Munich, 1865.*

It is sobering to consider where Wagner might stand in the pantheon of opera composers if he had been captured and condemned to death (as well he might have been) in the collapse of the Dresden uprising of 1849. By then, he had written four major works, from *Rienzi* to *Lohengrin*. All of them had made significant advances on the process initiated by Hoffmann, Spohr, Weber, and Marschner—the process of developing German Romantic opera. In *Der fliegende Holländer* Wagner had gone vastly further than they had in integrating the music and the drama into a compelling whole. There were very few "numbers" that could be lifted out. The orchestra had become the principal narrator, characterizing the atmosphere, the situations, and the personalities through its recurring themes. *Tannhäuser* went further still in its Venusberg music, but it also looked back to more traditional forms of opera. It used grand "arias" and choruses, not in the set-piece way of the eighteenth century, but nevertheless in a recognizably operatic tradition (which was one of the reasons for its greater popularity with audiences). *Lohengrin* was yet another advance, employing many of the techniques of French *grand opéra*, but encasing them within a score that was essentially "through-composed." None of these operas made use of leitmotifs except in isolated instances, but their structure, their liberal use of melody, and their orchestral textures contained the seeds of what was to come. Had there been no successors, they would certainly be seen as the zenith of German Romantic opera.

Tristan, however, was a giant leap forward. Music, words, and dramatic action were now completely integrated, and the harmonic structure of the work was nothing less than revolutionary. Wagner wrote a vast, panoramic symphony in which the music, vocal and orchestral, delineated a psychological drama of great intensity. The musical leitmotifs, continually recurring and developing, provided the underpinning for the whole complex drama. The forbidden love of Tristan and Isolde struggled free, exploded in ecstasy, and was finally transfigured in the *Liebestod* (love death). The entire story, interior and exterior, was told in music of great tension, and often of great beauty. It was no wonder, in retrospect, that Wagner invaded the unfamiliar territory of chromatic harmonies to depict the subtle psychological development of his protagonists (much more subtle than traditional forms of tonality would have allowed). And it was no wonder that audiences at the time were bemused by what they heard: it was unfamiliar, but it was also very powerful.

Wagner's behavior in Munich, and his influence on the young king, had quickly made him enemies. At the end of the year in which *Tristan* was performed, he was forced to leave Bavaria, to the utter desolation of Ludwig. But the patronage continued unabated. Wagner settled on the banks of Lake Lucerne at a house called Tribschen (rent paid annually in advance by Ludwig), and there he spent what were probably the six happiest and most productive years of his life, mostly with Cosima. *Die Meistersinger* and *Siegfried* were completed; *Götterdämmerung* and the orchestral piece the *Siegfried Idyll* were written; there were also books on opera, on conducting, and on Beethoven; the children Eva and Siegfried were born; and in 1870 Cosima and Wagner finally married.

During this period, too, there were premieres in Munich of *Die Meistersinger* (probably the greatest single triumph of Wagner's life) and of *Das Rheingold* and *Die Walküre*. Wagner himself was not present at either of the last two. They had been composed for a nonexistent theater of his imagination. He did not want them publicly performed at the Court Theater in Munich, where they could not be heard or seen to advantage. The "theater by the Rhine" that Wagner had foretold in 1851 after his flight from Dresden was still not a reality, though it continued to be a possibility. As early as 1865, Ludwig had summoned Gottfried Semper, the architect of the Dresden opera house, and commissioned him to design such a theater on the heights above the river Isar in Munich. For four miserable years, poor Semper was ground between Wagner and the king, and between the king and his ministers, until in 1870 he sued the Bavarian government for damages and his expenses.

Wagner had repeatedly lied to Ludwig about the nature of his relationship with Cosima. Slowly but surely, with Wagner absent in Tribschen and his enemies in the Bavarian civil service gaining more and more influence, Ludwig came to distinguish between the two Wagners—the artist, whom he worshiped, and the man, whom he had begun to distrust.

In the meantime, quite independently, Wagner had found the site for his new theater. In

Cosima, Siegfried, and Wagner, c. 1872.

1871, he informed Ludwig that Bayreuth, which was within Ludwig's kingdom of Bavaria, would be the home of a German national theater. There, Wagner's works would be performed under his own exclusive direction.

It was no coincidence that this announcement came in a year that began with the proclamation at Versailles of the German Reich. This was the culmination of the Franco-Prussian War, during which Bismarck's army had crushingly defeated the French at Sedan. Now, at last, Germany was whole, and Wagner saw himself as the poet laureate and supreme musician of "die heil'ge deutsche Kunst."

On his fifty-ninth birthday, on a green hill within the city boundaries of Bayreuth, Wagner laid the foundation stone of his theater, the Festspielhaus. Later that day (it poured rain incessantly), he conducted a performance of Beethoven's Ninth Symphony in the old Rococo opera house in Bayreuth, the ancient court theater of the margraves. It was an optimistic beginning to what turned out to be a nightmare. For two years, Cosima and Wagner worked heroically to raise the money to pay for the new theater, organizing concerts all over Germany. In the end, faced with ruin and the theater only half built, they were once again rescued by Ludwig. He ordered the Bavarian treasury to loan the necessary funds. Many years later, the loan was repaid in full.

Wagner built the Festspielhaus at Bayreuth specifically for the performance of his own works, but he did not build it as a shrine or a museum. It was to be a workshop. And that is what it has almost always been. The exception was the period immediately after Wagner's death, when Cosima zealously protected her husband's legacy and rigidly enforced what she knew to have been his original intentions. It was not until 1906, twenty-three years after Wagner's death, that she resigned the running of the festival to her son, Siegfried. Siegfried was a sweet and liberal-minded man, a fine conductor and an able composer, much admired by critics as difficult to please as Albert Schweitzer and George Bernard Shaw. He died in 1930, the same year as his mother, so we cannot know what he might have made of Bayreuth if Cosima had not been there to cast her long shadow. Production in his time was still naturalistic: Wagner's original stage directions were fairly rigorously enforced, while the revolutionary ideas of Adolphe Appia and other experimenters in staging and scenic design were ruled out of court.

But one of Richard Wagner's most famous injunctions was "Kinder, schafft neues!" (Children, try something new). Fortunately for the progress of *dramma per musica*, it is an injunction his grandchildren have taken very much to heart. Since it reopened after World War II in 1951, Bayreuth has been one of opera's principal workshops.

What Wagner created on top of the green hill at Bayreuth was certainly something new. Its

The Festspielhaus in Bayreuth. Engraving made in 1876, the year of the first complete production of the Ring *cycle.*

most famous innovation was the almost invisible orchestra in its sunken and covered pit. In his preface to the published libretto of the *Ring*, Wagner wrote:

> Imagine an orchestra which produces a clear, pure sound, free from the extraneous noises which necessarily accompany the production of an instrumental tone, which is filtered through an acoustic screen. Imagine the advantageous position of the singer who can establish personal contact, as it were, with the audience. Imagine also how comfortably the singer will be able to enunciate, and you will agree with the efficiency and superiority of my acoustic-archetonic design.[16]

Audiences would agree, but not necessarily the singers. Birgit Nilsson, among the greatest of modern Brünnhildes, has another point of view:

"That famous covered pit can be treacherous for singers; from the auditorium, the orchestra sound appears damped, but the hood throws it towards the stage. We feel swamped by a sonic tidal wave and, while fighting this illusion, try not to push our voices over that huge orchestra."[17]

Wagner turned Germany upside down looking for suitable singers for the *Ring*. As early as 1872, he and Cosima made a five-week tour of the country, visiting sixteen opera houses. They found precisely one female singer of any interest. Eventually, however, a cast and an orchestra were pieced together. It was made clear to the participants that this was an honor, not a commercial enterprise: "Will you please let me know if you wish to claim expenses and, if so, to what extent. . . . Please note that all participants will have to give up any thought of financial gain, and indeed the will to make sacrifices should be taken for granted."[18] On these terms, the singers and the orchestral players came to Bayreuth, not once, but twice. They came for six weeks in the summer of 1875 to rehearse. And they returned the follow-

Wagner's Die Meistersinger *at the Metropolitan Opera, New York, 1995. Directed by Otto Schenk, designed by Günther Schneider-Siemssen. Act III, Scene 1: the Quintet, with Birgitta Svendén as Magdalene, Lars Magnusson as David, Karita Mattila as Eva, Bernd Weikl as Hans Sachs, and Ben Heppner as Walther.*

"Bayreuth has left me with disagreeable recollections. . . . After the last notes of GÖTTERDÄMMERUNG *I felt as though I had been let out of prison. The* NIBELUNGEN *may be a magnificent work, but it is certain there never was anything so endlessly and wearisomely spun out. . . . Yet the* NIBELUNGEN RING *is an event of the greatest importance to the world, an epoch-making work of art."*

— *Pyotr Tchaikovsky (pictured at right)*

"Wagner's most recent reform does not represent an enrichment, an extention, a renewal of music; it is, on the contrary, a distortion, a perversion of basic musical laws, a style contrary to the nature of human hearing and feeling. . . . That it will ever become popular in the way of Mozart's or Weber's operas are popular appears improbable."

— *1876 review of the* RING *by Eduard Hanslick (pictured in the caricature below)*

ing year for eight weeks of rehearsal, followed by three complete performances of the *Ring* cycle in three consecutive weeks—the first time the great work had been performed as a whole.

Der Ring des Nibelungen (The Ring of the Nibelung) consists of four separate operas—the prologue *Das Rheingold*, followed by *Die Walküre*, *Siegfried*, and *Götterdämmerung* (Twilight of the Gods)—fifteen or sixteen hours of music in all. It is mythological. It is about gods, and giants, and a race of dwarfs (the Nibelung) who labor in the center of the Earth. It is universal, for all times and all ages. It is open to diverse interpretations, and various people at various times have subjected it to all kinds of weird and wonderful analyses and stage productions. There have been naturalistic productions, surrealistic productions, neoclassical productions, even "deconstructive" productions. It has been set in the past, the present, and the future—sometimes all three in the same production. It is claimed to be an attack on capitalism, a sexual interpretation of history, a psychological drama of inner discovery—and some people have even thought it is a story about gods, and giants, and a race of dwarfs.

Whatever it is about, it is a monumental work of art with an enduring fascination. Franz Liszt, in a speech at the end of that first Bayreuth Festival in 1876, put it very simply: "Other countries greet Dante and Shakespeare. So"—turning to Wagner—"I am your most obedient servant."

The "invitations to a great dramatic festi-

val" had finally gone out. People came from all over the world—the great, the musical, and sometimes just the curious. Ludwig came, of course ("You are the God-man who cannot fail, who cannot err," he wrote, "the true artist who, by God's grace, has brought down from Heaven the holy flame to inspire, ennoble and redeem us on earth"[19]). The kaiser himself came (he lasted through two operas before military maneuvers called him away). The emperor of Brazil was there, and dozens of lesser royalty. So were Nietzsche, and Tchaikovsky, and Grieg, and Bruckner, and Saint-Saëns; and Theodore Steinway came from America, having paid for his ticket with the gift of a piano. Sixty newspaper correspondents came from all over the world (both the *New York Times* and the *New York Tribune* sent reviewers), and four thousand people bought tickets. It was certainly the most remarkable gathering in the story of opera.

Whether they liked what they saw or hated it (and few were neutral), everyone was impressed by the scale of the production. Wagner had commissioned the set designs from Joseph Hoffmann, a well-known painter of historical subjects who had recently designed both *Die Zauberflöte* and *Der Freischütz* for the brand-new Hofoper in Vienna. Hoffmann's *Ring* designs were richly detailed and quite stunning on paper, but they were evidently not so impressive when translated to the stage by the set builders, the Brückner brothers. In his review,[20] Eduard Hanslick of *Die neue freie Presse* included a long list of ways in which the production had failed to live up to Wagner's description of it as a "model production." They ranged from missed opportunities to an embarrassing catalogue of mishaps on stage. Hanslick (admittedly not a fan of Wagner, though he claimed to be an admirer) singled out one failure that many other critics noted—the lighting. The Festspielhaus at Bayreuth had the misfortune to be built just three years before Edison invented the incandescent lamp, so Wagner had to rely principally on gas lighting in this first production. He magnified the ineptness of the lighting crew by having the auditorium completely darkened during the performance—a most unusual stipulation at that time.

It was easy to find fault with such a grand conception, but there was much to admire as well. Today, in the museum at Haus Wahnfried (the house Wagner built in Bayreuth and into which he and Cosima had moved in 1874), you can see the original swimming machines Wagner himself designed for the Rhinemaidens. The three Rhine-maidens are of peculiar importance to the *Ring*. They are the first characters to appear at the beginning of *Das Rheingold* and the last to be seen in the immolation at the end of *Götterdämmerung*. It is the gold they guard in the depths of the river Rhine around which the whole story revolves: the theft of the gold, its being made into a ring (a ring that is cursed), and the consequent destruction of the world in the mad scramble of greed, envy, and jealousy to possess the ring. Wagner wanted the Rhinemaidens to seem to be swimming as they sang. Nowadays, with modern lighting and stage technology, it can be done relatively easily (though not always effectively). In 1876, Wagner decided that machines were needed to hold the singers above the stage to make it appear that they were really swimming. Everyone, even Hanslick, agreed that the effect was quite amazing. Lilli Lehmann, who was one of the Rhinemaidens in those per-formances, recalled the experience with mixed emotions: "When one considers that the Rhine-maidens were shunted around on the tops of spe-cially manufactured swimming machines, squeezed into tight corsets, one might appreciate the phys-ical effort that was required of us, quite apart from our musical performance."[21]

Hans von Bülow was not asked to conduct the *Ring* in 1876. How could he be? Instead, that task was given to Hans Richter, whom Wagner had known from Tribschen days and who had

ABOVE: *Wagner's* DAS RHEINGOLD *at the Metropolitan Opera, 1989. Directed by Otto Schenk, designed by Günther Schneider-Siemssen. Loge confronts the gods—with Siegfried Jersualem as Loge (right) and James Morris as Wotan (center).*

LEFT: *The first* RING *cycle, Bayreuth, 1876. The Rhinemaidens as seen from the audience: Minna Lammert and the sisters Lilli and Marie Lehmann, who sang from the top of stage machines specially designed to make it appear that they were swimming.*

been an assistant to Bülow in Munich when *Die Meistersinger* was first performed. The concertmaster of his pickup orchestra at Bayreuth was the great violinist August Wilhelmj (best known today because he adapted part of a suite by Bach into what we know as the "Air on the G-string").

As for the singers, they may have been hard to find, but Wagner was able to assemble what he himself regarded as a very creditable cast. There was of course no Schnorr von Carolsfeld: the role of Siegfried would undoubtedly have been his. Albert Niemann seemed the logical alternative. He was the Tannhäuser who had been savaged by the Jockey Club in Paris fifteen years earlier. Niemann certainly thought he should have had the part, but Wagner wanted him for Siegmund, and he did not believe that Siegmund and Siegfried should be sung by the same person in a single cycle. As a result, Niemann was the only difficult and discontented member of the large cast. The Siegfried who was finally selected, Georg Unger, turned out to be a mistake, though not a catastrophic one. He had been spotted by Richter in Mannheim, and Wagner agreed that he had the physique and voice to sing Siegfried. After several months of intensive coaching, however, they discovered too late that he lacked the other essential ingredient, intelligence. The choice of a Brünnhilde was equally difficult but more happily solved. Amalie Materna was not widely known outside Vienna, where she was a permanent member of

the company. Wagner was attracted by her powerful voice and her considerable beauty, but in order to get her to Bayreuth he was forced to submit to blackmail by the director of the Vienna Opera. Wagner had to spend six weeks in Vienna at the end of 1875, when he could least afford the time, rehearsing new productions of *Tannhäuser* and *Lohengrin*. In return, he got his Brünnhilde. The last of the big roles—Wotan and the Wanderer (which is the form in which Wotan, the lord of the gods, appears in *Siegfried*)—was sung by a veteran Wagnerian, Franz Betz. He had been the first Sachs in Munich.

The enormity of Wagner's achievement, and the grandness of the whole design, can best be seen in the length of time it took him to bring the *Ring* to fulfillment. He had begun work on it in Dresden in 1848. At that stage it was conceived as a single opera—*Siegfrieds Tod* (Siegfried's Death), which eventually became *Götterdämmerung*. The texts of the four operas were therefore written in reverse order, as Wagner extended the story back into Siegfried's early life and antecedents. The poem of *Das Rheingold* was completed in 1852. The music, on the other hand, was written in the correct order. It took him twenty years, between 1854 and 1874, but there was a twelve-year interruption (1857–69) while he concentrated on *Tristan* and *Meistersinger*.

Those two operas—one a huge psycho-

logical drama built around a tragic love story, the other a genuine comic masterpiece—illustrated the scope of Wagner's craft and its ability to deal, equally effectively, with such different moods and atmospheres. It was true that *Meistersinger* had very serious underlying themes, but comedy and laughter were essential elements of that work. Wagner's technique—his use of leitmotifs, his massive sonic structures, his unfailing ability to manufacture melody—was as well able to create comic drama as it was tragic drama. That was remarkable in itself.

The *Ring*, however, was of such cosmic design that it stood apart from all other operatic works ever composed. Its dramatic wholeness was achieved despite the long period of its creation, and it was only surprising that Wagner's own development was so little evident within it. In retrospect, and knowing that the twelve-year break in composition came between Acts II and III of *Siegfried*, it was possible to detect a change of emphasis. The music, perhaps, became more dominant, the leitmotifs were used more profusely and ever more subtly. Whether or not that was so, the musical and dramatic intensity of the *Ring* had been there from the very beginning—literally,

from the very first bars, composed in 1854. The orchestral prelude to *Das Rheingold* begins with four bars for double basses, alone, playing a sustained E-flat. They are joined by bassoons playing a B-flat, and the chord is held for an astonishing 132

Three men who, with Wagner, made Parsifal *possible: Karl Brandt, the stage manager; Hermann Levi, the conductor; and Paul von Joukowsky, the designer. All three were Jewish.*

bars. With the possible exception of the storm scene at the beginning of Verdi's *Otello*, no one had written, or would ever write, such a dramatic opening. It was pure music drama.

After the first production of the *Ring*, invitations did not go out from Bayreuth again for six years. Most of that time was spent in increasingly desperate attempts to pay off the debt accumulated by the 1876 production. It was finally paid by yet another loan from Ludwig, but only after Wagner had threatened to move to America. In the meantime, Wagner had written his last opera, *Parsifal*, and the Bayreuth Festival of 1882 was devoted entirely to performances of that work. *Parsifal* was another part of the story Wagner had already touched on in *Lohengrin*—the story of the Holy Grail. He described it as *Bühenenweihfestspeil* (sacred festival drama). Certainly, it was different from everything else he had written, but the essential technique was the same—the massive symphonic scoring, the use of leitmotifs, the complete integration of words, music, and drama. In this final example of his craft, however, Wagner's technique was refined to the point that it appeared seamless and almost hypnotic in its intensity.

As for the subject matter, *Parsifal*, like the *Ring*, was open to various interpretations. It was a pious work of Christian mysticism. Or it was a celebration of a homoerotic ideal. Or it was an Aryan statement of Christianity's superiority to its Judaic roots. It might be any of those things, but concerning *Parsifal* (which was not the case with the *Ring*), Wagner himself made a definitive statement about the work in his own production of it in 1882.

Even the dreaded Hanslick was impressed by the designs. They had been executed by a young Russian painter (though German was his native language) called Paul von Joukowsky. Wagner met him in Italy in 1880, and he quickly became an intimate member of the family circle. For two years before the staging of *Parsifal*, Wagner therefore had the advantage of being in almost daily contact with his designer, so that there was every reason to believe that the end result (it was the eighth set of designs Joukowsky had submitted) was very close indeed to Wagner's vision. Some of those 1882 designs, those for the Grail scenes, remained in use at Bayreuth right up to 1933.

True to his description of it as a sacred festival play, Wagner staged *Parsifal* as a naturalistic, and very pious, drama. Partly because the Wagner/Joukowsky production was so successful, partly because Bayreuth had a legal monopoly on staged productions of the work until 1913 (a copyright that the Met and other North American companies willfully ignored in the first decade of the century), *Parsifal* was almost always staged in the same way, until 1951, when the composer's own grandson spectacularly and brilliantly broke the mold. But there is little would-be revisionists can do about *Parsifal*, except debase it, if they ignore the central fact that it aspires to be a sacred drama.

The conductor in 1882 was Hermann Levi—like Bülow, a Wagner disciple, but unlike Bülow, a Jew, the son of a rabbi. Wagner was virulently anti-Semitic in his writings: it was the most repugnant side of his character. But Hermann Levi was prepared to overlook this, and even continued to do so when Wagner attempted to convert him to Christianity.

In the winter of 1881, Levi had another problem, and a pressing one. He had to assemble an orchestra capable of playing *Parsifal* at Bayreuth the following summer. Among others, he needed a first horn player, and the one he wanted was that prince among horn players, Franz Strauss. We last encountered him in Munich in 1864 (the year his son, Richard, was born) preparing to play the *Tristan* score for the first time and complaining vigorously about Wagner and his writing for the horn. In 1881, Richard was seventeen and already showing considerable talent as a composer. That winter, Franz had the unusual experience of play-

Wagner's PARSIFAL *at the Metropolitan Opera, New York, 1991. With Plácido Domingo as Parsifal and Jessye Norman as Kundry.*

ing the horn in the Munich Court Orchestra at the first performance of his son's D minor Symphony, which was received with tumultuous applause. A proud and grateful father, Franz asked how he could repay the conductor for his kindness in scheduling the work. "Very simply," replied Hermann Levi: "by coming to Bayreuth next summer to play *Parsifal*."

Franz Strauss honored the commitment and hated every moment of it. More important, he took his son Richard with him to Bayreuth that summer. The two composers—sixty-nine-year-old Richard Wagner and eighteen-year-old Richard Strauss—did not meet.

The following year, three months short of his seventieth birthday, Wagner had a massive heart attack and died in Venice. By then, few people doubted his genius, and most serious students of music and drama must have agreed with Liszt's judgment that he stood with Dante and with Shakespeare. In Wagner's case, however, there was a problem that has never entirely gone away: how to divorce the humanity and the nobility of his works from the many unattractive aspects of his character. Was it not true that his personal life was immoral and self-centered, that he lived an extravagant and luxurious life on the proceeds of money he solicited from his friends and patrons, and that he was deeply prejudiced and unashamedly anti-Semitic?

All those charges were true, though it was sometimes possible to defend him, partially, from some of them. Yes, his relationships with women could certainly be described as immoral, if judged by the standards of contemporary society, but Wagner did not believe in those standards, and he saw no reason to pretend that he did. He did not believe in marriage, for instance (he thought it denigrated women and made them no more than vassals of their husbands), but he accepted in full his responsibility to look after Minna long after the marriage had failed and right up to her death. As for his penchant for silks and satins: Wagner suffered from erysipelas, a very painful disease that caused the skin to react violently when wools or other coarser substances came in contact with it.

But the charges of anti-Semitism were impossible to counteract because Wagner himself gave them so much substance. His 1850 essay "Das Judentum in der Musik" (Judaism in Music)[22] was as repellent then as it is now. His defenders maintained that it did no more than reflect the views of most Germans at that time. If that was so, then they failed to explain why Wagner had found it necessary to fuel the flames of prejudice by publishing the pamphlet in the first place, and by republishing it in extended form nineteen years later. Nor was it good enough for the defenders to argue that the pamphlet was really only an attack on one Jew, Meyerbeer, whom Wagner disliked for purely artistic reasons. On the contrary: the essay violently attacked all Jews. Indeed, not until the Third Reich did any major German artist express his prejudices so arrogantly or so viciously as Wagner did.

So there has always been present in any estimation of Wagner the age-old question of whether or not it is possible to divorce the artist's personal beliefs from his art. In the case of Wagner, posterity has made no bones about it. Yes, it is possible to divorce the two, and the worldwide popularity of Wagner's works has grown exponentially, despite the horrifying events of the mid-twentieth century.

AFTER WAGNER

For forty-seven years after Wagner's death, his widow, Cosima, guarded his legacy at Bayreuth. In the early years, she conducted her artistic supervision of productions from a curtained box at the side of the stage. From there, she sent a stream of detailed notes to singers, conductors, and stage managers. In 1886, she came out into the open by staging her own production of *Tristan*. She tolerated very little change or innovation. The operas were staged according to her own strict construction of what she deemed to have been the "master's" wishes, and in this way she imposed what amounted to a straitjacket on Bayreuth production. Nevertheless, it was greatly to her credit that by 1901 all Wagner's works from *Der fliegende Holländer* onward had been staged in the Festspielhaus, and that the Festival was an established institution, taking place every year, or every other year, with the exception of the decade during and after World War I.

Already, by the time of Wagner's death, the operas were being quite widely seen outside Bayreuth. Much of this was due to a remarkable producer and impresario called Angelo Neumann. As a singer at the Vienna Opera, he had been directed by Wagner, whom he admired but did not worship. In 1878, just two years after the Bayreuth premiere, Neumann staged the entire *Ring* cycle in Wagner's birthplace, Leipzig. He later took the production to Berlin and, in 1882, to London, and then on a European tour through six countries. After its initial 1876 production, the *Ring* was not seen again at Bayreuth until 1896, but by then it had been performed in many of the opera capitals of the world. The Metropolitan in New York first saw it complete in 1889, with Lilli

Lehmann as Brünnhilde. Often, Wagner's own associates were the missionaries—Anton Seidl in New York; Hans Richter in Vienna and London; and Hermann Levi and Franz Fischer in Munich.

These men were ideally equipped to be missionaries. They had worked under Wagner at Bayreuth, they had helped him prepare his last scores for the stage, and they had watched him direct the first performances. But there were also, inevitably, a number of Wagner imitators whose history was not so glorious. Chief among them was August Bungert, a man of Wagnerian-size ambitions but seriously lacking in talent. He wrote a cycle of operas based on Homer's *Odyssey*. They were performed in Dresden and one or two other German cities from 1896, uniting critics and audiences in universal disdain. But Bungert had powerful support, not least from Carmen Sylva, the queen of Romania. In 1911, she became patroness of the Bungert-Bund, an association founded to promote his works. Bungert's ambition knew few bounds and included a plan to build a Bayreuth of his own on the banks of the Rhine at Bad Godesberg: it was to be dedicated to performances of *Der homerische Welt* (The Homeric World). Not even the queen could make that wild dream come true.

There were other, and much more important, followers of Wagner. Peter Cornelius was one of them. The work for which he is remembered with gratitude is a comedy, *Der Barbier von Baghdad*. There is nothing Wagnerian about it. But Cornelius was a disciple of *Zukunftmusik* (the music of the future). He worked for both Liszt at Weimar and Wagner at Munich, and he tried, in vain, to make his own contribution to the new music. Neither *Der Cid* nor *Gunlöd* proved worthy of its inspiration. The Hungarian Karl Goldmark was another composer who worked in Wagner's shadow, though he could not be said to be a disciple. As with Cornelius, it was his first opera that made his reputation. *Die Königin von Saba* (The Queen of Sheba) was staged in Vienna in 1875, the year before the first Bayreuth *Ring*, and its star was Wagner's Brünnhilde, Amalie Materna. Musically, it certainly owed something to Wagner (it was hard not to be influenced by what he was doing), but it owed much more to the *grand opéra* tradition of Paris, and not a little to traditional Jewish music as well. Goldmark wrote five more operas, all produced in Vienna, but none of them had anything like the same success.

Much more successful (though too often

forgotten as an opera composer) was Hugo Wolf. He is revered as a composer of some of the most beautiful songs ever composed for the human voice, but he had opera ambitions as well, and he was heavily influenced by Wagner. Wolf died in 1903, aged only forty-two, but his one completed opera, *Der Corregidor* (The Governor), is a worthy survivor despite its dreadful libretto. Written for enormous forces (a super-Wagnerian-sized orchestra), it was an adaptation of Pedro Antonio de Alarcón's Spanish story *El sombrero de tres picos* (The Three-Cornered Hat).

One man, more than any other, survived Wagner and Bayreuth and still managed to emerge as a fine post-Wagnerian composer. Engelbert Humperdinck was employed by Wagner to copy the *Parsifal* score for publication, but he was a great deal more than a copyist, and Wagner knew it. Humperdinck was given the responsibility of being Siegfried Wagner's one and only music teacher—a responsibility he carried out with evident success, since Siegfried became an important conductor and quite a popular composer in his own right. But Humperdinck also had it in him to write operas, and he wrote one, *Hänsel und Gretel*, which had the most startling and immediate success. In 1893, ten years after Wagner's death, at a time when the Italians seemed to be having it all their own way (Verdi's career was just ending, Puccini's just beginning), Humperdinck produced a fairy-tale opera based on German folklore. The work owed much to Wagner's example. It was full of melodies but not too dense. The premiere in Weimar was followed within months by performances all over Germany as well as in London and New York. From that day to this, its popularity has never waned.

The conductor of the Weimar premiere of *Hänsel und Gretel* was Richard Strauss. Still not thirty years old, he had become a conductor and composer of considerable stature. Two of his tone poems—*Tod und Verklärung* (Death and Transfiguration) and *Don Juan*—had caused a stir among musicians and been well received by the public. His base at this time was in Weimar, where he was *Kapellmeister*. The year 1894 was important for him: in the spring, his first opera was staged in Weimar; in the summer, he conducted for the first time at Bayreuth; in the autumn, he was married.

The common element in these events was Pauline de Ahna. She sang the leading female role of Freihild in Strauss's *Guntram*; she was the Elisabeth of his Bayreuth *Tannhäuser*; and in the autumn she was Strauss's bride. *Guntram* was not a great success. In fact, it was not a success at all— "a testimony to my hair-raising naivety in those days," Strauss later explained.[23] Written to his own libretto, it was pseudo-Wagnerian both in subject matter and in music. Strauss was glad to forget it. The Bayreuth *Tannhäuser*, on the other hand, was a considerable triumph.

Cosima Wagner, to her credit, had not shut out the son of Franz Strauss. He had helped to rehearse *Parsifal* in 1889, and when Cosima herself produced *Tannhäuser* for the 1891 festival, Strauss had gone into print with an appreciation. It was not surprising that he should be asked to conduct the revival in 1894.

A new era in German opera was beginning, and Strauss would dominate it almost as completely, and just as controversially, as Wagner had dominated the previous one. But with this difference— that throughout Strauss's long career the music of Wagner remained one of the major preoccupations of the opera world. A generation of Wagnerian singers had already grown up, and it was being added to all the time, with Bayreuth as the principal nursery. Audiences in every country wanted to hear and experience the Wagner operas. Even allowing for the interruptions of two world wars, they were a twentieth-century phenomenon.

What this meant, more than anything, was that German was an established and internationally recognized language of opera. This had not been true when Mozart wrote *Die Zauberflöte*, or when Beethoven wrote *Fidelio*. At that time, German *Singspiel* was popular enough within the German-speaking lands, but the operatic universe was still fundamentally Italian. Weber and his contemporaries had begun the transition. Wagner had completed it. Richard Strauss and an important band of twentieth-century German composers would be the beneficiaries.

Unlike German, French had been a language of opera ever since the middle of the seventeenth century. It had never challenged Italian for international dominance, and even within France it had its detractors as an operatic language. The nineteenth century proved those detractors to be conspicuously wrong, and it proved that French opera could be, and often was, as popular as Italian opera in the world's theaters.

Opera in Nineteenth-Century Paris

Verdi coined the phrase "la grande boutique" to describe the Paris Opéra, and not without reason. During the nineteenth century, Paris became the cosmopolitan capital of European opera. It was the showcase — the city to which everyone came, whether willingly, like Rossini, Bellini, Donizetti, Meyerbeer, and Offenbach, or somewhat grudgingly, like Wagner and Verdi. By the mid-century, Paris had thirty different theaters presenting some kind of musical drama. They ranged from the grand goings-on at the Opéra to the intimate and hilarious concoctions of Offenbach's Bouffes-Parisiens. There was French opera in profusion, and there was foreign opera, too — most notably in the great years of the Théâtre-Italien, when the art of *bel canto* was celebrated to its highest degree. There was *grand opéra*, there was *opéra-comique*, there was *opéra-ballet*, there was *opérette*, and (aside from all the labeling) there was a steady devel-

PRECEDING PAGES: *Meyerbeer's* ROBERT LE DIABLE *at the Paris Opéra, 1985. This huge production, with six hundred costumes, a chorus of ninety-six, and a corps de ballet of forty, was staged by Pétrika Ionesco, with designs by Ionesco and Florica Malureanu. It featured Alain Vanzo as Robert, June Anderson as Isabelle, and Samuel Ramey as Bertram.*

opment that led eventually to some of the greatest creations of lyric opera—from Berlioz's *Les troyens* to Debussy's *Pelléas et Melisande,* via Gounod's *Faust,* Bizet's *Carmen,* and a hugely popular supply of works by Massenet.

The essential preliminaries to all this activity were the shedding of the straitjacket in which Lully and his successors had imprisoned "serious" French opera, and the opening of the door to outside influences. Both processes were well under way before the Revolution. It was already clear that the future of French opera would not lie with Lullian *tragédie lyrique.* It was much more likely to lie with the rival tradition of *opéra-comique*—more flexible, more capable of development, and more all-embracing, since it was by no means limited to comic opera: it included any musical dramatic work in which there was spoken dialogue.

THE REVOLUTIONARY ERA

The outside influences came in many different forms. In the 1770s, the German-speaking Gluck brought his reform program to Paris and staged his six French operas. Their effect was enormous and, for *tragédie lyrique,* more or less spelled the end. Right up to his death in 1787, Gluck maintained his contacts with the French capital, often through the medium of Vienna's court composer, Antonio Salieri, whom Gluck introduced to Paris and with whom he was said to have collaborated on at least one opera. By that time, Italian composers were already in the ascendant at the Opéra-

Comique. Between 1755 and 1775 Egidio Duni dominated the theater's output with a stream of light and lively works like *La fille mal gardée.* Niccolò Piccinni, who genuinely deserved to be compared with his Neapolitan confreres, Paisiello and Cimarosa, was hugely popular until the denouement of his unwanted confrontation with Gluck (see the chapter "From Gluck to Mozart"). Yet another Italian, Antonio Sacchini, less talented than either Duni or Piccinni, nevertheless chalked up the single most popular opera to be performed in Paris before, during, and for a long time after, the Revolution. Sacchini did not live to see *Oedipe à Colone* staged in 1787, nor could he have guessed that it would have 583 performances at the Opéra during the next fifty-seven years—a statistic no other composer came close to matching.

Duni, Piccinni, and Sacchini were important in their time, but their long-term influence was small compared to that of André Grétry. Grétry was a Belgian composer, trained in Rome. He arrived in Paris in 1767 and proceeded to write more than fifty operas in the next forty years, right through the Revolution and into the Napoleonic years beyond. Many of them were acceptable and popular comedies, high on melody, low on other musical ideas, but he also developed a gift for more serious dramatic works (the most famous was *Richard Coeur-de-Lion* in 1784) in which he began to lead French opera into the more exciting territory it was to inhabit for most of the nineteenth century.

Paradoxically, the Revolutionary times of

the 1790s were great years for Parisian theater, and therefore for opera. The violence and uncertainty of daily life were accompanied (to begin with, at least) by a remarkable freedom. At the start of 1791, the Assembly abolished the system of monopoly that had been in place since the time of Louis XIV. The Opéra thus lost its elevated and protected position, as well as the subsidies all other musical theaters had had to pay it from their earnings. It kept going, but mainly on a diet of rather safe operas about Roman history: the celebration of *la gloire* was replaced by the glorification of republicanism, and not just ancient Greek or Roman republicanism. Successive Revolutionary governments came to realize that opera, as a popular entertainment, could be helpful to their cause. So a series of regrettable productions with titles like *Le triomphe de la République* and *La réunion du 10 août* were advertised as being "of, by, and for the people."[1] At one stage, an edict was in force making it possible for any member of an audience to stop a performance, on demand, in order to have an approved Revolutionary hymn performed, including the popular new "Marseillaise."[2]

Despite the incipient chaos, some startlingly original works were staged at the Opéra-Comique, including several by Étienne Méhul. Méhul was a genuine dramatist, one of the first opera composers to use musical themes to characterize situations and personalities. Later, he would become a Romantic composer almost before that term was invented, but his operas in the 1790s were psychological dramas that owed little or nothing to the Revolutionary atmosphere in which they were written. The first of them, *Euphrosine* in 1790, had the added bonus of a duet which quickly became a hit tune: "Gardez-vous de la jalousie."

The chief considerations for staging opera in these years were finely balanced between political correctness, on the one hand, and commercial viability, on the other. Spectacle had always been an important element in French opera; now, in a highly competitive atmosphere, it became essential to survival. The Opéra-Comique unexpectedly found itself in cutthroat competition with a brand-new theater. This was the Théâtre Feydeau, built in 1789 as a home for Italian opera in Paris. The timing for such a venture, at the very beginning of the Revolution, was unfortunate, but the will to survive among the theater's employees was impressive. They quickly dropped the Italian affil-

iation and redoubled their efforts to provide their supporters with better music and bigger spectacles than the Opéra-Comique could offer. It was a suicidal contest that ended with the two theaters having to merge in 1801. Méhul with his psychological dramas, Nicolas Dalayrac with a series of immensely popular light comedies, and Henri-Montan Berton with a particularly thrilling opera about nuns (entitled *Les rigueurs du cloître*) delighted audiences at the Opéra-Comique. But the Feydeau's overall record was probably better. What was certain was that the Feydeau possessed, in the person of its music director, Luigi Cherubini, the most important opera composer in Paris, and probably the most successful one in Europe.

Cherubini was yet another Italian who made Paris his home. He arrived there in 1788 at the age of twenty-eight, having already written thirteen Italian operas in what was then the prevailing Neapolitan style. He lived in Paris for more than fifty years, right up to his death in 1842, effectively dominating the musical life of the city. He flourished during the Revolution and the Directory; he survived the Napoleonic years, despite a falling-out with the emperor himself; and he eventually became a famously irascible director of the Paris conservatoire. His popularity extended far beyond France: the London and Viennese theaters vied with each other to stage his latest works, and Beethoven and Goethe (but not Berlioz, who had suffered under him at the conservatoire) were two of his professional admirers.

All this seems strange now because Cherubini's operas are not often performed. His reputation has faded and is now outshone by those of his great contemporaries—Mozart, who was only four years older, and Beethoven, who was ten years younger. It is hard to understand how an opera like *Les deux journées* (known as *The Watercarrier* in English) could have done so much better at the box office in Vienna than the early performances of Beethoven's *Fidelio*. It is even harder to understand how his three large-scale epic operas— *Lodoïska* (1791), *Élisa* (1794), and *Faniska* (1806) —could have enjoyed so much success in Paris and Vienna. The explanation lies in the dates. Cherubini staged these works thirty years before Auber, Rossini, and Meyerbeer inaugurated the era of *grand opéra*. Audiences were seeing something new and quite extraordinarily impressive.

With the exception of *Médée* (which provided a starring role for Maria Callas a hundred

THE OSSIAN MYTH

Costume drawings by Bethélémy for Le Sueur's OSSIAN, OU LES BARDES *at the Paris Opéra, 1804. Jean-François Le Sueur (1760–1837) wrote the opera at the request of Napoleon, who was imbued with the Ossian myth. Ossian was a legendary Gaelic bard of the third century A.D. His major work* (Fingal: An Ancient Epic Poem in Six Books, Composed by Ossian, the Son of Fingal) *was "rediscovered" in the 1760s, but it turned out to be a fraud—the work of a Scottish writer called James MacPherson (1736–1796). MacPherson was roundly denounced by Dr. Johnson, but Ossian "mania" nevertheless swept through Europe. Étienne-Nicolas Méhul was another composer who wrote an opera about it* (UTHAL, 1806): *his score used no violins in an effort to conjure up a suitably gloomy and mysterious atmosphere. MacPherson survived the scandal, became a Member of Parliament, and was buried in Westminster Abbey (at his own expense). The enthusiasm for Ossian led Goethe to quote Ossian at length in* The Sorrows of Young Werther.

and fifty years later), Cherubini's operas did not deal with mythological subjects. They were set in real places, at recognizable moments in history, and the plots were often exciting. *Élisa* was set in Switzerland, with an avalanche providing a dramatic high point. *Lodoïska* was set on the Russian border of Poland and ended with a castle going up in flames. *Les deux journées* was set in Paris during the time of Cardinal Mazarin. *Lodoïska*, *Les deux journées*, and *Faniska* all featured heroes or heroines who, like Berton's nuns, were rescued from a fate worse than death.

The Feydeau and the Opéra-Comique thus launched what was to be a dramatic change in French opera—a foretaste of the Romantic movement just around the corner, a prophecy of what, in the hands of greater dramatists, would become *grand opéra*. They extended the bounds of *opéra-comique* into areas that had not previously been thought of as "operatic"—the exotic and the supernatural, the epic and the recognizably real. Myth and fairy-tale were by no means discarded, but they were clearly thought of as less exciting—and excitement was the hallmark of French opera in these dangerous and unpredictable times.

Cherubini led the pack, but he was by no means alone. André Grétry followed up his *Richard Coeur-de-Lion* by having a go at Russian history in *Pierre Le Grand* (1790), and then at Swiss history in *Guillaume Tell* (1791, anticipating both Schiller and Rossini). A highly talented colleague of Cherubini at the Feydeau, Jean-François Le Sueur, wrote some very dramatic operas with intriguing

titles like *Télémaque* and *Ossian*. Even Méhul eventually turned away from his passionate and tragic dramas to mine the Bible for more epic source material. The result, *Joseph*, was an opera that remained in the international repertoire well into the twentieth century.

In the meantime, Napoleon had restored decorum to the French capital. Like his predecessors in the Directory, he believed that theater and opera were important opinion-formers, and he took steps to place them officially under his own control. A decree of June 1806 directed that "the productions of the Opéra, the Comédie-Française and the Opéra-Comique shall be determined by the Minister of the Interior."[3] Napoleon's personal taste was decidedly Italianate, but he shared with the Paris public a love for pomp and grandeur.[4] French opera responded by becoming bigger, and louder, and its leader was once again an Italian émigré.

Gaspare Spontini's career was a brilliant exercise in adapting his talents (which were considerable) to whatever political, social, and musical styles were in fashion. He had learned his art in Naples, writing operas in the light Neapolitan style of the day. He fled Naples in 1798 as Napoleon's armies converged on the city. Five years later, he wound up in Paris and became a favorite of Napoleon's wife, the empress Joséphine. This was no small feat in itself, but what was a much greater achievement was the speed with which Spontini learned an altogether new style of opera. He carefully studied what Cherubini and Méhul and Le Sueur were doing, and he had the good fortune to team up with Étienne de Jouy, a playwright who would later become the official librettist of the Paris Opéra and Rossini's collaborator for *Guillaume Tell*. Jouy provided Spontini with three increasingly ambitious librettos. The one-act *Milton*, based on the life of the English poet, was a modest start in 1804, but three years later *La vestale* (The Vestal Virgin) brought Spontini lasting fame and the award of a prize, offered by Napoleon. Then came *Fernand Cortez* (1809), a work of stunning stage effects and enormous set pieces—a cavalry charge, the torching of the Spanish fleet, a human sacrifice. Jouy successfully argued that the introduction of horses on stage would create in the audience the same surprise that the Aztecs must have experienced when confronted by Cortez's mounted legions.[5] He was right: the sensation was enormous. It was *grand opéra* in the making, and audiences loved it. So did two of the severest musical judges of the next generation, Berlioz and Wagner, though the critics of the time were somewhat nonplussed by the very large role Spontini gave his orchestra in the overall storytelling.

Spontini was nothing if not a survivor—some would say a turncoat. No sooner was Napoleon defeated and exiled than Spontini was composing equally huge, but much less successful, works to glorify the restoration of the Bourbon monarchy. *Olimpie*, a story about the daughter of Alexander the Great (it included a huge battle scene, a bacchanal, and even an apotheosis), failed to win popular support in 1819. But just as his luck was running out in Paris, Spontini was summoned to Berlin by the Prussian king, Friederich Wil-

helm III. He survived there for twenty years as court composer—argumentative, pompous, and justly famous. His earlier works were regularly performed all over Europe, but time had passed him by; the concentration now was on a new generation of composers. When Spontini staged *Olimpie* in Berlin in 1821, it was submerged within weeks by the brilliant premiere of Weber's *Der Freischütz*.

Even with Spontini gone, the French opera scene was dominated by Italians. Luigi Cherubini, his composing days behind him, presided officiously at the conservatoire, but the center of Italian influence had shifted, once again, to the Théâtre-Italien. It had been reestablished in 1801, with Napoleon's blessing, for the performance of Italian opera, in Italian. Since 1812, its director had been Ferdinando Paer, a mildly distinguished

Rosa Ponselle (1897–1981) in Florence after a performance of Spontini's La vestale. *Ponselle, who had one of the most beautiful voices of the twentieth century, rarely sang outside America. She was Julia in the Met's first production of* La vestale *in 1925 and sang the role again for her only foray into Italy (at the Maggio Musicale, Florence, 1933).*

Italian composer who had been a favorite of Napoleon. In 1824, greatly to his annoyance, Paer was persuaded to share his directorship with Paris's newest Italian émigré, Giaocchino Rossini.

ROSSINI IN PARIS

Rossini was still only thirty-two years old, yet he was already an elder statesman of music. The first of his operas to be performed in Paris had been *L'italiana in Algeri* as recently as 1817, but now, as he sought to perfect his command of the language before attempting to compose in French (which he was bound by his contract to do), he staged a dazzling series of productions of his Italian works with singers all Paris wanted to hear. Pasta was the greatest draw, until she was overtaken by María Malibran, with Henriette Sontag not far behind. The biggest sensation of all, however, was the Paris debut of a young tenor who had sung for Rossini in Naples, Giovanni Battista Rubini. His performances in *Cenerentola*, *Otello*, and *La donna del lago* inaugurated an extraordinary chapter in the history of the Théâtre-Italien. Rossini was formally director of the theater (and a very indifferent one) for only two years, but he remained the dominant presence for twenty years after that, right through the ascendancies of Bellini and Donizetti and the

stunning achievements of the "Puritani Quartet." Never before or since has so much star power been on display at any one time. Rossini's first "command" opera in Paris (his last in Italian) was a glorious example of the style. *Il viaggio a Reims* was written for the coronation of Charles X in 1825. It was hardly an opera, more a vast cantata, and it had only four performances. Yet it contained no fewer than ten virtuoso roles for a cast led by Pasta, the Italian tenor Domenico Donzelli, and the French bass Nicolas Levasseur.

Rossini's contribution to French opera was brief but startling. All of his French works were written for the Opéra between 1826 and 1829. *Le siège de Corinthe* was an adaptation of his earlier Italian work *Maometto II*, and *Moïse et Pharaon* was similarly adapted from *Mosè in Egitto*. Both these works were given massive productions at the Opéra, and both were well served by French stars—the tenor Adolphe Nourrit as Néoclès in *Corinthe*, and Levasseur in the title role of *Moïse*. The mystery of the quick disappearance of *Il viaggio* was explained (in part, at least) by the unveiling of Rossini's next work. *Le comte Ory* was a return to his scintillating comic mode, and it remained a Paris favorite for many years. Four numbers from *Il viaggio* were recycled for it. Nothing, however, could have prepared Rossini-watchers for what came next. Just a year after *Ory* had delighted the Opéra audience with its outrageous storyline and its glorious ensemble finales, so reminiscent of *Il barbiere* and *Cenerentola*, Rossini staged his biggest and his final operatic work, *Guillaume Tell*. It was *grand opéra*.

The term *grand opéra* is inescapably connected with this period of French opera, and most of all with the name of Giacomo Meyerbeer. Rossini had been responsible for introducing the German Meyerbeer to Paris in 1825 when he staged *Il crociato in Egitto* (The Crusader in Egypt) at the Théâtre-Italien. It was the last of Meyerbeer's Italian operas, written very much in the Rossinian style of *Tancredi*, with a *castrato* leading role. The next opera Meyerbeer wrote, *Robert le diable* in 1831, was the work that, more than any other, defined the style and essence of *grand opéra*—huge five-act dramas on historical subjects, with massive orchestras, big choruses and ballets, featuring large voices and enormous spectacles. But Meyerbeer was not the pioneer. That honor had fallen to Daniel Auber with his 1828 opera *La muette de Portici* (The Mute Girl of Portici), and it was quickly followed by Rossini's *Guillaume Tell* in 1829.

By any standards, *Tell* was an enormous opera. Étienne de Jouy freely adapted Schiller's play, and the Opéra gave it a staging worthy of its scale. But no one, least of all Rossini, doubted that there were longueurs. Moreover, the tenor role of the hero Arnold proved too much even for Nourrit and had to wait eight years for the emergence of a singer, Gilbert-Louis Duprez, capable of doing it justice. Within it, however, *Tell* contained some of Rossini's most glorious music—and not just the famous overture. Audiences at the Opéra received it with a frenzy of acclaim. They liked the epic story of the Swiss hero leading his nation's resistance to the Austrian invaders, and they were thrilled by its majestic settings in the mountains, and by its big ballets, its grand choruses, and its orchestral set pieces, as well as the vocal writing, which was pure Rossini. The leading critic of the time, Théophile Gautier, wrote of Rossini: "He is historic . . . from today his name can be placed alongside those of Palestrina, Haydn, Gluck, Mozart, Weber, and Beethoven."[6] No one knew, of course, that it was the last time Rossini would write for the opera stage. He was only thirty-seven, and he still had more than half his life to live.

Rossini had arrived in Paris in the early days of the Bourbon Restoration. As it turned out, they were also its dying days, because in July of 1830 the reactionary and tyrannical Bourbon king, Charles X, fled into exile, and the duc d'Orléans was crowned as Louis-Philippe. The age of the bourgeoisie had arrived, and Louis-Philippe, the "citizen king," with his plain gray hat and his furled umbrella, became the symbol of the age.

So, too, did the Paris Opéra. Since 1822, it had been housed in the rue Le Peletier, where it would remain until 1873. In those five decades, it wrote a chapter in the story of opera that was at various times glorious and scandalous, but always *grand*.

Design for Robert Bruce, *Paris Opéra, 1846. Rossini's* Robert Bruce *is not an opera with which we are familiar, largely because Rossini did not actually write it. But that did not prevent the Paris Opéra from performing it, in 1846. It was, in fact, an elaborate* pasticcio *(or medly) of Rossinian music, mostly based on his 1819 opera* La donna del lago, *jammed into a plotline vaguely resembling the story of the fourteenth-century Scottish hero Robert Bruce. Rossini grudgingly connived in the production, and it did him much harm with the critics, notably Hector Berlioz. It was, however, a commercial success.*

Grand Opéra in Paris

The Opéra had already been in existence for more than a hundred and fifty years. Only once had it been in profit. That, characteristically, had been during Lully's directorship. The recurring problems were overspending and debt—despite the monopoly granted by the monarchy, despite an enormous state subsidy, and despite a royalty it received by law from "all theaters of the second rank" and "from all amusements of whatever kind they may be" (these royalties ranged from five percent of the revenues of a rival opera production to twenty percent of the revenues from balls or concerts).[7] The Revolutionary governments of the 1790s terminated all such monopolies and subsidies, but by 1811 they had been restored by Napoleon. So had the management's tradition of overspending. Government-appointed superintendents turned out to be ineffective. The last of them before the July Revolution of 1830, the vicomte de la Rochefoucauld, was the most incompetent of all. He wished to raise the moral tone. Gautier wrote scathingly of him as the "unfortunate and virginal Vicomte who lengthened the skirts of the dancers at the Opéra and with his own hand applied a modest plaster to the middle of all the statues."[8] So in 1830, when the bourgeoisie finally got control of the government, change was quick and radical. A government decree stated that "The administration of the Académie Royale de Musique, known as the Opéra, shall be entrusted to a director-entrepreneur, who shall manage it for six years at his own risk and fortune."[9]

The man selected, after intensive lobbying on his own behalf, was Louis Véron, a doctor of medicine, enriched by ownership of a patent for chest ointment, and, as he proudly stated in the title of his memoirs, "un bourgeois de Paris."[10]

Whatever else one may say about him, Véron was a brilliant administrator—a "hands-on" manager. He was also an outstanding publicist, a no-holds-barred entrepreneur, and an unblushing giver of bribes. As a showman he would compare favorably with his American contemporary Phineas T. Barnum. Like Barnum, he knew how to make money.

He was lucky, too. When he took over the Opéra in 1831, having put down a deposit of 250,000 livres, he inherited most of the equipment, physical and human, that he would need to turn it into a paying proposition. The house itself was only ten years old—a handsome two-thousand-seater with gas lighting. Véron reduced the number of boxes and increased the amount of seating available at the box office. The stage machinery was modern, and would be made more so by the introduction of wondrous new inventions—the so-called *spectacles d'optique*. The orchestra, under François Habeneck, was reputed to be one of the best in France; the chorus master was Fromental Halévy, future composer of *La juive;* and the ballet company was led by the greatest ballerina of the age, Marie Taglioni.

Best of all, the government decided to continue its subsidy to the Opéra—less than it used to be, and on a descending scale year by year, but sufficient to insure Dr. Véron against losses, which he would have had to bear himself. In fact, he made huge profits, and he did so by making the Opéra the most talked-about institution in Paris, and himself its most visible personality. He drove around in an elegant carriage drawn by two magnificent English-bred horses; he always wore a large white cravat; he entertained extravagantly; and he crossed a great many palms with gold, including those of leading journalists. On a visit to London he wined and dined the Austrian ballerinas Fanny and Therese Elssler. He was attempting to persuade Fanny Elssler to join the Opéra as a counterattraction to Marie Taglioni. Jewels were served with the dessert, a ploy that momentarily phased the modest Austrian sisters. But only momentarily.[11] Fanny Elssler moved to Paris and caused a sensation as great as Taglioni.

The evidence of contemporaries indicates that the standard of performances in Véron's day was generally high, but the director was not prepared to rely on the house's artistic reputation alone in order to sell tickets. He instituted a system of backstage passes to allow ticket holders more intimate glimpses of the stars, especially the ballerinas. He held frequent and very magnificent balls in the theater, with tickets available to everyone, not just the aristocracy. Most famously, he made use of the claque.

One of the ugliest sounds to be heard in an opera house, then and now, is the sound of an organized group in the audience, a claque giving vent to its prejudices. In 1815, it had happened to Rossini in Rome on the opening night of *Il barbiere di Siviglia.* In 1861, it would happen to Wagner at the Paris Opéra, when the Jockey Club shouted down his production of *Tannhäuser.* In modern times, it happens all too often in leading houses throughout the world. It is not a pleasant thing. But it has an ancient and not altogether dishonorable history. The earliest claques (Suetonius recorded them in the time of Emperor Nero) were employed to support performers, not to denigrate them. Very early in the history of opera, in seventeenth-century Venice just after the time of Monteverdi, there were reports of organized groups of supporters in certain theaters. But Paris in the 1820s is the first time we hear of the genuine *claqueurs*—the paid supporters. There was even an agency in Paris with the title L'Assurance des Succès Dramatiques.

Véron did not need an agency. The Opéra employed its own *chef de claque*. His job was to recruit and organize a group of *claqueurs*, to situate them strategically around the opera house, and to direct their interjections in minute detail. It was an elaborate process, an art form in itself. The *claqueurs* were hired as specialists: there were *tapageurs* (for vigorous applause), *connaisseurs* (knowing exclamations of approval), *pleureurs* (tears of emotion), *bisseurs* (encores), and *chatouilleurs* (witty sallies). In addition, there were *commissaires* and *chauffeurs* who were the equivalents of the modern "spin doctors": they mixed with the audience before and after the performance and during the intervals, exclaiming loudly at the triumphs taking place on stage.[12]

The Opéra paid the *chef de claque* in tickets; on a big night he might be given as many as a hundred. The dancers, singers, conductors, and even some composers, paid him in cash, and sometimes with additional tickets. No one of any consequence could afford to perform at the Opéra without first making sure that the *chef de claque* had had his palm greased, generously. He was said to earn at least as much as the highest-paid performer.

Auguste Levasseur, who was Véron's *chef de claque*, was a legend in his own time. "Large, robust, a veritable Hercules in size, and gifted with an extraordinary pair of hands, he was created and put into the world to be a *claqueur*," wrote one observer.[13] Those hands may have been good for clapping, but Auguste's art consisted of much more than just unleashing a storm of applause whenever he gave the signal: he was probably Véron's closest adviser. He examined scores and librettos in advance and gave the director his opinion (though he was no musician at all—nor was Véron); he attended rehearsals; and he was often called upon to counsel dancers and singers on the finer points of their performances. Moreover, he was good at it. In his memoirs, Hector Berlioz praised him effusively: "One has often admired, but not enough in my opinion, the marvelous talent with which Auguste directs the great works of the modern repertoire and the excellent advice that he gives on many occasions to the authors."[14]

No claque has ever been so well organized, or so benevolent, as Auguste's. Modern claques have tended to breed counter-claques—never more so than at La Scala, where one such encounter at a Callas performance ended with a brawl and two men in prison. Too many great singers still have to undergo the unnerving experience of encountering a wall of booing, regardless of whether they are singing well or badly. At least (we hope), the claques are no longer paid.[15] An Italian tariff of 1919 is a vivid reminder of how bad it used to be:

applause for gentleman's entry	25 lire
ditto for a lady	15 lire
ordinary applause	10 lire
insistent applause (pro rata)	15—17 lire
interruptions with "Bene!" or "Bravo!"	5 lire
a "bis"[encore]	50 lire
wild enthusiasm	by arrangement[16]

Whether or not Meyerbeer's operas would have succeeded so brilliantly without Auguste and his *claqueurs* is impossible to know. At the very least, the practice provided insurance against failure. But there were two other resources Meyerbeer and his fellow composers needed much more, and they were resources that Dr. Véron was always able to provide. The first was a dramatist with the literary skills and the imagination to write the librettos. The second was a technical team with the expertise to create the massive spectacles called for by the dramas.

The librettist was Eugène Scribe, surely the most prolific dramatist there has ever been. When he died in 1861, in his seventieth year, his published works amounted to seventy-six volumes. He had collaborated with almost every great opera composer of the nineteenth century, with the exception of Wagner. He wrote for Rossini, Bellini, and Donizetti; for Cherubini and Boïeldieu; for Auber, Halévy, Hérold, and Meyerbeer; for Cilea, Zandonai, and Verdi; for Gounod and Offenbach. And that is by no means a complete list.

Eugène Scribe (1791—1861). Caricature by Benjamin, 1841. Scribe was so prolific as a librettist and playwright that the cartoonists loved to depict him as an accumulator of wealth. This caricature shows him surrounded by sacks of droits *(author's rights) and pigeonholes labeled "comic situations," "puns," "couplets," and other tools of the writer's trade.*

He wrote plays as well, masses of them. It is claimed that one theater alone, the Gymnase, produced at least a hundred of his plays between 1820 and 1830, even while he was writing others for the Théâtre-Français.[17]

No one would have the temerity to compare Scribe with the greatest dramatists of his generation, but it is important to see him in the context of what was going on in French theater at the time. When Scribe joined the Opéra as resident librettist in 1828, his two great contemporaries, Alexandre Dumas *père* and Victor Hugo, were in the process of revolutionizing the French stage. In 1829, Dumas produced his landmark play *Henri III et sa cour*, and the following year, amid controversy and even violence, Hugo staged the first great work of French Romantic theater, *Hernani*. At the very same time and in the same city, Scribe was playing a major role in changing the face of French opera.

A partial catalogue of Scribe's first eight years at the Opéra chronicles the change. He announced himself in 1828 with the libretto for Auber's *La muette de Portici*. The story of the fishermen's revolt in Naples in 1647 was told with much local color; it featured an eruption of Mount Vesuvius in the final scene. Scribe was not involved with Rossini's *Guillaume Tell* the next year, for which Jouy wrote the libretto, but he was very much involved with Meyerbeer's first Paris opera, *Robert le diable* in 1831. Here were medieval knights, a Sicilian setting, and a large dose of the supernatural—the Romantic movement arrived at the Opéra in tandem with *grand opéra*. Auber's *Gustave III*, the story of the very recent Swedish king (he had been dead only forty years) was the same masked-ball/assassination story that Verdi later set. Then came what was probably the most daring and powerful libretto of them all—*La juive* (The Jewish Woman) for Fromental Halévy. It was a story of religious prejudice and persecution in fifteenth-century Switzerland, with the heroine finally being put to death in a cauldron of flaming oil. And in 1836, again for Meyerbeer, there was *Les Huguenots*, another story of religious persecution, this time in France, ending with the St. Bartholomew's Day Massacre.

This was a far cry from the mythological stories that had dominated French opera for so much of its history. Scribe's talents were those of the storyteller. His librettos moved along from event to event, with little pause for characteriza-tion. To the extent that characterization existed, it had to be a function of the music. But however grand or subtle the music, none of these operas would have succeeded without the spectacle — and that was the other thing Véron could supply.

Techniques of stage production had ebbed and flowed in the two centuries since the Florentine *camerata*. The amazing mechanical sophistication of Venetian theaters in the time of Monteverdi and Torelli had proved to be only a passing phase in Italy. It had given way to a style in which the virtuoso singer was the chief attraction, and there is nothing singers like less than being upstaged by the scenery. But in France, the Venetian mechanics, imported and imitated by Lully, had maintained their importance. The mythological operas of Rameau and his contemporaries relied heavily on scenic effects—on magical transformations and ghostly apparitions—and much emphasis was placed on the effectiveness of costumes and backcloths. Lighting by candles was cumbersome by modern standards, but a great deal of ingenuity was expended on it. Soon after the Revolution, with melodrama established as a popular element of both theater and opera, the audience's expectations of the mise-en-scène became ever more demanding.

Technology came to the rescue. A form of entertainment known as *spectacles d'optique* began to appear in Paris. As early as 1787, panoramas had been demonstrated. A series of panoramic paintings would be displayed, each of them depicting a number of scenes within an overall story; a narrator, out of sight, provided commentary. Louis Daguerre, the photographic pioneer, began to use perspective in his panoramas, and then, as gas lighting replaced candles, he enthralled the public with his first "dioramas." For these, the panoramic paintings were partly opaque and partly transparent; carefully choreographed lighting revealed each segment of the action at the right moment. The audience sat on a large turntable so that its attention could be directed to whichever part of the panorama contained the current action. No actors were involved: it was simply the painting, the lighting, and their combined effect.[18]

This was exciting, but it was not happening at the Opéra. There, the mise-en-scène had fallen into disrepute under the superintendency of the Vicomte de la Rochefoucauld. It took the arrival of Edmond Duponchel, an architect with a passion for theater, to change it. He was even-

Drawing by Pierre-Luc-Charles Cicéri for Act II of the original production of Meyerbeer's ROBERT LE DIABLE, *Paris Opéra, 1831. "Nonnes, qui reposez"—Bertram summons the dead nuns from their graves.*

tually Véron's successor, but his greatest contribution to the Opéra was to import the magic of *spectacles d'optique* to its stage. Together with his more famous assistant, Pierre-Luc-Charles Cicéri, he produced his coup in time for the staging of Auber's *La muette de Portici* in 1828. The Neapolitan beach scene thrilled the audience; the Viceroy's palace amazed it; the eruption of Vesuvius practically blew it away. The next year, Rossini's *Guillaume Tell* was given the same treatment, only slightly less startling. Then, with Meyerbeer's *Robert le diable* in 1831, the set designers entered opera's hall of fame. The cloister scene, in which statues came to life and the dead rose from their graves, was as chilling and awesome a sight as audiences could easily endure. The opera's ending, when the evil Bertram disappeared in a cloud of fire and brimstone, almost literally brought down the house.

All this razzmatazz was fine, but it would have meant little without musicians and singers to inspire it. In this department, by great good fortune, Paris was suffering an embarrassment of riches in the 1830s. At the Théâtre-Italien the great *bel canto* operas of Bellini, Donizetti, and Rossini were in their heyday, performed by a group of singers whose fame was the equivalent of modern movie stars'. The Opéra-Comique was slightly less starry than the Italien, but immensely popular. There, Daniel Auber was king. In a long career (he died in 1871 in his ninetieth year), Auber wrote forty-four operas, most of them for the Opéra-Comique and most of them with Scribe as librettist. His fame was by no means confined to France. *Fra Diavolo*, his 1830 opera about a Neapolitan bandit chief, was given in London and Philadelphia within a year of its Paris premiere and remained a popular repertoire opera for many years. François-Adrien Boïeldieu contributed *La dame blanche* in 1825, an opera set in Scotland with a libretto by Scribe (of course) based on novels by Walter Scott; it was one of the most enduringly popular works of the century. Ferdinand Hérold died very young in 1833, but his last work for the stage, *Le pré aux clercs* (The Clerks' Meadow), had no fewer than 145 performances at the Opéra-Comique in a single year. Donizetti wrote *La fille du régiment* for the same theater in 1840, and the list of lesser composers is long and by no means undistinguished—Halévy, Adam, Flotow, Balfe, among many others.

It was a plethora of operatic activity, and it was all taking place in Paris at the time when the bourgeoisie came into its own. The man of the moment turned out to be Giacomo Meyerbeer.

MEYERBEER

He was neither French nor Italian. He was a German Jew from Berlin whose given name was Jakob Beer. As a young man he had had very little success in his own country. It was Antonio Salieri, Mozart's old sparring partner, who advised him to go to Italy. Meyerbeer arrived in Venice as a twenty-five-year-old, at a time when Rossini's *Tancredi* was playing at La Fenice, and it was the inspiration of this work that caused him to start all over again and to study the art of the *opera seria*. Between 1818 and 1824 he wrote thirteen operas in the style of Rossini, of which the last, *Il crociato in Egitto* (The Crusader in Egypt) brought him international celebrity and his introduction to Paris at the Théâtre-Italien.

Meyerbeer understood instinctively that Paris was where he had to be. He made it his home and began the long process of assimilating all things French—culture, language and history. This was a man who was a few months older than Rossini, who had already once undergone the rigors of changing his musical nationality, when he moved from Germany to Italy, and who had finally achieved international fame in his mid-thirties. Yet he was prepared to go through the process all over again, and to suffer the necessary five-year creative silence before he was ready to write an opera in his new language. That speaks of a powerfully motivated man.

Meyerbeer may have been an assimilator, but he was not an imitator. As a musician he was a craftsman, perhaps, rather than a great original, but as a dramatist he had few peers until Verdi and Wagner produced their mature works. His passion was theater, and just as he conquered three very different musical styles—German, Italian, and French—so he adapted those styles to the demands of the drama. He was the Cecil B. DeMille of his day, an orchestrator of vast forces who supervised every detail of the productions. His letters to Scribe are like those of Verdi to Piave and Richard Strauss to Hofmannsthal—ordering, checking, and revising the librettos almost down to the punctuation. The set designers at the Paris Opéra—Duponchel, Cicéri, and their colleagues—were treated as his collaborators, not his servants, and he himself was always there to oversee the staging, bringing together the individual elements of the set pieces for maximum effect to create the ensembles, the ballets, and the choruses.

Among much other music, Meyerbeer's legacy to *grand opéra* consisted of four principal works: *Robert le diable* (1831), *Les Huguenots* (1836), *Le prophète* (1849), and the posthumous *L'africaine* (1865). All of them were painted on large historical canvases, and the subject matter was often daring. After the Faust-like tale of *Robert*, *Les Huguenots* brought its audience face-to-face with religious

persecution in sixteenth-century France, culminating in the St. Bartholomew's Day Massacre of 1572, one of those great crimes that still reverberated down the years. *Le prophète* was also about religious strife, this time in Holland, during the Anabaptist uprising in the 1530s. And *L'africaine* (The African Girl), even more ambitious, was set in Portugal and India, as well as at sea: it was the story of Vasco da Gama.

The shared characteristic of these operas, apart from their scale and length, was the opportunity they gave to stage directors, dancers, chorus, and singers to arouse the audience (with or without the help of Auguste and his men) to demonstrations of enormous enthusiasm. Whatever they may have thought about the individual ingredients, most observers agreed that Meyerbeer's operas were hugely exciting events: they invited audiences to suspend their critical faculties.

Stars of the Opéra

Meyerbeer's operas "had better not be sung at all than indifferently," wrote Gustave Kobbé in his *Complete Opera Book*.[19] Meyerbeer's letters and diaries show a man who was constantly going to theaters to see and hear new singers, as concerned with their acting abilities as with their musicianship. Paris was awash with fine singers in the 1830s, but many of them—the Malibrans and Rubinis and Sontags—were there to sing at the long-running *bel canto* festival at the Théâtre-Italien. The wide-open spaces of the Opéra and the huge orchestrations of Meyerbeer were not for them. But there was talent enough to go around, and much of it was already employed at the Opéra when Meyerbeer arrived.

The soprano Laure Cinti-Damoreau was high on the list. She had the unique distinction of being the leading lady in each of the first three *grands opéras*, each for a different composer: *La muette de Portici* for Auber, *Guillaume Tell* for Rossini, and *Robert le diable* for Meyerbeer. The other big soprano role in *Robert* was given to Julie Dorus-Gras, a recent arrival from her home in Belgium. She came with a story to tell. She had been singing Elvira in a Brussels performance of *La muette de Portici* on a night in September 1830, when the performance had ignited a revolt in the Low Countries. The story of the Neapolitan fishermen's insurrection two centuries before had touched a nerve with the populace and inspired a revolution.

In short order, however, these two singers were superseded by a much greater star. She was

Cornélie Falcon, a tall, black-haired French-woman who bewitched the Paris Opéra from the moment she arrived as a twenty-year-old straight from the conservatoire. As with Malibran, it was the combination of her voice and her presence that made her so attractive. Donizetti, one of her greatest admirers, described the voice as "veiled," and *falcon* is a term still used to describe such a voice. She quickly became the outstanding Alice in *Robert*, and a famous interpreter of Donna Anna in Mozart's *Don Giovanni*. She created the blazing role of Rachel in Halévy's *La juive*, and she was Meyerbeer's Valentine in *Les Huguenots*. But Cornélie Falcon was not, in the end, a real star: she was a meteor. Her career ended abruptly after six years, when she lost her voice. Her disappearance from the stage of the Opéra more or less coincided with the arrival of a much more powerful lady (though a lesser singer). This was Rosine Stoltz, who dominated the Opéra for ten years by the simple expedient of becoming the mistress of the theater's manager, Léon Pillet. Her power was demonstrated in the number of leading mezzo-soprano roles composers wrote to accommodate her (Donizetti's *La favorite* and *Dom Sébastien* were prime examples). Stoltz was as unscrupulous as she was ambitious, and as successful as any prima donna has ever been in the amassing of titles. Successive marriages (after Pillet) made her a baroness, a countess, and a princess. She might have gone even farther had she succeeded in making Dom Pedro, the opera-loving emperor of Brazil, her husband instead of just her lover.

Stoltz was blamed (rightly or wrongly, it is not known) for the fact that Jenny Lind never sang at the Paris Opéra. But Lind did sing for Meyerbeer; indeed, he wrote a role especially for her. *Ein Feldlager in Schlesien* (The Encampment in Silesia) was the only one of Meyerbeer's mature operas not to originate in Paris. He wrote it in 1844 for his native city, Berlin, where he was the nonresident *Generalmusikdirektor* throughout much of the 1840s. It was a very Prussian opera, based on an episode in the life of Frederick the Great. In various revisions it was also known as *Vielka* in Vienna, and *L'étoile du nord* in Paris, where it played at the Opéra-Comique rather than the Opéra. But by that time (1854), the "Swedish Nightingale," still in her early thirties, had already been retired from the opera stage for five years.

María Malibran was also lost to opera—dead at the age of twenty-eight—but her younger

sister, Pauline, was in the middle of a great career. Known by her married name of Viardot, Pauline's soprano voice was even lower than her sister's; today it would be called mezzo-soprano. She had managed the (soprano) role of Valentine in *Les Huguenots* with great success, but in 1849, with *Le prophète*, Meyerbeer wrote a leading role that was tailored to Pauline's voice. At the Paris Opéra she created Fidès, the prophet's mother, to great acclaim. In her long life (she lived to be eighty-eight) she was renowned not just as a singer and teacher, but also as a composer of operettas and as a poet and painter. For many years she lived with the Russian writer Ivan Turgenev, who wrote her librettos.

Of the male singers at the Paris Opéra, three stood out. One of them was Nicolas Prosper Levasseur, a bass whose career was going nowhere until Auber, Rossini, Donizetti, and Meyerbeer began to provide him with great dramatic roles. He was nearly forty when he joined the Opéra in 1828, but he sang there for twenty-five years, creating all the great bass roles of *grand opéra*. His influence was great, but it was nothing compared to that of Adolphe Nourrit.

Nourrit was the tenor who had had trouble with the role of Arnold in Rossini's *Guillaume*

Cornélie Falcon (1812–1897). Donizetti wrote of her, "After she sang for a short time, her voice seemed veiled."

Tell, but that was no reflection on him—most tenors have trouble with that role. He learned his art from Manuel García, father of María Malibran and Pauline Viardot, and himself the first Almaviva in *Il barbiere di Siviglia*. Nourrit, like Cornélie Falcon with whom he sang so often, had the musical instinct to realize that the old Italian style in which Garcia had trained him would not suffice in the new world of *grand opéra*. A critic writing in *La revue musicale* in 1829 (just after the unhappy *Guillaume Tell* experience) noted that Nourrit was "the first to understand that something besides declamation is possible at the Opéra, and to take a just middle ground between the exaggerated dramatic expression of the old French school and the excessive embellishments of the Italian singers."[20] Nourrit was more than just a singer: he gave advice (which they took) to both Halévy and Meyerbeer on the construction of their operas; he wrote the words of several arias attributed to Scribe; and he created dance scenarios for both Taglioni and Fanny Elssler. More than all of this, he had been a popular hero of the 1830 Revolution: he had marched at the head of a column, and he had sung the "Marseillaise" and other patriotic songs for the crowds. Eventually, and far too early, he was eclipsed at the Opéra by the arrival of a greater tenor, Gilbert-Louis Duprez—one of the few who never had any trouble with Rossini's Arnold.

Duprez's voice was one of the wonders of

the age. By the time he arrived at the Paris Opéra in 1837, he had already created the role of Edgardo in Donizetti's *Lucia di Lammermoor* (a major test for any lyric tenor), but his voice was also large enough and strong enough to take over Nourrit's *grand opéra* roles in works by Halévy and Meyerbeer. He was the star of two other premieres at the Opéra: Donizetti's *La favorite* and Berlioz's *Benvenuto Cellini*. But Duprez's greatest fame was as the first tenor to sing his high C's from the chest—rather than falsetto, which was the usual practice of the time. Nourrit, who could not compete, left the Opéra immediately upon Duprez's arrival and unhappily ended his life less than two years later by leaping out of a window in Naples. He was only thirty-seven. Duprez, on the other hand, lived to be ninety—a famous teacher and a composer of forgotten operas.

When Meyerbeer needed a tenor for the part of John of Leyden in *Le prophète*, neither Nourrit (who was dead) nor Duprez (who had retired from the stage to teach at the conservatoire) was available. Gustave Roger, whom Meyerbeer had not previously heard, had been singing with Pauline Viardot in London: he was more or less forced on Meyerbeer by Pauline's husband and manager, Louis Viardot. It turned out to be a piece of great good fortune. Roger was given a series of extraordinary ovations on opening night, every bit as great as those extended to Viardot, and almost as great as those accorded to the scenery.

Le prophète outdid even *Les Huguenots* in its initial success at the Opéra, and the scenic effects were certainly part of the reason. Indeed, if the conflagration at the end of the opera, in which the prophet blows up himself and his mother as well as a battalion of imperial troops, is never mentioned in the music, spectators at the Paris Opéra could be excused for not noticing that fact. But *Le prophète* was even more famous for its ballet, which was performed on roller skates. "Les Patineurs" (The Skaters) is in the repertoires of many leading dance companies to this day, but it is rarely seen, as Meyerbeer intended it should be, as part of his opera. In Paris it set off the craze for roller skating on what were advertised as "Prophet skates." It is a reminder that, however fine the leading singers were deemed to be at the Opéra (even the Falcons and the Viardots, the Nourrits

and the Duprezes), they were frequently upstaged by the ballerinas. Contemporary accounts leave no doubt that the greatest individual sensation of *Robert le diable* in 1831 was Marie Taglioni in the dancing role of the evil abbess.

Meyerbeer's final contribution to *grand opéra* turned out to be posthumous. He completed the score of *L'africaine*, on which he had worked for almost twenty years, the day before he died in 1864. It was staged at the Opéra the next year. Meyerbeer himself thought it was the finest thing he had ever written. Parisian audiences did not share that view, but they did think it was the most amazing thing they had ever seen. The ending of Act III, in which Don Pedro's ship was wrecked and sunk by a massive storm, gave the *spectacles d'optique* team the best opportunity it had ever had, and it took extravagant advantage of it.

So this was the age of *grand opéra* in Paris—an extraordinary chapter in the history of *dramma per musica*. It was the first time that a major opera house had blatantly based its policy on the assumption that the music was only as important as the spectacle. It was a collaboration by a group of people—of whom Véron, Duponchel, Cicéri,

Scribe, and Meyerbeer were the leaders—for whom the commercial success of a work was at least as vital as its artistic success. It was wildly popular, and it remained popular for most of the nineteenth century, not just in Paris but in theaters like New York's Metropolitan Opera, which were able to mount spectacular productions with a roster of stars to match. At the height of its international popularity, Meyerbeer's last opera, *L'africaine*, was staged in London, New York, St. Petersburg, Berlin, Madrid, Lvov, Vienna, Budapest, Havana, and Sydney—all of them within twelve months of the Paris premiere.[21]

Not only was *grand opéra* popular, it was also highly influential. Wagner, Berlioz, and others wrote endlessly about it. But it would take a musician of much greater stature than Meyerbeer and his colleagues to bring it to its zenith. That musician was Giuseppe Verdi. He never liked "la grande boutique," but he spent a great deal of time in Paris between 1847 and 1857, and he wanted to succeed there. He never did—certainly not by his standards. *Jérusalem* in 1847 was a French adaptation of his earlier *I lombardi*. Then, in 1855, he wrote a brand-new work in French, clearly modeled on

The Act III finale of Meyerbeer's L'africaine. *Engraving after the first performance, April 28, 1865. The sinking of the ship was one of the most spectacular pieces of staging at the Paris Opéra.*

the *grand opéra* style. *Les vêpres siciliennes* (The Sicilian Vespers) was about the massacre of a French army of occupation in medieval Sicily—not exactly a tactful subject to choose for Paris, though it was certainly *grand*. Finally, in 1867, two years after the posthumous premiere of Meyerbeer's *L'africaine*, Verdi returned to Paris with *Don Carlos*, arguably the finest of all *grands opéras*.

Don Carlos was politely, but rather coolly, received in Paris (and it was not performed there again until 1963). But in London and Bologna, it was greeted with great enthusiasm, and its Italian version, first seen at La Scala in 1884, was always popular. Verdi swore he would never again write for the Paris Opéra, and he never did. The plain fact, however, is that between the mature Verdi and the mature Meyerbeer there was a musical chasm that has been recognized by twentieth-century operagoers. That is the most important reason why Verdi's operas so dominate the modern repertoire and why Meyerbeer's are performed only rarely, and generally in shortened and edited form.

Nevertheless, what happened at the Paris Opéra in the forty years between Auber's *La muette de Portici* and Verdi's *Don Carlos* was not an ephemeral thing. It had lasting importance in the story of opera because it revealed the real potential for *dramma per musica* when words, music, and spectacle were combined in a single streamlined entity. Verdi's *Otello* and Wagner's *Tristan und Isolde* would certainly have come about whether or not Cicéri and Scribe and Meyerbeer had dominated the Paris Opéra in the middle years of the century, but audiences might not have been as receptive to those works if their expectations had not been fed by the experience of Parisian *grand opéra*.

THE CASE OF BERLIOZ

Grand opéra was essentially cosmopolitan. It was not specifically French—not in a nationalist sense, at any rate. It had few roots in the folklore of France, and no particular reason for being in the French language except that it had originated in Paris. But there were other currents flowing around the world of French music at this time.

Surely the greatest French musician of the nineteenth century was Hector Berlioz, yet when he died in 1869 it seemed that he had contributed little to operatic history. It took a hundred years and a revival of his works in Britain (of all countries) to show how false that judgment had been.

The years of Berlioz's maturity coincided almost exactly with the reign of Meyerbeer at the Opéra. That one fact alone might have accounted for Berlioz's being absent from the operatic scene. But he was not absent. In 1838, he composed *Benvenuto Cellini* for the Opéra. It had twenty-nine rehearsals and only seven performances. In 1862, he composed *Béatrice et Bénédict* for the Baden Festival in Germany, but it was not performed in Paris until twenty years after his death. And between 1856 and 1858, he labored over one of the greatest works in operatic history: *Les troyens*. It was never performed in his lifetime, unless you count a truncated version of Part II, which was given twenty-one performances at the Théâtre-Lyrique in 1863.

Such a miserable record of performances requires some form of explanation. One reason, no doubt, was that Berlioz made his living as a music critic, and a pretty vicious one at that; he had many enemies. The great bulk of his own work, of course, was not operatic, yet opera was very important to him. He was perhaps the most theatrical by temperament of all the Romantic musicians of the era, and drama was ever present in his thinking and his experience. He was constantly at the theater, a frequent (and loquacious) visitor to the Opéra. Most of his music was dramatic in conception, if not in form, from the program symphony the *Symphonie fantastique* to the "dramatic legend" *La damnation de Faust*. But his operas did not fit tidily into any convenient format. *Benvenuto Cellini*, based on the life of the great Florentine goldsmith and sculptor of the sixteenth century, was neither *grand* nor comic—though it contained scenes of high comedy (with the pope as the chief comedian) and one of the grandest scenes in all opera, the Roman Carnival. *Les troyens*, on the other hand, was grander than anything ever conceived by Meyerbeer and larger in scale than *Tristan und Isolde*, on which Wagner was working at precisely the same time.

Already wounded by the failure of *Cellini*, Berlioz nursed the idea of an epic work drawn from the second and fourth books of Virgil's *Aeneid*: "To me the subject seems magnificent and deeply moving—sure proof that Parisians would think it flat and tedious"[22] (he did not have a high opinion of his audience). Nevertheless, urged on by Liszt, Berlioz devoted just over two years of his life to the project and completed it in April 1858.

Les troyens is a homage to two of the literary gods in Berlioz's life: Virgil, whom he had stud-

ied on his father's knee, and Shakespeare, for whom he had conceived a passion while he was in love with the English actress Harriet Smithson. Shakespeare's love scene between Jessica and Lorenzo in *The Merchant of Venice*,

> In such a night
> Stood Dido with a willow in her
> /hand
> Upon the wild sea-banks, and waft
> /her love
> To come again to Carthage

became, in Berlioz's hands, "Nuit d'ivresse et d'extase infinie"—a love duet between Aeneas, the Trojan hero, and Dido, the queen of Carthage, that bears comparison with the love duet in *Tristan*, or with any other love duet in opera.

There were occasional performances of *Les troyens* in the hundred years after Berlioz's death, but they were mostly in translations and almost always in edited and truncated versions. Not until 1957 was a production staged, at London's Royal Opera House, that would have been entirely recognizable to the composer (though it was in English), and not until the centenary in 1969 of the composer's death was the work restored to its full glory by Colin Davis, with an authentic version of the orchestral score prepared by Hugh Macdonald. Throughout the intervening period, the world

Berlioz's Benvenuto Cellini *at Covent Garden, London, 1966. Directed by John Dexter, designed by Beni Montrésor. Nicolai Gedda sang the title role.*

of opera was denied full access to one of its central works. It was as though *Tristan und Isolde* had never been properly seen or heard until the mid-twentieth century. The only comparable loss in music was the disappearance of Bach's *St. Matthew Passion* until its rediscovery by Felix Mendelssohn.

Berlioz had no Bayreuth and no King Ludwig. Nor did he have ready access to the opera houses of Paris—denied as a result of his own vitriolic pen, as much as anything else. It was certainly true that the forces required to perform *Les troyens* were very large (though less than those for the *Ring* and not much more than those required for the operas of Meyerbeer and Halévy). But the real reason for the neglect of *Les troyens* was none of the above. It was rumor, pure and simple—the unverified, widely accepted rumor that *Les troyens*, while it had some good things in it, was quite unstageable. Wagner suffered from the same kind of rumors, of course, but he had the good fortune to be able to prove them wrong. Berlioz did not.

Just as Berlioz towers over his French contemporaries, so *Les troyens* towers over all other French operas of the nineteenth century. But that was not understood at the time. When Berlioz died, in 1869, Charles Gounod remarked that, like his namesake Hector, Berlioz had died beneath the walls of Troy, and there was a certain truth in that. Others—Gounod himself, and Bizet, Massenet, Saint-Saëns, Chabrier, Lalo, Delibes, and Thomas —were perceived as having contributed a great deal more than Berlioz had to French opera.

THE TRIUMPH OF FRENCH OPERA

Initially, these young composers were not helped by the conservatism of the main Parisian theaters. Between 1852 and 1870, the Opéra staged only five new French operas. The Opéra-Comique was not much better: it existed on a diet of successful works from the first half of the century—a profusion of Auber, Boïeldieu, and Adam. But intriguing things were happening in French music, and eventually, during the last three decades of the century, the major houses woke up to the fact and profited greatly from it. They no longer had much competition from the Théâtre-Italien. In the early 1880s, that great institution finally went out of business. In eight decades, it had run through eight separate homes, four bankruptcies, and more than twenty changes of management. Its production standards had generally been low (in a city that

prided itself on the mise-en-scène), but at times, most notably between 1825 and 1845, it had generated tremendous excitement—the excitement of some of the greatest voices the world of opera had ever known.

The Opéra in rue Le Peletier burned down in 1873. It was quickly replaced by Charles Garnier's magnificent new theater, and younger composers, notably Gounod and Massenet, came to dominate it. The Opéra-Comique had similar misadventures with fire, but it never ceased to operate for long. It was there that works as varied as *Carmen* by Bizet, *Lakmé* by Delibes, *Manon* by Massenet, *Le roi d'Ys* by Lalo, and *Les contes d'Hoffmann* (The Tales of Hoffmann) by Offenbach first saw the light of day. Meanwhile, at the Bouffes-Parisiens, just off the Champs-Élysées, Jacques Offenbach established a form of musical theater whose popularity could only be compared to that of Broadway in the twentieth century. And amid all this activity, the two most popular operas ever written came into being: *Faust* and *Carmen*.

In 1869, only four years after the rapturous reception of Meyerbeer's *L'africaine*, Charles Gounod revised his *Faust* in preparation for its new production at the Opéra. The work was already ten years old and very successful. It had played in London and New York as well as in Paris, but its Paris home had always been the Théâtre-Lyrique rather than one of the major opera houses. Now, for its staging at the Opéra, Gounod composed recitatives to replace its spoken dialogue and added the compulsory ballet. In this, its final form, *Faust* was formally enthroned at the Paris Opéra, where it has reigned ever since. It became one of the most notable French exports of the nineteenth and twentieth centuries. It was the opera chosen to inaugurate the original Metropolitan Opera House in New York in 1883, and the frequency of its performance there led, in time, to a not-so-frivolous suggestion that the splendid theater should be renamed the "Faustspielhaus."[23]

Sugary and sentimental it might have been, but Gounod lavished on *Faust* a torrent of melodies. In its final version, with ballet and recitatives and grand choruses and a five-act format, it observed the conventions of *grand opéra*, but it was not dramatic or epic in the way that Meyerbeer's operas had been. It was something much more enduring: a masterpiece of an essentially lyrical kind.

Even before *Faust*, Gounod had established himself as a writer of *opéras-comiques*. *Le médecin mal-*

gré lui (The Doctor Despite Himself) was a charming comedy based on Molière's popular play, and it had won him the affection of Parisian audiences. But the success of *Faust* changed everything. He sought to replicate it in a series of large-scale works, of which *Roméo et Juliette* and *Mireille* are the survivors. Neither of them approached *Faust*, though *Roméo*, which played at the Théâtre-Lyrique during the Great Universal Exposition of 1867, contained some of his finest music and had a considerable success. To all these works Gounod brought two very important skills: his talent for melody, of course, but also a method of setting verse that was freer and less predictable than that of his predecessors. He was not yet fifty when he completed *Roméo*, and he would live for another twenty years, but there were no more successful operas. The two sides of his life, the religious and the worldly, seemed to compete for supremacy. As a young man, he had served a novitiate in a monastery (he liked to be addressed as the "Abbé Gounod"), but he was also an active admirer of women—a "philandering monk," as some of his amused colleagues described him. In the end, he chose to concentrate on his religious music.

Meanwhile, another greatly talented French composer had come and gone. Georges Bizet was only thirty-six when he died in 1875, but in that year he staged the only opera that has come within striking distance of *Faust* so far as worldwide popularity is concerned. As tastes and fashions have changed, the popularity of *Faust* has faded. But *Carmen* has not.

What *Carmen* had in common with *Faust* was a wonderful excess of melody, but there the comparison ended. *Faust* was immediately recognized by audiences as a brilliantly executed product of a genre with which they were familiar and with which they felt entirely comfortable. *Carmen*, on the other hand, made them uncomfortable. It was seemingly about real people in real places; it portrayed a seamy tragedy; worst of all, the crime of passion that climaxed the tragedy was played out onstage, with nothing left to the imagination. This was not like the safe thrill of observing the Opéra's *spectacles d'optique*. This was instead alto-

Gounod's FAUST *at the Welsh National Opera, 1996. Directed by Christopher Alden, designed by Bruno Schwengl. With Paul Charles Clarke as Faust and Alastair Miles as Méphistophélès.*

gether too real, too shocking, certainly not what was expected in the opera house. It was, in fact, the forerunner of a short-lived school of opera that would be known by its Italian name, *verismo* (realistic). It became one of the most popular forms of opera ever created, but it is also a commodity in short supply. Few composers have had the dramatic skills to confront it successfully.

Carmen first played at the Opéra-Comique, because it had spoken dialogue, and was coolly received. There were forty-eight performances, but the later audiences were small and not overly enthusiastic. Bizet died three months after the premiere without knowing the extent of his achievement. Not until it had been successfully staged in Brussels, Vienna, London, and New York did *Carmen* return triumphantly to Paris in 1883. As the only opera of his maturity—the earlier *Les pêcheurs de perles* (The Pearlfishers), *La jolie fille de Perth* (The Fair Maid of Perth), and *Djamileh* all contained some wonderful music set to frighteningly dreadful librettos—*Carmen* was a testament to what might have been.

"That little fellow is about to walk all over us," Bizet remarked shortly before his death.[24] The little fellow in question was Jules Massenet, and Bizet was right. Massenet, ever intent on pleasing his public and every bit as commercial as Meyerbeer, turned out twenty-seven crowd-pleasing operas between 1877 and 1910. *Manon* and *Werther* are the two that have traveled best, but in his day, and for about thirty years thereafter, Massenet's

popularity was enormous. He possessed a wonderful facility for writing music. There was nothing onerous or difficult about it for him, yet he was not merely facile either. "Yes," he told his colleague Vincent d'Indy, "we must always agree with the public,"[25] so he wrote operas that combined elements of many successful styles—Tchaikovskyan, Wagnerian, sometimes approaching the near-*verismo* example of Bizet. And if the public liked it, then so did the singers. Every one of Massenet's principal operas contained at least one major role for a great singer: *Thaïs, Le Cid, Hérodiade,* and *Don Quichotte* all afford the sorts of roles singers longed for. "That little fellow" became extremely rich.

No other French composer of the period approached the triumphs of Massenet or the impact of Gounod and Bizet, but several had substantial successes. At a time when Verdi was extending the Italian repertoire by leaps and bounds, and Wagner was dominating the German scene, and Russian and Czech composers were finally finding their voices, French opera rode the crest of a wave. It was no longer dependent on resident foreigners. Instead, there was a whole generation of native French composers vying to get their works produced at one of Paris's many musical theaters. Camille Saint-Saëns succeeded with *Samson et Dalila* (though it was first produced for Weimar and did not reach Paris until thirteen years later, in 1890). Ambroise Thomas succeeded with *Mignon* and *Hamlet.* So did Emmanuel Chabrier

with *L'étoile* (The Star) and *Le roi malgré lui* (The Reluctant King). And Léo Delibes garnished his reputation as the finest ballet composer of the generation (after Tchaikovsky) with *Lakmé,* an opera that exploited the fashion for things Eastern.

All these operas, and many more that have not endured, received expensive, elaborate, and generally magnificent productions. The mise-en-scène continued to be one of the glories of French opera, with long rehearsal schedules sometimes leaving time for relatively few public performances. And all this happened against the background of multiple revolutions (1830, 1848, 1870), a coup d'état (1851), occupation by an alien power (1870), and a brief rule by the Commune in 1871. Paris was a living theater in itself.

Wagner was not popular in Paris—neither before the Franco-Prussian War of 1870 nor afterward. The Jockey Club disposed of *Tannhäuser* in 1861, and the next attempt to stage one of his works at the Opéra, *Lohengrin* in 1891, was greeted by rioting outside the theater. But Wagner's influence on French composers could not be denied. "Le Petit Bayreuth" was a phrase often used to identify those thought to be tarred with that brush. Chabrier was probably the most obvious. His 1886 opera *Gwendoline* was an epic tale of medieval England full of eccentric (some would say "liberated") harmony, and threaded throughout with leitmotifs. Wagner had set an agenda that could not be ignored, and many other French composers could be accused of complicity: Saint-Saëns and Massenet, for certain. Some critics even claimed that Gounod's *Faust* was in large part an exercise in Wagnerian harmony, orchestral narrative, and thematic development. If so, it did not make the work any less French, or any less good.

THE LEADING FRENCH SINGERS

French opera required French singers—or French-taught singers, at least—and for them, the last quarter of the nineteenth century was an outstanding time. It was epitomized by the de Reszke brothers: Jean was the greatest tenor of the age, and Édouard, one of the greatest basses. They came from Poland, but it was in Paris, and with French music, that they made their names. Jean was the true successor of Nourrit and Duprez, but with a wider range than either. His first biographer, Clara Leiser,[26] suggested that his breakthrough resulted from the happy accident of his being in a music shop reading through scores (and

Mᵐᵉ SIBYL SANDERSON & M. DELMAS
dans « Thaïs », à l'Opéra

MASSENET'S THAÏS

ABOVE: *Poster for the premiere at the Paris Opéra, 1894.*

LEFT: *Sibyl Sanderson as Thaïs at the Paris Opéra. Cover of* Le petit journal, *1894. The creator of the role of Thaïs, Sanderson, an American, was also said to be Massenet's favorite Manon.*

singing away at the top of his voice) when
Massenet came by to order some sheet music.
Hearing the young man's voice, and being in
urgent need of a tenor to sing John the Baptist in
his new opera *Hérodiade*, Massenet offered him the
role on the spot. An unlikely story—but de
Reszke did sing in the premiere of *Hérodiade*, and
Massenet subsequently wrote the title role of *Le
Cid* especially for him. De Reszke was blessed with
more than just a great voice: he had the looks of a
matinée idol ("one of the beautiful ones," George
Bernard Shaw said), and he enjoyed tremendous
success on both sides of the Atlantic in parts as
varied as Radamès in *Aida*, Vasco da Gama in
L'africaine, Faust and Roméo in Gounod's operas,
and Tristan, Siegfried, and Lohengrin in Wagner's. With all this prodigious talent to support, he
adopted the habit of keeping a throat specialist on
hand so that his vocal cords could be constantly
sprayed.[27] He was, his colleagues reported, a very
nervous performer.[28]

Édouard de Reszke had none of his broth-
er's dedication or finesse (he was plain stupid, said
Shaw), but he possessed, by all accounts, one of
the greatest bass voices ever heard on the opera
stage, with a range of roles that is breathtaking by modern standards—from Gounod's
Méphistophélès to Wagner's Hagen, from
Mozart's Leporello to Bellini's Giorgio in *I puritani*. Like his brother Jean, he was handsome to a
fault, very tall with an imposing stage presence,
but unlike Jean, singing on stage was no great
effort for him: he loved it. Sadly, he died during
the third year of World War I, living in poverty
in a cave near the family estates in Poland.

In 1884–85, there were performances of
Hérodiade in Paris in which no fewer than three de
Reszkes appeared—the two brothers as well as
their younger sister Joséphine. She was a soprano
who sang mainly at the Paris Opéra from 1875
until her marriage and retirement ten years later.

The de Reszke brothers were French by
adoption, but there were several other outstanding male singers of that generation who were
French by birth. One was Pol Plançon, a bass
whose repertoire duplicated Édouard de Reszke's
but whose vocal technique was more spectacular.
Contemporaries described him as a *bel canto* singer
whose runs and trills were the envy of many sopranos. He had the even more uncommon distinction
of being dismissed from the Opéra, in 1893, on
account of his sexual predilections (he was homo-

sexual), but he continued his singing career to great
acclaim in London and New York. Until the
appearance of the great Russian bass Fyodor
Chaliapin in the early years of the new century, no
one was more closely identified with Gounod's
Méphistophélès than was Plançon.

Jean-Baptiste Faure was another famous
Méphistophélès, but he was more of a bass-baritone (what the French called a *baryton-noble*). He
created the roles of Nélusko in *L'africaine* for
Meyerbeer and Posa in *Don Carlos* for Verdi, as
well as the title role in Thomas's *Hamlet*. Faure was
greatly admired as Rossini's Guillaume Tell and
Mozart's Don Giovanni. By the time he retired
from the stage in 1886 (to write two important
books about the art of singing), his place had been
taken by two baritones whose careers outshone
even his. Jean Lassalle was certainly the more
musical of them. The doyen of opera writers at
that time, Herman Klein, called him "the posses-
sor of probably the noblest male voice that France
produced during the nineteenth century."[29] Lassalle was also a close friend of the de Reszke
brothers and sang with them repeatedly in Europe
and America. But his fame was exceeded, and outlasted, by that of his contemporary, Victor Mau-

rel. Like all these international stars, Maurel sang in the German and Italian repertoires as well as the French, but in his case it was the Italian repertoire that gave him a place in history: he was chosen by Verdi to create the two greatest baritone roles in Italian opera, Iago and Falstaff. There could be no greater compliment than that. Maurel's voice was never considered to be as beautiful an instrument as Lassalle's or Faure's, but Maurel had the advantage of being a good actor as well. Reviews of his performances almost always dwelt on his contribution to the drama and the force of his presence on the stage.

If you were a female singer at this time, and if you had ambitions to conquer the world of opera, then at some time or another you would probably have had to face what was likely to be an unpleasant experience: a spell at the École Marchesi in the rue Jouffroy in Paris. The presiding genius of the École was Madame Mathilde Marchesi de Castrone, aptly described by one of her most noted pupils, Emma Eames, as the "ideal Prussian drill master."[30] Marchesi had started life in Frankfurt as Fraulein Graumann. She was a pupil of the greatest voice teacher of the century, Manuel García the Younger. It was García who first noticed her abilities as a teacher, and eventually he handed over most of his pupils to her. In the rue Jouffroy, for more than thirty years at the end of the nineteenth century and the beginning of the twentieth, she trained and drilled a roster of remarkable voices. They included those of Nellie Melba, Emma Calvé, Mary Garden, and Emma Eames. Not many of them lasted long at the rue Jouffroy (Mary Garden left almost before she arrived), but none of them ever forgot the experience (and, in the case of Emma Eames, never forgave it either).

The Marchesi method was unique, and somewhat dangerous. It went against all the accepted Italian methods of the day, including García's, by concentrating on what is called *placement*—on "placing" the voice high on the breath so as to maximize the brilliance of the tones. There is a very early cylinder recording, made during a live performance at the Metropolitan Opera by the house librarian, Lionel Mapleson, in which Melba sings the queen's aria from *Les Huguenots*. It is the finest example we have of the Marchesi method in action—a staggering demonstration of virtuosity and power, and this is clear despite the appalling background noise that necessarily disfigures Mapleson's recordings.[31] The danger of the Marchesi method was the damage it could do to the top of the voice if the method was insufficiently practiced, or the voice insufficiently strong.

Adelina Patti was the greatest diva of the last quarter of the nineteenth century. Although she rarely appeared in her native Italy, her repertoire was largely Italian. It encompassed all the great coloratura parts of the *bel canto* age, along with some dramatic roles as modern as Aida. In French, she sang Meyerbeer, Gounod, Thomas's Mignon, and even Carmen, and she appeared regularly, though expensively, in Paris. In the 1880s, she was earning as much as five thousand dollars a performance in America. When it was pointed out to her that this was more than the president of the United States earned in a year, she said, "Well, let him sing!" As Patti's career moved toward its close, Nellie Melba's took off. She was Australia's first significant contribution to the story of opera. For forty years, Melba, and later Enrico Caruso, were the most celebrated singers in the world. But not far behind were three women—a Frenchwoman, an American, and a Scot—who could all claim to belong to the French tradition. Like Melba, they were all pupils of Marchesi.

Emma Calvé was the Frenchwoman. To most people she was simply Carmen. The Marchesi method never did her a lot of good (she was there for only six months), and her singing voice was much higher than most Carmens', but she had a personality, both on and off the stage, that made her a favorite wherever she went.

The American was Emma Eames, a woman with rare beauty and an exquisite voice. Headstrong, and no doubt badly advised, she encountered vocal problems that eventually forced her retirement at the age of forty-four. In her rather scurrilous and self-serving memoirs, she put most of the blame on Madame Marchesi's method, but it might have been more appropriate to have questioned her own choice of roles. An ill-fated attempt to sing Tosca at New York's Metropolitan lasted four performances before she withdrew with "Toscalitis," as one critic tactfully described it.[32] Another (not so tactful) critic remarked of her chilly acting style in *Aida*: "Last night there was skating on the Nile."[33]

The Scot was Mary Garden. She defied all the known laws of the diva: she was tiny (no more than five feet and less than a hundred pounds); she

Mary Garden (1874–1967) as Jean in Le jongleur de Notre-Dame, *a role Massenet wrote for a tenor. The composer confessed himself "somewhat bemused" when Garden, very definitely a soprano, sang the role at the New York premiere (Hammerstein's Manhattan Opera, 1908). For Garden, and the audience, it was a great success, and she repeated the role many times during the next twenty years.*

was a natural and brilliant actress; and her voice appeared never to tire and never to give her any problems. The critics did not like the voice much—at times they were fairly cutting about it—but it was more than adequate to sustain her in a long career as a much-loved opera personality in Paris and New York, and most of all in Chicago. In another peculiarity for an international star, her repertoire was almost entirely French. More than anyone else, perhaps, she was identified with the operas of Massenet and those of a number of contemporary French composers, many now forgotten. If there is a single role with which her name will always be connected, it is the one she created at the Opéra-Comique in 1902: Mélisande.

DEBUSSY'S PELLÉAS ET MÉLISANDE

Ever since its first performance, Claude Debussy's opera *Pelléas et Mélisande* has caused division in the opera world. It has been passionately admired by some, and greatly reviled by many more. It belongs to no known category; it is entirely original.

"No place, no time, no big scene"—that was Debussy's prescription for an opera plot.[34] He found what he was looking for in the play *Pelléas et Mélisande,* written by the Belgian poet Maurice Maeterlinck in 1892. From it, he created an opera that was the very antithesis of *grand opéra.* There were twelve scenes, or tableaux, but the score was composed as a continuous whole, complete with orchestral interludes, with no breathless pauses for big numbers. The characters were timeless and mythic, but their dialogue was sparse and understated, not overblown and melodramatic as in the more conventional librettos of Scribe and his followers. The result was something strange and new, even for a generation that was coming to terms with Richard Wagner. It took Debussy nine years to complete the work, and its premiere at the Opéra-Comique in 1902 was accompanied by a great deal of controversy.

A large part of the trouble was caused by Maurice Maeterlinck. He had approved Debussy's plans for the opera and had dozed fitfully, prodded awake by his wife-to-be, when Debussy came to play through the score at the piano. The future Mrs. Maeterlinck was a well-known actress, Georgette Leblanc, and both she and Maeterlinck were under the impression that she would sing the part of Mélisande in the premiere at the Opéra-Comique. One day, however, they opened their

newspaper in Brussels and discovered that Mary Garden, not Leblanc, had been cast in the role. Their fury knew no bounds: they disavowed the opera; they wrote letters of denunciation to the newspapers; they inspired demonstrations outside the Opéra-Comique in an effort to disrupt rehearsals; and they devoutly wished for the opera's failure.

The premiere was only mildly successful, but the public controversy had served to cloak *Pelléas et Mélisande* in an aura of mystery, so that, within a comparatively short time, it became very successful at the box office. Mary Garden's performance was not the least of its attractions. For her, it was a wonderful vehicle. During rehearsals, Debussy had urged the singers to forget they were singers: he wanted them to concentrate on the words and the speech patterns, just as Musorgsky had before him and Janáček would after him. The diminutive figure of Mary Garden gave the role of Mélisande a naturalness and a vulnerability that might have eluded her more robust colleagues.

There was no doubt, of course, that Wagner was a major influence on Debussy. The obvious comparison was with *Tristan*—the symphonic treatment, the orchestral narrative, the story of forbidden love. But, in fact, the lovers were very different. Wagner's were certainly bewildered by what was happening to them, yet they were always able to articulate their feelings—at length. Maeterlinck's lovers had no such ability. Their speeches were brief, ambiguous, sometimes incomplete, often ending in questions. They could not find words for their emotions. It was left to Debussy's music to do that, in a subtle and imaginative way. It complemented the strange disorientation of the lovers, contrasted it with the angry certainties of Golaud (Mélisande's husband), and suggested in music what the participants could not bring themselves to say. Where speech was necessary, its natural patterns of inflection were taken up by the music, so that this most "unreal" drama was never far from reality—closer, perhaps, than *Tristan* had ever been.

The opera world was divided about *Pelléas.* There were those who believed it was the ultimate realization of *dramma per musica.* Others were profoundly bored by it. Those divisions remain to this day. It was Debussy's only excursion into opera (his only completed one, at any rate). In 1902 it stood alone, without precedent and unclassifiable. It remains unique.

Debussy's PELLÉAS ET MÉLISANDE *at the Metropolitan Opera, New York, 1995. Directed by Jonathan Miller, designed by John Conklin. With Frederica Von Stade as Mélisande and Dwayne Croft as Pelléas.*

OPERA OF THE PEOPLE

*I*TALY, FRANCE, AND GERMANY WERE NOT THE ONLY COUNTRIES TO HAVE ESTABLISHED NATIVE FORMS OF OPERA BY THE END OF THE NINETEENTH CENTURY, THOUGH THEY WERE CERTAINLY THE MOST IMPORTANT. THE NINETEENTH CENTURY WAS AN AGE OF NATIONALISM, WHEN SMALLER NATIONS STRUGGLED TO ESTABLISH THEIR IDENTITIES, BOTH POLITICALLY AND CULTURALLY. THE "CONCERT OF EUROPE" (AS THE POLITICIANS CALLED IT) DID NOT ALLOW FOR RADICAL CHANGE IN THE BALANCE OF POWER, YET THERE WAS WITHIN IT AN IMPLICIT RECOGNITION THAT CULTURAL NATIONHOOD WAS NOT A BAD THING — PROVIDED, OF COURSE, IT DID NOT GET IN THE WAY OF THE GREAT POWERS. THUS POLAND, EVEN THOUGH IT WAS PARTITIONED FOR MUCH OF THE CENTURY, MADE GREAT STRIDES IN CELEBRATING ITS ANCIENT HERITAGE AND DISTINCTIVE CULTURE. THE SAME WAS TRUE OF HUNGARY AND BOHEMIA, CROATIA AND SLOVENIA, EVEN THOUGH THEY ALL REMAINED UNDER HABSBURG RULE. IT WAS TRUE ALSO IN RUSSIA, WHERE THE AUTOCRATIC CZARS EXCHANGED THEIR WESTERN-DIRECTED CULTURAL POLICIES

for a new concern with Russian arts. In all these countries, the lyric stage had a significant nationalist role to play—becoming the opera of the people.

By definition, a national opera was one written in the vernacular language of the populace and rooted in the folklore of the land. There was no better example than *opéra-comique*. It had developed out of France's medieval agricultural fairs as a form of popular entertainment featuring music, theater, vaudeville, and a great deal of audience participation. It was crude, and in many ways more theatrical than musical, but it was an important part of the folk culture of France, and it was the basis for what, in the eighteenth century, became a very sophisticated, and very French, form of opera.

France was not the first country outside Italy to develop such an opera. Even while *opéra-comique* was fighting for its life in the face of Louis XIV's resolute disapproval, the royal court of Spain was busy creating an altogether different form of opera—one that was entirely Spanish, and one that would eventually, two centuries later, acquire genuine grassroots popularity.

ZARZUELA IN SPAIN

In the woods outside Madrid, the Habsburg kings of Spain built one of their great palaces. It was called La Zarzuela, *zarza* being the Spanish word for the bramble bushes that were such a feature of the woods. Here, in the mid-seventeenth century, during the long reign of Philip IV, a form of court entertainment was developed in which words, music, and dance were almost equally important, and in all of which the dominant rhythms were distinctively Spanish. The new entertainment caught on and spread far afield, at a time when Spain was extending its empire throughout the Americas. The entertainment was identified by the name of its first venue: *zarzuela*.

In more than three centuries, the fortunes of *zarzuela* have gone up and down, often matching the fortunes of the country and its peoples. To listen to *zarzuela* is to know you are in Spain, but to listen to it with a Spanish ear is to know in which province of Spain you are. You may recognize the various Iberian rhythms celebrated by the music—*seguidillas, habañeras, boleros, paso dobles, malagueñas*—but a Spaniard will know whether the idiom in which you are hearing them is Catalan, Basque, Galician, Navarrese, Asturian, or even Cuban. In true *zarzuela,* the idioms are never mixed.

This was the art form that took hold in Philip IV's palace outside Madrid, but at that stage, in the late seventeenth century, it was strictly a court entertainment. It did not last long (in fact, it lasted longer in Mexico, Peru, and other Spanish colonies than it did in the mother country). When the Bourbon dynasty inherited the Spanish throne in 1700, Italian opera became dominant and *zarzuela* was displaced. Philip V imported the great Italian *castrato* Farinelli and gave him charge of the court theater. For a century and a half, there was little in the way of native Spanish musical theater, and almost nothing that could be described as Spanish opera. The *tonadilla*—a short, comic, usually satirical entertainment based on popular dances and folk songs—had a brief run of popularity in the eighteenth century, but it was, eventually, the *zarzuela* that returned to favor, in the middle of the nineteenth century. It was no accident that it happened in the aftermath of Spain's defeat of Napoleon—after the whole nation had risen to defend itself—and this time, it was not confined to the court, or even to the main cities: it became the musical theater of the nation.

Zarzuelas contain spoken dialogue as well as music, dancing as well as singing, and they often include audience participation. But there is another, more "serious" form: *zarzuela grande*, a full-evening entertainment, normally in three acts. Always struggling against the imposition of Italian opera from above, the *zarzuela* remained for too long confined to the Spanish-speaking world, until, in the late twentieth century, a brilliant generation of Spanish singers on the international opera scene began to introduce the *zarzuela* to new audiences. No one did more than Plácido Domingo, who grew up in the midst of *zarzuela*: his mother and father ran their own *zarzuela* touring company.

Ironically, many of the members of that great generation of Spanish singers—Victoria de los Angeles, Teresa Berganza, Montserrat Caballé, and Pilar Lorengar; Alfredo Kraus, José Carreras, Jaime Aragall, and Juan Pons, as well as Domingo—frequently found themselves singing operas about Spain that were written by French, Austrian, Italian, and even American composers. Stand outside the Teatro de la Maestranza in Seville, opened in 1991, and you are within a few hundred yards of the settings of some of international opera's most important works. The theater looks out over the bullring where Bizet's Carmen met her death at the hands of Don José; on the outskirts of the city is the fortress where Beethoven's Florestan was imprisoned in *Fidelio*; Seville is the

setting for Verdi's *La forza del destino* and Donizetti's *La favorite*; and it is the city of Figaro in both Mozart's and Rossini's operas about the barber. Yet none of these operas, of course, is Spanish.

Spain's greatest opera composer was Vicente Martín y Soler, a contemporary of Mozart and one of Da Ponte's chief collaborators. But Martín y Soler wrote his mature works in Italian, never in Spanish. Even today, there are only two or three genuinely Spanish operas that have a place, and that a small one, in the international repertoire: Manuel de Falla's *La vida breve* (Life Is Brief) and his marionette opera *El retablo de Maese Pedro* (Master Peter's Puppet Show), both written in the early twentieth century; and even more recently, Roberto Gerhard's *The Duenna* (though that has an English libretto). But this brief list leaves out the entire genre of *zarzuela*. For a hundred and fifty years, Spanish composers and dramatists have been creating *zarzuela* and *zarzuela*-based operas that are only now beginning to receive wide recognition beyond Spain and Latin America. Names like F. A. Barbieri, Manuel Penella, Jerónimo Giménez, and Amadeo Vives are getting long-overdue entries in dictionaries of opera.

It could be argued that *zarzuela* is one of those forms of the art, like operetta and some American musicals, that were not originally written for the opera house but got there in the end. *Zarzuela*, however, and certainly *zarzuela grande*, does belong there. It is the peculiarly Spanish form of the art in which Spanish music and the Spanish language are united to create opera for the people and of the people. It is a distinctive contribution to *dramma per musica*, the more powerful because it arises directly out of the folk roots of cultures rich in both drama and music.

Polish Opera

The same could be said of the operas that were eventually developed in Eastern and Central Europe. They, too, came to fruition in the nineteenth century, but their antecedents went back much further—in the case of Poland to the very beginnings of opera. Prince Władisław Zygmunt, who later became Władisław IV of Poland, visited Florence in 1625 and was present at the premiere of the first opera written by a female composer, *La liberazione di Ruggerio dall'isola d'Alcina* by Francesca Caccini. Back in Warsaw, Władisław founded an Italian opera company. But there was little, if anything, that could be called Polish opera,

Stanisław Moniuszko (1819—1872), national composer of Poland.

and this remained true throughout the long period of Saxon domination in the eighteenth century.

A great deal of opera was performed in Warsaw (there were twice-weekly performances at the Operainia, the public theater), but it was mostly Italian, and it was generally performed by singers imported from the elector's court in Dresden.

Poland's geographical position put it at the center of European conflicts, constantly attacked and partitioned by its powerful neighbors. It was a state of affairs that lasted into the late twentieth century. Despite political disruptions, however, Polish opera began to establish itself at the very beginning of the nineteenth century. It happened largely because of the activities of an actor-manager named Wojciech Bogusławski (he was also a fine singer) and two native composers, Józef Elsner and Karol Kurpiński. In 1807, when the French army occupied Warsaw, Napoleon himself attended one of Elsner's operas, following it in a French translation.

The real hero of Polish opera, however, was Stanisław Moniuszko. The operas he composed between 1848 and his death in 1872 fit precisely the definition of national opera: written in the vernacular, based on the dance tunes and folk images of the country, and calculated to stir the national sensibilities of their audience. Two of them remain popular to this day. *Halka*, set in the Polish countryside and almost Donizettian in its construction, was a tale of unrequited love, madness, and suicide. *The Haunted Manor*, on the other hand, was written soon after the failure of the Poles' revolt against their Russian masters in 1864. It owed more to Weber—a love story revolving around a ghostly plot, with a wonderful tenor aria (the so-called "aria with chimes") and a very popular *mazurka*. But its overt nationalism and call to Polish pride were too much for the Russians: they suppressed it after only three performances.

Moniuszko's example was followed by a veritable outpouring of Polish opera in the turbulent decades that led up to the onset, in the twentieth century, of Nazism and then communism. Of all the musicians involved in it, one stood out as the successor to Moniuszko (and Chopin), and that was Karol Szymanowski. His finest opera, *King Roger*, first performed in 1926, was Polish in its language and origins, but its theme was universal, its drama stylized, its music complex and often chromatic. No subsequent Polish composer has quite equaled that achievement, though

Krzysztof Penderecki's *The Devils of Loudun* created a considerable stir following its 1969 premiere in Hamburg.

The heartland of Polish opera still belonged with Monuiszko. His ability to articulate the longings of the Polish people was powerful in its own day, and is powerful still. As much as anyone, he truly wrote the "opera of the people."

So, too (and at the very same time), did Bedřich Smetana in Bohemia.

CZECH OPERA

Since the fourteenth century, the Habsburg dynasty had ruled its European empire from Vienna. Bohemia, only a few miles to the east, had become a part of the empire in the sixteenth century. It was an ancient kingdom in its own right, and Habsburg emperors traditionally made the short journey to Prague soon after their accessions so that they could have a second coronation, as kings and queens of Bohemia. It was for one such occasion—the coronation of Leopold II in 1791—that the city of Prague had commissioned Mozart to write *La clemenza di Tito*. He accepted the commission with delight because Prague, much more than Vienna, had taken him to its heart. It was the city where *Figaro* had had its first popular success, and it was the city for which he had written *Don Giovanni*. A quarter of a century later, Weber, too, would spend important years in Prague. They were the years 1813—16, immediately before he moved to Dresden, when he was formulating the ideas that would lead to *Der Freischütz* and the development of German Romantic opera. So Prague and its State Theater, later known as the Tyl Theater, already had a place in opera history.

That place however, derived from the performance of Italian and German opera. It had nothing to do with Czech opera, of which there was virtually no such thing, owing to Austrian control of Bohemia. But by the middle of the nineteenth century, the empire of the Habsburgs was in retreat. Austrian armies were on the defensive in Italy, and the German states were moving toward unification. In Bohemia, Czech nationalism was coming to the fore. In 1848, the year of revolutions throughout Europe, Czech patriots went to the barricades in defiance of the Austrian army. Among them was a twenty-four-year-old musician called Bedřich Smetana. Like most of his colleagues, he had been brought up to speak the German language of the occupiers. He had to teach himself the language of his forebears, which was Czech.

The 1848 revolt in Prague was a hopeless cause, doomed to failure, just like its counterpart in Dresden the following year. When Richard Wagner escaped from Dresden, it was Franz Liszt who hid him and helped him eventually to get away to exile in Switzerland. And it was Liszt, in rather less dramatic circumstances, who also looked after Smetana. They had met in Prague in 1843, soon after Smetana first went there to study at the conservatory and to take up a position as music teacher to the family of Count Thun. His association with the revolutionaries put an end to his chances of holding down any such job in the future. So Liszt, who knew Smetana for the fine pianist that he was, helped him and his young wife, Katharina Kolar, who was also a talented pianist, to set up a music school of their own in Prague. It provided a living, and Smetana was able to augment it as his reputation as an international recitalist grew, but his own compositions made no headway at all with the public. So in 1856, he accepted the post of chief conductor to the Philharmonic Society of Göteborg in Sweden, and it was there, ironically, that he began to compose in the idiom we now recognize as his own. Except for summer visits, he did not return home until the Austrians had been forced to grant Bohemia political autonomy in 1860.

One of the by-products of the new autonomy in Prague was a commitment to build a national opera house: a Bohemian theater for Bohemian music and drama. For almost two centuries, the official language of the country had been German. All that could be counted in the way of specifically Czech operas were a few not very distinguished or widely heard pieces by František Škroup. When Smetana returned to Prague in 1861, Škroup was just leaving—to become conductor of a German opera company in Rotterdam, which is where he died two years later. So there was an urgent need for original Czech operas to be written if the new theater was to become a reality in more than name only. It was not completed until 1881, and in the meantime Smetana and his colleagues made do with a tiny temporary theater that was constructed for them. It was pointedly called the Provisional Theater. During his six years in charge of the theater, Smetana put on eighty-two different operas; thirty-three of them were new productions that he himself conducted.

Despite the difficulties, Smetana saw the opportunity for national opera and seized it. He had been much influenced by Mikhail Glinka's Russian opera *Ivan Susanin* (also known as *A Life for the Czar*), and that was the inspiration for the work he completed in 1863, *The Brandenburgers in Bohemia*. It was a fiercely nationalistic work about the thirteenth-century expulsion from Bohemia of the occupying Brandenburgers—a rather delicate subject for Prague's Austrian overlords. When it was finally performed at the Provisional Theater at the beginning of 1866, it was reasonably well received, but within months it had been superseded by Smetana's next opera, *The Bartered Bride*.

The Bartered Bride was a romantic comedy that sparkled with the melodies and dance tunes of Bohemia. Slowly, but very surely, it won the hearts of the Bohemian people, and people much farther afield as well. Yet it was not really what Smetana was about. It was a story of peasant village life, folksy and charming, filled with with the dance rhythms of the countryside: the polka, the furiant, and the *skočná*. But Smetana was now the principal conductor of the Provisional Theater: he saw his role on a more epic scale, as the composer of heroic dramas that might better be compared to those of Wagner or Verdi. *The Bartered Bride*, he later claimed, was no more than a transitional piece, written without much enthusiasm. In large part, this was a reaction to the disappointing reception for his loftier, grander works. *The Brandenburgers* had been one such, but there were two subsequent works—*Dalibor* and *Libuše*—that would eventually be recognized (in his own country, if not elsewhere) as the justification for his estimate of himself.

Dalibor was based on a fifteenth-century legend about a Bohemian hero who symbolized the yearning for national independence. At the time of its first production in 1868 it was accused of "Wagnerism" and it had a very limited success. Half a century later, when Czech independence finally became a reality after World War I, *Dalibor* did become immensely popular. But for Smetana, who labored so mightily at the Provisional Theater, the initial reception was like a slap in the face.

After *Dalibor*, he returned to the more folksy and much more popular theme of village life with *The Kiss*, but he had already composed another epic and its premiere waited only for the official opening of the new National Theater. It was a long

SMETANA'S <u>LIBUŠE</u>—A CZECH
NATIONAL OPERA

ABOVE: *Set design for Act I of the original
production, 1881. The lime tree, which
dominates the set, was an important symbol
of Czech nationhood. In this scene, Libuše
gives judgment under the tree. In a later
scene Přemsyl, a simple countryman who
will become Libuše's husband and will father
the first Czech dynasty, sings to a lime tree
of his fears and premonitions.*

RIGHT: *Gabriela Beňačková, a modern
interpreter of the title role, at the National
Theater, Prague, 1983.*

Princess Libuše, who founded a Bohemian dynasty. After tackling the very modern subject of a female ruler, the work ended with a majestic prophecy of Bohemia's history for more than a thousand years. *Libuše* was essentially Czech and has rarely been performed elsewhere.

Smetana was present at the beginning of what turned out to be a long struggle for Czech independence—a struggle that would seem to end in 1919, only to be renewed against new oppressors in the 1930s and for more than half a century thereafter.

Although the foundations Smetana had laid for Czech opera were substantial, it was obviously important that they should be quickly added to. As though to emphasize the point, the German minority in Prague built its own opera house in 1887, the Neues Deutsches Theater. Today, ironically, it bears Smetana's name, but in the late 1880s it symbolized the might of German opera and German culture—as opposed to Czech opera and Czech culture. Angelo Neumann, who had already been responsible for introducing Wagner's operas to several European countries, was the new theater's first manager.

Leoš Janáček was eventually the composer who took up the cause of Czech opera at the beginning of the twentieth century, and produced a body of work even more substantial than that of Smetana. In the meantime, two other composers, both Czech but more broadly European in outlook, made important contributions. Zdeněk Fibich was one of them. He grew up in a German-speaking household and acquired most of his musical education in Germany. He eventually wrote six operas in Czech, but only two of them were set in Bohemia. Fibich preferred adaptations of Schiller, Byron, and Shakespeare to the legends and folklore of his native land. Nevertheless, his most successful opera was *Šárka* in 1897, and it was decidedly Czech. It took up the story of Czech history more or less where Smetana had left off in *Libuše*, and it had an obvious emotional appeal. Although Fibich did not know it (and almost no one else in Bohemia did either), Janáček had written his first opera eleven years earlier, and it was the same story—*Šárka*. In 1888, however, Janáček was still an unknown, working quietly in the Moravian city of Brno, and his version of *Šárka* would not be performed until 1925. By then, Fibich had been dead for quarter of a century and his operas were rarely performed.

wait, but finally, in 1881, the theater opened, with *Libuše* as its first production. The building burned down after only twelve performances. It was quickly rebuilt and reopened in 1883, once again with *Libuše*. Exactly a hundred years later, during the last decade of communism, yet another reopening of the same theater was dedicated with the same opera. Smetana had done what he had promised; he had written an enduring Czech epic.

Not strictly speaking an opera, *Libuše* was more a festival pageant in six tableaux. It told the story of a Bohemian princess in pagan times,

Fibich, in any case, had already been overshadowed by his great contemporary, Antonín Dvořák. Indeed, by the time Smetana died, in 1884, Dvořák was already well launched on his career. Although he wrote thirteen operas, his worldwide fame owed little to them. "I consider opera the most suitable form for the nation," he wrote in 1904. "I am viewed as a composer of symphonies and yet I proved long years ago that my main bias is toward dramatic creation."[1] That was true. Indeed, after his return from America in 1895 (the highlight of that three-year visit was the premiere of his last symphony, *From the New World*), he devoted most of his time and effort to opera.

Dvořák's fame as an international composer worked against him in his native land. There was a strong feeling in Prague that anyone who spent so much time bathing in publicity and hero worship in England and America could not be Smetana's true successor. Like Fibich, he had written his first opera in German, but the Czech operas that followed reflected a wide variety of subject matter. The most successful were small-scale comedies about Bohemian village life. The grander epics, *Vanda* and *Dimitrij*, were not concerned with Czech stories at all.

Dimitrij was actually a sequel to the story of Boris Godunov, though Dvořák had no knowledge of Musorgsky's opera when he wrote it. His two finest and most enduring operas, however, were both written after his return from America and were both based on folk stories. *The Devil and Kate*, half fairy-tale and half village comedy, was clearly written by a symphonist (and one who owed a good deal to Wagner), but its story of a woman who gets the better of a rather stupid Devil had great appeal and is still popular today. *Rusalka*, on the other hand, was Dvořák's claim to greatness as an opera composer. The story of the water nymph who loved a mortal was an adaptation of the Undine legend that E. T. A. Hoffmann and Albert Lortzing had made use of many years before, but the music Dvořák wrote for it was passionate, melodic, and wonderfully integrated with the drama. Rusalka's "Hymn to the Moon" quickly became a popular concert piece. It took longer for the work as a whole to win wide acceptance outside the Czech lands, but by the late twentieth century it could certainly be accounted a repertoire work.

Dvořák was always a recognized figure in the world of music. That was not true of Janáček,

either during his lifetime or for some thirty years thereafter. It was one of the wonderful discoveries of the last half of the twentieth century that Janáček was not just a rather obscure composer of his native land, but an opera composer of great genius—greater than that of any of his Czech predecessors.

Janáček was only thirteen years younger than Dvořák, but while Dvořák was striding the international scene, Janáček was quietly running a music school in the ancient city of Brno, a hundred miles southeast of Prague. He was a genuine scholar. Like Béla Bartók and Zoltán Kodály in Hungary, and Ralph Vaughan Williams in England, he traveled throughout his country hearing and recording the folk songs of every region. He listened especially to what he called the "speech melodies"—the patterns and rhythms of the words people used in everyday speech in many dialects. And these "speech melodies" became the basis for the music of his dramatic work. One of the characteristics of a Janáček opera is that the singers declaim their words in rhythmic patterns, often very dramatically, while the melody is frequently carried by the orchestra. In operas like *Jenůfa* and *Katya Kabanova*, *The Makropulos Affair* and *The Cunning Little Vixen*, Janáček developed a new and original method of attacking the old Florentine conundrum of *dramma per musica*.

Janáček was a native of Moravia. It is a part of the Czech Republic but very different from Prague. Lachian, the Moravian dialect in which he wrote most of his operas, was not readily understood or encouraged in Prague. One of his biographers, Erik Chisholm, likened this to the difficulties of English people in understanding the Scottish dialect of Robert Burns.[2] Nor was a composer from Brno able to command the attention that might have been available to lesser talents who happened to be from the capital. So Janáček's first important opera, *Jenůfa*, completed in 1903 and performed in Brno in 1904, had to wait twelve more years before it was performed in Prague (by which time Janáček was already sixty-two). In part, it was his own fault. A few years earlier, he had written a highly critical review of an opera by the Czech composer Karel Kovařovic—not knowing that Kovařovic would shortly become director of the National Theater in Prague. Although Kovařovic was a great champion of Czech music, particularly that of Smetana and Dvořák, he was not interested in performing a work by Janáček, however well it had been received in Brno. And even when he did finally relent, in 1916, it was on the condition that the work should first be "edited"—by Kovařovic himself. The elimination of the overture, some reorchestration, and a number of other tiny "edits" thus secured for Karel Kovařovic, and after him for his widow, a handsome royalty on a work that he could never have created himself.[3]

Nevertheless, the performance in Prague was a great success and led almost immediately to performances, in a German translation, in Vienna and Cologne—amazingly, during the last days of World War I. Janáček must have been elated, but his only operatic output since composing *Jenůfa* had been two not-so-successful pieces—*Fate*, and the sublimely weird *Adventures of Mr. Brouček*. He was in his early sixties and it might have seemed unlikely that he had much more to offer.

But he did, and we probably owe it to his infatuation with a twenty-five-year-old woman, Kamila Stösslová, whom he met on holiday in Luhačovice in 1917. Janáček's own marriage, dating from 1880, had been tempestuous and troubled. In Kamila, nearly forty years younger than himself, he found his ideal of womanhood. She was already married, and there is no evidence that Janáček's love for her was ever consummated: indeed, it was probably a very one-sided relationship. But it lasted for the rest of Janáček's life, and it is clear from his letters that he considered Kamila his muse.

In these last ten years of his life, Janáček wrote four magnificent operas, all highly dramatic but immensely varied in their style and subject matter. Two of them were products of his deep attachment to all things Russian, and to Russian literature in particular. *Katya Kabanova* was a lyrical small-town love story drawn from Alexander Ostrovsky's Russian play *The Thunderstorm*. *From The House of the Dead* was an intensely moving compression of Dostoyevsky's epic novel of imprisonment in Siberia. In common with many Czech nationalists and intellectuals of the time, Janáček looked to the Russian example of political independence and cultural autonomy as a model, unlike the Czech experience of constantly living in the shadow of German and Austrian oppression.

The Katya of *Katya Kabanova* was clearly inspired by Kamila Stösslová. So, in a rather different way, was Emilia Marty, the character at the center of *The Makropulos Affair*. This is an "elixir of life" story, set in Prague and adapted from a contemporary Czech play by Karel Čapek. Emilia, who drank the elixir when she was sixteen, has reappeared in a new guise once every seventy years: she is 337 years old at the time in which the opera is set, 1922.

The Cunning Little Vixen, composed between *Katya* and *Makropulos*, is even more exotic. Janáček read a newspaper column written in verse by a local journalist. It was about country life in Moravia. Both animal and human characters were featured, and all of them were treated as equals. From this, Janáček developed a pantheistic opera that was entirely original. The story concerns a vixen, and a forester who captures her and tries to domesticate her. The vixen escapes, marries a fox, but is accidentally killed by a poacher. At the end of the opera, as the forester sits in the clearing where he first saw his vixen, he catches sight of a young fox cub. "I'll catch you like I did your mother," he sings, "only this time I'll bring you up better, so that people don't talk about you and me in the newspapers."

Janáček belonged squarely in the twentieth century. His music was not at all atonal—in fact it owed more to Wagner than it ever did to his own contemporaries—but it was sparse, often jagged, and became lyrical only infrequently. It was hardly surprising that it took so long to become accepted. The "speech melodies" on which it was based were Czech—or if not Czech, Moravian—and translation was not kind to them, even though the early translations to German were done by Janáček's friend Max Brod. It took the efforts of latter-day devotees—in particular the Czech conductor Rafael Kubelik and the Australian conductor Charles Mackerras—to place Janáček firmly in the consciousness of the opera world and to win for his works their rightful place in the mainstream repertoire.

Janáček died in 1928. His natural successor would have been Bohuslav Martinů, whose early music was also deeply rooted in Bohemian folklore. But Martinů was doomed to spend most of his life abroad—first by choice, later because National Socialism, and then socialist realism, were anathema. Martinů's best-known work, *The Greek Passion* (1961), owes very little to his Czech nationality.

Here, then—from Smetana, who had to teach himself his native language; through Dvořák, the internationally renowned Czech composer;

to Janáček, the Moravian scholar of "speech melodies"—is a clearly defined tradition of national opera, rooted in the culture, the folklore, and the languages of a single country.

HUNGARY

Like Bohemia, Hungary was a Habsburg possession for most of the eighteenth and nineteenth centuries, and just as Smetana could be seen as the father of Czech opera, so Ferenc Erkel clearly played that role in nineteenth-century Hungary.

Opera came late to Budapest—not until about 1740. It was invariably Italian or German opera, sometimes in Hungarian translation, and it was generally performed by visiting companies. The Hungarian experience was different from Bohemia's in one important respect. Whereas in Bohemia the native aristocracy was generally muted

after the disaster of the 1620 rebellion, the Hungarian aristocracy was always in the vanguard of the nationalist movement, and it played an important role in the encouragement of opera as well. It was at Esterháza that Haydn enjoyed his prolific years as an opera composer, and it was at Nagyvárad that Dittersdorf made his early impact in the service of the bishop of Grosswardein. But this was still Italian and German opera, not Hungarian.

Budapest's enthusiasm for opera became clear in the early nineteenth century. Works by Italian, German, and French composers were staged at the National Theater very soon after their first appearances in Naples, Paris, or Vienna. Pioneer works in Hungarian, written by Hungarian composers, began to be heard in the 1820s. These were the foundations upon which Erkel built. Beginning slightly earlier than Smetana, and end-

Janáček's THE CUNNING LITTLE VIXEN *at the English National Opera, London, 1995. Production (1980) directed by David Pountney, designed by Maria Bjørnson.*

ing slightly later, he developed an operatic style that was peculiarly Hungarian, yet relied very little on the folklore of the country.

Erkel's principal contribution consisted of two operas, both of them on patriotic themes drawn from earlier Magyar history, and both of them dominated by a uniquely Hungarian musical style known as *verbunkos*. There is no adequate translation. At its most literal, it might be called "recruitment." It seems to have originated in the dances performed by hussars, normally to Gypsy music, in order to attract recruits to the army. Fast or slow, its main feature was always a march rhythm, but it was by no means confined to military occasions. Like the more famous *csárdás*, it was capable of characterizing many different moods and situations, and that is how Erkel used it.

Erkel was a virtuoso pianist, but not so virtuosic that his talents could compare with those of his compatriot and contemporary, Franz Liszt. Luckily for him, he was also a theater conductor, so in 1838, when Liszt was already embarked on his European career as a recitalist, Erkel became chief conductor of the Hungarian National Theater in Pest. *Hunyadi László* in 1844 was the first of his operas to have significant success. The story of a Magyar hero of the fifteenth century, it established Erkel once and for all as a patriotic composer identified with the anti-Austrian feelings of the Hungarian people. It was almost twenty years before he achieved a similar success, but when he did, in 1861, it was an opera called *Governor Bánk*. If anything, it exceeded the popularity of *Hunyadi László*.

By this time, Erkel was firmly established as the leading patriotic composer of the Hungarian nation. He had written the national anthem, and he had written the national operas. Moreover, as the presiding eminence of the National Theater, and of the fine new Opera House, when it opened in 1884, he was able to encourage many other Hungarian composers to write operas. Few of them had significant successes, and none to compare with his own, but at least ethnic Hungarian opera was being performed. It also helped Erkel to keep his theaters firmly closed to the works of Richard Wagner (though that omission was quickly corrected at the National Theater when Hans Richter succeeded Erkel in 1871).

Where Moniuszko in Poland, and Smetana and Dvořák in Bohemia, had mined a rich vein of native folklore, Erkel's nationalism was based much more on simple patriotism. It was true that his use

of *verbunkos* gave his operas a decidedly ethnic feel, but there was nothing very profound about their musical roots. There were, however, two men—Béla Bartók and Zoltán Kodály—who came after Erkel and who explored folk culture with the same thoroughness that Janáček exhibited in Moravia and Ralph Vaughan Williams in England. Neither of them, unfortunately, was dedicated to opera in the way that Janáček was. Bartók's only opera, *Bluebeard's Castle*, was written in 1911 and owed more to Debussy, Schoenberg, and Freud than it did to anything Hungarian. Kodály, on the other hand, wrote three specifically Hungarian works, all of them making use of his intimate knowledge of the folklore and folk music of his country. *Háry János*, written in 1926, remains the best known and the most frequently performed. Many other composers have written operas in Hungarian, several of them with more popular success than Bartók, or even Kodály, but the Hungarian tradition is essentially like that of Poland; it follows from one central figure—with the promise that a genuine "opera of the people" will continue to be explored.

The operas of Poland, Bohemia, and Hungary grew out of nationalist movements unleashed by the experiences of occupation and repression. Russia, on the other hand, was a sovereign nation. The founding of its native opera also had to await the nineteenth century, but when it finally emerged it moved quickly onto the international stage as an expression of nationalism that was uniquely Russian, but universal in its appeal.

RUSSIA

There is no sound so singular as the sound of Russian opera. Listen to the early phonograph recordings of Fyodor Chaliapin, or sit in the auditoriums of the modern Bolshoi and Maryinsky (Kirov) Theaters, and you can instantly detect a distinctive national sound. It is something at once musical, linguistic, and cultural.

It was not always so. Until as late as 1836, there were few noteworthy Russian operas. There had been performances of opera in St. Petersburg for at least a hundred years, but they were almost always of Italian or French works. Empress Anna Ivanova began the tradition in 1735, when she appointed the Italian composer Francesco Araia as *maestro di cappella*. Araia spent more than twenty years in Russia, regularly composing new works for performance at the court. Many of these were operas, but only one of them was written to a Russian text. And that is more than could be said for Araia's successors, who included several of Mozart's great contemporaries—Cimarosa, Martín y Soler, Sarti, and Paisiello. The Italian influence was dominant, and stifling.

Nevertheless, there *was* such a thing as Russian opera, and Catherine the Great, who ruled Russia for thirty-five years at the end of the eighteenth century, was largely responsible. At the same time that she imported distinguished foreigners to organize the court music, she also began to foster a native strain of Russian opera. She even contributed to it herself by writing librettos for selected composers to set (they could hardly refuse). There was a reason for her efforts, and they were not as altruistic as they might have seemed. Catherine was an autocrat, German by birth, but never ceased to think of herself as a woman of the Enlightenment. Like Rousseau and Diderot, she saw opera as a legitimate vehicle for the propagation of political and social ideas. Her librettos were a mixture of patriotic stories and moralistic social commentary—even, when it suited her, political satire: *The False Hero Kosome-*

tovich was a none-too-subtle attack on Gustavus III of Sweden, against whose armies she had to defend Russia.

Opera houses have always had a propensity for burning down—too much wood, too many flaming candles—but nowhere more so than in Russia. St. Petersburg's Maryinsky Theater, later known as the Kirov, and Moscow's Bolshoi Theater stand today on sites where a series of predecessors have stood, and burned, since Catherine's time. Nowadays, these theaters are as famous for their ballet companies as they are for opera, but in Catherine's time they housed all forms of dramatic presentations, with or without music. The same actors frequently appeared in both opera and spoken drama. The greatest tragic actor of Catherine's day was a man known as Shusherin. Among his most famous roles was the lead in one of the first Russian operas, *The Miller—Magician, Deceiver, and Matchmaker* by Mikhail Sokolovsky, first performed at the Petrovsky Theater in Moscow in 1779. At about the same time, and in the same theater, Catherine might have heard the greatest Russian opera singer of the day, Repina, playing the lead in a straight play.

Catherine must also have been aware of something else. As the official history of the Bolshoi Theater puts it:

> The Petrovsky Theater troupe was frequently augmented by talented serf actors and actresses, and occasionally by entire serf theater companies purchased by the theater management from landowners. . . . In 1806 [ten years after Catherine's death] the serf actors at the theater were given their freedom.[4]

Catherine's encouragement of Russian opera was significant, but limited. It was always secondary to her admiration for the French, Italian, and German models. When she discovered a particularly promising Russian composer, Dimitri Bortnyansky, she sent him to Italy to study. And when Bortnyansky returned to be *maestro di cappella* in St. Petersburg, he composed operas in French, not Russian.

The arrival of Russian opera can be dated very precisely—to an evening in December 1836, when Czar Nicholas I and members of his family were guests of honor at the glittering premiere

OPPOSITE: *Glinka's* A LIFE FOR THE CZAR *(also known as* IVAN SUSANIN*) at the Bolshoi, Moscow, 1982. Directed by Nicolai Kuznetsov.*

of Mikhail Glinka's opera *Ivan Susanin*. Tchaikovsky, writing half a century later, remarked on how sudden and unexpected the change had been. With no warning, with no track record to indicate that he was capable of it (up to that moment, Tchaikovsky said, the composer had been no more than a "dilettante" in the world of music), Glinka delivered the first great Russian opera. It was, Tchaikovsky said, the "acorn" from which the "oak" of Russian opera would grow.[5]

In 1836, *Ivan Susanin* was immediately recognized as a landmark, and no one in Russia doubted that judgment until the Revolution—witness the fact that performances of *Ivan Susanin* opened every opera season in Moscow and St. Petersburg until 1913. It was a Russian opera, by a Russian composer, about an important moment in Russian history. Susanin had been a real-life hero—a peasant who had risked his life in 1612 to save the life of the very first Romanov czar by misdirecting a contingent of the Polish army. Nicholas I, after watching a rehearsal, suggested that the title should be changed to *A Life for the Czar*, and that is how it has always been known in the West.

Glinka was not the first composer to tackle the story of Susanin. In 1799, a young Italian musician named Catterino Cavos had been brought to St. Petersburg as conductor of the Imperial Opera (he lived there the remaining forty years of his life). In 1815, in the euphoria following Napoleon's defeat, Cavos used the heroic story of Susanin to reflect the nationalistic feelings of the moment. Cavos's opera did not make a great

impression, but it must have been galling for him, only twenty years later, to find another (and, at that time, quite inconsequential) composer using the same story, and scoring a magnificent success with it. It says much for Catterino Cavos that he not only helped Glinka prepare the opera for performance but he also conducted the premiere.

Mikhail Glinka was well connected. Tchaikovsky's judgment that, until *A Life for the Czar*, he had "composed nothing but banalities,"[6] was not inaccurate, but he had traveled in Europe, he had met Donizetti and Bellini in Milan and Berlioz in Rome, and he had studied at firsthand both the *bel canto* school of Italian opera and the Romantic movement in Germany. Their influences were clearly present in *A Life for the Czar*, but so were those of Glinka's upbringing—a lonely childhood on his grandparents' estate near Smolensk. It was the musical influences of those early years—the folk songs he heard on the estate, the music of the Orthodox Church, the sound of bells—that remained with him and stubbornly refused to go away when he began to immerse himself in Western music. They could be heard in the great choruses of *A Life for the Czar*—the "Bridal Chorus" and, above all, the "Slavsya Chorus," with which the work ended. Most important was the Russian language. What few Russian operas there had been until that time had contained spoken dialogue, rather like German *Singspiel*. Glinka, by contrast, wrote recitatives, thus making the Russian language an integral part of his musical fabric.

He also made use of Russian literature. Nikolay Gogol and Aleksandr Pushkin were two of his great contemporaries, and immediately after the success of *A Life for the Czar*, Glinka invited Pushkin to collaborate with him on the adaptation of one of his fairy-tale poems, *Ruslan and Lyudmila*. Unfortunately, Pushkin died in 1837, and as a result, Glinka worked from an adaptation that had no real structure and was dramatically weak. Nevertheless, *Ruslan and Lyudmila* not only contained some of his finest music; it also began the tradition of basing Russian operas on works of Russian literature. "After Pushkin" was an acknowledgment that would appear in the credits of works by Musorgsky, Tchaikovsky, Rimsky-Korsakov, Rachmaninoff, Stravinsky, and many others.

Glinka died in 1857, aged only fifty-two, but he had planted the acorn. It grew, although it had to do so in the face of fierce competition from Italophiles. Giovanni Battista Rubini, the great-

Aleksandr Pushkin (1799–1837). Portrait by V. A. Tropinin. Many of the most important Russian operas of the nineteenth century were adapted from Pushkin's works, including RUSLAN AND LYUDMILA *(Glinka),* THE STONE GUEST *(Dargomyzhsky),* EUGENE ONEGIN *and* THE QUEEN OF SPADES *(Tchaikovsky),* BORIS GODUNOV *(Musorgsky), and three operas by Rimsky-Korsakov.*

est Italian tenor of the time, performed regularly in St. Petersburg for staggeringly large fees, and in 1862 Verdi himself was commissioned to write *La forza del destino* for the imperial theater. Nonetheless, these were the years when Russian opera prospered.

The first to benefit from Glinka's example was Aleksandr Dargomyzhsky. He was largely self-taught and would probably have been no more than a pale imitator of the French fashion for *grand opéra* had it not been for Glinka's encouragement. Dargomyzhsky had little of Glinka's talent as a composer, and even less talent as a dramatist, but he was able to articulate a principle that would be of enormous importance to Musorgsky, Rimsky-Korsakov, and their successors. "The note must express the word,"[7] he said: the music of a Russian opera should echo the sounds and rhythms of the Russian language. Thus, more than fifty years before Janáček sought his "speech melodies" in the Moravian dialect, Dargomyzhsky was doing much the same thing in the Russian language. Unfortunately, he was not very good at it in practice. He set Pushkin's play *The Stone Guest* practically word for word as Pushkin had written it—an almost continuous recitative, devoid of any form of melodic lyricism. Few operas have achieved, let alone sustained, such heights of boredom. When, twenty years later, Musorgsky came to set another Pushkin play, *Boris Godunov*, he was able to create a genuine Russian classic—partly because he adopted Dargomyzhsky's instruction to reproduce in music "human speech in all its finest shadings," but also because he had precisely the gifts of melodic lyricism that Dargomyzhsky so notably lacked.

In the history of Russian opera, Aleksandr Dargomyzhsky is much more celebrated than Mily Balakirev. Yet Balakirev, a rude tyrant of a man who never wrote an opera, was probably the most important single influence on the course of Russian opera after Glinka. He arrived in St. Petersburg as an eighteen-year-old and made an immediate impression with both his piano playing and his compositions. Glinka himself was impressed. But Balakirev's activities as a musician were fitful. Quite early on, he began to suffer from bouts of acute depression. In between, there were periods of frenetic activity. There was something in his personality, despite his arrogance, that attracted his peers and made him their undisputed

leader. Gradually, he assembled around himself a group of young musicians, none of whom were professionals, all of whom were self-taught, and all of whom, at the time Balakirev got to know them between 1856 and 1862, had other professions. Three of them were in the armed services, one was a distinguished chemist.

César Cui was the first to come under Balakirev's influence. He was an army engineer and musically the least talented of the group. His fifteen operas have mostly disappeared, though *William Ratcliff*, first performed at the Maryinsky Theater in 1869, was, at the time, an inspiration to his colleagues. It was based on a play by Heinrich Heine about a Scottish family, and it seems now to be an unlikely subject for someone of such pronounced nationalist views. But Cui was always a paradox. As a writer and critic (and as the unofficial spokesman for the group), he did much to propagate the Russian nationalist sentiments to which Balakirev and his friends subscribed; as a composer, he was generally attracted to Romantic, often French, subjects.

The next to join the group was Modest Musorgsky. At the time he met Balakirev, he was an eighteen-year-old ensign in the prestigious Preobrajensky Regiment. So great was Balakirev's influence on him that he quickly resigned his commission and dedicated himself to his real interest in life, music. He could afford to: he came from a wealthy landed family. But all that changed in 1861, when the serfs were emancipated in Russia. From that time on, Musorgsky had to support himself, and his increasingly severe drinking habit, by taking lowly jobs in the civil service.

The only member of the group who would ultimately make his living as a musician was Nicolay Rimsky-Korsakov. When he first met Balakirev, in 1861, he was a seventeen-year-old naval cadet with an overwhelming ambition to compose music, but without any of the basic instrumental skills you would normally expect of a composer. Indeed, ten years later, when he was sufficiently established as a composer to be made professor of composition at the St. Petersburg conservatory, he had, by his own admission, the greatest difficulty in keeping ahead of his students. By the time he died in 1908, however, he was universally acknowledged as the doyen of Russian music— a composer of genuine distinction, and a teacher who bridged the years between the early pioneering days and the arrival of a new, self-confident generation of Russian composers in the early twentieth century. Glazunov, Stravinsky, and Prokofiev were just three of his famous pupils.

The last member of Balakirev's group was the chemist, Aleksandr Borodin. As a musician, he acknowledged himself a dilettante, but as a scientist he was in the first rank—a professor at the academy of medicine in St. Petersburg and a frequent guest speaker at seminars and conferences all over Europe. Composition was a hobby, carried on joyously and chaotically among the friends and family who constantly invaded his home on the grounds of the academy. His greatest work, the opera *Prince Igor*, remained unfinished at his death in 1887, after eighteen years on the drawing board. It was completed and orchestrated by Glazunov and Rimsky-Korsakov.

For almost fifteen years in the 1860s and 1870s, these five men—Balakirev, Cui, Musorgsky, Rimsky-Korsakov, and Borodin—were the core members of a group of amateur musicians who studied together in their spare time and evolved a philosophy of Russian music that built on Glinka's example. They were short on technique, and they knew it, but they had very firm ideas about what they should be doing—and equally firm ideas about what they should not be doing. They were opposed to the prevailing fashions of opera in the West, both the vocal ornamentations of French and Italian opera, and the imposition of leitmotifs (or constantly recurring themes) that had become fashionable with Mendelssohn and Berlioz and was being taken even further by Wagner. They were especially opposed to the academic teaching of music in Russia, which they felt was based entirely on Western principles. This meant they were opposed to the Rubinstein brothers, Anton and Nicholas. The Rubinsteins were both great pianists. Anton, the more famous, was also a prolific composer in the Romantic style (not a Russian composer, Cui scathingly remarked, but "merely a Russian who composes"[8]). The brothers had something else that Balakirev and his group lacked: platforms from which to influence and even direct the development of Russian music. In 1862, Anton Rubinstein founded the St. Petersburg conservatory. Two years later, Nicholas founded the Moscow conservatory.

The strength of Balakirev and his friends was not so much what they stood against, but what they stood for. César Cui and Balakirev himself were fond of using phrases like "truth in music" and "intrinsic worth," but what it came down to was Russian nationalism: the search for a way of expressing Russian themes and stories in musical forms and sounds that had their roots in Russia's own cultures. It was no accident that Aleksandr Dargomyzhsky, who labored so long to marry the Russian language to a new form of music, was a peripheral member of Balakirev's group (they often met in Dargomyzhsky's house), and it was certainly no accident that the operas created by members of the group were unmistakably Russian in sound and substance.

In 1863, perhaps as a riposte to the establishment of Anton Rubinstein's conservatory, Balakirev founded the Free Music School in St. Petersburg. Its avowed purpose was to give concerts of Russian music, interspersed with occasional works of the approved German masters. This was in harmony with a growing conviction among Russian intellectuals that their own culture was so closely related to those of the other Slav peoples—Czechs, Serbs, Poles, Bulgarians—that the interests of Russian artists ought properly to encompass the whole Slav world. This Slavophile movement, in turn, coincided with a series of wars against Turkey, aimed at the liberation of Bulgaria. A popular feeling developed in St. Petersburg and Moscow that all the Slav nations might one day be united—under Russia. In this spirit, Balakirev himself visited Prague in 1866 and conducted successful performances of Glinka's two great operas, *Ruslan and Lyudmila* and *A Life for the Czar* (having first had to sit through a chaotic performance of *A Life for the Czar* conducted by Smetana). In a reciprocal gesture the next year, Balakirev invited Czech musicians to the Free Music School in St. Petersburg for a concert of their music, together with works by himself, Cui, Musorgsky, Borodin, and Rimsky-Korsakov. It was after this concert that the Russian critic Vladimir Stasov, another occasional member of Balakirev's group, wrote smugly that Russia possessed its own *moguchaya kuchka*—literally, its Mighty Heap, but usually translated as the Mighty Handful or Mighty Five. The name stuck (though the five composers themselves never used it), and it quickly came to embody the idea of Russian nationalism in music.

The Slav cultures to the west were not the only objects of this nationalism. There were also the cultures of eastern Russia and its neighboring lands. Balakirev himself made several journeys into the Caucasus, collecting and adapting folk tunes of the region (his setting of "The Song of the Volga Boatmen" was probably the most popular single item in his legacy), but it was eventually Rimsky-Korsakov who made most use of the exotic and magical folk cultures of these eastern territories. From his symphonic suite *Scheherezade* (1887) to his very last opera, *The Golden Cockerel* (1908), they played a large part in his output.

The first member of the Mighty Handful to make his mark in the world of opera was Musorgsky. He wrote *Boris Godunov* in a period of fifteen months in 1868–69, only to have it rejected by the opera house. It was not until 1874 that the revised opera was performed in full at the Maryinsky Theater—a popular success, a critical failure. In retrospect, neither of those judgments can have been surprising. *Boris Godunov* was popular because, based on a Pushkin play, it was an epic of Russian history—the story of a man who seized the throne of the czars at the very end of the sixteenth century and clung to it for seven years, pursued by his demons and by a claimant to the throne whom he thought he had caused to be murdered many years previously. The canvas of the opera was the czarist Russia of an earlier era—crude and cruel, but still Mother Russia. It was a time and a place entirely recognizable to audiences at the Maryinsky Theater in 1874.

To the critics, however, Musorgsky's work was hardly recognizable as opera—that is, opera as they knew it. It was made up of a series of individual tableaux, some written in verse, some in prose, with no attempt to make them flow into each other in the customary way. As for the music, it was often harsh in its harmonies and roughly orchestrated. Yet Musorgsky had achieved what Dargomyzhsky had preached but been unable to achieve himself: the creation of a musical language to match the sound and the inflections of the Russian language. To the tutored, conventional ear, it was strange. Even César Cui found it odd, and said so in print: he characterized *Boris* as "a crude tone poem" with overtones of "Wagnerism."[9] Musorgsky was furious. The Mighty Handful began to fall apart.

Between 1874 and 1882, *Boris* was given a total of only twenty-five performances at the Maryinsky, and then it was withdrawn. By that time, Musorgsky was already dead, destroyed by his drinking and his melancholy. *Boris*, however, was anything but dead. Rimsky-Korsakov took it upon himself, as a labor of love, to edit and reorchestrate the opera, even to rewrite bits of it. It was in the Rimsky version that most countries outside Russia heard the opera for the first time, and acclaimed it. Not until the 1930s (and not generally in performance until four decades after that) was the Musorgsky score of 1874 restored as the orthodox version.

More than any other opera in the repertoire, *Boris* is a showcase for basses. It has three splendid roles—the monk Pimen, the vagabond Varlaam, and Czar Boris himself. The first Varlaam was Osip Petrov, sixty-eight years old but still the dean of Russian basses; for more than thirty years he had been a famous Ivan Susanin in Glinka's opera. The first Boris was Ivan Melnikov—a baritone rather than a true bass—who also created the title role of Borodin's *Prince Igor* and was one of Tchaikovsky's favorite singers. But if there is one singer with whom the role of Boris is indissolubly linked, it must be Fyodor Chaliapin. In the first thirty years of the twentieth century, he sang it all over the world—and not only sang it: he acted it and impersonated it in a way that transfixed audiences. This was no mere opera singer trying to remember to act: this was a man with a histrionic genius. The proof of his acting

Osip Petrov (1807–1878). Petrov was the greatest Russian bass of his day, an inspiration to the generation of emerging opera composers. He was the first Ivan Susanin and the first Ruslan for Glinka; the first Miller in Rusalka *and Leporello in* The Stone Guest *for Dargomyzhsky; the first Varlaam in* Boris Godunov *for Musorgsky (at the age of sixty-eight); and the first Mayor in* Vakula the Smith *for Tchaikovsky (at sixty-nine).*

can still be seen in the film of *Don Quixote*, directed by G. W. Pabst, where Chaliapin played the great Cervantes character. And the proof of the voice can still be heard in the recordings he made in his later years—a huge, commanding voice, unarguably Russian.

Even before *Boris* had been given its first performance, Musorgsky was deeply involved in another opera project. *Khovanshchina* dealt with a period of Russian history almost a hundred years after Boris Godunov's time. It revolved around a recurring theme of Russian history: the struggle between the old and the new, between the reactionary and the revolutionary. In this case, Musorgsky placed the action in the 1680s, in the years just before Peter the Great overthrew the forces of reaction (represented by the Khovansky family on the one hand, and the Old Believers on the other) and became the first great czar of the modern era. Once again, Musorgsky wrote his own libretto, except that this time he never really wrote it: he amassed it from protracted researches over several years. *Khovanshchina* contained some wonderful lyrical music, but it never reached the heights of *Boris*. Musorgsky left it unfinished at his death, and once again it was Rimsky-Korsakov who completed it for him (Shostakovitch did a new, and better, version in 1959). *Sarochinsky Fair* was also left uncompleted—a bucolic village opera, based on a story of Gogol's and originally intended as a vehicle for the aging bass Osip Petrov, but he, too, died before it was finished.

This chronicle of unfinished works is easily explained by one look at Ilya Repin's portrait of Musorgsky, painted less than two weeks before the composer died in 1881. It is the picture of a forty-two-year-old dipsomaniac: a man with a natural, untutored genius, destroyed by alcohol and massive depression. Along with the daguerreotype of Donizetti, made thirty-six years earlier as the Italian composer relapsed into terminal madness, it is one of the saddest pictures in the story of opera.

No other member of the Mighty Handful had the sheer operatic genius of Musorgsky, but Aleksandr Borodin was probably the one with the most natural gift for music. Unfortunately for music, his working life was devoted to science, and he, too, died relatively young, at fifty-four. All told, he completed only about forty works.

As the illegitimate son of a prince, Borodin had all the advantages of a superior education. As an outstanding scientist, he traveled widely and spoke four languages. But music had always been his passion, and while it is certainly true to say that he was a spare-time musician, it is not good enough to describe music merely as his hobby. For Borodin, meeting Balakirev and his circle in 1862 was a heaven-sent opportunity. It enabled him to explore musical ideas and techniques with people as interested, but as untaught, as himself. Sometimes these explorations were very basic: Borodin and Rimsky-Korsakov investigated the instruments of the orchestra by borrowing two or three at a time and spending weekends scraping, blowing, and thumping them to find out how they worked and what sounds they could make.

Borodin, perhaps even more than Rimsky-Korsakov, had an instinct and an ear for orchestral sounds. If Tchaikovsky wrote the greatest

Modest Musorgsky (1839–1881). Portrait by Ilya Repin, painted just before the composer's death.

Aleksandr Borodin (1833–1887).

that united the critical faculties of the Mighty Handful, it was Borodin's opera *Prince Igor*. "While controversy rages among us on every other subject," Borodin wrote, "all, so far, are pleased with *Igor*."[10] And they knew it intimately. From the time he began it in 1869 to the time of his death in 1887, when it was still incomplete (the music was composed but not yet fully orchestrated), they had constantly listened to him playing bits of it. Glazunov, then in his early twenties and a pupil of Rimsky-Korsakov's, was able to reconstruct the overture from memory; Borodin had never bothered to write it down.

Prince Igor goes even further back into Russian history than does *Boris Godunov*, to a time in the twelfth century when Igor, Prince of Seversk, was attempting (unsuccessfully) to subdue a Tartar tribe called the Polovtsians. It is a massive, sprawling, undisciplined work, lacking the benefit of a properly structured libretto (Borodin put it together himself, working from an early Russian chronicle), yet it contains a series of magnificent set pieces, of which the "Polovtsian Dances" is only the best known. Like *Boris*, it is Russian through and through—in its language and in its music. And like *Boris*, it benefited from the championship of Chaliapin when it came to be performed outside Russia in the early years of the twentieth century—a towering presence in the role of Khan Konchak, the Polovtsian leader.

No member of the Mighty Handful did more for his colleagues than Rimsky-Korsakov, though his editing and completion of their works laid him open to much retrospective criticism, as he knew it would. It could also be said that his "defection" to the conservatory in 1871 was the event that made the breakup of the Mighty Handful inevitable. Musorgsky, in particular, saw it as treachery. But that was to overlook the truth, which was that Rimsky was simply more successful than the others; he would hardly have been invited to assume so prestigious and important a professorship otherwise. Borodin alone among the Handful, so successful in his own professional world, appears not to have held it against him. Rimsky's first successful opera, *The Maid of Pskov* (sometimes known as *Ivan the Terrible*) was performed only two years after his arrival at the conservatory—one year before *Boris*.

In all, Rimsky-Korsakov wrote fourteen operas. They represented a corpus of operatic work far more significant than that of any of his

Russian symphonies of the period, then Borodin was not far behind—and no one in Russia wrote finer string quartets. Some of his colleagues darkly suspected that his European travels had subjected him to too many Western influences. Vladimir Stasov and Musorgsky tried to dissuade him from tackling string quartets at all, on the grounds that the form was Teutonic and academic, just the sort of thing you might expect to come out of the Rubinstein brothers' conservatories. Borodin proved them wrong. But if there was one work

contemporaries, including Tchaikovsky. And far from proving him a traitor to the ideals of Balakirev's group, they demonstrated that Rimsky was the one who most thoroughly practiced those ideals. He never achieved a single impact such as that of *Boris*, but he enormously enriched the store of Russian opera. There were heroic, historical operas, such as *The Maid of Pskov* and *The Czar's Bride*. There were "peasant" operas, such as *Christmas Eve* and *May Night*. Most of all, there were the fairy-tale operas that explored the exotic and magical world of Russian folklore—*Sadko*, *The Invisible City of Kitezh*, *The Golden Cockerel*, and several others. And there was one opera, *Mozart and Salieri*, though based on a play by Pushkin, that was no more Russian than most of Catherine the Great's commissions in the previous century.

Musorgsky was angry at Rimsky for joining the conservatory. He would have been even angrier if he had lived long enough to witness the event that triggered Rimsky's obsession with opera during the last two decades of his life. Almost the greatest single sin known to the Mighty Handful was what César Cui called "Wagnerism." At the very time that Balakirev and his friends were meeting in St. Petersburg and pioneering their own form of opera, Richard Wagner was finally realizing his dreams in Germany. It was during this period that *Tristan*, *Die Meistersinger*, and the first operas of the *Ring* cycle were all given their first performances. Few Russians got to see them, but much was heard of them. In 1889, however, Rimsky-Korsakov, score in hand, did finally see the *Ring*—the entire cycle, performed in St. Petersburg by Angelo Neumann's touring company. That experience, by his own admission, inspired him to devote more and more of his energies to opera. He already had four operas to his credit, but now, beginning with *Mlada* (1892) and ending with the posthumous production of *The Golden Cockerel* in 1909, he set about adding to the repertoire of Russian opera as no one had before. At the same time, he passed on to his pupils, who included Stravinsky and Prokofiev, his passionate concern for Russian music and drama.

Less than three years separated Rimsky's death in 1908 from Stravinsky's unveiling of the ballet *The Firebird* in Paris—not an opera, to be sure, but the beginning of something new and wonderful in Russian musical theater.

❧

Pyotr Tchaikovsky was an exact contemporary of the Mighty Handful, but he stands apart from them, by reason of his genius and his universality. He was every bit as Russian as they were, and just as much in debt to Glinka, but there the resemblance ended. A supremely gifted child from a fairly affluent background, he waited until he was twenty-one before deciding to make music his career. He was a product of the Rubinstein brothers' conservatories, a pupil of Anton's in St. Petersburg and later a member of Nicholas's teaching faculty in Moscow. His complicated personal life, increasingly tortured as the years went on, made him something of a vagabond, uncomfortable at home in Russia, hopelessly homesick when he was abroad. He traveled extensively in France and Germany, absorbing the music of those countries and keeping himself up to date with current developments. He knew Wagner's music at firsthand: he was actually present in Bayreuth for the very first complete performance of the *Ring* cycle in 1876 (admired the enterprise, hated the method). But it was earlier music that had the firmest hold on him: Mozart was always his hero, with Gluck and Haydn some way behind.

Tchaikovsky's work is so rich in symphonic and orchestral masterpieces that it is easy to overlook the extent of his theatrical work. He composed ten operas, along with the three great ballet scores *Swan Lake*, *The Sleeping Beauty*, and *Nutcracker*. After the contemporary French composer Léo

Pyotr Tchaikovsky (1840–1893) and his bride, Antonina Milyukova, in 1877.

Nikolay Rimsky-Korsakov (1844–1908).

Delibes, whom he much admired, Tchaikovsky was the first significant composer of the modern era to write original music for ballet. It was wonderfully dramatic music, better known and more popular than anything he ever wrote for opera, and it graphically demonstrated the glorious gift he possessed in such quantity: the gift of melody.

By the time he went to Bayreuth in 1876 (he was thirty-six years old), Tchaikovsky had already composed two operas, neither of them notable in retrospect. Although nothing remains of it now, he had also spent several months in 1863–64 setting scenes from Pushkin's play *Boris Godunov*, five years before Musorgsky began work on the same subject. But it was in Paris, en route to Bayreuth, that he had what he himself described as his most important operatic experience. He attended a performance of Bizet's *Carmen*.[11] It had been staged for the first time the previous year and had had a cool reception from the Parisian audience. What fascinated Tchaikovsky was not just the copious melody and the realistic story line: *Carmen* also had

an underlying theme that corresponded to something deeply embedded in his own consciousness and that was increasingly to dominate the remaining years of his life—the theme of fate.

In the "Card Trio" at the beginning of Act III, Carmen turns over the cards to see how they lie. "Spades—a grave!" she exclaims. "What matters it? If you are to die, try the cards a hundred times, they will fall the same—spades, a grave."

Although he desperately wanted to reject it, and tried hard in his music to do so, Tchaikovsky lived in fear of his own mortal destiny. Moreover, he was in the invidious social position of recognizing himself as a homosexual, yet having to deny it. Homosexuality was illegal in czarist Russia, as in most other countries, and Tchaikovsky came from a social and educational background in which any public knowledge of his sexual preference would have been fatal to his career. With denial his only option, marriage seemed the best course. Unfortunately, he allowed himself to be drawn into a marriage with a much younger woman that

was completely unsuitable. Within days, he fled in panic and attempted to commit suicide.

Tchaikovsky wrote much of his most expressive, emotional, and understanding music for women, whether ballerinas or singers. There is no better example than the role of Tatyana in *Eugene Onegin*, the opera he wrote in the immediate aftermath of his disastrous marriage. He clearly empathized with the young woman's awakening sexuality, her attraction to the older, more mature Onegin, and the thwarting of her impulsive advances. Pushkin's story contained all the elements that Tchaikovsky required to write a lyrical music drama of sustained power—from the early scenes of Tatyana's infatuation, to the final curtain, when Onegin, returned as suitor, is rejected with dignity and sadness. Tchaikovsky never again reached the heights of dramatic and emotional intensity he scaled in *Eugene Onegin*—not in his operas, anyway. *Onegin* was not received with any great acclaim in Moscow in 1879, but five years later, in St. Petersburg, it was seen for what it was—a Russian classic.[12]

There had been other operas in the interim: *The Waid of Orleans*, a large-scale work in the style of French *grand opéra*; and *Mazeppa*, a much more successful, and more Russian, work about a real-

life traitor in the time of Peter the Great. Tchaikovsky was now fashionable in St. Petersburg. The new czar, Aleksandr III, was an admirer and wished to see his work performed. But Tchaikovsky's own mood grew steadily more pessimistic. His diaries began to speak of the "flat-nosed horror," by which he meant death.

In 1885, he rented a house in Maidanovo, near the village of Klin—fifty miles from Moscow, on the main railway line to St. Petersburg. Tchaikovsky loved the surrounding coun-

Tchaikovsky's last home, in the village of Klin, is preserved much as he left it when he set out for St. Petersburg in 1893 for the premiere of the Sixth Symphony. This is the living room, where Tchaikovsky also composed.

tryside: it represented all that was best about "my adored Mother Russia." It was his only real home during the last eight years of his life—the place where he did most of his composing, and where he took long afternoon walks every day he was there. In the spring of 1892, soon after his return from America, where he had conducted the concert that opened New York's Carnegie Hall, he moved from the rented house in Maidanovo to a house in nearby Klin—a house that is still scrupulously preserved just as Tchaikovsky left it when he traveled to St. Petersburg in October 1893 to conduct the premiere of his Sixth Symphony, the *Pathétique*. He would never return. His books, his pipes, his pens, his piano, even his clothes, are as he left them. On the walls are his pictures. Above his bed hangs a brooding watercolor whose title is *Melancholy*.

In this solitary setting among the forests of Maidanovo and Klin, Tchaikovsky fought with his demons, and in his music he wrote a commentary on his life—his fears, his joys, and his ever-growing concern with fate. The fairy-tale worlds of his ballets *The Sleeping Beauty* and *Nutcracker* belong to this period (the latter paired with a one-act opera, *Iolanta*, about which Tchaikovsky confessed, "Medieval dukes and knights and ladies captivate my imagination, but not my *heart*"[13]). In the last two symphonies, the Fifth and Sixth, he laid bare his soul—what he called his "complete resignation before Fate." And in *The Queen of Spades*, all unknowingly, he foretold his own end.

He cannot have written *The Queen of Spades* without thinking back to Carmen's prophecy, "Spades—a grave." His brother Modest wrote the libretto, loosely based upon Pushkin's story, but giving it now a tragic ending. In order to win the hand of Lisa, Hermann requires the secret of three cards—a secret known only to Lisa's grandmother, the old countess. When Hermann confronts her, she dies of fright. But later, when her ghost appears to him, he thinks he has the secret—"three, seven, ace." At the card table, the formula seems to be working out—until the final card turns out to be, not the ace, but the queen of spades. It is the dead countess's revenge. Hermann, driven mad, commits suicide.

At its first performance in St. Petersburg, the opera was a triumph. The role of Hermann was created by Nicolai Figner, the most admired Russian tenor of the day, probably better known in Italy and England than he was in Russia. Figner's wife, the Italian soprano Medea Mei, was the Lisa. It was a much more conventional piece than *Eugene Onegin*—more dramatic, with more obvious set pieces. But it lacked the lyricism and the inwardness of *Onegin*, and posterity's judgment has always been that it is second, not first, among Tchaikovsky's operas.

Whether or not Tchaikovsky himself, like his character Hermann, committed suicide is an open question. He died in St. Petersburg in November 1893, just eight days after conducting the first performance of the Sixth Symphony. The official explanation was that he died of cholera as a result of drinking tainted water. That has always seemed doubtful, in view of the circumstantial evidence, including the destruction of many pages of Tchaikovsky's diaries. Rimsky-Korsakov, writing some years later, noted that there had been free access to the requiems for Tchaikovsky (unheard-of when cholera was the cause of death), and that he had even witnessed one person being allowed to kiss the body on the face and head.[14]

In 1978, the Russian scholar Alexandra Orlova made public an account of Tchaikovsky's death that had been given her by Aleksandr Voitov of the Russian Museum in St. Petersburg, a man old enough to have been a witness.[15] In this version, Tchaikovsky took arsenic on the instructions of a so-called "court of honor" composed of former classmates from the school of jurisprudence. They had hastily formed themselves into a court, and commanded Tchaikovsky's appearance before it. One of their number, a senior official in the imperial service, had intercepted a letter to the czar in which a member of the aristocracy charged that Tchaikovsky had had a homosexual liaison with his nephew. Tchaikovsky (the theory goes) took the "honorable" way out. True or not, the story makes some sense in light of what we know of Tchaikovsky.

Not the least of Tchaikovsky's contributions to Russian opera was his fame. More than anyone else, he put Russian music on the map and caused people all over the world to be curious about what other music there might be in that vast land. What they found, among other things, was an emerging school of Russian opera that must have taken them by surprise if Tchaikovsky's music was all they had heard up to that time. Russian opera, they discovered, was rough-hewn, nationalistic, and extremely difficult to categorize in the generally accepted formulas of the day. Most of all, when sung in Russian, which was by no means always the case in the great opera houses of the world, it had a sound that was more than just distinctive: it was unique.

It was not only in the great imperial theaters of Moscow and St. Petersburg that these events took place. As early as Catherine the Great's time, there had been wealthy private patrons who owned their own theater companies. These companies were very often composed entirely of serfs, and most of them were in the provinces rather than the capital cities. Later on, at the time when Tchaikovsky and the Mighty Handful were going about their business, a man named Savva Mamontov founded a company that deserved almost as much credit for the promotion of opera in Russia as did the Bolshoi and the Maryinsky. Mamontov was a remarkable character. He made his fortune building railways, and he spent it on the arts. His two great passions were the paintings of Aleksandr Golovin and the music of the Mighty Handful. The opera company he formed (it was known as the Mamontov company) performed in Nizhni Novgorod as well as in Moscow, and it was responsible for the Russian premieres of many contemporary operas that could not yet be seen in the imperial theaters—*Aida* and *Faust* among them. He also gave opportunities to Russian singers. The most famous beneficiary was Fyodor Chaliapin, who spent two years with the Mamontov company, singing many of his greatest roles for the first time: Boris, Ivan the Terrible, Susanin, Dosifey (in Mussorgsky's *Khovanshchina*), and Salieri in Rimsky-Korsakov's *Mozart and Salieri* (a part he created).

Savva Mamontov made another great contribution to Russian theater: he persuaded major artists, including his protégé Golovin and artists of the distinction of Nicolay Roerich, to design sets for productions at the imperial theaters. The magnificent, bold curtains and backcloths for *Swan Lake*, *Boris*, *Onegin*, *Igor*, and other productions in

Design by Aleksandr Golovin for Rimsky-Korsakov's The Maid of Pskov (Ivan the Terrible) *at the Théâtre du Châtelet, Paris, 1909.*

the early years of the twentieth century were a memorial to Mamontov and a foretaste of what Léon Bakst and Aleksandr Benois were about to do for Sergei Diaghilev in Western Europe (see the chapter "On the Twentieth Century").

Something else of great significance for the future of opera was happening in Russia at this time. From Gogol and Pushkin, through Turgenev and Dostoyevsky, to Chekhov and Tolstoy, the nineteenth century had been a brilliant era of Russian literature and drama. But it had not been such a brilliant era for the production and presentation of drama. The stage was still bound by the contrived, overly dramatic conventions of the previous century. Then, in June 1897, two men who rebelled against those conventions met for the first time. They met in a Moscow restaurant, the Slavyansky Bazaar, and they talked without stopping for seventeen hours. Their names were Vladimir Nemirovich-Danchenko and Konstantin Stanislavsky.[16] The next year they founded the Moscow Art Theater.

What Stanislavsky and Nemirovich-Dan-

chenko strove for was a much more naturalistic style of acting and staging. Stanislavsky's actors were required to achieve total identification with the characters they played. It was no longer good enough to go on stage and temporarily impersonate someone: you had to assume the character's personality and way of thinking; you had to play the character from inside, not outside. One of the early productions of the Moscow Art Theater was a staging of Chekhov's play *The Seagull*, a work that had not previously enjoyed much success. It was perfect for Stanislavsky's purposes: it had virtually no plot, it revolved around three complicated love triangles, and it had at its center the symbolism of the seagull. The production caused a sensation. There were dissenters, of course, and ironically they included Chekhov himself, despite the fact that his wife was one of the actresses. But the style—and more important, the method—that Stanislavsky created at the Moscow Art Theater had a tremendous impact on all forms of theatrical presentation.

Of those theatrical forms, opera was far and

away the hardest to reform. It was true that you could sometimes see great singers who were also good actors (Chaliapin was an outstanding example), but the tradition of the Bolshoi's early years, when the company was composed of actors who also sang, was long forgotten. The accepted conventions of opera at the end of the nineteenth century—and much of the music that was being written for it—called for voices of great power and stamina, and that, it was generally agreed, meant singers of considerable bulk and awkwardness. Stanislavsky's prescription for changing this was to try to develop a new style of singing, in which words and their meaning could be given greater importance. It was the logical consequence of all the effort and dedication the Mighty Handful had invested in creating music that complemented the Russian language. In 1918, Stanislavsky founded his own opera studio and began experimenting with productions of works as varied as Cimarosa's *Il matrimonio segreto* (The Secret Marriage) and Musorgsky's *Boris Godunov*. When he died in 1938 he was working on *Madama Butterfly*.

Later in the twentieth century, when theater and opera finally came to feed each other, Stanislavsky's ideas would have an impact far beyond Russia. In the same way, it was another Russian of the same vintage, Sergei Diaghilev, who would revolutionize the concept of design and staging throughout the world of musical theater.

ABOVE: *Design by Natalia Gontcharova for Rimsky-Korsakov's* LE COQ D'OR, *Paris, 1914.*

LEFT: *Konstantin Stanislavsky (1863–1938). "The whole point,"* Stanislavsky wrote, *"is to convert a concert in costume, which is what most opera performances are nowadays, into a genuine dramatic spectacle."*

An Interlude with Realism

February 1893 was a memorable month in the life of Giulio Ricordi, music publisher of Milan. In the first nine days of the month, two of his long-term projects came to fruition. In one of them, Ricordi had the utmost confidence: it could not fail. For the other (and it would be the more important to him in the long run), he had high hopes, but it was by no means a certainty.

The worrying one came first. At the Teatro Regio in Turin, on the first day of the month, a young composer in whom Ricordi had been investing his firm's money for almost ten years (to the great discomfort of his fellow directors) was staging his third opera. The composer's name was Giacomo Puccini. He was thirty-four years old, and he still had not had a significant success. He needed one now, and Ricordi needed it every bit as much if he was to justify his actions to his board.

The sure-fire success was to happen at La Scala, Milan, nine days later. It was the premiere of the latest, and

surely the last, opera to be written by the most
famous client of G. Ricordi & Co.: Giuseppe
Verdi. The great maestro was in his eightieth year,
and for the last six of them, ever since the triumphant opening of *Otello* in 1887, Ricordi had
been quietly conspiring with Verdi's wife, Giuseppina, and his librettist, Arrigo Boito, to bring this
final work to completion.

As things turned out, Puccini's *Manon Lescaut*
was a triumphant success in Turin, and Verdi's
Falstaff, though it was not quite what the Milanese
public had expected, was received with all the antic-
ipated reverence, ecstasy, and jubilation.

While these events undoubtedly made
Ricordi a happy man, and a much richer one, too,
they also served to answer a question that had
obsessed Italians for almost two decades. Who
would be Verdi's successor? There were several
contenders, collectively known as the *giovane scuola*
(the young school). Their progress was closely
monitored, not just by music critics and music
publishers, but by the general public as well. Verdi
himself, cloistered on his estate at Sant'Agata, had
a healthy interest in the matter.

About the time that *Manon Lescaut* confirmed Ricordi's faith in Puccini, a Milan pho-
tographer published a portrait of "Verdi and the
Young School." It showed Verdi sitting in a box
at La Scala, accompanied by five of the composers

thought most likely to follow in his footsteps:
Boito, Mascagni, Giordano, Leoncavallo, and, sitting closest to Verdi, Puccini. The picture was not
a real photograph: it was a composite constructed
from several individual pictures, which doubtless
explained why the composers were so studiously
looking anywhere but at each other.

There were others who might have been
added to the picture. Francesco Cilea had a right
to be there. So did Alfredo Catalani, though he
would die later the same year. It nevertheless captured an extraordinary moment in the story of
Italian opera, a sort of interlude between the
respective reigns of Verdi and Puccini. It was a time
when music publishers could, and did, assume the
role of kingmakers, and when a short-lived, but
very potent, form of opera blossomed and faded,
all in the space of twenty years.

This new form of opera was called *verismo*
(realism). Traditionally, opera had avoided reality: it had been about mythology, ancient history,
and idealized romance. When it had taken on real
historical stories, as Meyerbeer, Verdi, and their
contemporaries had done, they had avoided the
seamy or controversial sides of the stories in deference to censors and impresarios. There had been
exceptions, of course. As early as 1642, Monteverdi
had stood the conventions on their head when he
had made a heroine out of Poppea as she slept her

way to the imperial throne. Ninety years later, Pergolesi had composed one of the best-loved of all comic operas, *La serva padrona*, the story of a serving girl who became mistress of the household. Mozart had featured "downstairs" as well as "upstairs" in his adaptation of Beaumarchais's play about Figaro, with "downstairs" being both cleverer and more virtuous. Verdi had depicted rather more of reality in *La traviata* than bourgeois morality was comfortable admitting to. Finally, in 1875, *verismo* had been prefigured by Bizet's *Carmen*—a highly realistic story about cigarette-factory girls, smugglers, bullfighters, and a very nasty onstage murder. Like most musical movements, *verismo* had its literary progenitors—Guy de Maupassant and Émile Zola in France; Charles Dickens in England, perhaps; and certainly Giovanni Verga in Italy.

But it was not simply literary fashions, nor even musical ones, that ignited the brief *verismo* movement in Italy. It had more to do with the commercial rivalry between the two biggest music publishers in Milan.

For the greater part of two centuries, the principal connection between opera and publishing had been the printing of librettos, rather than music scores. Librettos were often written by distinguished poets and dramatists whose works were published almost as a matter of course. Thus, the texts of Ottavio Rinuccini, the very first librettist of opera, had all been printed, but the scores of Monteverdi and his contemporaries existed generally only in manuscript. There were occasional exceptions. Lully, whose music was recognized and promoted by Louis XIV as an "official" branch of French culture, had his scores published in magnificent editions by Ballard, the leading woodblock printer of Paris. But most composers had to rely on their own manuscript scores and hand-copied parts.

Music copying, all of it done by hand, was a cottage industry. By definition, it had to be done by musicians, so for orchestral players it was often a welcome way of augmenting meager earnings. One such at the very beginning of the nineteenth century was Giovanni Ricordi. He was a violinist and occasional conductor at the Fiando Theater in Milan, and a music copyist in his spare time. Still in his early twenties, he saw the business potential for a genuine music publisher in Milan, a city where music was a way of life and where the latest song or the latest tune would seem to have a ready-made market. So Ricordi went to Leipzig

for a year, to the firm of Breitkopf & Hartel, Beethoven's publishers, to learn the craft of music engraving. When he returned to Milan in 1808, he immediately opened a shop and set himself up as a publisher: G. Ricordi & Co.

Giovanni Ricordi had been right about the business opportunity, of course, but one of the principal reasons for his success was his own standing as a musician. It enabled him to become a close friend of Rossini and the publisher of his music. Thirty years later, with his ear close to the ground at La Scala, he was one of the first to recognize the promise of Verdi and to make sure that he, too, would be a client of the firm—its avenue to prosperity and power.

Verdi dealt with three generations of Ricordis: Giovanni, whom he knew only slightly but respected greatly; Tito, who was a close friend and trusted business partner for the greater part of his career; and Giulio, Tito's son, who came into Verdi's life as a very young man and was eventually responsible for suggesting, persuading, and gently cajoling Verdi into writing the two great operas of his old age. By the time Giulio took over the firm from his ailing father in 1887, the Ricordi firm was already highly profitable; *Aida*, more than anything else, had seen to that. But it was also true to say that the Ricordis had made Verdi very rich. He was an excellent and hardheaded businessman on his own behalf, but the contracts he dictated for his operas could only have been as lucrative as they were because there was a marketing system in place that was able to promote and sell his wares. That system was G. Ricordi & Co.

Any successful business attracts competitors. In the case of Ricordi, there were two principal opponents in Milan. One was the publishing firm of Lucca. In his early days, before he settled into his long-term relationship with the Ricordis, Verdi had written three operas for Lucca, of which *Attila* was the most important. That was before he discovered how much he disliked Francesco Lucca and his much younger wife, Giovannina. Dislike turned to hatred when the Luccas became the Italian publishers and agents of Richard Wagner. Giovannina succeeded her husband on his death in 1872 and proceeded to conduct a loud and aggressive campaign on behalf of Wagner's music in Italy (with considerable success), but in 1888 she called it a day and sold the entire business to Ricordi.

A much more substantial competitor was Edoardo Sonzogno. His family had been in the

business of publishing long before Giovanni Ricordi opened his shop in 1808, but the Sonzognos' business was book publishing and the printing of pamphlets; they did not become involved in music publishing until the 1870s, by which time the Ricordis were showing just how profitable it could be. Edoardo Sonzogno knew that Ricordi's wealth was based on its ownership of Verdi's works; that much was obvious to everyone. It became Sonzogno's obsession that there must, somewhere, be a successor to Verdi—and that the successor must become a Sonzogno client.[1]

The most visible organ of the Sonzogno publishing empire was its popular daily newspaper in Milan, *Il secolo.* It was largely on the advice of the paper's music critic, Amintore Galli, that Sonzogno had gone into the business of music publishing, in 1874. Now, in 1883, Galli proposed a strategy for finding Verdi's successor. It was not entirely original, but neither was it expected to end in embarrassment and failure.

Galli's idea was for Sonzogno to launch a nationwide competition for a new one-act opera. The winning entry would be published (by Son-

toire piece today, had had a triumphant premiere at La Scala in 1876. This eminent jury eventually announced two winners rather than one. Both of them have long since been forgotten. In making its decision, the jury overlooked the entry of Giacomo Puccini.

At the time of the competition, Puccini was twenty-five years old. Like Verdi, he had come to Milan to pursue his studies at a more mature age than most music students. Unlike Verdi, he had been accepted by the conservatory despite his age. No one doubted that he was an outstanding student—Ponchielli was one of his professors. The piece he wrote for the competition was called *Le willis* (later known as *Le villi*). It was an adaptation of the same story on which the popular ballet *Giselle* had been based. To be fair to the jury, Puccini's manuscript was pretty illegible. It was written in haste, and Puccini's handwriting all his life was notoriously hard to read, sometimes impenetrable. But that did not alter the fact that a lot of influential people in the music business knew Puccini had submitted an entry, and that it had been rejected in favor of what appeared to be two rather undistinguished works.

The jury's decision was final, of course, but Puccini's friends, led by the playwright Ferdinando Fontana, who had been the librettist of *Le willis*, were not prepared to leave it at that. Fontana arranged for a private performance of the work and invited a number of influential people. They, in turn, raised the money for *Le willis* to be given

zogno, of course) and given public performances, and its composer would become a long-term client of Sonzogno's. Twenty-eight entries were received, and a distinguished jury was empaneled to choose a winner. Galli was on the jury; so was Franco Faccio, La Scala's outstanding conductor and a fine composer in his own right; and so was Amilcare Ponchielli, professor of composition at the Milan conservatory and composer of one of the few really successful Italian operas of the last few years, other than those of Verdi. Ponchielli's *La Gioconda* (The Joyful Girl), still a popular reper-

Giulio Ricordi (1840–1912) in the 1880s.

a series of public performances at Milan's Teatro Dal Verme in the early summer of 1884. One of those who attended these performances was Giulio Ricordi. Within a matter of days, he had purchased the publishing rights and, more important, he had commissioned Puccini to write another opera. Instead of paying an advance, he made the much more lavish offer of a regular stipend throughout the process of composition.

The catastrophe for Sonzogno seems much greater in retrospect than it did at the time. It was almost five years before Puccini's new opera, *Edgar*, reached the stage of La Scala, and then it was a failure. It was at this point that his fellow directors implored Giulio Ricordi to cancel Puccini's salary and cut the firm's losses on the young composer. But Ricordi had greater faith. He patiently waited almost four more years before his hopes were eventually realized in Turin in that first week of February 1893.

Cav and Pag

Meanwhile, in 1888, Sonzogno had held a second competition, and a much more successful one. This time there were seventy-three entries, and a clearcut winner: Pietro Mascagni's *Cavalleria rusticana* (Rustic Chivalry). It was given its premiere in Rome in 1890, and it has been a favorite ever since.

More than any previous opera, *Cavalleria rusticana* deserved the description *verismo*. Mascagni based it on a story (later a play) by Italy's leading writer of the realist school, Giovanni Verga. The setting was a Sicilian village on Easter morning, and it contained all the elements of tabloid realism: passion, violence, romance, a mother's love, illegitimacy, religion. All the action was packed into one act, seventy-five minutes of concentrated drama highlighted by some of the finest set pieces ever composed for the opera stage, the "Easter Chorus" being perhaps the most popular.

Although he was five years younger than Puccini, with whom he had shared rooms at the Milan conservatory, Mascagni was the first to achieve fame. But it was short-lived, and it derived mainly from *Cavalleria rusticana*, which he spent the rest of his life trying to emulate. *L'amico Fritz* (Friend Fritz) is occasionally performed today. *Iris*, a Japanese story, has never had much of a following, but it did better than *Le maschere* (The Masks), which was booed off the stage in both Verona and Genoa. In his later days, sadly, Mascagni became a mouthpiece for Italian fascism. He composed a

huge, bombastic work called *Nerone* (Nero) in honor of Mussolini, and died a lonely and unpopular old man in 1945.

Cavalleria rusticana had many imitators but few successors. One of the few legitimate successors was Ruggero Leoncavallo's *I pagliacci* (The Clowns). Leoncavallo was Neapolitan and very well traveled. As a young man (he was a year and a half older than Puccini), he wrote an opera called *Chatterton* and invested his entire worldly wealth in its production. The impresario ran off with the money before the opera was actually performed, and Leoncavallo found himself penniless. He spent several years traveling around Egypt, Greece, Turkey, Germany, Belgium, and the Netherlands, earning his keep as a café pianist. Eventually, he came to rest in Paris, where he became a fervent student of the works of Wagner. He conceived the very un-Neapolitan idea of composing a Wagnerian-sized trilogy of operas about the Italian Renaissance. He devoted six years of his life to this epic, finally returning to Italy in 1887 with the first opera, *I Medici*, composed and ready for production. Giulio Ricordi expressed interest, but then there were delays and more delays. It became clear that Ricordi was not going to publish the opera, let alone get it performed. In despair, Leoncavallo consulted Ricordi's star client, Puccini, and it was Puccini who suggested doing a shorter piece, a one-act opera. Leoncavallo took the advice and sent the manuscript, not surprisingly, to Sonzogno rather than Ricordi. Sonzogno thus became the proud owner of two of the best short operas ever written.

I pagliacci was Leoncavallo's own dramatization of the true story of a recent crime of passion in a small Calabrian village.[2] It was the perfect pairing for *Cavalleria*. Indeed, within a year of *I pagliacci*'s premiere in Milan in 1892, Sonzogno had united the two operas on a single bill at the Teatro Costanzi in Rome. "*Cav* and *Pag*" became a phrase in every operagoer's vocabulary.

Like Mascagni, Leoncavallo was never able to repeat his success, but he came close—or he might have if fate, in the form of Giacomo Puccini, had not intervened. The origins of the story went back to the summer of 1891,[3] when neither of them had yet achieved great success, though both were on the verge of it. Puccini was in the throes of *Manon Lescaut* and Leoncavallo was equally immersed in *I pagliacci*. In order to escape the hot Milanese summer, they each took a cottage in the village of Vacallo in the Italian Tyrol. It was while they were there that Leoncavallo mentioned to Puccini another project he had in mind. There may even have been a suggestion that it should be a collaboration, with Leoncavallo writing the libretto and Puccini the music (Leoncavallo had actually contributed to the libretto of *Manon Lescaut*, though there were so many contributors to that libretto that when Ricordi published it he omitted to credit anyone at all). But Puccini seems to have expressed no great enthusiasm for the new project at the time.

Almost two years went by. Leoncavallo had his great success with *I pagliacci*; Puccini followed him a few months later with *Manon Lescaut*. Then, on an afternoon in March 1893, the two of them met by chance while strolling in the Galleria in Milan. They made a very nasty discovery: they were both working on adaptations of the same book, Henry Mürger's *Scènes de la vie de bohème*. The world was shortly to be richer by not one, but two operas called *La bohème*. Mürger's book was certainly the one Leoncavallo had mentioned in the Tyrol. Although Puccini had not been interested at the time, the idea had come back to haunt him, and he had commissioned a libretto from Luigi Illica and Giuseppe Giacosa, completely unaware that Leoncavallo was still pursuing the idea. (Mürger's book was in the public domain, so the issue of exclusivity did not arise.)

Warfare was waged—not so much between the two composers (though it was the end of their friendship) as between their rival publishers. Sonzogno, as the owner of the daily newspaper *Il secolo*, published an announcement that his man, Leoncavallo, had begun work on the opera and claimed the rights. The next day, Puccini wrote to a rival newspaper, *Corriere della sera*, wondering what the fuss was about: why should they not both write their operas, and let the public decide between them?

That was what happened. Giulio Ricordi used the public speculation to whip his normally slow client into action (Puccini had probably not written a note of the music at the time of the meeting in the Galleria), and the Puccini version was the first to reach the stage, in Turin in 1896. Fifteen months later, when Leoncavallo's version was produced in Venice, he had a very reasonable success, but by that time, unfortunately for Leoncavallo and Sonzogno, a good many Italians were already whistling the tunes of *La bohème*—Puccini's *La bohème*.

Not that Puccini had had an uncritical success. That was a luxury he never again enjoyed after *Manon Lescaut*. Compared to his earlier work, *La bohème* was written in a conversational vein, and the music was somewhat impressionistic—not what had been expected. Puccini was dissatisfied with both the production and the casting at the premiere

Pietro Mascagni (1863–1945) conducting Cavalleria rusticana. *Caricature by Liberio Prosperi (Vanity Fair, 1893).*

Caricature of Ruggero Leoncavallo (1858–1919).

in Turin and worked hard to improve on them for subsequent productions. In Livorno, not far from his native city of Lucca, he auditioned a young tenor called Enrico Caruso for the role of Rodolfo: "Who sent you to me? God?" Puccini is said to have remarked at the end of the audition.[4] Eventually (but not quite yet), Caruso, and the conductor of *La bohème* at its premiere, Arturo Toscanini, would become, with Puccini himself, the three most celebrated Italian musicians of the age.

La bohème made Puccini famous, and it made both Ricordi and Puccini very rich. Out of the proceeds, Puccini built a small lodge on the shores of Lake Massaciuccoli in the village of Torre del Lago. It was a place he had been visiting for several years—a place where he could find some peace and quiet for composing, where he could indulge his favorite hobbies (duck hunting and poker), and where he could keep his private life private. There was some need for this. Ever since the time of *Edgar*, Puccini had been living with Elvira Gemignani. She, too, came from Lucca, and in 1886 she had borne him a son, Antonio. Unfortunately, she was married, to a wholesale merchant. It was not until he died, in 1904, that Elvira and Puccini were able to marry. In the meantime, Torre del Lago provided a wonderful haven as Puccini, remorselessly pursued by Giulio Ricordi, worked slowly but surely to create more operatic heroines to follow in the footsteps of

Mimì. There would be Tosca, Butterfly, Minnie, and eventually Liù.

OTHER VERISMO COMPOSERS

In the prologue to *I pagliacci*, one of the principal characters, Tonio, boldly announced the subject matter of the opera. In doing so, he defined *verismo*. It was, he sang, a "squarcio di vita"—a "slice of life."

No one else was to have the success Mascagni and Leoncavallo had had with the genre, but many tried. One of them was Umberto Giordano, a legitimate member of the *giovane scuola*, and a runner-up to Mascagni in the Sonzogno competition of 1888 (his entry, *Marina,* had been cited for distinction). Giordano tackled the seamy side of life in an opera aptly named *Mala vita,* but it had no great success. In *Andrea Chénier,* however, produced in the same year as *La bohème,* he had a triumph at La Scala. It was *grand opéra,* but it also demonstrated elements of *verismo*—a French Revolutionary background, real historical characters, and a dénouement at the guillotine. Two years later, his *Fedora* had an almost equal success, somewhat exaggerated by the fact that it was Caruso's first big starring role in Milan. *Fedora* was probably the most ambitious of all the *verismo* operas, an international murder mystery set in St. Petersburg, Paris, and Switzerland. Thereafter, Giordano's career flagged. He lived until 1948, a greatly honored personage in the world of Italian music, but

The "other" LA BOHÈME: *a production of Leoncavallo's* LA BOHÈME *at the Wexford Festival, Ireland, 1994. Directed by Reto Nickler. With (from left) Jean-Pierre Furlan as Marcello, Patryk Wroblewski as Rodolfo, and Jungwon Park as Mimì. In Leoncavallo's version, Marcello and Musetta have the principal roles; Rodolfo is a baritone, Marcello a tenor.*

he never recaptured the glory days of *Chénier*. In 1915, still juggling with *verismo* and the French Revolutionary period, he wrote an opera for New York's Metropolitan about the proprietress of a Paris laundry whose Revolutionary exploits enabled her, years later, to present the emperor Napoleon with an unpaid bill incurred at her laundry when he was a lowly lieutenant. It was called *Madame Sans-Gêne* (Madame Free-and-Easy). Geraldine Farrar sang the title role and Toscanini conducted, but it managed only fourteen performances in four seasons.

Francesco Cilea was another who tried *verismo*. The only one of his operas to remain in the repertoire is *Adriana Lecouvreur*, another opera based on a real historical character—an eighteenth-century actress at the Comédie-Française in Paris. The title role was, and remains, a marvelous vehicle for great divas near the end of their careers: Renata Tebaldi, Licia Albanese, Renata Scotto, Montserrat Caballé, and Mirella Freni have all, at various times, made the role their own.

Perhaps the unluckiest composer of them all was Alfredo Catalani. Like Verdi and Puccini, he was a client of Ricordi, but not by choice. He

had originally been published by Lucca and had passed to Ricordi when Giovannina Lucca sold her business in 1888. It was a time of unparalleled power for music publishers, and Catalani, playing third fiddle behind Verdi and Puccini in the Ricordi camp, suffered more than most. He had

had a modest success with *Loreley*, and then, in 1892, a much more significant success at La Scala with an opera called *La Wally*. It was undoubtedly of the *verismo* school, though not typical of it—a romantic story set in the Tyrol, ending with the deaths of Wally and her lover in a huge avalanche, but lacking the seamy side of life expected in true *verismo*. It won a lot of hearts at La Scala (including Toscanini's: he would name his daughter Wally), and the Teatro Regio in Turin decided to give it the next season. That idea was vetoed by Giulio Ricordi, who wanted the Regio to concentrate its resources on the world premiere of Puccini's *Manon Lescaut*, also scheduled for that season. To make sure he got his way, Ricordi threatened to raise the rental fees on a number of other operas the Regio was to present during the season, including *Aida*, *Rigoletto*, and *Die Meistersinger*, all of which were owned in Italy by Ricordi. The Regio caved in, and Catalani, not yet forty, died later that year, a thoroughly embittered man.

Verismo was not entirely an Italian phenomenon. Jules Massenet climbed on the bandwagon with *La navarraise* in 1894; so did his pupil Gustave Charpentier with *Louise* in 1900. In Germany, it seemed for a while that Eugen d'Albert might be the one to watch. His *Tiefland* (The Lowlands) in 1903 contained a cunning mixture of German Romanticism and fashionable *verismo*, including a very nasty strangling. But d'Albert, who had actually been born in Scotland, never quite lived up to other people's expectations of him.

Meanwhile, one member of the *giovane scuola*, the senior member, declined to join the *verismo* movement at all. Arrigo Boito had started out as everyone's favorite in the Verdi succession. The son of an Italian painter and a Polish countess, he had been blessed with one of the most brilliant minds of his generation. As a young man, he had served with Garibaldi and had become a leading member of the artistic reform movement centered in Milan in the 1870s—the so-called *scapigliatura* (disheveled). He was only twenty-six when his opera *Mefistofele* was produced at La Scala—a failure in its original version, but much more successful in later revisions and still a popular piece today. But Boito's gifts were literary as well as musical, and in the 1880s and 1890s, while other members of the *giovane scuola* were staking their claims with new operas, Boito was the junior partner in one of the most productive collaborations in opera: he wrote the librettos for *Otello* and *Falstaff*, the two great works of Verdi's old age. Even when *Falstaff* was completed, Boito sought to continue the partnership: he began work on yet another Shakespearian adaptation, *King Lear*. Verdi,

Catalani's La Wally *at the Muziektheater, Amsterdam, 1993. Directed by Tim Albery, designed by Hildegard Bechtler. With Janet Cessna as Wally and Barry McCauley as Hagenbach. The opera is set in the Tyrolean Alps.*

Gomes's Il guarany *at the Bonn Opera, 1994. Directed by Werner Herzog, designed by Maurizio Balò. With Plácido Domingo as Pery.*

meanwhile, urged him to concentrate on composing, but Boito had developed something of a writer's block. For the last thirty years of his life, he struggled with an opera called *Nerone*, set in ancient Rome (the same subject that Mascagni later used to glorify Mussolini). Boito never finished it. When he died, in 1918, the huge, sprawling manuscript was picked up by his friends Arturo Toscanini and Vincenzo Tommasini; they edited it into a performing version that was given at La Scala in 1924 and then quietly dropped.

Other stars had briefly shone. In the early 1870s, when Verdi was still busy with *Aida* and Boito was wondering how he could salvage *Mefistofele*, it had seemed possible that Carlos Gomes, a Brazilian composer then based in Italy, might be the successor. Gomes was an exotic figure in Milan. He had been sent there by Brazil's opera-loving emperor, Dom Pedro II. In 1870, Gomes had a great success with *Il guarany* (Gomes's grandmother had been a member of the Guarany Indian tribe). It was the opera in which Victor Maurel, the future Iago and Falstaff, had made his La Scala debut. But Gomes never again reached those heights. By the time La Scala mounted his *Maria Tudor,* in 1879, he had lost momentum, and he soon returned to Brazil. Meanwhile, Stefano

Gobatti had appeared in Bologna, only twenty years old, had had a remarkable triumph with his opera *I goti* (The Goths), and had disappeared almost without trace.[5]

In the end, of course, no one could step into Verdi's giant-size shoes, and members of the *giovane scuola* were always careful to acknowledge it. But by 1896, when *La bohème* confirmed the promise of *Manon Lescaut*, it was clear that Giacomo Puccini was the outstanding composer of the next generation. Backed by his prodigious talent, and the very considerable power of Ricordi, Puccini was ensconced at Torre del Lago and already at work on the story of Floria Tosca.

PUCCINI'S MATURE CAREER

Puccini never really belonged to the *verismo* school. Only one of his operas, the one-act *Il tabarro* (The Cloak), quite late in his career, can truly be placed in that category. But most of his other operas did contain elements of *verismo*. The milieu of the four students in *La bohème*, for example, was essentially autobiographical—based on the life Puccini had lived at the Milan conservatory when he shared rooms with Pietro Mascagni.[6] They had run up large bills on credit at their local restaurant (it was called the Aida rather than the Café Momus), and

at one stage Puccini had even pawned his coat, as Colline does in the opera (but, in Puccini's case, because he wanted to take a pretty young dancer out for the evening). *Tosca*, too, had strong elements of realism. The Roman locations were real places; the events of the opera took place at an actual historical moment, in June 1800; and the principal character, the opera singer Floria Tosca, was a thoroughly believable heroine, just as the police chief, Scarpia, was a very credible villain. In the same way, the audience at the Metropolitan Opera in 1910 must instantly have recognized the Wild West setting at the world premiere of *La fanciulla del West* (The Girl of the Golden West).

Not everything went smoothly for Puccini. The premiere of *Madama Butterfly* at La Scala in 1904 was a fiasco. Coming in the wake of *Tosca*, it was not the sort of opera the public expected from Puccini (it was one of his great talents always to do the unexpected). Nor did the audience much like the Japanese settings. Worse still, it was too long. Intermittent booing finally gave way to a storm of laughter and catcalls when poor Rosina Storchio, who was creating the role of the heroine, Cio-Cio-San, brought out the child called Sorrow. That was too much. Storchio swore she would never again sing the role at La Scala, and she never did, despite the fact that Puccini subsequently revised and shortened the opera into a version that quickly became an international hit.

In the same year as *Butterfly*, Elvira Gemignani's unwanted husband finally expired, and she and Puccini were able to get married. Puccini was now forty-six years old, an international celebrity who increasingly valued the privacy of his lakeside retreat at Torre del Lago. The peace of that place was frequently interrupted by Puccini's duck-hunting expeditions (Ricordi reported that the duck population of Lake Massaciuccoli was decimated for a generation), but in 1908 the peace was interrupted by a much less welcome event.

Elvira Puccini probably had had good cause to be jealous in the past. Puccini, by his own admission, loved beautiful women. Unfortunately, Elvira's jealousy came to a climax when it was least justified: she decided that Puccini was having an affair with their seventeen-year-old maid, a local girl named Doria Manfredi. She hounded Doria to her death, persuading her to commit suicide by taking poison. (At the autopsy, it was established that Doria was a virgin.) Pursued through the courts by Doria's father, Madame Puccini was eventually sentenced to five months in prison for her part in the death—while Puccini, locked in a hotel room in Rome, wept compulsively for days.

What a plot for an opera. And maybe— just maybe—that is what it became. The last scene Puccini ever wrote, just before his death from cancer eighteen years later, was the scene in which Liù, the slave girl in *Turandot*, took her own life rather than betray her lover to Turandot, the "ice-cold princess." Doria Manfredi could not have been far from Puccini's thoughts when he wrote that scene for Liù.

In 1912, two years after the premiere of *La fanciulla*, Puccini suffered another personal loss. Giulio Ricordi had been his friend and champion throughout his professional life—"the only person," Puccini wrote, "who inspires me with trust, and to whom I can confide what is going through my mind."[7] More even than his father or grandfather before him, Giulio Ricordi had demonstrated what could be done when business acumen, at times very aggressive, was allied to his own genuine musicianship and gift for personal relations. Giulio's son Tito, who was a concert pianist in his own right, possessed none of his father's patience or diplomacy. He had been the producer of *Tosca* in 1900 and deserved much credit for the opera's success, but as head of the family firm he soon fell out with his chief client. Puccini actually left Ricordi's for a time, during which he composed *La rondine* (The Swallow) for Monte Carlo in 1917 (it had originally been intended as an operetta for Vienna, but the war had prevented its production there). By the time Puccini patched up the quarrel with Tito and returned to the Ricordi fold, Tito's tenure was almost over. He was forced out in 1919, and the family lost control of the firm. It eventually became a limited company in 1952.

There were other collaborators in Puccini's professional life almost as important as Giulio Ricordi. Two of them were Giuseppe Giacosa and Luigi Illica. Together, they wrote the librettos for the three most enduring of Puccini's operas—*La bohème*, *Tosca*, and *Madama Butterfly*. Giacosa was the poet and "versifier." Illica created the story lines and scenarios, and also wrote detailed stage directions to go with them. It was a delicate, and at times explosive, combination, with Puccini not helping much by frequently changing his mind. Giulio Ricordi's diplomatic skills were in constant demand.

With Arturo Toscanini, however, Ricordi had no influence at all. Those two giants of Ital-

ian music did not like each other. Toscanini's obsession, first and always, was with the music. He cared not at all for the politics of the business, or its commercial aspects. Intolerant of the vanities of singers, he was extremely sparing with their encores. And he had a famous temper.

Toscanini's relationship with Puccini blew hot and cold at various times, but mainly it was good. He recognized in Puccini a musical and dramatic genius that had no peer in its day, and he was its most faithful servant. When they disagreed, it was intense, but brief. During one such falling out, Puccini was distressed to discover that Toscanini's name had not been dropped from his Christmas-present list. As a result, the traditional Puccini gift of *panettone* (fruitcake) had been duly

PUCCINI'S DIFFICULT PREMIERES (2)

Cover of the published score for Puccini's MADAMA BUTTERFLY, 1904. *Puccini's composition of* BUTTERFLY *was interrupted by a serious car accident in 1903. The first-night fiasco was totally unexpected by Puccini and the performers, and may have been caused in part by a claque organized by Ricordi's rival publisher, Sonzogno. The shortened version, first performed in Brescia three months later, was a triumph.*

mailed to the conductor. Puccini dispatched a telegram: "PANETTONE SENT BY MISTAKE—PUCCINI." By return came a telegram from the maestro: "PANETTONE EATEN BY MISTAKE—TOSCANINI."[8]

PUCCINI'S SINGERS

At the center of Puccini's concern were the singers. For them, he wrote a series of wonderful roles that have been central to the careers of almost all great singers ever since. In particular, from *Manon Lescaut* to *Turandot*, via Mimì, Tosca, Butterfly, and Minnie, he created heroines that every dramatic soprano would want to sing. Musically, they were demanding roles; dramatically, they could be dangerous. A robust prima donna affecting to die of consumption, or impersonating a Japanese geisha, was in grave danger of appearing ludicrous to an audience that had become familiar with the naturalistic conventions of *verismo*. On the other hand, the musical opportunities were so great that even Nellie Melba—a singer renowned for her inability to act—could, and did, become a famous Mimì.

For the creators of these roles, Puccini generally chose lyric sopranos whose training and skills exemplified what was now the Verdian tradition: the sort of sopranos who were outstanding as Gilda in *Rigoletto* and Violetta in *La traviata*, and who therefore had more than a passing acquaintance with the problems of acting and singing at one and the same time. Cesira Ferrani was such a one. She came from Turin, so it was fitting that the two roles she created for Puccini, Manon

Nellie Melba (1861–1931) as Mimì in Puccini's LA BOHÈME.

Lescaut and Mimì, should both have had their premieres in that city. Manon suited her perfectly, but she was never as comfortable with Mimì, which may have been one reason for the less than ecstatic reception of *La bohème* at its premiere. Not until it reached Palermo, two years later, was its true potential revealed, and the revelation had a lot to do with the husband-and-wife partnership of Adelina Stehle and Edoardo Garbin, who sang Mimì and Rodolfo. They had been the first Nanetta and Fenton in Verdi's *Falstaff*, and Stehle had also created the role of Nedda in *I pagliacci*.

The first Tosca, Hariclea Darclée, was a Romanian singer who had studied with Faure in Paris. She had become an overnight sensation in 1888, when she replaced Patti in a performance of Gounod's *Roméo et Juliette* at the Opéra. Her powerful voice was much admired in Italy. She created La Wally for Catalani in 1892 (he dedicated the score to her), and a few years later she became the resident prima donna in Rome. That was how she came to originate Iris for Mascagni (in his Japanese-inspired opera of 1898) and Tosca for Puccini, both of them commissioned for Rome's Teatro Costanzi. The premiere of *Tosca*, produced by Tito Ricordi, was a success, and Darclée spent much of the remainder of her career capitalizing on it. She sang it at La Scala under Toscanini and, as the years went by and vocal decline set in, in almost any opera house around the world that would have her.

Playing the part of Floria Tosca was something most singers could be expected to do with a good deal of credibility. Tosca was, after all, an opera singer. But Cio-Cio-San (Madame Butterfly) posed altogether greater problems. Rosina Storchio, the recipient of so much abuse at the first performance, was a petite, mischievous-looking woman—a great favorite of both Puccini and Toscanini—and she was popular in Italy for many years. The failure of *Butterfly* was certainly not her fault, and she sang it with great success elsewhere. By then, of course, she was singing it in Puccini's revised version, which had had its premiere in Brescia only a few months after the fiasco at La Scala. The Cio-Cio-San in Brescia was a Polish soprano, Salomea Krusceniski—a very different singer from Storchio. Krusceniski would eventually become the reigning Brünnhilde, Isolde, and Salome at La Scala.

The woman who gave Butterfly new dimensions, as she did most of the roles she sang, was Emmy Destinn. Few singers have been more adored by the public than she was, and few have been more admired by musicians. She was Strauss's own choice to sing *Salome* in Berlin less than a year after that opera's tumultuous opening in Dresden; five years earlier, in 1901, Cosima Wagner had invited her to sing Senta in the first Bayreuth production of *Der fliegende Holländer;* she sang Mozart, Tchaikovsky, Smetana, Meyerbeer, and the *verismo* school with equal success. But her greatest fame was reserved for her performances at Covent Garden and the Met of Verdi's Aida and Puccini's heroines. It was out of gratitude to her for these performances that Puccini wrote the role of Minnie for her in *La fanciulla del West.* Despite physical limitations as an actress, Emmy Destinn had a bewitching stage presence to add to the glories of a great dramatic voice.

Destinn came from Prague, Bohemia, then part of the Austro-Hungarian Empire, and although she made her career mainly in Berlin, London, and New York, she never ceased to be a Czech patriot. During World War I, which interrupted her career, she went home to Bohemia and established herself as an organizer of the Czech independence movement. A young airman, bailing out over her castle, stayed to become her husband (for a time).[9] After the war, having changed her name to Ema Destinnova, she returned to the stage for eight more years.

Destinn's principal rival as a Puccini heroine in New York was America's own Geraldine Farrar. For sixteen seasons she was a phenomenon at the Met—a very beautiful woman (she starred in several silent films) with a lyric soprano voice that perfectly encompassed the music of Massenet, Gounod, Bizet, and Puccini most of all. She was the Met's first Butterfly, as well as a much-loved Mimì and Tosca—a more vulnerable and appealing figure than Destinn, even if she lacked Destinn's awesome vocal equipment. Farrar's supporters at the Met adopted the name "Gerry-flappers"; they were much in evidence whenever she sang.

These women, and a long line of distinguished successors, had good reason to praise the name of Puccini. So did male singers, and especially tenors. For them he wrote a series of great romantic leads, peppered with showstopping arias—from "Che gelida manina" (Your tiny hand

Enrico Caruso (1873—1921) on board ship in 1920.

after his death in Brussels in 1924, by the composer Franco Alfano, nominated for the task by Toscanini. At the La Scala premiere in 1926 Toscanini chose not to include the new ending. When he came to the place in the score where Puccini had given up, as the funeral music for Liù died away, he stopped the orchestra, turned to the audience and said "The opera ends here, because at this point the Maestro died."[10] At subsequent performances, Alfano's ending (or a version of it) has always been given.

In 1922, two years before he died, Puccini wrote pessimistically about the future of opera: "Melody is no longer practical, or if it is, it is vulgar. People believe the symphonic element must rule, and I, instead, believe this is the end of opera."[11]

It was very far from the end of opera, but it did mark the end of a glorious period in Italian opera. This time, there was no *giovane scuola*, no successor to that great line of composers that had begun with Rossini and had now ended with Puccini.

In retrospect, the fifty-year period between 1876 and the posthumous performance of *Turandot* in 1926 can be seen as the richest, most productive period in the whole four-hundred-year story of opera. It began with the opening of Bayreuth and the culmination of all that Richard Wagner had worked for. It proceeded through the final glorious years of Giuseppe Verdi; the rebirth of French opera; the maturing of Russian opera in the works

ABOVE: *Geraldine Farrar (1882–1967) as Puccini's* BUTTERFLY. *Farrar was the Metropolitan Opera's first Butterfly, in 1907, with Caruso as Pinkerton.*

RIGHT: *Emmy Destinn (1878–1930) as Minnie in the premiere of Puccini's* LA FANCIULLA DEL WEST *at the Metropolitan Opera, New York, 1910.*

OPPOSITE, ABOVE: *Puccini's* TURANDOT *at La Scala, Milan, 1958. Directed by Margherita Wallman, sets by Nicola Benois, costumes by Nicola Benois and Chou Ling.*

OPPOSITE, BELOW: *The posthumous premiere of Puccini's* TURANDOT *at La Scala, Milan, 1926. Rosa Raisa was Turandot, Miguel Fleta was Calaf, and Maria Zamboni was Liù. Mussolini declined to attend the premiere because Toscanini refused to play the "Fascist Hymn" at the beginning of the performance.*

is frozen) in *La bohème* to "Nessun dorma" (None shall sleep) in *Turandot*. And it was Puccini's good fortune that, in the last years of the nineteenth century, an Italian lyric tenor emerged whose talents and inclinations were perfectly suited to his music. Enrico Caruso's fame, which was vastly increased by the gramophone, was greater than that of any of the prime donnas with whom he sang. Caruso was both a friend and a muse to Puccini. His story is told in the chapter "On the Twentieth Century."

PUCCINI'S FINAL WORKS

The last of Puccini's operas to be staged in his own lifetime was actually three operas in one evening, collectively known as *Il trittico*. The trio consisted of *Il tabarro* (The Cloak), a true example of *verismo*; *Suor Angelica*, a wonderful vehicle for female singers (Geraldine Farrar created the title role); and *Gianni Schicchi*, an old-fashioned comic opera that contained the popular aria "O mio babbino caro" (O my beloved papa). The premiere took place at the Met in 1918, just five weeks after the end of World War I. Thereafter, Puccini had time for only one more opera, *Turandot*—though he never quite finished it. It was set in ancient China and based on one of Carlo Gozzi's fables. It contained a rich supply of Puccinian melody and an exotic plot within which was a simple and affecting love story. Because of his advancing cancer, Puccini never completed the final scene. It was done for him,

of Tchaikovsky and the Mighty Handful; and the brief flowering of the *verismo* school in Italy. Then, with the dawning of the twentieth century, Puccini and Richard Strauss continued and developed their respective traditions, so that it looked as though nothing would change. But in truth a great deal had changed. The generation of singers represented by Caruso and Melba and Chaliapin and Lilli Lehmann turned out to be the last generation that regularly and as a matter of course sang new operas. From now on, the regular diet for a singer would be nineteenth-century works. The twentieth century added to the repertoire, but more slowly and with evident labor, and what it added was altogether different. Melody often went missing, leaving a curious and sometimes indigestible gap in the operagoer's experience between the tuneful works of three centuries and the tougher meat of the twentieth century.

But melody would return. It happened on Broadway, in the commercial box-office-driven theater that was dedicated to supplying the public with what it most wanted. That did not just mean escapism and romance: there would be a healthy injection of *verismo* as well—in musicals like *Porgy and Bess* and *West Side Story*. Eventually, they would reach the opera house, and play an important part in the story of twentieth-century opera.

POPULAR MUSICAL THEATER

*O*PERA HAS ALMOST ALWAYS BEEN TAGGED WITH AN ELITIST LABEL. ITS BEGINNINGS IN MEDICI FLORENCE WERE UNDENIABLY ELITIST, AND IT HAS ALWAYS, BY ITS NATURE, BEEN AN EXPENSIVE ENTERTAINMENT TO PRODUCE, AND THEREFORE TO ATTEND. NEVERTHELESS, ITS ORIGINAL DEFINITION, *IL DRAMMA PER MUSICA,* WAS BROAD ENOUGH AND LOOSE ENOUGH TO ALLOW IT TO DEVELOP INTO MORE POPULAR AREAS. MUCH OF THIS ACTIVITY — WHAT MIGHT BE CALLED "CROSSOVER" — DID NOT BEGIN IN THE OPERA HOUSE, AND WAS NOT ORIGINALLY INTENDED FOR OPERA'S REGULAR AUDIENCE, BUT IT GOT THERE IN THE END. THE EARLIEST EXAMPLE WAS FRENCH *OPÉRA-COMIQUE.* IT EMERGED FROM THE POPULAR ENTERTAINMENTS OF FRANCE'S MEDIEVAL AGRICULTURAL FAIRS. DESPITE ANY NUMBER OF OFFICIAL ATTEMPTS TO HAVE IT RESTRICTED, OR EVEN ABOLISHED, IT EVENTUALLY BECAME AN IMPORTANT STRAND OF FRENCH OPERA. SIMILAR DEVELOPMENTS COULD BE SEEN IN GERMAN *SINGSPIEL,* IN FRENCH AND GERMAN OPERETTA, IN SPANISH *ZARZUELA,*

RIGHT: *Gay's* THE BEGGAR'S OPERA
*in a BBC television production, 1984.
Directed by Jonathan Miller. With Carol
Hall as Polly, Roger Daltrey as MacHeath,
and Rosemary Ashe as Lucy.*

PREVIOUS PAGES: *Gershwin's* PORGY AND
BESS *at the Metropolitan Opera, New York,
1985, fifty years after the work's premiere
in Boston. Directed by Nathaniel Merrill,
designed by Robert O'Hearn. With Simon
Estes as Porgy.*

and in the American, German, and British musicals of the twentieth century. All of them reached
the opera house in the end, and they had an
important characteristic in common: they were
commercial. This popular side of opera has always
been governed by the box office, and that has
meant melody.

BALLAD OPERA

One of the earliest examples was the English ballad opera. It became hugely popular in London

during the second quarter of the eighteenth century. This was the London memorialized by the
artist William Hogarth. In a series of pictures he
called "moralities," Hogarth captured forever the
spirit of the times—the squalor, the filth, and the
poverty, as well as the grandeur, the affluence, and
the gaiety of the city.

Ballad operas came into being as a direct
riposte to what was going on at the King's Theatre. That was where Handel ruled, turning out a
series of formal *opere serie* in Italian, featuring the

THE BEGGAR'S OPERA, ACT III, SCENE XI, *by William Hogarth, c. 1729. Lavinia Fenton is Polly (in white). Her future husband, the Duke of Bolton, sits in the audience (extreme right).*

great *castrati* and prima donnas of the period. Ballad operas, as their name implied, were written in a thoroughly English folk idiom, but the best of them were also intended to make fun of the artificial form of opera that Handel represented. With a mixture of spoken dialogue and popular ballad music, they portrayed the real London of the streets, the London of Hogarth.

Not far from the King's Theatre was a rival establishment, considerably more "down-market." The Lincoln's Inn Fields Theatre was owned by John Rich. He had a small inheritance from his father, which included a royal patent giving him the right to build a new theater "any place within our Cities of London and Westminster."[1] If he was to build his new theater, John Rich needed to make some money quickly.

His opportunity came when a playwright named John Gay, who had written the libretto for Handel's *Acis and Galatea*, approached him with a work that was a blatant send-up of Handel and the conventions of Italian opera. Its subject matter was provided by the lower end of London society—the thieves, the prostitutes, and the corrupt officials responsible for the administration of justice—and its music was drawn from the popular treasury of English ballads, most of which would have been well known to the audience. It was called *The Beggar's Opera*. As a journalist of the day so aptly put it, "It made Rich gay and Gay rich."

The Beggar's Opera had an enormous success at Lincoln's Inn Fields. It gave John Rich the financial means to use the rights granted him by his royal patent to build a new theater. The site he chose was at Covent Garden, and his theater was the first incarnation of what is now the Royal Opera House. Rich did not build it for opera. It opened in 1732 with William Congreve's play *The Way of the World*, and the first musical work performed there a few weeks later was, not unnaturally, *The Beggar's Opera*.

More than two hundred and fifty years later, the popularity of John Gay's bawdy, boisterous ballad opera remains undimmed in England. The lead role of MacHeath, the highwayman, has been a film role for Laurence Olivier and a television role for one of the late twentieth century's pop idols, Roger Daltrey. In their very different ways, they coped with the attentions of Polly Peachum and Lucy Lockitt, both of whom believe themselves to be Mrs. MacHeath.

The original Polly in 1728 was Lavinia Fenton. She was immortalized in a painting commissioned from Hogarth by John Rich. It depicted a scene from *The Beggar's Opera*—the scene in Newgate Prison, where MacHeath is confronted simultaneously by his two "wives." Polly is appealing to her father, but her gesture and her eyes suggest she is more interested in the attentions of a gentleman in the audience. The gentleman in question was the duke of Bolton: he is reputed to have sat in the same seat at every performance. Soon after the picture was painted, he and Lavinia ran off together.[2] She remained his mistress for twenty-three years and bore him three sons—until, finally, his wife died and Lavinia at last became the duchess of Bolton.

Ballad operas remained popular in England throughout the eighteenth century, a time when opera in England consisted almost exclusively of imported Italian opera, almost always sung by Italian singers. The ballad opera tradition was *sui generis:* it had no succession, no line of development. But it was exportable, and in Germany, in particular, it had an influence on the development of *Singspiel.*

The *Singspiel* (literally, song-play) consisted of musical numbers interwoven with spoken dialogue. It was in evidence by the middle of the seventeenth century, but it was in the early eighteenth century, in cities like Hamburg and Leipzig, that it became popular. It was, at that time, the only form of native German opera. *Singspiele* were reinforced by imported and translated *opéras-comiques* from France and ballad operas from England, and they were soon institutionalized as a legitimate form of opera. All the great German composers, including Haydn and Mozart, wrote them, and it was Mozart, predictably, who brought the art to its zenith—first with *Die Entführung aus dem Serail* (The Abduction from the Seraglio), then with *Der Schauspieldirektor* (The Impresario), and finally with *Die Zauberflöte* (The Magic Flute).

France had a rather similar form of theater—*vaudeville.* It probably originated in the songs of the valleys around Vire (*vaux de Vire*) in the fifteenth century,[3] and it had certainly been an element in the agricultural fairs from which *opéra-comique* had sprung, but by the mid-nineteenth century it was a distinct form of entertainment in its own right, with a format resembling the old ballad operas of London.

Paris was by now the busiest opera city in Europe. The Opéra, the Théâtre-Italien, and the Opéra-Comique were all in their heyday, but they were only three of almost thirty Parisian theaters specializing in musical entertainment. *Vaudeville* was a major part of this scene. Eugène Scribe, the literary architect of *grand opéra*, was also the mainspring of *vaudeville.* He wrote literally hundreds of comedies, most of them with inscrutable plots, and all of them partly set to music. The music was not original; it was "borrowed," rather as the music of the ballad operas of England had been borrowed.

Onto this crowded Parisian stage stepped Jacques Offenbach.

OPERETTA IN PARIS

Offenbach was not French. He was German, a Jew, born Jakob Offenbach in Cologne. In later life, he would sometimes refer to himself as "Monsieur O de Cologne." His father, a synagogue cantor, sent him to the Paris conservatoire at the early age of fourteen. He studied there for only one year (it was during the last days of Luigi Cherubini's long directorship of the conservatoire), but he made his home in Paris for the rest of his life. Offenbach's ambitions had little to do with the sort of academic music taught by Cherubini, but they had a great deal to do with theater. Still only in his middle teens, he began earning a living as a cellist in the orchestra of the Opéra-Comique and as an occasional composer of dance music and light numbers for the fashionable *café-concerts.* Slowly, but very surely, he established a reputation. In 1850, aged thirty-one, he became resident conductor of the Comédie-Française— not as good a position as the Opéra-Comique, but it gave him a podium, which he used, as often as possible, to introduce his own music. Nevertheless, it was frustrating. Neither the Comédie-Française, which was not primarily a musical theater, nor the Opéra-Comique, which was, would perform his full-length works. So he came up with another plan—or, rather, he copied one from a rival composer.

Florimond Ronger was better known by his stage name, Hervé. He was slightly younger than Offenbach, and not as talented as a composer, but he combined the roles of actor, librettist, producer, and composer. In 1854, Hervé, similarly frustrated by the major theaters, came up with the idea of owning his own theater. He founded Les Folies Nouvelles and began staging lighthearted works by himself and others (they included some of the early cancans). Offenbach wrote him a charmingly odd little work about cannibals called *La reine des îles.*

So it was hardly a surprise when the following report appeared in the Paris newspaper *Le Figaro* in May 1855: "Our friend Jacques Offenbach, the cellist, conductor of the Théâtre-Française, has just leased a new theater that he will manage, opposite the Olympic Circus, enticingly named 'Bouffes-Parisiens.' The title says everything about the repertoire. It is a theater more than anything consecrated to openhearted laughter, to light and smart melody, to bold refrains."

The Théâtre des Bouffes-Parisiens was a tiny theater just off the Champs-Élysées. It seated only fifty, and its auditorium was so steeply raked that people had to hang on to their seats for safety. But, so far as Offenbach was concerned, it was his. He ran it. He decided what was performed. Most of all, he wrote for it.[4]

Both his timing and his choice of location were impeccable. The theater was right next door to the huge exhibition site where, in that very summer of 1855, all the world came to see the great Paris International Exhibition. The new emperor of France, Louis-Napoleon, was a frequent visitor; Queen Victoria came from England ("delighted, enchanted," she informed her diary); even Giuseppe Verdi was in town, for the premiere of his new opera commissioned for the Exhibition year, *Les vêpres siciliennes*.

From the beginning, the Bouffes-Parisiens was a sellout, and Offenbach gave his audiences much to entertain them and much to laugh about. He quickly obtained the use of another theater of similar size, the Théâtre des Jeunes-Élèves, close to the Théâtre-Italien; it was more suitable for winter performances than the Bouffes-Parisiens, which was built only of wood. Within two years, Offenbach took the company on tour to London and Lyons, and to Marseilles and Berlin the following year. He staged a double bill of Mozart's *Der Schauspieldirektor* and Rossini's one-act *Il Signor Bruschino*—this was the occasion on which Rossini declared that he was delighted to do anything for the "Mozart of the Champs-Élysées."[5] But there were still frustrations. The chief of them was the licensing laws in Paris, which restricted him to only four actors on stage, and no chorus. By 1858, in his third season, it was clear that Offenbach would need a miracle if he was to keep the enterprise afloat. The miracle came in two parts. The first was the lifting of the licensing laws. The second Offenbach supplied himself by writing and staging *Orphée aux enfers* (Orpheus in the Underworld).

Offenbach had staked a great deal on the success of *Orphée*, but to begin with it looked as though it might not achieve much more than a

six- or eight-week run. There was no doubting that audiences enjoyed it, especially the famous cancan. But the critics had been lukewarm on opening night, and the word of mouth was that it was not just "naughty," but actually in bad taste. One of the unscheduled successes of the production was the performance of an extremely eccentric actor from the Opéra-Comique. He was called Bache, and no one, least of all the other actors, knew quite what he was going to do at any time. Offenbach, perhaps recognizing a kindred spirit, wrote a special role for Bache—the part of John Styx—and a song that became a showstopper: "Couplets du roi Béotie" (When I Was King of Beotia). Nevertheless, it was an expensive production (scenery and costumes by Gustave Doré) in a small theater; after six weeks, the box office was badly in need of a boost.

It got it from Jules Janin, the pompous and widely read critic of the *Journal des débats*. Janin visited the production six weeks into its run and was deeply offended—"a profanation of holy and glorious Antiquity,"[6] he wrote. Nothing could have been better calculated to arouse the interest of Parisians. The box office instantly sold out, and *Orphée* made Offenbach a rich man. More than that: the newspaper cartoonists, for whom Offenbach's physical characteristics were an irresistible

Top: *Jacques Offenbach (1819—1880), a caricaturist's dream.*

Bottom: *Caricature of Offenbach, by T. Thomas.*

gift, made him a celebrity far beyond the world of theater. And if the Bouffes-Parisiens never again looked back, neither did the idea of operetta.

Literally, *operetta* (or the French *opérette*) means "little opera." It is a word that has conveyed different things at different times in different places, but nothing better defines it than Offenbach's enormous output. He wrote one "orthodox" opera, *Les contes d'Hoffmann* (The Tales of Hoffmann), not quite finished at the time of his death in 1880, but the rest of his work can properly be described as operetta. He ceased to be director of the Bouffes-Parisiens in 1862, four years after *Orphée*, but he never stopped composing and he never stopped delighting his audiences in Paris, London, Vienna, and many other cities on both sides of the Atlantic. *La belle Hélène*, *La vie parisienne*, and *La périchole* (about a street singer in Peru) were some of his most famous titles.

The peak of Offenbach's international renown was reached in 1867, another landmark year in the brief history of France's Second Empire. Once again, it was an exhibition year in Paris—this time, the Great Universal Exposition. The Bouffes-Parisiens was still in business, but most of Offenbach's works now played in larger theaters. For 1867 he had a commission from the Théâtre des Variétés. Together with his two most trusted and prolific librettists, Henri Meilhac and Ludovic Halévy (they would shortly write *Carmen* for Bizet), Offenbach wrote *La grande-duchesse de Gérolstein*.

Twelve years before, in 1855, the Paris Exhibition had provided an opportune background against which to open a new theater. But this time, Offenbach's latest operetta was almost as great a draw as the Exhibition itself. The czar of Russia was in the theater only three hours after arriving in the city. The prince of Wales (one day to be King Edward VII of England) arrived without a ticket and had to make a personal plea to the show's star, Hortense Schneider, before he eventually got a seat. Even Otto von Bismarck went to see it (this was three years before the Franco-Prussian War). In that balmy summer of 1867, *La grande-duchesse de Gérolstein* was the toast of Paris.

Hortense Schneider was the grand duchess. Back at the beginning of Offenbach's venture at the Bouffes-Parisiens, in the very first month he was there in 1855, the then twenty-two-year-old Hortense had gone to visit Offenbach at his home. She persuaded him to let her sing for him as an audition. She sang only a few notes before Offenbach stopped her and offered her a contract on the spot. By 1867, she was by far the greatest star of the operetta world—a prima donna to match any prima donna in the world of opera. She played royalty on the stage, and she expected to be treated as royalty off the stage. Arriving one day at the Exposition, she announced that she wished to drive around in her carriage. That, she was unwisely told, was a privilege granted only to royalty. "I am the grand duchess of Gérolstein," she informed the officials.[7] She drove around in her carriage.

VIENNESE OPERETTA

In all the excitement of Hortense Schneider's performance at the Théâtre des Variétés, and all the foreign visitors to the Universal Exposition, it might have been easy to overlook a good-looking man, in his early forties, who was in Paris that summer to conduct waltzes at a restaurant close to the Exposition site. But it was highly unlikely that he would be overlooked, because he bore the most famous name in music—Johann Strauss the Younger, Vienna's very own "waltz king." In Paris, in that summer of 1867, he created a sensation with one of his newest pieces, the "Blue Danube" waltz. He and Offenbach had met before, three years earlier in Vienna, and they had liked each other. But up to this point, Strauss had been content with his waltzes and his polkas and his marches: he had not yet ventured into operetta.

The fact that Strauss's name was so well known in 1867 was not entirely on his own account. It was his father, Johann Strauss the Elder, who had created the Strauss family legend. Between 1825 and his death in 1849, Strauss the Elder was the most famous orchestra leader in Europe. He had grown up in a music hall managed by his father, at a time when the waltz was the newest and the most fashionable dance around.

The waltz was a peculiarly Viennese invention. It had been derived from an old German-Austrian dance in ¾ time called the *Ländler*, and it had begun to be heard in Vienna in Mozart's time. In 1786, in his opera *Una cosa rara* (A Rare Thing), the Spanish composer Vicente Martín y Soler had used a waltz: it had made a great impression—so much so that Mozart had quoted it in his next opera, *Don Giovanni* (perhaps alluding thereby to the fact that the success of *Una cosa rara*, which had a libretto by Da Ponte, had caused his own little offering, *Le nozze di Figaro*, to be taken off after only

Hortense Schneider (1833–1920) as the Grand Duchess of Gérolstein.

and Josef, to have musical training, too. At the age of nineteen, Johann the Younger established his own ensemble, playing nightly at Dommayer's Restaurant in Hietzig, a suburb of Vienna. His father did not like it, but he could not do much about it, and when he died five years later, in 1849, Johann the Younger united their two orchestras and began his unrivaled reign as the waltz king. It was to last for exactly fifty years.

The waltz king and the Mozart of the Champs-Élysées met for the first time in Vienna in 1864. Offenbach had been invited to visit the city by a journalists' club, the Concordia, which had had the bright idea of commissioning two waltzes for its annual ball at the Sofiensaal. Offenbach called his the "Abendblätter" (Evening Papers) and Strauss called his the "Morgenblätter" (Morning Papers). A few days after the ball, they met in a Viennese café, the Goldener Lamm, to make each other's acquaintance. It was supposedly at this meeting that Offenbach suggested to Strauss that he ought to try his hand at operetta.[8]

Offenbach's operettas were already popular in Vienna. He had first visited the city in 1858, with his Bouffes-Parisiens company; now, on the same visit during which he met Strauss, he signed an exclusive three-year contract for the performance of his works at the Theater an der Wien (the theater Schikaneder had built at the very beginning of the century). But operetta was not just a French import in Vienna: a native tradition was already growing up, and it was led by Franz von Suppé. Nowadays, Suppé's fame depends chiefly on a number of tuneful orchestral overtures, but in Vienna in the 1850s and 1860s he was the pioneer of local Viennese operetta. It owed much to the example of Offenbach (and not a little to Donizetti, who was a distant relative of Suppé's), but it was definitely Viennese. Of his many works, the most famous, composed in 1865, was *Die schöne Galathée* (The Beautiful Galatea), a one-act piece with a brilliant overture dominated by a wonderful waltz tune, and a style and story that obviously owed a good deal to Offenbach's *La belle Hélène*.

It was five years before Strauss took up Offenbach's challenge to write an operetta. In 1871, after abandoning an earlier project, he finally brought *Indigo und die vierzig Räuber* (Indigo and the Forty Thieves) to the stage of the Theater an der Wien. It had a good success, but it was not until 1874, ten years after the meeting at the Goldener

a few weeks in the repertoire). By the time Strauss the Elder persuaded his father to allow him to take up music as a career, the waltz was one of Vienna's most popular dances.

Strauss the Elder teamed up with a friend, Josef Lanner, and together they formed a small orchestra of twelve players. Within a few years, they split up. Lanner and Strauss went their own ways, each forming his own orchestra, and the two became the most celebrated competitors in Vienna. What distinguished Strauss was his organizational ability. He was soon employing two hundred musicians and providing orchestras for up to six separate balls each night. He was also a very skillful composer. The "Radetzky March" was just one of many Strauss tunes everyone knew.

Johann Strauss the Elder forbade his son to become a musician. But it was not that easy. Father Strauss was not only managing a large concern; he was also committed to touring engagements outside Vienna—in Berlin, Paris, and London, his orchestra had major successes—and, complicating matters, he had left his wife and taken up with another woman. So Johann the Younger found it relatively easy to get himself a musical education, and to arrange for his younger brothers, Eduard

Strauss's DIE FLEDERMAUS *at Covent Garden, London, 1983. Directed by Leopold Lindtberg and Richard Gregson, designed by Julia Trevelyan Oman. With Hildegarde Heichele, Hermann Prey, and Doris Soffel. The party at Prince Orlofsky's.*

Lamm, that he produced anything to rival Offenbach. *Die Fledermaus* (The Bat) is the most famous of all operettas, and it was no coincidence that Offenbach's two great librettists, Meilhac and Halévy, had a hand in it.

In Paris, in 1872, the two had written a play, called *Le réveillon,* about a New Year's Eve party. Somewhat adapted, and with the locales altered, it became the basis for *Die Fledermaus.* But, strange to say, *Die Fledermaus* was not an immediate success. It did respectable business at the Theater an der Wien (anything by Strauss would), and it did somewhat better in Berlin later in the year, but the atmosphere in Europe had changed: the carefree attitudes of the 1850s and 1860s had been brought up against cold reality. The Franco-Prussian War of 1870 had had something to do with it; so, in a more personal way for many people, had the crash of the Vienna stock market in May 1873. Moreover, *Die Fledermaus* was not quite as escapist as it might have seemed from the music. It was set in contemporary times and performed in modern dress—something that was as unusual in operetta as it was in opera, and something that appeared to make audiences uncomfortable (as did the title, which was generally thought to be unattractive). Nor did it help that the leading man died onstage one night in the middle of the initial run at the Theater an der Wien.[9] Moreover, there were many who criticized the long, and mainly spoken, final scene—a virtuoso turn for a genuinely great comedian, but a dreadful embarrassment if the performer was anything less than a virtuoso.

Die Fledermaus never needed to be rescued, however. A work that included so much melody, wit, and gaiety was not easily going to be condemned to the refuse dump. It was quite often performed on both sides of the Atlantic in Strauss's time and after, but it was not until Max Reinhardt's revival in Berlin in 1928 that it really took off. Reinhardt played fast and loose with certain elements of the piece (including the score, which was "revised" by Erich Korngold), but the production was so spectacular, and the performances so engaging, that Strauss was exceedingly well served. The whole production took place on a revolving stage, so that one splendid set after another was revealed at staggering speed. (The turntable was borrowed two years later, apparently without Reinhardt's permission, for a Broadway production that starred a certain Archie Leach—better known to history as Cary Grant.)[10] *Die*

Fledermaus was firmly established in the repertoire of every opera house in the world.

Strauss never again wrote anything to match *Die Fledermaus,* though he came close with *Der Zigeunerbaron* (The Gypsy Baron) in 1885. The truth was that Strauss, unlike Offenbach, was never really a man of the theater. He was a composer of wonderful melodies, but he found it hard to think of them in a dramatic context. He frequently composed the individual songs without any ref-

erence to the rest of the plot; sometimes he did not even know what the plot was. *Eine Nacht in Venedig* (A Night in Venice) was a case in point. The Berlin premiere in 1883 was practically drowned out by the laughter and catcalls of the audience. The hilarity was aimed not at the music but at the lyrics. One of them, to the beautiful "Lagunen-Waltzer," began with the memorable couplet: "At night the cats are gray/And tenderly sing meow." Afterward, Strauss wrote to a friend:

"I never saw the libretto dialogue, only the words of the songs. So I put too much nobility into some parts of it, and that was unsuitable to the whole. . . . At the last rehearsals, when I discovered the whole story, I was simply horrified."[11]

Offenbach had successors—Charles Lecocq and André Messager were among them—but Paris never really sustained an operetta tradition in the twentieth century. Vienna, on the other hand, did. No one could step directly into Strauss's

Lehár's Die lustige Witwe *at the San Diego Opera, 1976. With Beverly Sills as Hanna Glawari.*

always been able to compete with *Die Fledermaus* for popularity—*Die lustige Witwe* (The Merry Widow). Its sheet-music sales alone were reputed to have made him a millionaire. In a long career (he died in 1948), he composed several other successful (and still successful) pieces, including *Der Graf von Luxemburg* (The Count of Luxembourg) and *Das Land des Lächelns* (The Land of Smiles), and he lived to see several of them committed to film— an altogether new experience for a composer.

Think of Lehár and it is hard not to think of the tenor Richard Tauber. On stage, on record, and on film, Tauber became one of the most popular international performers of his day. He began his career as a singer in his native Austria just before the outbreak of World War I, establishing a considerable reputation in the tenor repertoire, especially that of Mozart. When he turned to operetta, his friends berated him for what they saw as a lapse of taste: his voice and his musicianship, they said, were too good for operetta. "I don't sing operetta," Tauber replied, "I sing Lehár."

OPERA IN ENGLAND

French and Viennese operetta grew up and thrived at precisely the same time that their older cousin, opera, was experiencing its grandest days. Offenbach and Johann Strauss the Younger were contemporaries of Verdi and Wagner, of Meyerbeer and Tchaikovsky, of Bizet and Smetana. All this creative activity took place on the mainland of Europe, but its impact was far wider. Latin America—particularly Mexico, Brazil, and Argentina— had proved a ready market. So, of course, had the English-speaking world. London had been an important opera center almost as long as Paris: New York was in the process of becoming one. But neither the United States nor Britain had yet contributed in any substantial way to the creation of *dramma per musica*.

By the middle of the nineteenth century, the theater John Rich had built in London's Covent Garden on the profits of *The Beggar's Opera* was in its second (and shortly after that, its third) incarnation: the first two burned down. Revealingly, it was not the home of the "Royal Opera": the resident company was called the "Royal *Italian* Opera." In 1862, the *Illustrated London News* noted with some asperity: "It can never be said that the musical drama holds its due place among the entertainments of the English metropolis, till it is established in a dwelling of its own, and till the

shoes, but two Hungarian composers had plans to do so. Emmerich Kálmán was one of them— the composer of *Die Czárdásfürstin* (known in England as The Gypsy Princess[12]) and many other popular works. But the man who dominated the world of operetta in the early years of the twentieth century was Franz Lehár. He had a closer connection to the Theater an der Wien than did any of his predecessors: he was its musical director. He had been brought up in Hungary amid the sounds of operetta. His father was a military bandmaster, and the band, of which Lehár was briefly a member, played through the entire repertoire of Strauss, Suppé, Offenbach, and Italian *opera buffa*. In 1905, six years after Strauss's death, Lehár wrote the one operetta that has almost

phrase 'the Opera' shall be applied, as in Paris, to the *national* opera, and not, as at present in London, to an entertainment which, however splendid and beautiful, is only an exotic."[13]

In point of fact, there *was* such a thing as an English opera company in London at this time. It was grandly called the Royal English Opera because it had the patronage of Queen Victoria, and it leased the Covent Garden theater for a few weeks each autumn between 1858 and 1864. It petered out for lack of support, but also (the truth had to be faced) because there was very little English opera available. Thomas Arne, a contemporary of Handel's, and the Irishman Michael Balfe in the nineteenth century were the only English-language opera composers of any real consequence between Henry Purcell, who had died in 1695, and Frederick Delius, who was born in 1862. Moreover, the real movers and shakers of the opera world, the star singers, were loath to sing in English.

Italian opera was a different matter. There were plenty of famous singers willing to sing in London—indeed, they had more or less controlled the commerce of opera in London since Handel's time. The leading figure among them in the middle years of the nineteenth century was Giulia Grisi. She arrived in London in 1834 as a renowned interpreter of the *bel canto* roles of Rossini, Bellini, and Donizetti—of all of whom she was a favorite, as was her sister Giuditta. In London, Grisi found she could be more than just a singer: she could virtually dictate what would be sung in the way of Italian opera—first at the King's Theatre, and later at Covent Garden, when the Royal Italian Opera was established there in 1847. Not only could she dictate what would be sung: she was generally able to decree who would sing it. For twenty-seven seasons, she reigned supreme. She had some celebrated battles with would-be usurpers (most notably Pauline Viardot, the sister of Maria Malibran[14]), but she almost always had her way. In particular, she was generally able to ensure that the leading tenor was her husband, Giovanni Mario. He was a handsome man and a fine actor with a voice of great beauty, an idol of the London public for many years.

Grisi's reign came to an end in 1861, when Covent Garden found itself a new, young, and very special prima donna. Her name was Adelina Patti. She had been born in Spain of Italian parents, but she had been brought up and educated entirely in New York. When Patti made her London debut in 1861, as Amina in Bellini's *La sonnambula* (one of Grisi's signature roles), she was only eighteen. She sang in London every season for the next twenty-four years. At the height of her fame she earned two hundred guineas a performance (and reputedly five thousand dollars a performance in America), and she had a clause in her contract excusing her from rehearsals. Truly, an opera director's nightmare.

In 1870, nine years into her London supremacy and already a tremendous star, Patti acquired a new agent. He was a twenty-four-year-old Englishman just setting up in business on London's Charing Cross Road. His name was Richard D'Oyly Carte, and he had acquired two other clients: Matthew Arnold and Oscar Wilde. A good enough start. But D'Oyly Carte's real ambition was to establish "English comic opera in a theatre devoted to that alone."[15] Patti, who was now married to the Marquis de Caux, was not going to be much help to him in fulfilling that ambition. Nor was Covent Garden.

But the city in which D'Oyly Carte was operating was ripe for such a development. Besides its opera house and its musical theaters, London had no fewer than two hundred music halls in active use at this time. Most of them were attached to pubs, like The Surrey in Southwark and The Bedford in Camden Town, and it was in them that Londoners from all levels of society could enjoy variety shows that featured anything from popular songs to novelty acts. What D'Oyly Carte wanted to add to this array was something that did not yet exist: an English version of the Théâtre des Variétés in Paris. He was a very determined young man. Within a year, he had taken on the management of the Royalty Theatre in London's Soho district, while continuing to look after his clients.

GILBERT AND SULLIVAN

At Christmas the next year, 1871, D'Oyly Carte visited one of the neighboring theaters in Soho, the Gaiety Theatre, to see a new comic opera called *Thespis, or The Gods Grown Old*. It was not a success—too long and too esoteric for its audience. We cannot even know what it sounded like, the music having long since been lost, but D'Oyly Carte felt at the time that it had been unfairly treated.

Four years went by. D'Oyly Carte was planning a production of Offenbach's operetta *La Périchole* at the Royalty. He needed a shorter piece to use as a curtain raiser. At this moment the librettist of the now forgotten *Thespis* appeared in

Cartoon from Punch, *1882. As these caricature figures suggest, Richard D'Oyly Carte (center) was vital to the relationship between Gilbert and Sullivan. Yet while Arthur Sullivan (left) was close to Carte, Gilbert (right) often thought of himself as the outsider.*

D'OYLY CARTE
OPERA COMPANY

THE GONDOLIERS

THE MIKADO

THE YEOMEN OF THE GUARD

D'Oyly Carte's office wanting some advice. His name was W. S. Gilbert. He was a successful poet and playwright, most famous for his *Bab Ballads,*[16] part of which he was now planning to expand into a libretto for a one-act operetta. D'Oyly Carte suggested he might think about getting together again with the man who had composed the music for *Thespis,* Arthur Sullivan. Sullivan's reputation, however, was as a "serious" musician. He was in his early thirties and had already composed a symphony, an oratorio, and a good deal of religious music. He was generally thought to be the most promising English musician of his time.

So, fully expecting a rebuff, Gilbert took his libretto to Sullivan. And Sullivan liked it. Thus D'Oyly Carte got his one-act curtain-raiser at the Royalty Theatre in 1875—and he got a hit as well. *Trial by Jury* ran for three hundred performances. The following year, he formed a new company for the express purpose of producing the operettas of "Gilbert and Sullivan."

From the start, the names were linked, for here truly was a partnership in which the librettist was as important as the composer. *Trial by Jury* got rave reviews because, among other reasons, Gilbert's lampooning of the legal profession had a deadly accuracy about it (he had spent six miserable years as a barrister before he turned to writing). The critic of the London *Times* opined that England had produced a rival to Offenbach[17]— but in that, at least, the *Times* was wrong. Gilbert and Sullivan's operettas would never have any real success outside the English-speaking world, and that, in itself, was a compliment to Gilbert. His librettos were witty, intricate, and highly topical, capable of keeping audiences amused even without the glorious music of Sullivan. You had to speak English to understand the nuances.

But the partnership consisted of three people, not two. D'Oyly Carte was the indispensable organizer, financier, impresario, and (when necessary) the mediator between the two creative forces. He staged every one of the thirteen operettas that followed *Trial by Jury*, from *H.M.S. Pinafore* in 1878 to *The Grand Duke* in 1896; he organized the triumphant visit to the United States for the American production of *Pinafore*, followed by the world premiere of *The Pirates of Penzance* in New York; he protected the writers' international copyrights, which by now had become an extremely important part of the potential earnings of composers and librettists; and finally, in 1881, he achieved his ambition of building a theater that would be devoted to English comic opera.

It was typical of D'Oyly Carte that his Savoy Theatre was state-of-the-art. It contained one tremendous innovation: electric lighting. On the night it was first used, about two months after the actual opening of the theater, D'Oyly Carte himself appeared on stage before a performance of *Patience*. In order to demonstrate how much safer it was than gas or candles, he carefully wrapped a lit electric light bulb in muslin and then smashed it to prove that the muslin would not burn. The muslin remained uncharred, but perhaps the greater miracle was that only one person in the audience of thirteen hundred fled the theater in terror.[18]

The Savoy Theatre was ideally placed, on the Strand next door to the Savoy Hotel, and it was here that the D'Oyly Carte company performed what came to be known as the "Savoy operas," the operettas of Gilbert and Sullivan. The tunes, and the jokes, of *Iolanthe*, *The Mikado*, *Ruddigore*, *The Yeomen of the Guard*, *The Gondoliers*, and all the others, quickly became part of the folklore of England, and of English-speaking countries far beyond.

BRECHT AND WEILL

If the names of Gilbert and Sullivan were forever linked, then so were those of Bertolt Brecht and Kurt Weill. Brought up in Germany in the early years of the twentieth century, and drawn to the bright lights of Berlin in the aftermath of World War I, they articulated the artificial gaiety and the profound bitterness of an entire generation, and not just in Germany.

Weill had trained as a classical musician: he was a pupil of both Engelbert Humperdinck and the great Italian pianist and composer Ferruccio Busoni. His music was clearly influenced by a number of familiar traditions—the classical symphony, the German *Singspiel*, folk music, and Vien-

nese operetta—but its dominant features were entirely contemporary: the rhythms of ragtime, jazz, and the blues competed with those of the dance bands and the more discordant sonorities of modern music. It was the sound of Berlin in the 1920s. It was here that Weill met Bertolt Brecht, a playwright and poet, already, by 1927, well known in Berlin for his Expressionist plays. Their first collaboration was intended to be a full-length opera, *Aufstieg und Fall der Stadt Mahagonny* (Rise and Fall of the City of Mahagonny), but in its first manifestation in 1927 it was no more than a "*Songspiel*" — a group of five songs called *Mahagonny*. Not until 1930 was the complete work staged in Leipzig.

Mahagonny was a slashing attack on American capitalist society. It reflected the furies of Weimar Germany and the strong Marxist convictions of Bertolt Brecht. Brecht began his study of Marxism in 1927; by 1930, when he finished *Mahagonny*, he was a virulent believer. One of the grand ironies of the piece was that, in order to preach their stern message, Brecht and Weill made use of that most reactionary and bourgeois form of *dramma per musica*, the opera—arias, recitatives, choruses—but all of it put into their own unique format.

By the time the full-length *Mahagonny* was staged, the Brecht/Weill partnership was already well established. In 1928, they had made a huge

Weill's RISE AND FALL OF THE CITY OF MAHAGONNY *at the Metropolitan Opera, New York, 1995. Directed (1979) by John Dexter, designed by Jocelyn Herbert. With Gary Lakes as Jimmy and Sherri Greenawald as Jenny.*

Lotte Lenya as Jenny in G. W. Pabst's 1931 film of Weill's THE THREEPENNY OPERA.

impression with *Die Dreigroschenoper* (The Threepenny Opera). It was based on the wonderful idea of taking the story of *The Beggar's Opera*, which was exactly two hundred years old in 1928, and transposing it to the slums of London at the beginning of the twentieth century. The highwayman MacHeath became Mack the Knife, and the jailer Lockitt was transformed into Police Chief Tiger Brown. Weill's music was mainly inspired by jazz. *Die Dreigroschenoper* had enormous success in Europe, but it was not well received in New York, in 1933. Yet twenty years later, when it returned to off-Broadway in a new translation by Marc Blitzstein, it ran for a record-breaking 2,500 performances. Weill's widow, Lotte Lenya, played the role of Jenny, which she had created in Berlin in 1928.

Kurt Weill did not live to see this triumph; he died in 1950. But he had lived the last fifteen years of his life in America, and he had become, in his own right, a great Broadway composer. Free of Hitler's Germany, and free of Brecht's influence as well, he set about creating what he called the "Broadway opera." Of his many productions, *Lady in the Dark* was the most successful in Broadway terms—a series of four dream sequences, co-written with Ira Gershwin to a book by Moss

Hart. It became a famous film role for Ginger Rogers. But one of Weill's last pieces, *Street Scene*, best demonstrated his idea of Broadway opera. Like German *Singspiel* and most Broadway musicals, *Street Scene* had spoken dialogue; it told the down-to-earth, sometimes violent, story of the inhabitants of a New York tenement building; it was *verismo*, in the truest sense of that description since the genre had been pioneered by Mascagni and Leoncavallo in the 1880s. *Street Scene* was Broadway, certainly, but it was not many years before opera houses in Europe and America were admitting that it was opera, too.

Which would have pleased Weill. In 1940, five years into his American residency and ten years before he died, he had given an interview to the *New York Sun*. In it, he had denounced the American opera establishment as being entombed in a museum of its own making. American opera, he had prophesied, would develop on Broadway, not in the opera houses.[19]

OPERA IN AMERICA

New Orleans had been the first real center of opera in North America, with regular performances of mainly French operas being given there as early as 1791. Boston, Philadelphia, and Chicago had been steady venues for touring companies throughout the nineteenth century, and although the vast majority of the operas given were European, there was such a thing as American opera. One of the first was a comedy called *The Temple of Minerva*; it was written by Francis Hopkinson, a signer of the Declaration of Independence, and it was seen by George Washington in 1781. But the major influence was inevitably Italian. Manuel García had taken a company, including his daughter María Malibran, to New York in 1825 and had given the first American performances of *Il barbiere di Siviglia* and *Don Giovanni*. The audience had included Mozart's librettist, Lorenzo Da Ponte, who was then living in New York and trying hard to get local opera companies launched. By mid-century, the United States had become a profitable touring base for major European singers. Jenny Lind had spectacularly proved the point in her 1850 tour sponsored by P. T. Barnum, and by 1854 Giulia Grisi and her husband, Giovanni Mario, were also on the bandwagon, with Adelina Patti not far behind.

New York had always been the principal

American city for opera. At the Park Theater from 1798, then at the Astor Place Opera House, then at the Academy of Music on Fourteenth Street, Italian (and later French and German) opera had flourished in a city dominated by European immigrants. Among many colorful personalities, the English impresario Colonel Mapleson had done more than most to ensure the success of the Academy. In fact, it was too successful: certain members of New York's upper crust found they could no longer be assured of boxes there, so they decided to build a new opera house. Together, they subscribed 800,000 dollars for the purpose, and the Metropolitan Opera House was constructed on Broadway between Thirty-ninth and Fortieth Streets. It opened in 1883. Other cities followed New York's example. Philadelphia's Academy of Music had actually been in use as early as 1857, but there was no permanent company in the city until the Philadelphia Civic Opera came into being in 1923. Chicago had its own opera company by 1910, with Mary Garden as its reigning diva for

the first twenty-one years. The San Francisco Opera was founded in 1923 and moved into its fine new home, the War Memorial Opera House, nine years later. New Orleans, Boston, and several other cities staged frequent, if erratic, opera seasons.

New York's Metropolitan had been built by and for its stockholders. The interior reflected that fact, with its famous horseshoe auditorium affording box holders an excellent view of each other. For nearly sixty years, the Met was run on a very un-European basis: the building was owned and maintained by the box holders, who leased it, rent-free, to a separate company, which was responsible for staging the operas (star singers had to be approved by the board of the "real estate company"). On the surface, it seemed like a system uniquely capable of self-destructing. But it worked. The Met became, at the beginning of the

ABOVE: *Playbill for the opening night of the original Metropolitan Opera House, New York, October 22, 1883.*

LEFT: *Marcella Sembrich (1858–1935) as Donizetti's Lucia. At the age of twenty-five, as Lucia, the Polish soprano made the Met's second night as memorable as the first. Later in the season, at a benefit, she amazed the audience by giving virtuoso performances in quick succession on the piano and the violin, followed by a stunning rendition of Amina's waking aria from Bellini's* La sonnambula.

twentieth century, a glittering symbol of opera's golden age.

It almost came unstuck. The first decade of the century was a time of vast expansion in the United States. But there were financial crashes in 1901 and 1907, and the times were uncertain. To this, the Metropolitan added troubles of its own. In 1906 many of its sets and costumes were lost during the earthquake in San Francisco, where the company, which included Caruso, was on tour. The beginning of 1907 was marked by the cancellation, after one performance, of a very expensive production of Richard Strauss's *Salome*: powerful box holders, led by J. P. Morgan, had found it morally offensive on opening night. Worse still, the Met had competition—powerful and effective competition. It came from Oscar Hammerstein (grandfather of one of the century's finest librettists). In 1906, Hammerstein had opened the Manhattan Opera House on West Thirty-fourth Street and had quickly established himself with stellar casts led by Mary Garden, Nellie Melba, Luisa Tetrazzini (who was making her first New York appearance), and the beautiful Lina Cavalieri. Cavalieri had been one of the Met's greatest draws—its first Fedora, its first Manon Lescaut, and its first Adriana Lecouvreur—but she forfeited her place on the Met's roster after she married the millionaire Winthrop Chanler. (He signed over his entire fortune to her,

and she left him within a week; Chanler's brother, resident in an asylum, sent him a charming note: "Who's looney now?"[20]).

From all these disasters and aggravations, the Met rescued itself. It appointed a new company, led by the banker Otto Kahn, to hold the lease on the theater. In 1908, it also appointed a new general manager, Giulio Gatti-Casazza from La Scala. And Gatti-Casazza brought with him Arturo Toscanini.

The immediate result, the "miracle" season of 1908–9, was a phenomenon, and the Met never looked back. Musical standards were higher than they had ever been, with Toscanini and Gustav Mahler sharing much of the conducting. Toscanini had had to lay down the law with some of the singers, notably the beauteous Geraldine Farrar. Farrar stopped his first rehearsal of *Butterfly* to inform him that he must follow her, since she was the star. "The stars are all in the heavens, mademoiselle," the maestro replied, "You are but a plain artist, and you must obey my direction."[21]

Oscar Hammerstein's Manhattan Opera, struggling to counter the Met's new assertiveness and at the same time to establish a secondary base in Philadelphia, overreached itself and was bought out by the Met in 1910 for 1.2 million dollars. Meanwhile, Toscanini was developing both the Italian and the French repertoires, and at the same time maintaining the Met's justified reputation for German opera (it would be lost, but only temporarily, during World War I).

The presiding genius of the Met's success was Gatti-Casazza. He ran the house for twenty-seven seasons, showing a profit on every one of them until 1932, when the Depression was at its worst. In all this time, he conducted business entirely in Italian,[22] though he was generally thought to understand English perfectly well. He staged as many as forty-five operas in every thirty-week season, including, it should be said, a number of new American operas; and he maintained the Met's extraordinary reputation for having practically every international opera star of any importance on its roster. This was made somewhat easier than it is today by the custom of contracting artists for entire seasons, or for half seasons. And as one generation went into retirement, another appeared. Although Enrico Caruso, Emmy Destinn, and Geraldine Farrar all disappeared in the early 1920s, Beniamino Gigli (no

OPPOSITE: *The old Metropolitan Opera House, New York, as it looked at the turn of the twentieth century.*

LEFT: *Lina Cavalieri (1874–1944). Early in her life, Cavalieri sold programs at the Rome Opera. She died in an air raid on Florence during World War II (after reportedly returning to her villa from the air-raid shelter in order to fetch her jewels). One of the most bewitching and sensational opera stars of her time, she was played by Gina Lollobrigida in the 1957 film* LA DONNA PIÙ BELLA DEL MONDO.

Caruso, but almost as popular), Maria Jeritza from Czechoslovakia, and America's own Rosa Ponselle were there to take up the burden. The aging but incomparable Fyodor Chaliapin sang with the company throughout the 1920s, and that was also the time when two of the greatest of all Wagnerian voices joined the roster: Friedrich Schorr and Lauritz Melchior (Kirsten Flagstad arrived in 1935). Rosa Ponselle was by no means the only American singer to ornament the Met's marquee: Lawrence Tibbett, Lily Pons (a Frenchwoman who became an American), and later Risë Stevens were the leaders of a formidable group.

Despite, or because of, all this activity, there were many who agreed with Kurt Weill that opera houses in the United States (and not just in the United States) had become museums. American opera would begin to come into its own toward the end of the twentieth century, when the com-

position of new operas—and a series of collaborations between composers, dramatists, and stage directors—brought about what may eventually be seen as a rebirth (certainly a rethinking) of the whole art form. But there was also some progress in the first part of the century. As early as 1910, Gatti-Casazza had offered a prize of 10,000 dollars for a new American opera. It was won by Horatio Parker of Yale, and the following year the Met staged his opera *Mona*. But the two most successful American premieres during these years were both operas in which Lawrence Tibbett starred: *Peter Ibbetson* (1931) by Deems Taylor, and *The Emperor Jones* by Louis Gruenberg (*Jones* was a considerable commercial success for the Met at a time when it most needed it, in 1933). Tibbett was a Californian with the unusual distinction of having risen through the ranks to stardom: he had begun as a very ordinary singer of very secondary roles. On the night in 1925 when Gatti-Casazza gave him his first major opportunity, as Ford in *Falstaff*, he received a fifteen-minute solo ovation at the end of the second act—an event so extraordinary that the *New York Times* made it a front-page story the next day.[23] From that time on, Tibbett's popularity at the Met never wavered.

It was not often that the Met, or any other opera house, made the front page. Broadway, on the other hand, was always in the news, and it was here, as Kurt Weill noted, that America had begun to make its distinctive contribution to opera in the 1920s and 1930s. Ironically, the Met was also located on Broadway, a few blocks south of Longacre Square (now Times Square)—a close, but officially disinterested, observer of the extraordinary range of talent Broadway commanded. Sigmund Romberg, Irving Berlin, Jerome Kern, George Gershwin, and Richard Rodgers were just a few of the great composers. They were joined by Ivor Novello and Noël Coward from Britain. And among the librettists, few could equal Lorenz Hart and Oscar Hammerstein II (whose grandfather had done so much to discomfort the Met in the first decade of the century).

Of all the fine works that filled Broadway's theaters in the 1920s and 1930s, two stand out as important landmarks in the development of American musical theater.

In 1927, Florenz Ziegfeld, the greatest of all Broadway producers, staged what he must have known would be a controversial show. It was written by Jerome Kern and Oscar Hammerstein II, and it was full of memorable tunes—from "Only Make Believe" to "Ol' Man River." But *Show Boat* was also brutally and sensationally truthful. Its themes of prejudice and racial intermixture caused shock and offense. They were meant to. Broadway was not just a place for sugar-coated confections: it was also a place for powerful drama and raw emotion.

That was emphasized in 1935 by George Gershwin, when he produced *Porgy and Bess* in Boston. He had written it as an opera, and he had hoped it would be staged by the Metropolitan Opera. It was—but not until 1985, fifty years after its first performance. By then, it was famous throughout the world; it had been staged as far afield as Leningrad, in the Soviet Union, where it was triumphantly performed by a visiting American company in 1955, at the height of the Cold War.

In 1935, George Gershwin was thirty-seven years old. Better than all his contemporaries, he symbolized the peculiarly American combination of a European musical heritage with a thorough immersion in the excitement of jazz, ragtime, and the blues. His songs, his revues, and his musical comedies were packing theaters on both sides of the Atlantic. He was the composer of *Rhapsody in Blue* for piano and jazz orchestra, and his works were equally celebrated in the concert hall—both his Piano Concerto and his symphonic work *An American in Paris* were given their premieres by the New York Symphony (which would later be united with the Philharmonic).

In 1926, while he was hard at work on a musical called *Oh, Kay!* (Gertrude Lawrence was to be its star), Gershwin, unable to sleep one night, picked up a novel from the current bestseller list, read it from cover to cover during the night, and the next day mailed a letter to the author suggesting they collaborate to turn it into an opera.[24] The novel was called *Porgy*, and its author was a former insurance salesman from Charleston, South Carolina, called DuBose Heyward. Heyward came from a somewhat impoverished family of Charleston's old aristocracy: his great-great-grandfather had been a signer of the Declaration of Independence. DuBose had decided to become a full-time writer only two years earlier, and *Porgy*, his first novel, had been inspired by a report he read in the *Charleston News and Courier*:

> Samuel Smalls, who is a cripple and is familiar to King Street, with his goat and cart, was held for the June term of Court of Sessions on an aggravated assault charge. It is alleged that on Saturday night he attempted to shoot Maggie Barnes at No. 4 Romney Street. His shots went wide of the mark. Smalls was up on a similar charge some months ago and was given a suspended sentence. Smalls had attempted to escape in his wagon and was run down and captured by the police patrol.[25]

Sammy Smalls, it was thought, lived on Cabbage Row. In the novel, Sammy became Porgy and Cabbage Row became Catfish Row. This is the story that George Gershwin, together with his

RIGHT: *Scene from the original production of
Rodgers and Hammerstein's* OKLAHOMA,
New York, 1943.

OPPOSITE: *Ken LeRoy and Chita Rivera in*
WEST SIDE STORY, *New York, 1957.
Music by Leonard Bernstein, lyrics by
Stephen Sondheim, choreography by Jerome
Robbins.*

brother Ira, who co-authored the lyrics with DuBose Heyward, turned into the first great American opera.

Gershwin died tragically young from a brain tumor only two years after the premiere of *Porgy and Bess*, but Broadway continued to be the seminal home of American musical theater. Shows like *Oklahoma*, *Carousel*, *West Side Story* and *My Fair Lady*, and, later on, a series of works by Stephen Sondheim and by Andrew Lloyd Webber, sustained a tradition of musical theater that was a legitimate and important development of the venerable idea of *dramma per musica*. No single work contributed more to this genre than Leonard Bernstein's *West Side Story*. Based on the Romeo and Juliet story, it combined *verismo* drama with virtuoso dance numbers and a continuous stream of unforgettable melodies. Sondheim's lyrics and Jerome Robbins's choreography were vital ingredients, but it was Bernstein's music, and his instinct for theater, that made it a music drama of such extraordinary power. The original Broadway production in 1957 was only a moderate success, but the 1961 film version quickly became, and will remain, a classic of the big screen (which is one reason why *West Side Story* has rarely been produced on the stage again—comparisons will always be invidious). Here was a contemporary story (set in 1950s New York) in which the action and the emotions were played out in artificial, unrealistic ways (singing and dancing), yet it was a drama in which hundreds of millions of people, all over the world, and in several generations, have become totally absorbed and absolutely accepting. This is the power of *dramma per musica* at its very best.

Broadway's musicals were the more welcome because they were produced against the background of an age of experimentation in the world of more "serious opera"—a world in which musicians had changed the language of music to such an extent that it was alien to a large part of opera's traditional audience. There was atonal music, and Expressionism, and serialism, and Minimalism, and much else that many found disturbing and often impenetrable. The exuberant melodies of Broadway stood in sharp contrast to all this, and it was not many years before Kurt Weill's bitter prophecy was proven right: the best of the "Broadway operas" found their way into the hallowed halls of opera houses—just as surely as had the works of Offenbach and Johann Strauss the Younger from the nineteenth century, and *The Beggar's Opera* and *Die Zauberflöte* from the eighteenth century.

It is an honorable tradition in the story of opera.

On the Twentieth Century

THE FIRST DECADE

*I*T SEEMED AT FIRST AS THOUGH NOTHING WOULD CHANGE—AS THOUGH THE WORLD OF NINETEENTH-CENTURY OPERA WOULD GLIDE EFFORTLESSLY INTO THE TWENTIETH CENTURY, AND THINGS WOULD GO ON WITHOUT REGARD FOR THE ARBITRARY ADJUSTMENT IN THE DATELINE. ONLY TWO WEEKS INTO THE NEW CENTURY, ON JANUARY 14, 1900, THE PREMIERE OF PUCCINI'S *TOSCA* WAS GIVEN IN ROME. IT WAS REPEATED A FEW MONTHS LATER AT LA SCALA, TO EVEN GREATER ACCLAIM.

LA SCALA WAS EMBARKED ON ONE OF ITS MOST GLORIOUS PERIODS, UNDER THE DIRECTION OF GIULIO GATTI-CASAZZA AND ARTURO TOSCANINI. BUT THERE WERE SIGNIFICANT SHIFTS IN THE REPERTOIRE. *OTELLO* WAS THE ONLY VERDI OPERA ON THE ROSTER IN 1900, WHEREAS THERE WERE TWO WAGNER OPERAS. VERDI HIM-SELF WAS STILL ALIVE, EIGHTY-SEVEN YEARS OLD AND LIVING IN RETIREMENT AT SANT'AGATA, A MAGNIFICENT, BROODING

presence in the world of opera. Richard Wagner had been dead for seventeen years, but Cosima, his widow, presided over Bayreuth with the single-minded determination that everything should be done exactly as the master had intended. The Wagner craze (for that is what it was) had spread right through Europe and across the Atlantic to both North and South America. French opera was also in its heyday: Gounod's *Faust* was everywhere; Bizet's *Carmen* had finally triumphed, even in Paris; and Massenet was surely the world's most popular active composer. Russian opera was just beginning to join the international repertoire, with the great bass voice of Fyodor Chaliapin as its foremost ambassador. Everywhere, the advances made in the nineteenth century were being consolidated.

Singers remained the biggest draw. Lilli Lehmann was the great Brünnhilde, Enrico Caruso was an idol in Italy and America, and the Australian Nellie Melba was behaving just as though she was the world's greatest diva—which she was. She traveled across the United States in her own Pullman railroad car with MELBA painted in large gold letters on its side and with a personal staff consisting of chef, waiter, porter, conductor, and maids. On the surface, little in the world of opera had changed.

And yet, in almost every area of human activity, the first decade of the new century pro-

PRECEDING PAGES: *The Presentation of the Rose from Strauss's* DER ROSENKAVALIER *at Covent Garden, London, 1985. Directed by John Schlesinger, sets by William Dudley, and costumes by Maria Björnson. With Barbara Bonney as Sophie and Anne Howells as Octavian.*

vided intimations of change. Freud published *The Interpretation of Dreams*; Einstein produced his theory of relativity; Picasso painted *Les desmoiselles d'Avignon*; the Wright brothers made the first successful airplane flight; Marconi transmitted a telegraphic radio message across the Atlantic; and Henry Ford founded his motor company.

There were similar intimations even within the tradition-bound world of opera. Some of them, like the gramophone, brought promise of progress. Caruso made his first recordings in 1902, and shortly afterward Verdi's *Il trovatore* became the first opera to have a full-length recording. But many more of the changes were deeply shocking, even scandalous. This was the decade of Claude Debussy's *Pelléas et Mélisande* (1902), Leos Janáček's *Jenůfa* (1904), Richard Strauss's *Salome* (1905) and *Elektra* (1909), and Arnold Schoenberg's *Erwartung* (1909). There was very little that was "nineteenth century" about these works. True, the shock did not come all at once. *Jenůfa* was known only in the Moravian city of Brno and would not be heard anywhere else until 1916. *Erwartung*, with its stunning abandonment of the tonal system that had buttressed Western music for hundreds of years, was not publicly staged until 1924. But they were all products of the first decade of the century—heralds of what was to come.

Pelléas caused a stir when it was given its Paris premiere in 1902, but that was nothing compared with what happened in Dresden three years later. In the 1840s the brand-new Semperoper had announced the Wagnerian era with premieres of *Rienzi*, *Der fliegende Holländer*, and *Tannhäuser*. Now, gloriously rebuilt after the fire of 1869, it announced the Straussian era with two equally shattering events. Wagner's works had caused shock. Strauss's two new operas caused scandal.

The first was *Salome*, in 1905. It was not just the erotic and sensuous music that caused the scandal; it was also the subject matter. Without benefit of librettist, Strauss took Oscar Wilde's French play, translated into German, and turned it into a psychological music drama of tremendous force. The "Dance of the Seven Veils," in which Salome gradually discarded each layer of her covering, was shocking enough. But the idea of Salome then kissing the severed head of John the Baptist was hard for audiences to take.

It was even harder for the singers. Marie Wittich, the first Salome, absolutely refused to carry out the movements required of her, saying,

"I'll do no such thing. I'm a decent woman."[1] Strauss referred to her as "Aunty Wittich," but he had to accept that a ballerina would stand in for her in the "Dance of the Seven Veils." Five years later, at the first London performance, the censor refused to let the head of John the Baptist be seen onstage: instead, the Finnish soprano Aino Ackte had to sing to what appeared to be a plum pudding rather than a severed head.[2] The composer Arnold Bax, who was present at the first performances in Dresden, reported that the Czech tenor Karel Burian "created a quite horrifying Herod, slobbering with lust, and apparently almost decomposing before our disgusted but fascinated eyes."[3]

The scandal in Dresden was quickly imported to other opera houses. Milan, Turin, Brussels, and Amsterdam all staged *Salome* within the year. So did Berlin, even though the kaiser had at first banned it. He relented on condition that, at the very end, the Star of Bethlehem should be seen leading the Magi to the infant Jesus (which was more than a little illogical since the events of the opera clearly took place during the adult life of Jesus). The kaiser refused to see the opera himself, but his opinion was relayed back to Strauss. "I'm sorry," the kaiser said. "I like him otherwise, but with this he will do himself a great deal of harm." Years later, Strauss reminisced, "The harm it did me enabled me to build the villa in Garmisch."[4]

In Vienna, Gustav Mahler tried in vain to persuade the authorities to allow *Salome* to be performed, but it was staged in nearby Graz, where Mahler, Puccini, and Adolf Hitler all saw it. New York saw it, too, at the Metropolitan Opera in 1907, but for only one performance. It caused such an outburst of fury from public and critics alike that it was instantly withdrawn from the repertoire by order of the board of directors. It was not seen at the Met again until 1934.

Four years after *Salome*, again in Dresden, Strauss staged *Elektra*, a work not quite as shocking as *Salome*, but almost. His infamy, and his bank balance, grew accordingly. The new opera was evidently no easier to sing than *Salome* had been. Ernestine Schumann-Heink, a mezzo-soprano whose fame was as great in America as it was in Europe, went to Dresden to create the role of Clytemnestra. She was not amused: "I will never sing the role again. It was frightful. . . . There is nothing beyond *Elektra*. We have lived and reached the furthest boundary in dramatic writing for the voice with Wagner. But Richard Strauss goes beyond him. His singing voices are lost. We have come to a full stop."[5]

These operas may no longer scandalize us by their content, but their music—so brutish and harsh in places, so sensuous and beautiful in others—still has the power to shock. This was the only time in his long career as an opera composer, almost at its beginning, that Strauss flirted with atonality (music not based in any one key), though he did not actually succumb to it. "The two operas," he wrote years later, "are unique in my life's work. In them I penetrated to the utmost limits of harmony, psychological polyphony . . . and of the receptivity of modern ears."[6]

"The receptivity of modern ears" became the central problem of twentieth-century opera.

There is a distinction between "twentieth-century opera" and "opera in the twentieth century." The first is limited to operas composed during the century. The second is a much broader term, embracing the whole phenomenon of opera, old and new, as a form of entertainment.

"Opera in the twentieth century" has thrived. It has been fueled by a treasury of works written in previous centuries, and it has been disseminated by new methods of communication—by the gramophone, radio, television, video recordings, satellite broadcasts, and compact discs—to literally millions of people around the world, many of whom will never enter an opera house.

"Twentieth-century opera," on the other hand, has had a tougher time. There have even been periods when the phrase itself has been a term of abuse. It is associated with the ideas and contradictions prefigured in that first decade—with unfamiliar sonorities, shocking dissonances, and a musical language that has frequently developed beyond the comprehension of ordinary listeners. Melody, the element most easily understood and enjoyed, has often been in short supply. Nevertheless, looked at in the context of the continuing exploration of *dramma per musica*, twentieth-century opera has had much to say and much to contribute.

The most prolific opera composers of the century may be Puccini, Janáček, Richard Strauss, and Benjamin Britten, but they have been joined by a host of others, and never more so than in the last quarter of the century. Other than in Germany, which has never ceased to be an innovative and industrious center, the sources of these operas have changed radically: Italian opera (after Puccini) has taken a back seat, whereas English-language opera has finally found its voice—American and British composers have made their first significant contributions. So have musicians from countries as far apart as Finland and Australia.

But these new works have found it hard to win acceptance from their audience. For three hundred years, operagoing had been dominated by the experience of seeing new or very recent operas, but now, in the twentieth century, the situation has been reversed. The repertoire looks backward rather than forward, and audiences have become overwhelmingly conservative.

CHANGES IN PRODUCTION   By 1900, the conditions in which opera was performed were beginning to equate to those we know today. For centuries, theaters had relied on candlelight and oil lamps; then, from about 1820, the use of coal gas had offered scenic designers much more sophisticated, and much safer, methods of lighting the stage. It had enabled them to develop the spectacular illusionist effects required in many Romantic operas, and to light the dioramas and moving panoramas that had created so much astonishment among theatergoers in the 1820s and 1830s. By the middle of the nineteenth century, gas had provided them with another tool, limelight—a very brilliant and intense light that could be produced by heating lime in a gas jet. But it was the advent of electricity that made the greatest difference. At first, before the invention of the dynamo and the filament, it could do little more than provide arc lights (projecting arcs of light between carbon poles—a technique that was used at the Paris Opéra as early as 1849 to simulate the sun in the first production of Meyerbeer's *Le prophète*). Then, in 1881, the Paris Opéra installed electric lighting in its auditorium and foyer, and in the same year Richard D'Oyly Carte unveiled the electric stage lighting in his new London theater, the Savoy. The major theaters of Europe, from Covent Garden to Bayreuth, very quickly switched over to electricity.[7]

Now, for the first time, it was possible to darken the auditorium during a performance. Instead of battling against a flood of house lights, the stage could be isolated as the focus of all attention. For the performers, it was one of the great breakthroughs in the story of opera, but for audiences it was a mixed blessing. Before, they had always been able to use roughly printed librettos and translations to follow the performance (that is why so many texts exist for early operas, while their music scores, most of which were reproduced only as handwritten parts for the musicians, have long since disappeared). In the twentieth century, until the invention of projected supertitles in the 1970s, those members of an audience who had failed to do their homework would sit in darkness and, too often, in incomprehension.

Electricity revolutionized stage production, too. It offered designers a whole new world of lighting effects. The spotlight, taking over from the arc lamp, was one of the most useful. Electricity also provided things like hydraulic lifts, mechanically driven scenery flies, and even revolving stages (the Residenztheater in Munich had one as early as 1896). These were useful innovations for scenic designers, but it took someone of vision to see the true potential of the new electrical technology. Adolphe Appia was such a visionary. He was a Swiss artist and philosopher, much attracted by Wagner's music but appalled by the visual character of Bayreuth productions. "If man is three-dimensional," he wrote, "scenery must be three-dimensional." For Appia, lighting was the key, for it was "the supreme scenic painter, the interpreter, the most significant plastic medium on the stage."[8] He believed that the naturalistic

sets and costumes at Bayreuth contradicted the universality of Wagner's works, particularly *Tristan* and the *Ring*. He advocated symbolic settings in which the lighting would provide clues to interpretation. He was never allowed to design at Bayreuth (Cosima prevented that), but it was his influence on young Wieland Wagner, the composer's grandson, that eventually led to one of the most important revolutions in the story of opera.

Appia believed passionately that the stage director ought to be at least the equal of the conductor. But the term "stage director" had never been a job description much recognized in the nineteenth century. It was generally the role of a stage manager to give the singers instructions about their exits and their entrances, and to marshal the chorus in appropriate groupings; the stage manager's most important task was to ensure that each singer was on stage in time to meet the next music cue. Not surprisingly, it was very often composers who took the lead in "directing" their own operas. Weber was one of the first to insist that singers should be given some indication of what the opera was about and how they should characterize their individual roles. Meyerbeer, Verdi, and most of all Wagner went a great deal further. As for acting, it was not an essential qualification for a singer. What we would now consider embarrassing poses and a lot of exaggerated emoting were the rule rather than the exception. With the fashion for *verismo* (or realistic) opera in the final years of the nineteenth century, the old and well-loved cari-

Fyodor Chaliapin as Ivan the Terrible, Paris, 1909. After Chaliapin's success as Boris in Paris in 1908, Diaghilev decided to stage a Rimsky-Korsakov opera in 1909, THE MAID OF PSKOV, which Diaghilev renamed IVAN THE TERRIBLE. Nicholas Roerich was the designer.

cature of the hapless opera singer trying to "act" became an even more horrifying reality.

Acting was only part of what was happening onstage. In the minds of most people, opera was as much associated with visual spectacle as it was with singers. From Giacomo Torelli in Monteverdi's Venice to Pierre-Luc-Charles Cicéri in Meyerbeer's Paris, the set designers had acquired a mystique of their own. Torelli's awesome machines had thrilled seventeenth-century audiences as much as Cicéri's grand illusions dazzled and amazed the nineteenth century. Stage designers were technicians, but they were also artists: boxes of tricks were useful, but their craft was intimately linked to the artistic fashion of the time— whether it was the marvels of the Baroque, or the more balanced classicism that succeeded it, or the emotional intensity of the Romantic movement, or the requirement to portray an earthy "reality" in the *verismo* vogue. Opera productions were showcases for the best designers—so why not for leading artists, too? Toward the end of the nineteenth century, painters like Henri de Toulouse-Lautrec and Pierre Bonnard began designing for the French stage, and in Russia Savva Mamontov commissioned artists as talented as Konstantin Korovin and Aleksandr Golovin to design for his opera company.

DIAGHILEV   It was out of Russia that the first great wave of theatrical innovation came in the twentieth century. At the same time that Konstantin Stanislavsky was experimenting with a more naturalistic style of acting at the Moscow Art Theater, the young Sergei Diaghilev was beginning his career as an international impresario. He is chiefly identified with the story of dance, but what he achieved had such far-reaching consequences for both music and theater that he had a profound effect on opera, too. The dance company he created in France in 1909, the Ballets Russes, became a focus for the avant-garde—not just in dance and music, but in theater design as well. Diaghilev commissioned sets and costumes from an honor roll of twentieth-century artists: Pablo Picasso, Georges Braque, Aleksandr Benois, Léon Bakst, Henri Matisse, Joan Miró, Giorgio de Chirico, to name just a few. And he commissioned new music from the most original composers of the day—from Igor Stravinsky, Maurice Ravel, Claude Debussy, Manuel de Falla, Sergei Prokofiev, and even from Richard Strauss.

Diaghilev's restless energy had not got him very far in Russia. He had wanted to be a musician, but the director of the St. Petersburg conservatory—Rimsky-Korsakov— had not been encouraging. Instead, Diaghilev had concentrated on art. A small inheritance allowed him to travel extensively in Western Europe, and in St. Petersburg he became the focal point of a group of artists and writers that included Benois and Bakst. They produced a magazine called *The World of Art*, publishing reviews and opinions that were not designed to appeal to the Russian establishment. Diaghilev's attempts to work with the Imperial Ballet came to nought, but he had already begun to discover his talents as an impresario. His presentation of several succesful art exhibitions led him eventually, in 1906, to Paris.

The first foray, an exhibition of Russian artists, satisfied him that there was an appetite in Paris for things Russian. The next year he was back again, this time with a series of concerts of Russian music. He brought Rimsky-Korsakov, Aleksandr Glazunov, and Sergei Rachmaninoff to conduct their own works, and he introduced Paris to Fyodor Chaliapin. Chaliapin was already a renowned international singer. He had appeared several times at La Scala, and he had spent the 1907–8 season at the Metropolitan Opera in New York (though he would not sing there again until 1921). It was, however, Diaghilev's 1908 production of *Boris Godunov* in Paris, with designs by Benois, that established Chaliapin once and for all in the European consciousness as one of the truly great singers.

Diaghilev's next season in Paris, 1909, was a mixture of opera and ballet, but it was the ballet that caught the public imagination. And no wonder: the company featured Anna Pavlova, Tamara Karsavina, and Vaslav Nijinsky, with Mikhail Fokine's ballet *Les sylphides* as the main attraction. It was the beginning of the Ballets Russes, and for the next twenty years, until his death in 1929, that company would be the focus of all Diaghilev's extraordinary powers of fundraising, talent-spotting, and creative vision. Aleksandr Benois, who knew him longest, summed up the vision: "It was no accident that what was afterward known as the Ballets Russes was originally conceived not by the professionals of the dance but by a circle of artists, linked together by the idea of Art as an entity. Everything followed from the common desire of several painters and musicians to see the fulfillment of the theatrical dreams which haunted them."9

Diaghilev was the one who made those dreams come true, and opera was an incidental beneficiary in many ways.

NEW OPERA IN THE TWENTIETH CENTURY

Composers were naturally attracted to Diaghilev, especially the more progressive ones. He commissioned them to write for the Ballets Russes, and they responded with some of the most important music of the century—music that announced not just a change of direction, but a revolution. Stravinsky would be right there in the vanguard, but another revolution was happening in the mind of Arnold Schoenberg. He was beginning to change the most basic element of music—its harmonic language.

Opera had seemed to be comparatively sheltered from the more "advanced" developments in contemporary music. It was true that Debussy's *Pelléas* and Strauss's *Salome* and *Elektra* had heralded changes, but there had been no immediate follow-up, and they might have appeared to have

been isolated events. Debussy wrote no more operas; Strauss abandoned what he called the "uttermost limits of harmony" for the enchanting world of *Der Rosenkavalier*; and the opulent, accessible music of Puccini continued to dominate the field of Italian opera right up to the composer's death in 1924—and afterward, with the posthumous premiere of *Turandot*. But all this was deceptive, and Puccini knew it. "Melody is no longer practicable," he had written; "I believe this is the end of opera."10 Strauss did not agree, but he too was suspicious, and sometimes dismissive, of the efforts of the innovators. When Schoenberg sent him the score of *Five Orchestral Pieces* in 1909, Strauss returned it with the comment, "Your pieces are such daring experiments in both content and sound that for the time being I cannot take the risk of presenting them to my ultra-conservative Berlin public."11 Five years later (according to Gustav Mahler's widow, Alma, who was at pains to repeat the remark to Schoenberg), Strauss said privately, "I think he would do better to shovel snow than to scribble on music paper."12 He was no more polite about Stravinsky, who showed some of his scores to Strauss in 1914. "Very fine," said Strauss, "but why do you put so many wrong notes in?"13

Stravinsky was the best example of a composer "hijacked" by ballet. In Russia in 1909 he had written the first act of an opera, *Le rossignol* (The Nightingale). He did not complete the last two acts until 1914, when he was living in Switzerland. In between, he wrote three of the classics of ballet for Diaghilev—*L'oiseau de feu* (The Firebird), *Petrushka*, and *Le sacre du printemps* (The Rite of Spring, which Strauss suggested might better have been called "un sacrilège du printemps"14). It was the premiere of *Le sacre* in 1913 that brought down on Stravinsky's head the wrath of a generation raised on nineteenth-century tradition: the performance was disrupted by almost continuous catcalls and whistles—a theatrical riot even worse than that which had accompanied the Paris premiere of Wagner's *Tannhäuser* more than fifty years before. An aging aristocrat, the comtesse de Pourtales, doyenne of Paris society, was heard to shout from her box: "This is the first time in sixty years that anyone has dared to make fun of me!"15 Alas, the comtesse was going to have to get used to being mocked by the twentieth century. The dissonances and jagged rhythms of *Le sacre* were a portent of much more to come.

Stravinsky lived to a great age (he died in 1971). Just as his friend Pablo Picasso explored the interior world of art and expressed it in different ways during the different stages of his lifelong experiment, so Stravinsky did with music. The unmistakable Russian nationalism of his early works, including those first three ballets for Diaghilev, was already light years removed from the Romanticism of Tchaikovsky and his Russian forebears. Stravinsky's nationalist music in turn gave way to a long experiment with neoclassical forms until, in the 1950s, he unexpectedly began to employ the so-called serial or twelve-tone method pioneered by Schoenberg and his pupils.

In addition to the ballets (first with Diaghilev, later in another great collaboration with George Balanchine in New York), Stravinsky wrote frequently for the stage, most often in unorthodox formats. He clearly had doubts about traditional opera, and about the position of singers within it. *L'histoire du soldat* (The Soldier's Tale) contained no singing at all, only speech and music and acting. *Renard* placed the singers in the orchestra, with their roles duplicated by dancers on stage. *Mavra* was a more orthodox *opera buffa*, but with no recitative, just a series of arias and ensembles. *Oedipus Rex* (sung in Latin, with a narration spoken by an actor in the audience's own language) was part oratorio, part opera, intensely formal and performed in masks. Only in *The Rake's Progress* in 1951 would he write an opera that sits easily within the tradition of *dramma per musica*, a fantastic moral tale set in eighteenth-century England. A subsequent project, an opera about the rebirth of the world after an atomic cataclysm, was aborted by the death of the librettist, Dylan Thomas.

Like Stravinsky, Claude Debussy had doubts about opera as a vehicle for his music ("There's too much singing in opera," he wrote[16]). Yet, also like Stravinsky, he left an indelible mark on the art form. After *Pelléas* in 1902 he completed no more operas, though several subsequent projects remained incomplete, including some commissions from the Metropolitan Opera.[17] But with *Pelléas*, Debussy had done enough. It erupted onto a French operatic scene dominated by the easygoing, traditional works of Massenet. It signaled the new century's absorption in the interior workings of the mind—in the findings of Sigmund Freud and the drama of Symbolism. It was *musik-drama* in Wagner's sense of that term, but the music was not the heavy Teutonic mixture of Bayreuth: it was the sensuous, orgiastic music of Impressionism. Whether you loved it or hated it, and there were plenty of fanatics in both camps, *Pelléas* was there, and it would not go away. (One of the more intriguing might-have-beens was what Puccini might have made of *Pelléas*: by the time he asked for the rights, the author, Maurice Maeterlinck, had already granted them to Debussy).

Pelléas, like *Tristan*, stood alone, but there were two later operas that bore comparison in more ways than one. Paul Dukas's *Ariane et Barbe-Bleue* (Ariadne and Bluebeard) was written in the immediate aftermath of *Pelléas*, and it owed even more to Maurice Maeterlinck, who had originally written the libretto in the hope that Edvard Grieg would set it. Dukas and Debussy were friends, familiar with each other's music and methods, and there was much in *Ariane* to remind listeners of *Pelléas*, even some direct quotations. But *Ariane* was a more conventional opera in sound and construction: there were "operatic" recitatives, long lines of melody, and a predominant key of F-sharp. It also contained, in the part of Ariadne, one of the most challenging mezzo-soprano roles in opera—a role that was created by Georgette Leblanc, Maeterlinck's wife and the singer who had so notoriously been denied the role of Mélisande by Debussy.

In 1911, four years after the premiere of *Ariane*, the story was used again, this time by the Hungarian composer Béla Bartók. Musically, his *Bluebeard's Castle* owed something to both Debussy and Dukas, but it probably owed a great deal more to the tone poems of Richard Strauss and to Bartók's own study of the folk music of his homeland. The libretto gave little indication of drama. It was a static piece with roles for only two singers, apparently not very theatrical, but Bartók's powerful score supplied drama enough. Its style might be labeled either Expressionist or Symbolist, but the music was forceful enough, and disturbing enough, to give the work an enduring place in the repertoire.

These three works—Debussy's *Pelléas*, Dukas's *Ariane*, and Bartók's *Bluebeard*—were the only major operatic works written by their respective composers. It was as if the effort and the aggravation of producing them were a block to further development (in the case of Bartók, this was almost literally true).

One of the sadnesses of the twentieth cen-

The text on the banner in the image reads:

Leave all love and hope behind

out of sight is out of mind

tury was that French opera, in general, seemed to suffer from a rather similar block. Massenet, it is true, continued composing right up to his death in 1912, and Darius Milhaud wrote fourteen operas, of which *Christophe Colomb* was a genuine hit in 1930, albeit in a German text. But no other French composer truly persevered. Maurice Ravel wrote two intriguing short operas, *L'heure espagnole* (The Spanish Hour, 1911) and *L'enfant et les sortilèges* (The Child and the Enchantments, 1925), that have proven popular. Francis Poulenc wrote one of the century's finest and most dramatic operas,

Les dialogues des Carmélites (1957). Olivier Messiaen's only opera, *Saint François d'Assisse* (1983), was commissioned by the Paris Opéra, and although it is an impressive score, it is in truth more of an oratorio than an opera. These, however, were rare examples of French works that found their way into the international repertoire.

If there was one country that should have been in the vanguard of opera in the twentieth century, it was Russia. With the groundwork successfully

The Bedlam scene from Stravinsky's The Rake's Progress *at the Glyndebourne Festival, 1975. Directed by John Cox, sets by David Hockney. With Leo Goeke as Tom Rakewell.*

laid by Glinka, Tchaikovsky, and the Mighty Handful, opera had begun to attract the talents of other members of the artistic community—painters, designers, writers, and stage directors. Stanislavsky and Nemirovich-Danchenko, working from their base at the Moscow Art Theater, began a fruitful collaboration with the Bolshoi: a distinctive style began to emerge. But it was a turbulent time in Russia. The abortive uprising of 1905 foretold the end of czarist rule, and it finally came when Lenin seized power in 1917. For most of the next seventy years, Russian artists were limited by the state-approved style known as socialist realism.

At the time of the Revolution, Stravinsky, Diaghilev, most of the greatest Russian dancers, and some of the artists, were already abroad, and would stay there. Sergei Prokofiev, the outstanding pianist and composer of the younger generation, joined them in 1917. The planned premiere of his first opera, *The Gambler*, a study of obsession, was actually canceled because of the onset of the Revolution. In the United States he found himself labeled the "Bolshevik pianist," and his music was not popular. "His fingers are steel, his wrists steel, his biceps and triceps steel, his scapula steel," reported the *New York Times*; "he is a tonal steel trust."[18] His piano playing amazed Americans, but his own music made little impression. For Chicago in 1921, however, he composed a fine opera—*The Love of Three Oranges*, based on an old commedia dell'arte story. It was a fairy-tale piece, set to strident, tuneful music that made the grotesque story accessible and funny. Yet only a year or two later he was composing a violent Expressionist work, *The Fiery Angel*, an opera of extraordinary dramatic power that was not performed until 1955.

Prokofiev found Paris, where he had the patronage of Diaghilev and the companionship of so many other Russian émigrés, a more sympathetic environment than America. But the lure of Mother Russia pulled him homeward, and in 1932 he returned to the Soviet Union for good.

There were danger signals for artists. The sense of innovation and adventure that had marked the first decade of the century had by now been undermined. The new Soviet rulers saw opera, and all the other arts, too, as tools of propaganda, just as Catherine the Great had in a previous generation. New Revolutionary operas were hard to come by, but old operas could always be adapted to politically correct librettos. Thus, Meyerbeer's *Les Huguenots* became *The Decembrists*, in honor of the 1825 revolt that had nearly toppled the monarchy, and *Tosca* became *Into Battle for the Commune*.[19]

But so long as the term *socialist realism* remained undefined—or, at any rate, ill-defined—it was possible for a certain amount of genuine invention to survive. In 1930, Dmitri Shostakovich's spiky opera *The Nose* was controversial, but apparently acceptable.

That changed when Shostakovich brought out his next opera, *The Lady Macbeth of Mtsensk*—a magnificent surrealistic work in which lyricism and melody were freely applied to a story about the murderous activities of a bored wife. *Lady Macbeth* was produced to acclaim (accompanied by suitable controversy about its subject matter) in Leningrad and Moscow, as well as in Cleveland, Philadelphia, and New York. The trouble began when Joseph Stalin attended a performance in Moscow in 1936: he walked out before the end, and two days later *Pravda* printed an editorial entitled "Chaos Instead of Music."[20] The opera was condemned as unmusical and "degenerate," and the editorial signaled Stalin's determination to crush all forms of Russian art that did not conform with his own idea of socialist realism. For Shostakovich, who was still only thirty, it was a devastating blow.

Prokofiev, meanwhile, in the 1930s and

Shostakovitch's The Lady Macbeth of Mtsensk *at the Metropolitan Opera, New York, 1994. Directed by Graham Vick, designed by Paul Brown. With Maria Ewing as Katerina.*

1940s was fired by a genuine and deep-seated patriotism. *I, Son of the Working Class* (sometimes known as *Semyon Kotko*) was a story of World War I set in his native Ukraine, where partisans, organized by the nascent village soviets, fought German invaders. His two great film scores, *Alexander Nevsky* and *Ivan the Terrible*, were both written for the director Sergei Eisenstein, both on familiar Russian themes. But Prokofiev did not consider himself limited to Russian stories, and certainly not to socialist realism—witness his 1940 opera *Betrothal in a Monastery*, based on *The Duenna* (1775) by Richard Sheridan, and two wonderful full-length ballets, *Romeo and Juliet* and *Cinderella*. Eventually, it was the German invasion of Russia in 1941 that precipitated his finest work. As Hitler's armies laid siege to Stalingrad, and as millions of Russians were dying in the defense of their country, Prokofiev relived the epic story of the last time this had happened to Russia: the winter of 1812, when General Kutuzov had defended Moscow against Napoleon's armies. He wrote *War and Peace*, an opera as grand as the Tolstoy novel on which it was based, and a work that compares favorably with any other opera written in the twentieth century.

Prokofiev never saw *War and Peace* per-

formed in its entirety. For Soviet composers, the world effectively came to an end in 1948 when the central committee of the Communist Party published a resolution criticizing Soviet music and musicians.[21] Their music, it said, contained "antidemocratic tendencies that are alien to the Soviet people and to its artistic tastes." The composers, meeting with Stalin's functionaries soon after, publicly admitted their "mistakes." It was an infamous moment in the history of twentieth-century music.

Ironically, these events occurred just as Prokofiev was completing his last opera, *The Story of a Real Man*. It was the heroic story of a Russian pilot shot down in World War II and his long struggle "to rejoin the human race" and become a "Soviet man," despite appalling injuries. The patriotic theme notwithstanding, the bureaucrats, fearful of Stalin's erratic judgments, canceled the first performance (it finally took place in 1960). And even after that, one final irony remained: when Prokofiev died, on March 5, 1953, the event was largely overlooked in the Soviet Union, and throughout the world, because Stalin also died that day, just fifty minutes after Prokofiev. Two years later, *War and Peace* was given a complete performance in Leningrad—and two years after that, it was given a network television production by NBC in the United States.

In later decades, Soviet communism slowly pulled back from the 1948 ultimatum. But much damage had been done, to at least two generations of Russian artists and musicians. Others, meanwhile, pursued their careers outside Russia. That, after all, was how the century had begun, with the brilliant career of Sergei Diaghilev.

In the first decade of the century, an intellectual and artistic agenda had been put forward, and despite all the traumas and upheavals of the century, despite all the scientific and technological developments, this was the agenda that governed the direction of music and the arts for the next fifty years, at least. Opera was profoundly affected because the agenda had included what amounted to an altogether new language of music.

Arnold Schoenberg cast a long shadow across the century. He altered the harmonic structure of music, and thereby changed its language. What had been a fairly accessible world of music—a world in which you did not need special training to appreciate, if not to understand—seemed to become a private world for professionals only. "I realize that I cannot be understood," Schoenberg wrote in 1924, "and I am content to make do with respect."[22] He got the respect of a generation of young musicians—who in turn lost the attention of much of their audience.

In the 1920s, Schoenberg developed a system of composing based on putting the twelve notes of the octave in an invented series, and then building up the piece by repeating the series in various transformations. Comparatively few composers followed Schoenberg all the way into his twelve-tone system, but it was impossible to be a twentieth-century musician and not be affected by the method's precursor, which is generally known as "atonality" (although Schoenberg loathed the term).

Ever since the beginnings of opera in the early years of the seventeenth century, the language of music had been governed by tonality: that is, music had generally been written in such a way that each section of it adhered to the notes of one of the major or minor scales, with the tonic, or keynote, of the scale being recognized as its governing factor. A composition might be written in C major. This meant no more than that the work began, and quite possibly ended, in that key, but it gave the music an overall unity, and it offered the listener a "key" to its understanding. The tonic key of Mozart's *Don Giovanni*, for instance, was D. The overture began in D minor, in music foretelling the fate that awaited Don Giovanni when the stone statue of the man he had murdered would come to life and drag him down to Hell—and that scene, too, at the end of the opera, returned to D minor. You did not have to be able to read music to appreciate that, and it was the method that all composers had used for three hundred years.

Schoenberg was the first major composer to abandon the method. Debussy, the Russian Aleksandr Scriabin, and even Franz Lizst, had tampered with it, but in 1908, in the finale to his Second String Quartet, Schoenberg demonstrated an entirely new way. It was "atonal" because there was no longer any governing key, no tonal center. Each note of the scale was given equal importance and allowed an independent existence since it no longer had to be related to a key center. As a result, the harmonic structure of music, often rendered in puzzling enough ways by the likes of Wagner and Strauss, was now totally unhinged. The sounds were strange and somewhat alien, and they became uncomfortable, harsh, and downright brutal when Schoenberg applied them, in the early years of atonality, to the sort of subject matter that then interested him: the Expressionistic world of the troubled psyche. *Erwartung* (Expectation), written in 1909, was a thirty-minute monodrama in which a deranged woman searched for her lover in a forest, eventually discovering his dead body.

Schoenberg's next stage of development came in the mid-1920s, when he began writing his music within the twelve-tone system (not always—sometimes he even reverted to a tonal system). The opera of his that is most often performed is *Moses und Aron*, a monumental work composed in the twelve-tone style but left unfinished, though it stands up perfectly well in the two acts he completed. Aside from the musical language, which can seem difficult, *Moses und Aron* had a special interest because it represented the religious and philosophical dilemmas of Schoenberg's own thinking—the tensions between Moses (the otherworldly philosopher-thinker) and Aaron (the pragmatic leader who must translate those thoughts into action). Most of the music was written in 1931–32, but it was given added meaning by the knowledge that Schoenberg returned to Judaism in 1933, after his experience of Nazism in Berlin. The drama of the work—the clash between Moses and Aaron—was acted out through the biblical stories of God's call to Moses through the Burning Bush, the disobedience of the Children of Israel in worshiping the Golden Calf, and finally Moses' smashing of the tablets of the Commandments and his confrontation with Aaron.

Schoenberg's influence on the world of opera, however, came not so much from his own operas as from those of his pupil Alban Berg. Berg, too, was an Austrian, from a comfortable, middle-class family, and it was apparent very early on that he was a gifted musician, though not a very focused one until he began studying with Schoenberg. Then (like his colleague, Anton von Webern) he became a disciple. He was never a prolific composer, and he was dogged by ill health, but his *Wozzeck* and *Lulu* were atonal music's most successful experiments in *dramma per musica*—certainly the most enduring.

Wozzeck was written on either side of World War I, in which Berg fought. Its unlikely source was an 1836 play by Georg Büchner, which told the tragic story of a soldier, Wozzeck, who is variously put upon by his captain, a doctor, and the drum major. The last of these characters is having an affair with Marie, the mother of Wozzeck's child. Wozzeck ends up murdering Marie and drowning himself. With the exception of an orchestral interlude, all the music was atonal. Berg also made use of *Sprechstimme*, a device Schoenberg had used a few years earlier in his song cycle *Pierrot lunaire* and would use again in *Moses und Aron*. It was neither speech nor song, but a combination of the two in which the speaker-singer declaimed to a rhythm, and in an intonation, that was precisely described in the score. The music of *Wozzeck* was strange and difficult, but it was undeniably powerful. It underscored the drama, and it elevated it, giving the story of Wozzeck a universality, a timelessness, and a peculiar poignancy that Büchner's original play had never achieved.

Musically, Berg's second opera, *Lulu*, was even more complex. It was written throughout in the twelve-tone (or serial) system that Schoenberg had developed in the 1920s, and it is the only significant opera in that system to have retained a regular place in the repertoire. It was based on two plays by Frank Wedekind. Its subject was Lulu, a femme fatale as fascinating as she is dangerous, who runs through three husbands and several acquaintances, all of whom come to violent ends, before she is herself murdered by Jack the Ripper.

Schoenberg's MOSES UND ARON *at the New York City Opera, 1990. Directed by Hans Neugebauer, designed by Achim Freyer. With Thomas Young as Aron (second from left), John Calvin West as the Priest, and Richard Cross as Moses (at right). This modern-dress production was originally staged in Cologne. The Golden Calf is visible at the back.*

When he died, in 1935, Berg had completed only the first two acts of *Lulu*, although the third was fully sketched and might easily have been rendered as a performing version. Schoenberg rejected the task (he found anti-Semitic references in the opera), and thereafter Berg's widow, Helene, refused to grant the rights to anyone. When she died in 1976, and mainly because of the energy and determination of Pierre Boulez, the third act was completed by Friedrich Cerha, an Austrian composer and scholar, and the opera was finally performed in its entirety.

Berg's *Wozzeck* and *Lulu*, and Schoenberg's *Erwartung* and *Moses und Aron*, were the high points in opera's experiment first with atonality, then with the twelve-tone system. All four operas won a place in the general repertoire, and they are likely to retain it, because of the way in which they express drama with, and through, music—which is what opera is all about.

The time when Schoenberg and Berg were writing these operas was a period of unparalleled turmoil in the German-speaking world. In the twenty years between 1914 and 1934, Germany moved from the high tide of imperial power, through the humiliation of defeat, the poverty of the Weimar Republic, and the rise of National Socialism, to the appointment of Adolf Hitler as chancellor. Yet these were years when more new operas were written in German than in any other language—and Strauss, Schoenberg, and Berg were by no means the most famous names. Kurt Weill, working with Bertolt Brecht in the frenetic atmosphere of Berlin, was more popular than any of them.

German audiences were not afraid of the new music. Franz Schreker's career was proof of that. His mystical operas, in which realism was almost always surrounded by fairy-tale settings, were at least as popular as most of Strauss's. *Der ferne Klang* (The Distant Sound) was well received in Frankfurt in 1912 (the year after *Rosenkavalier*),

and *Die Gezeichneten* (Those Who Are Stigmatized) and *Der Schatzgräber* (The Treasure Seeker) were even better received after World War I. Schreker's music was certainly "progressive" — being largely devoid of traditional harmony — yet he used it to create drama that clearly touched a nerve in the consciousness of his audience. The same could be said a few years later of Schreker's pupil, Ernst Krenek. Krenek lived through the first ninety-one years of the century and his music went through every imaginable phase, including atonality and serialism, but he is best remembered for the huge success in 1927 of *Jonny spielt auf* (Jonny Strikes Up), perhaps the most sensational success of any new opera in the twentieth century. In its first year of life, it had more than thirty separate productions in German-speaking countries, and within two years it had been performed in twenty foreign cities as well, including a production at the Metropolitan Opera House. *Jonny* was conveniently advertised as a "jazz opera" because Krenek used a form of jazz to contrast with several other musical styles, including some very advanced Schoenbergian passages, but once again, as with Schreker's operas, the success of the piece lay in its accessibility to the audience. *Jonny* contained, in addition to a jazz band, such modern phenomena as a radio broadcast, a police-car chase, and death by railway locomotive (not to mention a singing glacier). *Jonny*'s success was enormous, but ephemeral.

Krenek never repeated that success. In 1934, while he was rehearsing his epic work *Karl V* at the Vienna Opera (he described it as "explicitly anti-Nazi, pro-Austrian, and Catholic"), he was forced to leave his country by the Nazis. Like Weill, Schoenberg, and so many others (Berg and Schreker were already dead), he made his new home in America.

So, too, did Paul Hindemith. His conflict with Nazism was the more inevitable because the central theme of his stage works was the responsibility of the creative artist in society. *Cardillac* (1926) was the cautionary tale of a master goldsmith who recognized no such responsibility: he murdered the purchasers of his work in order to keep the treasures for himself. *Mathis der Maler* (Mathis the Painter), on the other hand, was about the painter Matthias Grünewald at the time of the Peasants' Revolt in 1524. The conflict at the center of the opera was between Grünewald's natural tendency to support the peasants, his appreciation

of the debt he owed to his own patron, the cardinal, and his disgust at the increasing violence of the revolutionaries. *Mathis* was written in 1934–35, but it could not be performed in Nazi Germany. Hindemith became a professor at Yale and an American citizen, and it was not until after his death in 1963 that his two principal operas began to win popularity in his native country. Like Schreker and Krenek, he wrote music that was certainly modern, but in his case it was informed by a remarkably eclectic use of the styles of previous centuries, from the Baroque to the Romantic.

Another German opera composer of this stormy period found postwar rehabilitation more difficult. Hans Pfitzner played no great role in the twentieth-century music revolution. He defiantly continued to compose in much more traditional style, using harmonic patterns that sounded decidedly conservative alongside those of most of his contemporaries. If he was musically close to any one German, it was perhaps to Richard Strauss, but he had none of Strauss's natural affinity for drama. His *Palestrina*, first produced in 1917, was an important opera, and one of epic proportions. It was about the Renaissance composer Giovanni Pierluigi Palestrina and the part he was supposed to have played at the Council of Trent in persuading the Roman Catholic Church not to desert the cause of polyphonic music. Huge, grand, and musically inventive, *Palestrina* was more like a vast cantata than a dramatic stage work: it lacked the essential drama that Strauss would certainly have insisted on. Pfitzner survived the Nazi period in Germany, but he did so (unlike Strauss) as an ardent supporter of the Third Reich. That certainly explained, in part, the hesitation in reviving his music in the postwar era, though *Palestrina* did eventually become a regular feature of the Munich Summer Festival, and it was the work chosen by London's Royal Opera to mark its own fiftieth anniversary in 1997.

All the controversy about the avant-garde could not disguise the fact that there was also a mainstream of twentieth-century opera. Four composers from different countries — Giacomo Puccini, Richard Strauss, Leoš Janáček, and Benjamin Britten — each produced a substantial body of work that became part of the essential repertoire.

Right up to his death in 1924, Puccini continued sublimely on his way, very little affected by

Hindemith's MATHIS DER MALER *at Covent Garden, London, 1995. Directed by Peter Sellars, scenic design by George Tsypin. With Alan Titus as Mathis.*

the innovations going on around him, although there are traces in his final opera, *Turandot*, of a certain degree of familiarity with Stravinsky. Richard Strauss was much more involved with recent developments, partly because he was one of the leading conductors in Europe, but also because he had himself led the way in the first decade of the century. There were those in the avant-garde who sneered at his subsequent operas, from *Der Rosenkavalier* in 1911 to *Capriccio* in 1942. They accused him of sacrificing experimentation for

accessibility. "Me, a renegade?" Strauss responded in his old age. "Is that what they say? And yet I was one of the first in that business, with *Elektra*."[23]

Although *Elektra* was the end of a phase in Strauss's musical development, it was also the beginning of something just as important in his dramatic development: it was his first collaboration with Hugo von Hofmannsthal. In the story of opera, there have been several great partnerships between composers and librettists—Gluck and Calzabigi, Meyerbeer and Scribe, Verdi and Piave,

Pfitzner's PALESTRINA *at Covent Garden, London, 1997. Directed by Nikolaus Lehnhoff, set designs by Tobias Hoheisel. With Thomas Moser in the title role. Giovanni Pierluigi Palestrina here dictates the* MISSA PAPAE MARCELLI, *the work which, it is hoped, will persuade Pope Pius IV and the Council of Trent that polyphonic church music should not be banned in favor of plainchant.*

Verdi and Boito, to name just a few—but the partnership between Strauss and Hofmannsthal was almost as important to opera as that between Mozart and Da Ponte had been in the 1780s.

Working with a librettist was not entirely new to Strauss. His one-act opera of 1901, *Feuersnot* (Fire Famine), had been based on a libretto by the philosopher Ernst von Wolzogen. It was not a happy experience. The story of the opera, set in medieval Munich, caused a good deal of derision, even though the music generally delighted. Strauss called it "an intermezzo against the theater, spurred by personal motives and reaping a small revenge on my beloved native city"[24] (Munich had conclusively rejected his first opera, *Guntram*). In the case of *Elektra*, Strauss was led to Hofmannsthal because he wished to make use of Hofmannsthal's own play based on the tragedy of Sophocles. The collaboration was a good experience for both of them, and even before *Elektra* was performed, they agreed they would work together again.

The world doubtless expected another psycho-drama or tragedy from them, certainly something perverse. But Richard Strauss was already the composer of the tone poems *Till Eulenspiegel* and *Don Quixote*. They were comedies, and he was anxious to return to that genre. What Hofmannsthal came up with was not simply a comedy: it was better than that.

Der Rosenkavalier is one of the sublime works in the story of opera. It is recognizably modern, but also, in some respects, the climax of the Romantic age. It is the work of a composer who had grown up during the high days of German Romanticism, who had conducted at the greatest shrines of that movement, but who had nonetheless established his own unique identity as the musician of a new age. *Der Rosenkavalier* is certainly not the only late Romantic opera Strauss would write, but in its place (Dresden) and its time (1911) it can be seen as a culmination of the German Romantic movement in opera—the epitaph to a great age.

Despite the fact that Strauss and Hofmannsthal never really liked each other, they wrote six operas together, from *Elektra* to *Arabella*, in a partnership that explored, perhaps more fully than any other partnership between composer and librettist, the age-old question of which came first, words or music. It was the theme of the Prologue to *Ariadne auf Naxos*, the opera that succeeded *Rosenkavalier*, and it was the entire subject matter

of Strauss's final opera, *Capriccio*, written a dozen years after Hofmannsthal's death. Strauss seemed to come to no conclusion in that work: the countess (who is opera) fails to make a choice between her two suitors, the poet and the composer. But to judge by Strauss's copious correspondence with Hofmannsthal, he never doubted that, in the world of opera, the composer was preeminent. Hofmannsthal, the wealthy Austrian playwright, was the perfect partner for him because he, too, seemed to understand that this was the way the relationship must work, and he honored it even when they tackled a work based on one of his own stories, *Die Frau ohne Schatten* (The Woman Without a Shadow).

Other than Puccini's, Richard Strauss's operas are the most frequently performed of all twentieth-century operas, and the ones most certain to endure into subsequent centuries. It is true that after *Salome* and *Elektra* he never again "penetrated to the uttermost limits of harmony," but he challenged himself and his audiences with a wide variety of styles and subjects. They varied from the lush Mozartean romances of *Rosenkavalier* and *Arabella*, to the autobiographical conversation-piece *Intermezzo*; from the extravagant comedy *Die schweigsame Frau* (The Silent Woman) to the huge, dense allegory, *Die Frau ohne Schatten*, which Strauss thought the best of all his operas, and which found a great deal of support in the second half of the century. All of them had one feature in common—the huge role in the drama assigned to the orchestra. As both composer and conductor, Strauss was a master of the orchestra, in a way that only Wagner, of all his predecessors, had equaled.

Like the rest of the world, Strauss paid little attention to the work of Leoš Janáček (see the chapter "Opera of the People"). Indeed, it was not until after World War II, almost twenty years after Janáček's own death, that it became apparent that this quiet man from the little-known province of Moravia had created a canon of work that was destined to be one of the most important in twentieth-century opera. Janáček's music, especially in his last years, was often harsh and bleak, but it was never atonal, and the jagged sounds were offset by passages of lyrical beauty derived from what he called the "speech melodies of nature"—the sounds of birds, forests, and all the natural elements around him. What his works needed, and what they got only after Janáček's

death, was the attention of committed stage directors in order to reveal them as compelling examples of *dramma per musica* at its best.

Benjamin Britten, by contrast, lived to see his operas go around the world—if tentatively at first, because the world was not used to English opera. There had been no such thing to speak of since Henry Purcell at the end of the seventeenth century, and Purcell's work had hardly reached beyond the English Channel. This finally changed in the twentieth century, when three factors came together to make it possible. The first was the arrival of a group of talented composers—Frederick Delius, Edward Elgar, Gustav Holst, and Ralph Vaughan Williams—who wrote music that was identifiably English. The second was the presence of a few forceful personalities (of whom Sir Henry Wood and Sir Thomas Beecham were the most outstanding) who were determined that England would finally become a land of music.

And the third was the appearance, in the 1930s and 1940s, of a small band of artists, designers, poets, and musicians who eventually became the English Opera Group.

The forgotten man who played such a large part in bringing this about was Rupert Doone. He had been a dancer in the Ballets Russes and an unashamed admirer of Diaghilev. Better than most, he appreciated what Diaghilev had done in bringing together so many branches of the arts in a single theatrical endeavor, and he saw no reason why the same thing should not be attempted in England. In the early 1930s he formed an association called Group Theatre. Its leading members included the poets W. H. Auden, Christopher Isherwood, Louis MacNeice, and Stephen Spender; the artists Robert Medley and John Piper; and a young musician named Benjamin Britten. As founder and chief producer of Group Theatre, Rupert Doone defined its objectives as exactly those he had seen Diaghilev achieve: the unification of many different artistic disciplines, including poetry, painting, design and music, to produce drama—be it straight drama or musical drama, dance or opera.[25]

World War II intervened, but Benjamin Britten did not forget Doone's ideal. Britten's first opera was a somewhat daring conception—a story about an American frontier hero, *Paul Bunyan*, written by two Englishmen (Britten and Auden) and produced at Columbia University in New York. It was soon withdrawn, but it had made an impression in at least one important quarter, because Britten returned to England in 1942 with a commission from Serge Koussevitsky, conductor of the Boston Symphony Orchestra. That commission became the opera *Peter Grimes*. Koussevitsky generously waived his rights, and it was given its first performance at the Sadler's Wells Theatre in London in 1945, conducted by Reginald Goodall, with Peter Pears in the title role. Many people date the rebirth of English opera from that night, and they are probably right, but it would have meant a great deal less had it not been quickly followed by another important event. In October 1946, Britten and his principal collaborators founded their own company, the English Opera Group. It existed for thirty years, and it was chiefly responsible for the ferment of English opera in those years. It commissioned and produced a large number of new operas by Britten, Lennox Berkeley, Harrison Birtwistle, William Walton, and others; it restaged works by Purcell; it established the Aldeburgh Festival in Britten's hometown; it founded an Opera Studio, an Opera School, and other national institutions; and by its touring, it introduced not just England, but many other countries as well, to English opera.

Within this company, under the undoubted leadership of Britten, a number of very talented artists came together. The leaders were the painter John Piper and the writer and director Eric Crozier. There was also Myfanwy Piper (who would write three of Britten's finest librettos), and the company's two leading singers, Peter Pears and Joan Cross. By the mid-1950s, they had been joined by Colin Graham, a producer and director of a younger generation who would foster new English-language opera on both sides of the Atlantic. At the outset, in 1946, Britten, Piper, and Crozier issued a manifesto:

We believe the time has come when England, which has never had a tradition of native opera but has always depended on foreign works, can create its own operas. Opera is as much a vital means of artistic expression as orchestral music, drama and painting, and the lack of it has meant an impoverishment of English artistic life.[26]

The English Opera Group concentrated on small-scale and chamber operas, and Britten wrote many of its most popular works—from *Albert Herring* and *The Turn of the Screw* to *A Midsummer Night's Dream* and *Death in Venice*. He also wrote larger works for Covent Garden—*Billy Budd*, which rivals *Grimes* for popularity in international opera houses, and *Gloriana*, written for the coronation of Queen Elizabeth II and much undervalued to this day.

Britten had enormous success in his lifetime, yet there was a sense in which he never ceased to feel like an outsider. Again and again he chose to write about loners—men who were rejected by society, or whose innocence was corrupted by more worldly forces. There was Peter Grimes, the persecuted fisherman; Albert Herring, the gullible greengrocer's lad; Billy Budd, the sailor who is unjustly hanged; Owen Wingrave, the pacifist; the haunted children of *The Turn of the Screw*; and Aschenbach, the homosexual, in *Death in Venice*. For each of them, Britten made a passionate and convincing case, both dramatically and musically. That is doubtless why his operas so quickly won a place in the international repertoire, and why they remain there—while so many of the works of his contemporaries, well received at first hearing, have encountered an uncertain future. Britten's musical language was original, certainly, but it was also accessible to the mainly conservative audiences that came to hear it, and always remained within the bounds of traditional tonality. It had an affinity with the human voice and the English language, and a remarkable ability to define characters and events in phrases that were both memorable and dramatic. If proof of Britten's accessibility was needed, it came from children who responded so readily to the works he wrote for them—notably *The Little Sweep*, which was contained within a play called *Let's Make an Opera*.

While Benjamin Britten was certainly the most successful composer of opera in English, he was by no means the only one involved in it. From the earliest years of the century, the Metropolitan Opera had staged occasional American operas, and had even commissioned some, but none of them had prospered. The one work that might have changed things—*Porgy and Bess* (1935)—had been written by George Gershwin as an "American folk opera," and he had intended it for the Metropolitan. Instead, it went via Boston to Broadway, and it took fifty years to reach the Met. Nonetheless, *Porgy* had all the ingredients to be the first great American opera, which it was.

No one else came close to Gershwin's achievement, but at least two composers, Carlisle Floyd and Douglas Moore, wrote American operas that deserved a wider audience. Floyd's *Susannah* (1955) was set in Tennessee, in the midst

of religious bigotry: its fluent Puccini-like score, interrupted by big hymn tunes and energetic square dances, was as American as Gershwin's *Porgy*, and almost as seductive. The same could be said of Moore's *The Ballad of Baby Doe* (1956), which was set in a silver-mining community in Colorado. Most of the other leading American composers of the time—Virgil Thomson, Aaron Copland, Samuel Barber—also tried their hands at opera, but none of them wrote works that captured the popular imagination, and certainly not in the way that their talented contemporaries—Richard Rodgers, Frederick Loewe, Leonard Bernstein—were able to do on Broadway.

Gian Carlo Menotti had more success. An Italian who had lived in the United States since he was sixteen, he brought to opera a combination of dramatic and musical talents that broke down barriers previously thought insuperable. In 1950, he neatly reversed the customary practice when he wrote a full-length opera, *The Consul*, and

Britten's A Midsummer Night's Dream *at the Glyndebourne Festival, 1984. Directed by Peter Hall, designed by John Bury. With Ileana Cotrubas as Tytania and James Bowman as Oberon.*

Birtwistle's THE MASK OF ORPHEUS *at the English National Opera, London, 1986. Directed by David Freeman, designed by Jocelyn Herbert.*

ran it successfully in the commercial theater, rather than in an opera house. The next year he wrote an opera that was seen not by thousands but by millions. *Amahl and the Night Visitors* was a children's opera inspired by a Hieronymous Bosch painting of the Adoration of the Magi, but what made it different was that it was written for television. Its original broadcast by the NBC network on Christmas Eve of 1951 was followed by countless other productions and recordings, in America and throughout the world. *Amahl* may have been seen by more people than any other single opera.

The English language was no longer an anomaly in opera. One composer who had long wanted to make use of it was Igor Stravinsky, then almost seventy years of age and since 1940 an American resident. With Auden as his principal librettist, he wrote *The Rake's Progress* (1951). It was the culmination of his long neoclassical period. Inspired by the eighteenth-century engravings of William Hogarth, the *Rake* was a much more "orthodox" operatic work than anything Stravinsky had written earlier. In some ways, it was a homage to Mozart and his predecessors (it even used "dry" recitative in a manner that would have been recognizable to the Florentine *camerata* of the 1590s), but Stravinsky's score was a complex document, working with Auden's words on many different levels. The first performance, in Venice, was by most accounts a lackluster affair and clearly did not do justice to the work. Since then, however, *The Rake's Progress* has become a well-loved repertoire work, and one that will certainly endure.

On the other side of the Atlantic, Benjamin Britten's example was already being followed up by other composers. In 1954, Covent Garden gave the premiere of William Walton's *Troilus and Cressida,* and the next year it presented one of the most intriguing operas in any language, Michael Tippett's *The Midsummer Marriage.* This was the first of five operas Tippett wrote in a remarkable forty-year odyssey. In them, he explored the heights and depths of human experience in a language entirely his own. Ever his own librettist, he wrote dramas that explored the world of emotions with a profundity that few composers have matched. His last opera, *New Year* (1989), might be seen as a bookend with *The Midsummer Marriage.* From the lyrical, bucolic world of the midsummer rite, he had moved all the way to the urban world of the midwinter rite, now accompanied by electric guitars, taped music, and Afro-Caribbean rap. But his own lyricism remained, and with it the optimistic view of human nature that made Tippett's operatic work so appealing.

Tippett's road was a characteristically solitary one, but many younger composers benefited from the activities of the English Opera Group (until, a year or two after Benjamin Britten's death in 1976, the government withdrew its subsidy and precipitated its closure). One of those composers was Harrison Birtwistle, who may have contributed most to English opera after Britten and Tippett, notably in two enormous works: *The Mask of Orpheus* in 1986 and *Gawain* in 1991. *Orpheus* was an invention of great originality in which opera's oldest story was used to explore the origins of myth and the invention of language. *Gawain*, on the other hand, was more traditional in structure—a version of the Green Knight story from the folklore of King Arthur. His next opera, *The Second Mrs. Kong* (1994), had a genuine popular success in Germany and Austria as well as in England. The common thread running through Birtwistle's work was clearly a fascination with myth, ancient and modern, and what made his operas so much more accessible than those of many of his contemporaries was their sense of wholeness: musical ideas inspired visual ideas, and together they made compelling theater. Many of those who found the music difficult on first hearing were seduced by its ability to make drama—*dramma per musica*, as the pioneers of opera defined it.

In twentieth-century Europe, government subsidy replaced the private patronage of courts and aristocrats. There were advantages—witness the existence of literally hundreds of public opera houses on the continent of Europe, most of them supported by national, provincial, and local governments, many of them deriving as little as a quarter of their income from the box office. But there were disadvantages, too: governments were reluctant and unreliable when it came to spending tax money for "elitist" forms of entertainment. In the United States, by contrast, these problems were minimized: government subsidy was negligible, and almost all funding of opera and other artistic enterprises came from a combination of private donations and box-office revenues. These contrasting conditions on either side of the Atlantic were reflected in different attitudes toward opera in general, and to the creative process in particular.

As postwar Western Europe grew prosperous, though still dominated by the shadow of the Cold War, it spawned a plethora of new operas. Some composers retreated into a very static form of music theater more suited to the concert hall than the opera house. Others (and they were the majority) determined to make maximum use of the resources made available by technology and by their own expanding sense of theater. Now, more

than at any time in the past, opera became a branch of theater. Operas were to be experienced, not just listened to. They frequently reflected the turbulent political and social conditions of the time. Not intended simply as entertainments, they had something to say, and a vigorous language, both musical and theatrical, in which to say it.

The operatic statement made by Luigi Nono in Venice in 1961 was called *Intolleranza 1960*. It featured an immigrant miner, an itinerant with no status in an intolerant and repressive society. The work attracted praise and abuse in almost equal proportions. The score, which included sections of electronic music on tape, was matched by a vast array of staged and projected images. As a piece of confrontational theater, it made an undoubted impact.

Four years later, in 1965, *Die Soldaten* (The Soldiers) was given its premiere in Cologne. The composer, Bernd Alois Zimmermann, had been born in the last months of World War I and had witnessed at firsthand all that militarism had brought upon his country. In an opera that somewhat recalled Berg's *Wozzeck* (and was based on a play even older than Büchner's), Zimmermann attacked the military profession in all its forms. The complex structure of the work—with scenes sometimes playing simultaneously in response to the multilayered score—was theatrically very effective, and *Die Soldaten* eventually won a place in the modern repertoire.

Hans Werner Henze was another German composer who felt compelled to write on antiwar and antimilitaristic themes. His 1976 opera *We Come to the River* was a collaboration with the English playwright Edward Bond. It was conceived on a massive scale (more than a hundred named roles, three orchestras, and a military band). There were times when three separate scenes were played simultaneously on the stage, each with its own musical setting and instrumentation. If that was difficult for the audience to comprehend, then so much more so was the strident left-wing ideology that ran through the work. Predictably, it aroused enthusiasm and derision in equally fanatical camps. *We Come to the River* was the first opera Henze had written in ten years, and the shock of it was all the greater because his previous operas had been so widely admired in Europe and America. From *König Hirsch* (King Stag) in 1956, through *Der Prinz von Homburg*, *Elegy for Young Lovers*, *Der junge Lord*, and *The Bassarids*, he had craft-

Zimmermann's Die Soldaten *at the National Theater, Munich, 1969. Directed by Vaclav Kaslik, designed by Josef Svoboda.*

ed a unique canon. All these works, in their different ways, contained biting political and social comment, but they were warmed by the lyricism that seemed to emanate from his adoptive home on Italy's Mediterranean coast. Together, they amounted to one of the most important operatic statements of the postwar years, comparable to the works of Tippett and Birtwistle, if not Britten. To that group of composers might be added the name of Aribert Reimann, a German composer whose love of the human voice enabled him to create a series of operas, most of them dark and brooding, that reflected the wary pessimism of his generation (he was born in Berlin in 1936). *Lear*, which he wrote for the baritone Dietrich Fischer-Dieskau in 1978, was the most widely performed.

If there was rage and despair in European

opera, there was also a questioning of life that was more grotesque, and even comic, in character. In 1978, the Hungarian composer György Ligeti wrote a surrealistic farce about life and death. *Le grand macabre* was set in "Breughelland." In a series of bizarre and brilliant inventions—ranging from a coloratura soprano chief-of-police to a magician who dissolves into thin air when he fails to achieve the end of the world—it depicted something uncomfortably related to reality. The work was widely performed in Europe, and its appeal was not just its theatrical impact. It was also, in some respects, an exploration of the phenomenon of opera itself. Beethoven, Baroque music, and even Monteverdi were all recalled, either explicitly or implicitly, within the score.

In a very different way, the Italian composer Luciano Berio also explored the world of opera and theater. In 1984 the Salzburg Festival gave the first performance of *Un re in ascolto* (A King Listens). It was, quite literally, about listening. Auditions for Shakespeare's *Tempest* in a theater representing the play's isle "full of noises" eventually enable the impresario to comprehend his own failures, both in the real theater and in the "other theater," where he searches for perfect love. The motif of listening was central to the whole work, so it was not an opera that relied on visual effects or technical coups: listening to the drama, and especially to the drama contained within Berio's score, was sufficient.

Karlheinz Stockhausen wrote no operas at all until 1977, when he was in his fiftieth year. At that stage he began work on *Licht: Die sieben Tage der Woche* (Light: The Seven Days of the Week). Eventually there will be seven separate operas, one for each day. But this is not a cycle like Wagner's *Ring*. At least one of the operas, *Samstag* (Saturday), is not even intended for performance in a theater. Stockhausen has given his operas no narrative story line, neither collectively nor even within themselves. What continuity there is is supplied by the presence of three principal characters. They appear in many different forms—sometimes as singers, sometimes as dancers, sometimes not in the flesh at all but represented by featured instruments. These characters have names (Michael, Eva, and Luzifer), but their only real essence is in musical formulas. It is opera in mythic form and with mythic proportions.

Where opera in Europe had once been dominated by Italian, French, and German composers, its creative sources were now spread much more evenly across the Continent. Britain was the most obvious newcomer, but there were others. Finland was one of them. Once a part of Sweden, then, in the nineteenth century, a grand duchy of the Russian empire, the Finnish people became in the twentieth century an independent nation. They transformed their ancient folklore into a flourishing contemporary culture, in which opera played a significant part. In the 1980s and 1990s, works by Joonas Kokkonen and Aulis Sallinen were being performed not only in Finland, but in many other European countries. Sallinen's *The King Goes Forth to France* (1984) was jointly commissioned by London's Royal Opera House and the BBC, together with the Savonlinna Festival in Finland, and has been staged as far afield as the Music Center Opera in Los Angeles.

A sampling such as the above gives a fair idea of the ferment in European opera in the last half of the century. To the average operagoer, brought up on the music of the nineteenth century, it was sometimes an uncomfortable experience. In his acceptance speech at the first Aspen Awards ceremony, in 1964, Benjamin Britten articulated the problem: "A musical experience needs three human beings at least. It requires a composer, a performer, and a listener, and unless these three take part together there is no musical experience. . . . It demands as much effort on the listener's part as the other two corners of the triangle, this holy triangle of composer, performer and listener."[27]

Whereas listeners in previous generations had often been seduced by melody and virtuoso singing, the chief attraction now was theater. Stage directors were finally on a par with conductors, so operagoers, even if they found the music difficult to comprehend, were generally guaranteed an interesting, often spectacular, evening in the theater. The staging of new operas involved risks—there was nothing new in that—but it was to the credit of European opera houses that so many risks were taken (and not always by state-subsidized theaters: an entirely private foundation like the Glyndebourne Festival was often in the vanguard). There was an excitement about it, and one of the features of late twentieth-century opera was that Britten's "listeners" began to return.

The excitement was not confined to Europe. In the United States there had long been places

where experimentation took its place alongside the regular repertoire—the Santa Fe Summer Festival was one, and St. Louis became another—but in 1976 a major contribution was made. It came in the form of *Einstein on the Beach* by Philip Glass, working in collaboration with the director-designer Robert Wilson. *Einstein* was defined by Wilson as a "theater of images." Two of opera's traditional building blocks, narrative and character-

Berio's Un re in ascolto *at the Chicago Lyric Opera, 1996. Directed by Graham Vick, designed by Chris Dyer. With Jean-Philippe Lafont as Prospero (wearing the crown).*

The dancer-choreographer Lucinda Childs is in the foreground (in white shirt). The partnership between Philip Glass, the composer, and Robert Wilson, the designer-director, in creating EINSTEIN *(1976) was closer, and more equal, than almost any such collaboration in the story of opera. Their starting points in the process of creation were generally drawings by Wilson, to which Glass responded with music—leading, in turn, to more drawings and redrawings, and to more music.*

ization, were entirely absent. A train, a courtroom, and a spaceship were the principal images of the work. Einstein himself was represented in a series of violin solos: the theory of relativity, it seemed, was being somehow played out, or tested, in each scene. The overall impression was of "performance art" rather than traditional opera, with Glass's music being one of several artistic impressions that contributed to the whole. *Einstein* was immensely successful and went on a world tour.

Philip Glass represented the Minimalist school of composers, so called because their music was based on maximum repetition of a minimum amount of material. After *Einstein*, his work became somewhat more conventional, but certainly not orthodox. *Satyagraha*, which was about Gandhi in South Africa and explored the theme of violence and nonviolence, and *Akhnaten*, which was about an ancient Egyptian pharaoh and explored the theme of religious orthodoxy and reaction, were apparently written as part of a trilogy with *Einstein* in which historical figures were used to dramatize great issues. In them Glass developed a melodic and harmonic style that might still be called Minimalist but was more operatic, particularly in the grand choral music of *Satyagraha*. This process continued in subsequent works, most especially in his 1992 commission from the Metropolitan Opera to mark the five hundredth anniversary of Columbus's arrival in America: *The Voyage* was an enthralling piece of theater, conceived and produced on a very large scale.

Minimalism absorbed many different influences—from ancient Eastern music to jazz and rock—but in the case of John Adams, the primary influence was classical, and generally Romantic. Working closely with the poet Alice Goodman and the stage director Peter Sellars, he created two operas that had great impact and considerable importance. Both *Nixon in China* (1987) and *The Death of Klinghoffer* (1991) were about very recent events, both of them dramatic and important in world politics. The idea that poetry and music (i.e., opera) could deal with such things was blasphemous to some, but hugely successful in practice. Moreover, the score of *Nixon in China* was easy to listen to. It was full of melody, wonderfully singable, and always dramatic. Alice Goodman's text, though written in verse, used contemporary language and provided Adams with rhythm and line that must have been a joy to set. Peter Sellars dared to give the work a realistic setting and cre-

ated stage pictures that instantly recalled the events of Nixon's historic 1972 journey to Beijing. It was one of the most revolutionary operas ever created, and one of the most interesting demonstrations of the potential that the art form continues to reveal to the adventurous.

American opera was on a roll. Large and small companies all over the continent were beginning to commission new works. Dominick Argento (*The Aspern Papers*), John Corigliano (*The Ghosts of Versailles*), and Conrad Susa (*The Dangerous Liaisons*) were just three of a great many composers who converted such commissions into critical and box-office success. In style and structure, their works tended to be more accessible than those of many of their European contemporaries. Melody was almost always a principal component. Consequently, these composers seemed to have fewer difficulties in acquiring listeners. Like the Europeans, they benefited from spectacular staging of their works and very often from nationwide television broadcasts as well.

Although it is true that "twentieth-century opera" has generally had a hard time winning over audiences, it is equally certain that, by the end of the century, it is alive and well, and prospering.

THE PHENOMENON OF OPERA IN THE TWENTIETH CENTURY

For its first three centuries, opera's principal raison d'être was the creation of new works. Audiences expected to see them; managements were required to provide them. Ironically, it was the very success of this policy—and the prodigality of the nineteenth century, in particular—that allowed the twentieth century to stand the axiom on its head. The principal business of opera houses now became the restaging of old works.

On the surface, there was nothing very new about this policy. Successful works had been transplanted from one theater to another, and from one country to another, since the earliest days of opera. They might be called "restagings," but they were rarely "new productions" in the modern meaning of that term. The billing generally used the phrase "in the original conception." It meant that the libretto's basic directions about location, period, and settings were probably being adhered to, and (if the original designs were still available) the style of costumes and backcloths was maintained as well. Sometimes there were production manuals available—detailed records of how the opera was

designed and staged at its first performance. They existed from as far back as Monteverdi's time, but they were rare. It was not until the nineteenth century that Parisian theaters began compiling *livrets de mise-en-scène*, which in turn inspired Verdi to print *dispozione seniche* for all his operas after *Les vêpres siciliennes.*

What was lacking in opera during these first three hundred years was the stage director. That role was variously played by the librettist or composer (if they were still alive and on hand), by the conductor (if he cared), by the theater's in-house librettist (often a hack writer who would be a doubtful guardian of an opera's integrity), or by the stage manager (who might or might not have a production manual to guide him). Things improved when French and German theaters began hiring permanent *régisseurs*, or *metteurs-en-scène*, in the early nineteenth century, but none of these people (with the notable exception of the original composers and librettists) had much concern with characterization and interpretation, let alone with an overall "concept" of the work. Conductors and singers were not much help. Many of

them played fast and loose with the original score, cutting freely and substituting arias by completely different composers if they thought it advantageous. Verdi was the first important composer to get contracts written in such a way that his scores could not be lacerated behind his back, yet even Richard Strauss was constantly complaining about conductors with blue pencils (Ernst von Schuch, the first conductor of *Der Rosenkavalier*, defended himself by saying he had cut "only eight minutes" from that score[28]).

THE RISE OF THE STAGE DIRECTOR   Whatever conductors might get up to, there would generally be very little attempt to rethink the dramatic content of a work, and when critics accused opera houses of being no more than "museums," they were often justified. What changed in the twentieth century was that opera finally became a genuine branch of theater: the drama got on equal terms with the music. It did not happen suddenly—in fact, it became fully apparent only after World War II—and it did not happen everywhere: "museums" continued to litter the opera world. Much of the innovation came from Germany, and its hallmark was the arrival on the opera scene of genuine stage directors. They often came to opera from the straight theater, sometimes from film and television as well, and it was no easier for them to share power with a conductor than it was for the conductor to share power with them. There were many well-documented battles. But it was the stage directors who took opera out of the museum and gave it new life as a vital and sometimes controversial branch of theater. The new production of an old opera by a distinguished director became almost as important an operatic event as the premiere of a new work.

At the very beginning of the twentieth century, at a time when the opera world was obsessed by two very different genres—Italian *verismo*, on the one hand, and Wagnerian *musik-drama*, on the other—the avant-garde world of theater began to impinge on opera. Adolphe Appia was already writing about stylized and symbolistic methods of staging Wagner's epic works, and in Russia Konstantin Stanislavsky was experimenting with naturalistic acting and staging at the Moscow Art Theater. Although Stanislavsky was a man of the

theater who did not turn his attention fully to opera until 1918 (and then in a country that was increasingly isolated), and Appia was a theorist whose ideas won no acceptance where it mattered—at Bayreuth—until after World War II, both Stanislavsky and Appia influenced the way theater, and therefore opera, would develop.

So did Gustav Mahler. As both music and artistic director of the Vienna State Opera from 1897 to 1907, he was responsible for a series of famous productions, many of them (especially the Mozart and Wagner productions) designed by Alfred Roller. Roller was an important Viennese artist whose theater designs relied on huge painted backcloths and curtains to establish tone and mood. The backcloths were stylized in an Appia-like way, but they were also traditional and generally Romantic; there was no "shock of the new" effect. Roller belonged to the *Jugendstil* school of artists, whose objectives included the ideal of uniting, or synthesizing, all the arts, in much the same way that Diaghilev and his colleagues were about to do in the Ballets Russes. To the extent that one could detect any universal trend in theater production in the first half of the twentieth century,

Corigliano's THE GHOSTS OF VERSAILLES *at the Metropolitan Opera, New York, 1991. Directed by Colin Graham, designed by John Conklin. Loosely based on the final part of Beaumarchais's Figaro trilogy,* GHOSTS *has been a sellout with audiences at the Met and in Chicago.*

it was generally bound up in this idea of synthesis, but there were so many advanced ideas taking over the world of art—Cubism, Expressionism, Futurism, Constructivism, and a battery of others—that the conservative world of opera tended to hold itself aloof.

There were centers of experiment (and outrage). Otto Klemperer's Krolloper in Berlin was one such, between 1927 and 1931. Many of its productions were based on the utopian ideas of the Bauhaus school. Much-loved operas were given radical new stagings: *Fidelio* in Cubist sets and *Die Fledermaus* in modern dress. *Der fliegende Holländer* was produced in totally Surrealist decor by Ewald Dülberg. It caused an uproar. In France, meanwhile, a successful group of Surrealist artists led by Giorgio de Chirico, Max Ernst, and Joan Miró, influenced musical theater for a time. But these were exceptions. Most opera companies sheltered behind tradition, until the appearance of a generation of powerful stage directors immediately after World War II.

Their forerunner was Max Reinhardt. An Austrian producer who specialized in Romantic spectacle, he was the first virtuoso theater director to stage operas. It was his theater productions of Oscar Wilde's *Salome* and Hofmannsthal's *Elektra* that had alerted Strauss to the potential of those plays as operas, so when the first production of *Der Rosenkavalier* appeared to be faltering at the Dresden Semperoper, in 1911, it was Strauss's idea to bring in Reinhardt. It was meant to be a Roller-Toller production: that is, the designs were by Alfred Roller and the staging by Professor Ernst Toller, the Semperoper's resident *régisseur*. Roller was more than capable of fulfilling his part of the task (in fact, the publisher made it a condition that other theaters could stage *Der Rosenkavalier* only if they used Roller's designs), but Professor Toller was hopelessly at sea with the sort of music drama Strauss and Hofmannsthal had in mind. Reinhardt came in—in secret, and on condition that he did not actually set foot on the stage. In three days, working behind locked doors, he created a comic, Romantic, and brilliant staging of the opera, the yardstick for all subsequent productions. His name did not appear on the credits; Toller's did.

The next year, Reinhardt staged the first production of *Ariadne* for Strauss, and the two of them were among the founders of the Salzburg Festival after World War I. Most of Reinhardt's subsequent music productions were of operettas, including some famous Offenbach and Johann Strauss productions in Berlin in the 1920s. But if he had done nothing more, in the Dresden *Rosenkavalier* he had established the importance of theatrical direction in opera.

There were other opera directors between the wars. They included Heinz Tietjen at Bayreuth. He combined with the designer Emil Preetorius in the years immediately after Cosima Wagner's death to replace the traditional Bayreuth style with a less naturalistic and more stylized, rather pompous, approach. Tietjen and Preetorius enjoyed budgets unheard of before or since (they were able to field a chorus of one hundred and one men for Act II of *Götterdämmerung*[29]). Their productions became huge theatrical spectacles—a far cry from the inner psychological dramas that Wieland Wagner would introduce after the war—but they deserved credit for breaking out of the straitjacket of naturalism imposed by Cosima in her late husband's name. The "lavishness of the Reinhardt school" (which was a criticism leveled at them by a junior member of the Wagner family) was also a recognition that they were injecting a truly theatrical element into the operas.[30]

German directors took the lead in revolutionizing opera in the 1950s. In what was then East Berlin, Walter Felsenstein began his long and brilliantly successful experiment in realistic theater. And at Bayreuth, Wieland Wagner demonstrated an approach that finally gave life to the theories of Adolphe Appia. Setting aside their very different philosophies, Felsenstein and Wieland Wagner had one crucial thing in common: they were great stage directors. Each of them stands at the head of a long list of disciples, followers, imitators, and emulators in the staging of opera.

Felsenstein was an Austrian. He took over the Komische Oper in East Berlin in 1947 and remained there until his death in 1975. He had no interest in singers who could not act, and that applied to members of the chorus, too. He believed that opera must be so realistic on stage that the audience would accept singing as a perfectly natural function of the actors: it had to appear to be as instinctive and as spontaneous as though the singers were speaking their parts. Each role was meticulously thought through and analyzed to fit within Felsenstein's psychological interpretation of the work as a whole, and that interpretation was based at least as much on the music as it was on the text. The fame of his productions (of operas

as varied as *Figaro*, *Otello*, and Janáček's *Cunning Little Vixen*) was so great that not even the building of the Berlin Wall in 1961 could keep the Komische Oper from being one of opera's most important houses. Felsenstein's leading pupils, Joachim Herz and Götz Friedrich, traveled more widely than their teacher and staged exciting and controversial productions in many of the capitalist centers of the world. The controversy often derived from the leftist ideology and the committed social criticism on which the productions were based. Whether or not the audiences liked these implications, they certainly recognized what they saw as theater of a very high order.

"Kinder, schafft neues!" (Children, try something new!) had been one of Richard Wagner's favorite sayings. His two grandsons took him literally. Beginning with their very first season, in 1951, Wieland and Wolfgang Wagner turned Bayreuth into what it has been ever since, one of opera's most exciting workshops. Wieland led the way—as stage director, scenic designer, and lighting designer—by creating new productions of his grandfather's operas that departed radically and forever from the Romantic Bayreuth style enforced for so many years by his grandmother. It was true that his father, Siegfried, had attempted to change the formula (but he had died in the same year as Cosima), and during the 1930s Tietjen and Preetorius had gone in for more stylized productions, but what Wieland did was so much more radical, and so much more successful, that both opera and the wider world of theater felt the impact for years afterward.

Wieland's preparation was thorough: he studied with the aging Alfred Roller; he read Appia's theoretical writings; he watched Tietjen and Preetorius working at Bayreuth in the thirties; in 1937, as a twenty-year-old, he designed Tietjen's production of *Parsifal*; and away from Bayreuth he designed several productions of works by his father, Siegfried. During the war, exempted from military service, he began to direct, first at Nuremberg, then in the old court theater at Altenburg, near Leipzig. There he was required to restage an old production of the *Ring*. The existing sets proved unusable, and since there was no money to replace them, he produced the entire cycle on a bare stage—a formative experience.[31]

After the war, the Bayreuth Festival was relaunched in 1951 with a new *Parsifal* and a new *Ring* cycle by Wieland Wagner, together with a traditional *Meistersinger* by Rudolf Hartmann. Wieland's productions showed at once that he had abandoned the old orthodoxies of Bayreuth. He presented the operas as timeless spiritual dramas. The settings were not truly abstract, but they were not what one would call realistic either. They often depicted real objects (trees, castles, mountaintops), but they also made use of symbols. The general visual effect was impressionistic, with lighting as the most important element—soft, diffuse, and immensely subtle, using the great height and size of the Bayreuth stage to awesome advantage. The most revolutionary change, perhaps, was the freeing of the singers (and the set designers, too) from a slavish dependence on the music. Wieland felt strongly, just as his grandmother had, that everything depended on the music, that Wagner had portrayed every part of the drama in the score, but (and here he departed from Cosima) it was not necessary for the singers to mark every single musical line with a complementary action. It was true that Wagner had written copious stage directions—but how, even with the most modern technology, could anyone adequately reproduce on stage the immolation of the world, as called for in *Götterdämmerung*? One of Bayreuth's principal historians, Geoffrey Skelton, was present at those first performances of the 1951 *Ring*:

> The end of this *Ring* was already apparent in its beginning, where in the second scene of *Rheingold* one became conscious of the circular platform, symbolic of the ring itself, on which the whole action of the cycle was to be played out.... In the course of the cycle the symbolic circular platform became increasingly obscured, as Wotan's own ambition became increasingly obscured by the unforeseen complications that beset his way to it. Only at the very end, after all had perished and the dreamlike projection of Valhalla had dissolved in flames, did the circle appear once more in its complete state, alone and empty and bathed in a dim blue-green light like a ring submerged in deep water. It was a symbol not only of the fatal ring but of the drama of greedy power come full circle.[32]

Wieland produced all his grandfather's major works at Bayreuth, some of them several times. "Every new production is a step on the way to an unknown goal," he wrote,[33] and his personal odyssey took him into fields well beyond Wagner and away from Bayreuth. He worked frequently at Stuttgart and occasionally elsewhere in Germany, staging controversial productions of works as distant from his grandfather's as Bizet's *Carmen* and Verdi's *Aida*. In his later years (he was only forty-nine when he died) he produced historic stagings of twentieth-century works—*Salome* and *Elektra*, *Lulu* and *Wozzeck*—in many of which, as at Bayreuth, the leading soprano roles were sung by one of the century's greatest singing actresses, Anja Silja.

Walter Felsenstein and Wieland Wagner were the first great masters of operatic stage direction—the first to have both the talent and the authority to impose their own vision on the works they staged. In Wieland's case, authority was evident—the hereditary right to stage his grandfather's works, and an opera house of his own in which to do it—but talent was much more important. At a time when the very idea of Wagnerian opera was anathema to many people inside Germany, and to millions outside, Wieland not only sustained it, but gave it an excitement and a relevance that it had never had before, and a potential audience vastly bigger, and much younger, than its prewar discipleship. What Wieland achieved in the ideal surroundings of Bayreuth, and Felsenstein in the less publicized environment of East Berlin, proved once and for all that opera was a dramatic medium with untold theatrical possibilities—a medium in which any stage director with an ear for music should want to work.

That precept was amply demonstrated at Bayreuth in the years following Wieland's death. His brother Wolfgang, who assumed sole control in 1966, continued to stage the operas himself from time to time, but he also developed the idea of Bayreuth as a workshop. Some of the greatest theater directors in Europe were brought in: the Frenchman Patrice Chéreau, the Englishman Peter Hall, and the Germans August Everding, Götz Friedrich, and Harry Kupfer were all handed the unique resources of Bayreuth and allowed to stage their own productions. Most of these were controversial. Audiences and critics were often sour, not to say rude, in their initial reception. But those same audiences and critics almost always returned to cheer in subsequent years. Bayreuth, like all good workshops, remained where the Wagner brothers had placed it in 1951—somewhat ahead of its public.

In the fifties and sixties, most of the world's great opera houses and festivals followed suit. Directors who had already made their reputations in theater and film were invited to stage operas. Giorgio Strehler, famous for his Brechtian interpretations at the Piccolo Teatro in Milan, became a leading producer at La Scala—and the founder of an experimental opera studio, the Piccolo Scala. In England, the young Peter Brook arrived at Covent Garden in 1948, having already established a reputation in Shakespeare. The Italian theater and film director Luchino Visconti was lured to opera houses by his admiration for Maria Callas: he staged spectacular productions for her at La Scala, as well as a series of grandly visual works at Spoleto and Covent Garden. Franco Zeffirelli, a pupil of Visconti and as multitalented as Wieland Wagner, created some of the most opulent productions, defying the vogue for antagonizing audiences in favor of a skill for seducing them. Günther Rennert also had a background in cinema: for more than three decades he was *intendant* and chief producer of companies (including Hamburg and Munich, and a spell as artistic adviser to the Glyndebourne Festival) where production standards were as important as musical standards. The Austrian Otto Schenk demonstrated how convincing nineteenth-century opera could be, even when it remained faithful to the original demands of the composer. The Frenchman Jean-Pierre Ponnelle shot through the operatic firmament like a brilliant meteor, staging productions of great visual charm and originality for opera houses, film, and television. In England, a stream of brilliant theater directors—Peter Hall, Jonathan Miller, Trevor Nunn, Elijah Moshinsky, Graham Vick—turned their talents to opera with very positive, and often stunning, results. And in the United States, the free spirit of Peter Sellars brought intellectual originality and tremendous theatrical flair to operas old and new.

These and many other directors made opera exciting. Not infrequently, they also made it controversial. There were arguments about authenticity, about faithfulness to the composers' and librettists' original intentions, and about a director's right to abandon those intentions in favor of radical reinterpretation. Audiences were deeply involved in these arguments. Regardless of their outcome, however, the stage director was now recognized as an essential link between *dramma* and *musica*. The only great surprise was that it had taken so long.

GREAT SINGERS OF THE CENTURY   Even in the first half of the century, singers had seen great changes in opera: their celebrity and their earning power had been substantially increased by the rise of the recording industry and radio. Caruso became an international icon, as famous as any star of the silent movies; Geraldine Farrar had legions of "Gerry-flappers" to cheer her every action at the Metropolitan Opera, on stage and off; Maria Jeritza was the toast of Vienna between

the wars, greeted everywhere she went by hysterical bands of supporters. And some of these singers were fine actors. The diminutive Mary Garden and the massive Fyodor Chaliapin (to take two extreme examples) were rightly renowned for their stage presence, for their ability to hypnotize audiences by their appearance on stage. There were other singers—great singers—who were notorious for their lack of acting skills. Luisa Tetrazzini, the Italian soprano, had a large and beautiful voice and wondrous technique, but her physical appearance severely limited her effectiveness as an actress. The Irish tenor John McCormack had an absolute block where acting was concerned—he simply could not do it. But whether they were good actors or bad, they were on their own, because in those early years of the century there were still no authoratative stage directors to unify the singers' performances. They might as well have been singing in different languages (and sometimes they were).

Nevertheless, the singers were the undoubted stars, and they sold the tickets. Adelina Patti, who earned as much as five thousand dollars a performance in America in the 1890s, put the singers' case succinctly in a telegram she sent to the organizers of the Norwich Music Festival in England. They had asked (greatly daring) why she required such a large fee to perform at a musical festival.

Act III of Wagner's DIE WALKÜRE *at the Bayreuth Festival, 1988. Directed by Harry Kupfer, designed by Hans Schavernoch and Reinhard Heinrich. Loge uses laser beams to encase the sleeping Brünnhilde in a cube of magic fire. Wotan (John Tomlinson) looks on.*

Nellie Melba (1861–1931).

Luisa Tetrazzini (1871–1940) as Doni-zetti's Lucia at the Metropolitan Opera, New York. In order to establish her right to sing at the Metropolitan, Tetrazzini had a celebrated confrontation with Oscar Hammerstein. He claimed she was exclusive to his own company, the Manhattan Opera. In court, Tetrazzini claimed the right to sing anywhere—includ-ing on the streets of San Francisco, if she so wished. On Christmas Eve, 1910, she did indeed sing on the streets of San Francisco—to an audience estimated at 250,000.

She wired back: "I am a Musical Festival."[34]

Few singers have ever attained such power as Patti's successor, Nellie Melba, or used it so ruthlessly. At Covent Garden she had a permanent dressing room with a notice on the door: "Melba. Silence! Silence!" It was kept locked and unused during her absences. She was no actress at all, yet she had a voice of surpassing beauty, trained by Marchesi in Paris and capable of covering an enor-mous range, from B-flat below the clef to high F.[35]

Melba's reign in London was undisputed from 1888 until 1907, but in the latter year, she unwisely went home to Australia for a much-needed holiday. In her absence, Covent Garden engaged the services of an Italian soprano who had already spent fifteen years performing in Italy and South America to no very great effect. Her name was Luisa Tetrazzini. In 1905, she had taken the city of San Francisco by storm in a seven-week season, but so long as Melba was in control at Covent Garden (and almost in control at the Met), it was not possible for Tetrazzini to perform in those houses. Melba's absence in 1907 was her opportunity, and she took maximum advantage. Tetrazzini made her famous debut as Violetta in *La traviata*, and she never looked back. She unfail-ingly enchanted her audiences with the quality of her voice and with her amazing achievements in the upper octave. She also had a great sense of fun: one of her favorite tricks during a performance was to bend down and adjust the hem of her dress while holding a high note.[36]

There were other great lyric sopranos in Tetrazzini's time. The one who came closest to challenging her supremacy was an Italian, Ameli-ta Galli-Curci, whose breathtaking vocal agility made her a genuine rival for a time. Meanwhile, at the Metropolitan Opera in New York, a spec-tacular "diva duel" was fought out between the American Geraldine Farrar and the Czech Emmy Destinn. These were immensely popular singers, but they were not quite the living legends that Melba and Tetrazzini were. No more were their immediate successors—Maria Jeritza from Czechoslovakia, who was a woman of great beauty, a significant actress, and a singer much favored by both Puccini and Richard Strauss; Lotte Lehmann (no relation to Lilli), a German soprano closely identified with the role of the Marschallin in *Der Rosenkavalier;* and two singers— the Italian Claudia Muzio and the American Rosa Ponselle—whose beautiful voices and superior techniques qualified them, in the opinion of many good judges, to be numbered among the greatest female singers of the century.

Led by Rossini, nineteenth-century composers had built up the repertoire for lyric tenors from almost nothing to a level that all other singers might envy. Jean de Reszke had retired very early in the new century, but by then, Enrico Caruso was already established. The legend Caruso cre-ated, both on record and in the opera house, has remained the yardstick by which all operatic tenors of the French and Italian schools are judged.

Caruso was the first singer to leave a sub-stantial legacy of recordings. Between 1902 and 1920, just a few months before his death at the age of forty-eight, he made 286 separate recordings. They illustrate the art of a great musician. Pláci-do Domingo has written of them: ". . . through-out my career, whenever I have had a problem with a piece of music I have turned to Caruso's record-ings, and they usually have shown me how to solve the problem."[37] Unlike Domingo, Caruso was not a great actor, though he worked hard at it, and he took insufficient care of his voice (he smoked strong Egyptian cigarettes). Nor had it always been easy for him. He had spent several years trying to win the respect of critics before he discovered his ability to appeal directly to the galleries. One night, when he was singing Nemorino in Donizetti's *L'elisir d'amore* during his first season at La Scala

(1900–1) the audience literally stopped the performance to cheer him. Even Toscanini, against all his principles, was forced to give him an encore.[38]

His voice was always a thing of beauty—rich and almost baritonal in the lower registers, full and thrilling at the top, though he had a "safety first" policy of avoiding the very highest notes whenever possible. He was fortunate to be singing at a time when new operas were still being created around him (by Cilea, Giordano, Puccini), but also when the nineteenth-century repertoire was available and always in demand to be repeated. The gramophone undoubtedly helped to make him famous—like Luciano Pavarotti in modern times, he recorded popular ballads and his native Neapolitan songs, as well as opera—but he was also a character to whom celebrity came easily. His sense of humor was a considerable asset: this was a man who could emerge from his hotel in his bedclothes in the middle of the San Francisco earthquake of 1906 and be instantly recognized by everyone (he informed the gentlemen of the press that he much preferred Vesuvius, which was more predictable than an earthquake, and that he would not be returning to San Francisco—a promise that he kept). But he was first and foremost a musician—a man for whom Toscanini and Puccini had huge respect as well as affection. Caruso chronicled their friendship in a series of drawings and caricatures

with which he wiled away the long hours of rehearsal.

From 1903, almost until his death in 1921, Caruso performed principally with the Metropolitan Opera in America. He was still at the height of his powers when he died of bronchial pneumonia. Despite his smoking and despite the abandon with which he had used the voice in his early years, no one ever heard him in decline.

The bass Fyodor Chaliapin was exactly the same age as Caruso (they were born in the same month), but they came from different traditions, worlds apart. Chaliapin had very little formal education: he came from a humble peasant family in Kazan and began singing in church choirs. The voice was astonishing, and it soon brought him to prominence. He was only seventeen when he made his opera debut, and twenty when he sang Gounod's Méphistophélès for the first time. The huge voice, covering both bass and baritone ranges, would have been sufficient on its own to assure him a great international career, but Chaliapin was also a powerful actor and a master of makeup and costume: he had an uncanny ability to assume both the physical and emotional characteristics of the characters he portrayed. Even in old photographs, it is clear that he simply *was* Boris, just as he was Ivan the Terrible, or Dosifey in Musorgsky's *Khovanshchina*. He first appeared outside Russia at La Scala in 1901 and was quickly recognized as the greatest bass in the world. He took with him—to Milan, Paris, Monte Carlo, London, and New York—the operas of Glinka and Musorgsky, Rimsky-Korsakov and Borodin, often introducing them to Western audiences. He continued to sing at the Bolshoi until 1920, but it was in the West that he made his greatest impression. He sang a very large repertoire, from Mozart to Massenet (even Colline in *La bohème*), but it was for the Russian roles that he was best remembered. No voice and no presence, not even Caruso's, was as distinctive as Chaliapin's, and it was still there for him when he sang his last performance, as Boris, in Monte Carlo in 1937.

There was, of course, one category of opera into which neither Caruso nor Chaliapin ventured, and that was Wagnerian music drama. It was popularly believed to be bad for the voice—downright dangerous. That was a myth, but a myth that unfortunately had some basis in fact. It was certainly not Wagner's intention. He always maintained he had written his operas to be sung in something approximating to the Italian *legato* style—with smooth delivery, binding the notes together so that there was no perceptible pause between them. Wagner said that one of the finest performances he ever heard was a *Tannhäuser* in Rome in which the Italian baritone Mattia Battistini sang Wolfram in pure *legato* style.[39] Like many of the sins of Wagnerism, the discouragement of *legato* in favor of the much more declamatory *Sprechgesang* (speech song) came about after the composer's death. The responsible party was Julius Kniese, the head of the music staff at Bayreuth—a strong personality who had a powerful influence on Cosima Wagner. The Bayreuth Bark, as it became known, was certainly not a healthy way for singers to make a living. It was sometimes, but not always, dramatic; when taken to extremes, it could be both unmusical and ugly.

Most of the best Wagner singers spent more time in the French and Italian repertoires than they did in the German, however, and more time singing Wagner in other opera houses than they did at Bayreuth. Lilli Lehmann was certainly the most famous Brünnhilde in the years immediately after Wagner's death, but she was equally famous as Norma and Lucia. She was the first soprano to sing the big Wagner roles at the same time as the coloratura roles of the *bel canto* school. Her immediate successors were not quite so bold, though Lillian Nordica (born Lillian Norton in Farmington, Maine) once sang Brünnhilde and the *Traviata* Violetta on successive nights. Nordica's career coincided with that of Olive Fremstad, a Swede who became an American, and whose life was the basis for Willa Cather's novel *The Song of the Lark*. Fremstad came slowly to the big Wagnerian roles. She was a pupil of Lilli Lehmann's, and it was Lehmann who suggested, and then supervised, her conversion from mezzo-soprano to soprano—a conversion that was completed in 1908 when she electrified the Metropolitan Opera House with a performance of Isolde conducted by Gustav Mahler.

In the interwar years, there emerged two dramatic sopranos whose superiority in the Wagner repertoire was such that they were thought of, first and foremost, as "Wagnerian sopranos." Frida Leider was a Berliner; she was the great Brünnhilde and Isolde of the interwar years, until, in the mid-1930s, her powers began to fade and she was overtaken by a soprano who became one of the best-loved singers in the whole story of opera, Kirsten Flagstad. For twenty years, from 1913 to 1933, Flagstad, a Norwegian, appeared only in Scandinavia, and she was on the point of retiring when she was invited to sing a small part at Bayreuth. Almost immediately, she blossomed into the radiant, powerful singer whose recordings are still the benchmark for her successors. Right up to her retirement in 1954, she was the Isolde, the Kundry, the Sieglinde, and the Brünnhilde of choice in all the major opera houses of the world.

One of the most frustrating experiences of Richard Wagner's life was the search for a true *heldentenor* (heroic tenor) to sing the roles of Tristan and Siegfried. Ludwig Schnorr von Carolsfeld was the answer to all his dreams when he came to Munich to be the first Tristan in 1865—only to die of rheumatic fever a few weeks later. Georg Unger, the first Siegfried, proved to be a mistake, and Wagner himself did not live to hear anyone do justice to that great role. As it turned out, he would probably have had to live until 1924 to make the discovery (he would have been 111). It was not that there were no adequate—even very good—Siegfrieds in between. The great Polish tenor Jean de Reszke was one; he learned German late in his career and sang Tristan and Siegfried with great success, though the effort probably contributed to what many people felt was a premature retirement in 1902. Leo Slezak, an Austrian, was another. He was six feet two, with a very striking physique: he looked everything a Siegfried ought to look, but he had a lyric voice rather than a true *heldentenor* and he wisely confined himself mainly to singing the earlier Wagner parts—Tannhäuser, Lohengrin, and Walter—with occasional forays into Siegmund and the young Siegfried.

But if Wagner had still been alive in 1924, as his widow Cosima was, he would have heard the only *heldentenor* of the twentieth century thought to have come close to Schnorr von Carolsfeld. His name was Lauritz Melchior and he came from Denmark. Michael Scott, a historian of singing, puts it succinctly: "When nature created Lauritz Melchior she broke the mold and having done so threw it away: never before had there been such a powerful tenor voice, at the same time so dark and so brilliant, and to this day he has had no succes-

sor."[40] Melchior was a huge man—no great actor, but that somehow seemed excusable when he was able to use his voice to such dramatic effect. As early as 1920, at a time when he was still unsure whether he was a baritone or a tenor, he sang in a radio concert with Nellie Melba. In the 1930s and 1940s, he performed regularly with Kirsten Flagstad—a partnership that has had no equal in Wagnerian folklore.

In many of those Flagstad/Melchior performances of the *Ring* operas, the Wotan was Friedrich Schorr. He was Hungarian by birth, though he later became an American, and it was his bass-baritone voice that set the standard for Wotan and Hans Sachs and the Dutchman in the interwar years. It was a big voice, as it had to be if it was not be drowned by the orchestra in Wotan's long narrations, but it was also noble and opulent, and very beautiful to listen to. Luckily, at about

Kirsten Flagstad (1895–1962) and Lauritz Melchior (1890–1973) in Tristan und Isolde *at the Metropolitan Opera, New York, November 1937. This photograph was taken at a stage rehearsal for the opening-night performance of the Met's 1937–38 season.*

the moment Schorr retired in 1943, another such voice was there to take its place. It belonged to Hans Hotter—a German singer of great intelligence, a fine actor, and a first-rate musician.

Hotter was there after World War II, as was Flagstad for a short time, to reestablish and maintain the traditions that had been built at Bayreuth and elsewhere. The Swedish soprano Birgit Nilsson took over from Flagstad in the 1950s as the outstanding Wagnerian soprano—a steely, penetrating voice of great power and stamina, capable of creating genuine excitement at climactic moments. But there was no replacement for Melchior, and

the search for the elusive *heldentenor* went on. Nevertheless, a wonderful generation of Wagner singers emerged, believable, acting singers who were coached by some of the best stage directors of the time. All opera benefited from the process, but none so markedly, perhaps, as Wagnerian opera.

The performance of Wagner's stage works is a phenomenon of the twentieth century. Despite two world wars, his operas retained, except for fairly brief periods, their commanding position in the international repertoire. For stage directors, for singers, and generally for audiences, too, they were seen as peaks of achievement, mountains that

had to be climbed, and many opera companies aspired to climb them. International opera houses like the Met or Covent Garden or the Vienna State Opera could command expensive talent, but some of the finest results were achieved by smaller companies. At the English National Opera in London, in the early 1970s, a production of the *Ring* cycle was mounted, in English, that was able to assemble all the necessary talents from its own resources—a staging that was both functional and memorable; an original translation, by Andrew Porter, that was remarkable on the one hand for its faithfulness to Wagner's speech patterns, on the other for its singability; a cast of singers that was genuinely able to meet the challenges of the roles, both musically and dramatically; and ample rehearsal time, spread over many months, for the orchestra and singers to learn their parts. Most of all, the English National Opera had, in Reginald Goodall, a conductor and teacher of vision, passion, and absolute devotion to Wagner's music dramas. He forged a series of performances that remain landmarks for everyone who saw them.

The most famous singer of the century was Maria Callas. In her short career (effectively, it went from 1947 to 1965), she epitomized much of the best, and a little of the worst, of opera in the twentieth century. She started out singing Isolde, Brünnhilde, Aida, Turandot, and other big dramatic roles; she turned herself into a great coloratura soprano of the *bel canto* operas; she lost a great deal of weight and became a magnificent, haunting actress, whose impersonations of Tosca, Lucia, Norma, and many others were not easily forgotten; and, finally, she became an international celebrity.

The man who saw the potential in Callas, and became her mentor, was Tullio Serafin. He was seventy years old by the time he began to work with her—a conductor who had made his opera debut in 1900 and was a major influence in most of the great opera houses of the world. He championed two things in particular: new opera (he conducted four world premieres at the Met) and the *bel canto* Italian repertoire. In 1948, he heard Callas, still only twenty-five, sing the *Walküre* Brünnhilde in Venice. Bellini's *I puritani* was due to be performed a few days later, and the scheduled soprano had canceled. Serafin suggested that Callas might sing it. She did, with surprising effect.

From then on, he coached her himself. To her naturally powerful and dramatic voice she added a coloratura of amazing accuracy and agility, and (when she wanted it) exquisite beauty.

Her Norma, her Violetta, her Tosca were just three of her impersonations that were unlikely to be forgotten by anyone who saw them. But the existing repertoire was too narrow for her. With the help of Serafin and another "old school" Italian conductor, Victor de Sabata, rarely performed works were revived for her—Spontini's *La vestale*, Donizetti's *Anna Bolena*, Bellini's *Il pirata*, Rossini's *Armida* and *Il turco in Italia*, and (in a famous 1953 production at the Florence Maggio Musicale) Cherubini's *Medée*.

Callas became an idol of the public to an extent that not even Caruso had been, and she did it in the high days of Hollywood. She had always been a decent actress, but now, with the help of stage directors like Visconti and Zeffirelli, she became a great one. In 1955, in Berlin under Herbert von Karajan, she created a Lucia as memorable as any creation of the dramatic stage. She did it for a score of other roles, too—for Violetta, for Tosca, for Norma. There is a film recording of Act II of *Tosca* at Covent Garden, with Tito Gobbi as Scarpia, that is truly mesmerizing in its power and dramatic intensity. It could be argued, and it frequently was, that her singing was uneven, but that was more than compensated for by the electricity of her presence. What penalty she paid, and what pains she endured, for her spectacular weight loss, no one can tell. Certainly, for all her fame, for all her notorious behavior as a prima donna, and her tempestuous career as a butterfly of high society, there was always a fragile side to Callas. It was part of her glamour, and part of the reason for her tragically early loss to the world of opera. She died in 1977, aged fifty-three.

Did she have rivals? That would depend on whom you asked. The Italian soprano Renata Tebaldi had an army of fans in Italy and America, and a talent that was certainly comparable—a voice of greater natural beauty, perhaps, but without the same stagecraft. She and Callas both made a great many recordings: Tebaldi's, mostly made in the studio, reveal a radiant soprano; those of Callas, many of them made on the stage during performances, are *dramma per musica* incarnate—not always lovely, but emotionally powerful and capable of drawing listeners irresistibly into the drama.

Callas changed opera. Her rediscovery of the early nineteenth-century repertoire opened up new roles for a generation of female singers. Joan Sutherland, Renata Scotto, Montserrat Caballé, Beverly Sills, and the mezzo-soprano Marilyn Horne all followed her into that enchanted world. But she also showed audiences that beautiful singing was not always sufficient unto itself on the opera stage. A generation of singers with phenomenal acting abilities emerged—Teresa Stratas, Anja Silja, Maria Ewing, Josephine Barstow, Hildegard Behrens (the list could be greatly extended)—and they created some of the most memorable stage impersonations of heroines, villains, and lovers.

The century that had begun with the phenomenon of Caruso drew to its close with an equal phenomenon—that of Luciano Pavarotti and Plácido Domingo—two tenors of very different accomplishments but parallel fame. The sweet, lyric voice of Pavarotti appealed even to the millions of people who would never enter an opera house or a concert hall. Domingo brought to the stage and the recording studio a huge repertoire of more than eighty roles, and the dedication of a singing actor who knew no peer. Separately and together, on the stage, on television, and on record, Pavarotti and Domingo brought a global excitement to opera that it had never previously known.

Caruso, Pavarotti, and Domingo were the superstars, but any operagoer of the second half of the twentieth century could name a host of male stars to put alongside them: Giuseppe di Stefano and Franco Corelli, Mario del Monaco and Jon Vickers (contrasting and brilliant Otellos), Nicolai Gedda and José Carreras, Carlo Bergonzi and Alfredo Kraus, René Kollo and Siegfried Jerusalem—these were all outstanding tenors by any standard. And they were joined by a generation of basses and baritones that was exceptional in its depth: the mighty voice of Boris Christoff; Gobbi's Italian successor, Renato Bruson; Bayreuth Wotans from George London to James Morris; the unique sound of Russian male singers, returning to the international circuit as the Cold War ended; and the wonderful versatility of singer-actors with the range of Samuel Ramey and John Tomlinson.

CONDUCTORS OF OPERA   All these singers owed much to stage directors, but they generally owed a great deal more to conductors. The conductor (and even more certainly, a resident music director) was first among equals in the opera house.

Ever since Monteverdi's day, opera performances had been directed either by the leader of the orchestra (normally from the harpsichord or pianoforte) or by a "conductor" who beat time on the floor with a long staff (in Lully's case, a lethal weapon). By the early nineteenth century, the staff had been replaced by a baton, and conductors stood on a podium in front of the orchestra. Beethoven used a baton, as did Weber; Berlioz was one of the first to conduct from a full score. But it was Wagner who made conducting into a virtuoso art. He imposed on orchestras not only the strictest discipline but also his personal interpretation of whatever work was played. Conductors who were not famous composers—men like Hans von Bülow, Hermann Levi, Hans Richter, and Anton Seidl—followed in Wagner's footsteps. Their presence sold tickets (Seidl was a cult figure in New York in the 1890s).

Arturo Toscanini, however, was different. In the first half of the century, he was a superstar in his own right—not so much because of his public persona (though that was formidable) but because he was a fanatical musician, a martinet, a man totally dedicated to giving performances that were technically proficient and emotionally powerful. He had started out as a cellist, and had even returned to the cello desk, at his own request, for the opening night of *Otello* in 1887. (That was after his conducting debut in Rio de Janeiro the previous year, when he had been co-opted out of the orchestra to lead a performance of *Aida* following public demonstrations against the scheduled conductor. He conducted the score from memory.) He led the world premieres of *I pagliacci* and *La bohème*, as well as the Italian premiere of *Götterdämmerung*, and in 1898 he became the principal conductor of La Scala. His long association with La Scala, and a similarly long association with the Metropolitan, were the main platforms for his enormous influence on the world of opera. It lasted until 1929, when he finally resigned from La Scala in protest against fascism. After that, he conducted fully staged performances only at Bayreuth and Salzburg, and then infrequently, and

it was left to his years with the NBC Orchestra in America for him to make his most enduring opera recordings.

The twentieth century has had a select corps of composers who were also great conductors— Gustav Mahler, Felix Weingartner, Richard Strauss, Leonard Bernstein—but Herbert von Karajan was the only conductor to approach Toscanini's fame. At the Vienna State Opera between 1956 and 1964, he regularly conducted an extraordinary ensemble that included Christa Ludwig, Walter Berry, Eberhard Waechter, and Birgit Nilsson. Later, at the Salzburg Festival, where he was both music and artistic director, he created a series of festival performances that were

rightly renowned for their musical values.

Most of all, opera owed a debt to a few great conductors who devoted significant parts of their careers to directing individual companies— Victor de Sabata at La Scala; Hans Knapperts- busch at Munich; Otto Klemperer at Berlin; Karl Böhm, Josef Krips, and Clemens Krauss at Vien- na; Rafael Kubelik and Georg Solti at Covent Garden; Claudio Abbado and Riccardo Muti at La Scala; and James Levine at the Metropolitan Opera. These men were more than just conduc- tors; they were "directors of music" who took responsibility not just for performances they con- ducted, but for the repertoire and standards of whole seasons (in some cases, whole decades). This

Joan Sutherland in Donizetti's LA FILLE DU RÉGIMENT *at the Metropolitan Opera, New York, 1983.*

was how the finest ensembles were assembled, the best orchestras and choruses were developed, and the greatest opera-house reputations were made.

RECORDING AND BROADCASTING Such conductors almost always brought with them an asset of enormous value to an opera company—a recording contract.

When Thomas Edison invented his phonograph in 1877, and Emile Berliner refined it into the gramophone in 1888 with its accompanying flat disc records, they created the potential for the greatest popularization of opera there had ever been. The early recordings were crude in many ways—the reproduction was unfaithful and scratchy, with the singers' voices having to compete with unwanted "surface noise." The first complete opera recording, *Il trovatore*, was made over a three-year period, in 1903–6, with sixteen different singers cropping up at various stages in the five principal parts. But these early recordings brought the voices of Caruso, Chaliapin, and many others into homes all over the world. And it was not just the singers who became famous; it was also the arias and songs they sang. The gramophone replaced the barrel organ as the prime disseminator of opera's greatest hits.

In the 1920s, radio began to make them even more accessible. Very soon, complete opera performances could be heard live throughout Europe and North America. *Hänsel und Gretel* was broadcast from Covent Garden in 1923; by 1925, there were broadcasts every week in New York.

In 1950, the recording business (and therefore opera) was transformed once more, when the first long-playing records were marketed. Suddenly, it was possible to hear twenty-five minutes on a single side without interruption; a whole opera could be contained on six or eight sides—or, twenty years later, on even fewer tape cassettes. Subsequently (but certainly not finally), the compact disc became available in 1983; the CD made it possible to put more than seventy minutes on a single disc, while digital technology was able to refurbish the recordings of a bygone era. Caruso came back into fashion.

The recording industry, of course, was concerned with the musical side of opera much more than it was with the dramatic side. Opera houses were sometimes guilty of casting performances with an eye to a recording contract rather than to

dramatic integrity, but the other side of the coin was that the recording industry enabled listeners to hear performances that were never seen on stage: Callas's Carmen, Freni's Tosca, or Pavarotti's Otello. Moreover, it was undeniably true that recording companies expended huge sums of money on historic recordings that had little chance of recouping their costs in the near term.

Television played an important role as well. As early as 1936, the BBC transmitted scenes from *Pickwick*, an opera by Albert Coates; *I pagliacci* was televised from Radio City Music Hall in New York in 1941. But it was after World War II that television came into its own. Opening night at the Metropolitan was transmitted live in 1948 (it was *Otello*), and the following year NBC established its Television Opera Theater, which continued for fifteen years and was responsible for a great many studio performances of operas, as well as a significant number of commissions, including Menotti's *Amahl and the Night Visitors*. The BBC was equally busy in Britain, as were RAI in Italy, ORF in Austria, and ZDF in Germany. For a time, there was an unfortunate emphasis, most notably in Germany, on recording the sound and the visual image separately, so that the singers (or even actors substituting for them) would mime their parts to prerecorded music. But by the 1970s, a generation of fine television directors, musically trained, had taken control and was regularly bringing opera into millions of homes—from the stages of great opera houses and, occasionally, in studio performances staged for the cameras (Benjamin Britten's *Owen Wingrave* was one of the most significant operas to be written especially for television). Television's stubborn problems with sound quality were increasingly offset by simultaneous stereo transmissions on FM radio, while many great performances (and some less than great) became permanently available on videotapes and discs. It was also now possible for millions of people all over the world to be hooked up by satellite to see (for instance) *Tosca* performed live by an international cast performing in its original Roman settings and in its actual dramatic time-scheme—or "The Three Tenors" ripping joyously into a series of opera's greatest hits as part of the World Cup celebrations for the world's most popular sport, soccer.

Television made opera accessible in another important way. It pioneered the use of subtitles on the screen, so that viewers could follow the

text in their own language. Ever since the advent of electricity in the 1880s, and the consequent lowering of lights in the auditorium, operagoers had been denied the use of librettos during the actual performance. Television's example, however imperfect, encouraged opera houses first to experiment with supertitles above the stage, and eventually to install them.

It was the combination of all these forces—composers, librettists, singers, conductors, stage directors, designers, opera houses, record companies, and the electronic media—that made opera in the twentieth century such an exciting experience and such a dynamic phenomenon. To them should be added one other category: scholars. Twentieth-century musicologists, researchers, and archivists added enormously to the number of works available to performers. The long-lost works of centuries past were resurrected. They often had to be reassembled from scattered sources, their provenance authenticated, and their parts arranged into performable editions. The operas of Monteverdi, Cavalli, Sacrati, Rossi, and Cesti once again became available to opera houses. So did more recent works—by Charpentier, Rossini, Spontini, and many others. Parallel with this movement, but not dependent on it, was a vogue for performances on period instruments, so that it was often possible to hear works from the first two centuries of opera in at least an approximation of what their composers intended.

Other centuries did more to create new operas, but no century contributed so much to the expansion and enlargement of the art form as did the twentieth. At the end of four hundred years of continuous development and experimentation, the phrase *il dramma per musica*—drama expressed through music—had been given new meaning and presence, and an awesome amount of potential.

"The Three Tenors" in rehearsal: Plácido Domingo, Jose Carreras, Luciano Pavarotti. Tokyo, 1996.

Notes to the Text

Bibliographical citations are given here when the sources of quotations are not clear from the context.

"Il dramma per musica"

1. Quoted in J. Rigbie Turner, *Four Centuries of Opera: Manuscripts and Printed Editions in the Pierpont Morgan Library* (New York, 1983), p. 1.

2. Girolamo Mei, *De modis musicis antiquorum* (Rome, 1568–73). In Book IV, basing his argument on Aristotle's *Poetics*, Mei stated his conclusion that the ancient Greek tragedies had been entirely sung.

3. In *Divining the Powers of Music* (New York, 1986), p. 49, Ruth Katz suggests that a better translation of *camerata* in this context might be "invisible college."

4. Pietro de' Bardi, letter to Giovanni Battista Doni (1634); original printed in Oliver Strunk, ed., *Source Readings in Music History* (New York, 1950).

5. Ibid. Pietro de' Bardi writes that Galilei was "the first to let us hear singing in *stile rappresentativo.*"

6. Jacopo Peri, Preface to *Euridice* (1601), ed. Howard Mayer Brown (Madison, Wis., 1981).

7. Ottavio Rinuccini, quoted in Turner, *Four Centuries of Opera,* p. 1.

8. Quoted in Denis Arnold, *Monteverdi* (London, 1963), p. 21.

9. Rodolfo Celletti, "The Poetics of the Marvelous," *Opera News* 59 (July 1994), p. 12.

10. Randolph Mickelson, interviewed by Brian Kellow, "The Singing Detective," *Opera News* 59 (July 1994), p. 18. Mickelson, the Venice-based musicologist and voice teacher, is quoted as saying: "Then in 1637 they open the Teatro San Cassiano in Venice, which I have read—I've never verified it—held 6,000, twice the size of the Met. Those singers must have come out of San Marco, because you have to have an *enormous* voice in a place that holds 6,000."

11. Peri, Preface to *Euridice.* Peri describes Vittoria Archilei as the "Euterpe of our age." Born in 1550, she sang in the Florentine *intermedi* of 1589 and was in her fiftieth year when she created Peri's Euridice.

12. Giovanni Faustini, Preface to *Egisto* (1643). Faustini apologizes for introducing the mad scene, explaining that he has done so in order to placate a "*personaggio grande*"; quoted in Ellen Rosand, *Opera in Seventeenth-Century Venice: The Creation of a Genre* (Berkeley, 1991), Appendix I.31a, p. 422.

13. See Rosand, *Opera in Seventeenth-Century Venice,* p. 224.

14. Alexandre-Toussaint de Limojon, Sier de Saint-Disdier, *La ville et la république de Venise* (Paris, 1680); quoted in Rosand, *Opera in Seventeenth-Century Venice* p. 235.

15. Quoted in Rosand, *Opera in Seventeenth-Century Venice,* p. 239.

16. *The Memoirs of John Evelyn,* ed. W. Bray (London, 1819), vol. 1, p. 191.

17. Niccola Sabbatini, *Pratica di fabricar scene, e machine ne'teatri* (Pesaro, 1638).

The Singers Take the Stage

1. See Michael Scott, *The Record of Singing* (Boston, 1993), vol. 1, p. 11. Scott quotes the diplomat L. de Hegermann-Lindencrone, who heard Moreschi sing in 1883: "The famous Morescha [*sic*] . . . has a tear in each note and a sigh in each breath."

2. Charles Burney, *Musical Tours in Europe* (1773), ed. Percy Scholes (Oxford, 1959), vol. 1, p. 78.

3. See Michael Scott, *The Record of Singing,* vol. 1, p. 10.

4. Rodolfo Celletti, "The Poetics of the Marvelous," *Opera News* 59 (July 1994), p. 14.

5. Samuel Sharp, quoted in William Weaver, *The Golden Century of Italian Opera: From Rossini to Puccini* (London and New York, 1988), p. 28.

6. Quoted in J. L. Le Cerf de la Viéville, *Comparaison de la musique italienne et de la musique françoise* (Brussels, 1704–6), rpt. ed. (1972), p. 113.

7. Quoted in Harold Rosenthal and John Warrack, *The Concise Oxford Dictionary of Opera* (Oxford, 1985, rpt. 1990), p. 408.

8. John Playford, 1698; quoted in Margaret Drabble, ed., *The Oxford Companion to English Literature* (Oxford, 1985), p. 798.

9. *The Spectator,* March 1711; quoted in Christopher Hogwood, *Handel* (London, 1984), p. 64.

10. The Reverend John Mainwaring, *Memoirs of the Life of the Late George Frederic Handel* (1760); quoted in Nicholas Anderson, *Baroque Music: From Monteverdi to Handel* (London, 1994), p. 143. Mainwaring's principal source was Handel's assistant, John Christopher Smith.

11. See John Rosselli, *Singers of Italian Opera: The History of a Profession* (Cambridge, 1992, pbk. 1995), chapter 3: "Women."

12. See Charles Neilson Gattey, *Queens of Song* (London, 1979), p. 2.

13. Théophile Gautier, *Mademoiselle de Maupin* (Paris, 1835). It was in the preface to this novel that Gautier expounded his doctrine of *l'art pour l'art* (art for art's sake).

14. Quoted in H. Sutherland Edwards, *The Prima Donna* (1888; rpt. New York, 1978), vol. 1, p. 25.

15. Quoted in Gattey, *Queens of Song,* p. 5.

16. *Daily Post* (London), September 7, 1741; quoted in Gattey, *Queens of Song,* p. 9.

17. Hasse had first met Mozart (then aged thirteen) two years previously in Vienna. He wrote to a friend that Mozart was "good-looking, vivacious, gracious and very well-mannered; when you make his acquaintance it is difficult not to like him. Certainly he will become a prodigy if as he grows older he continues to make the necessary progress. . . ."; letter reproduced in Otto Erick Deutsch, ed., *Mozart: Die Dokumente seines Lebens* (Kassel, 1961).

FROM GLUCK TO MOZART

1. Raniero de' Calzabigi, *Dissertazione . . . sulle Poesie drammatiche del signor abate Pietro Metastasio* (1755).

2. See *The Collected Correspondence and Papers of Christoph Willibald Gluck*, ed. Hedwig and E. H. Mueller (New York, 1962).

3. Printed in full in Alfred Einstein, *Gluck* (rev. ed., London, 1964).

4. See *The Writings of Benjamin Franklin*, ed. Albert Henry Smyth (New York, 1905–7).

5. Quoted in Gustav Kobbé, *Complete Opera Book* (1922), 10th ed., revised and edited by the Earl of Harewood (London, 1987), p. 72.

6. Joseph Haydn, letter to Franz Roth, December 1787; quoted in H. C. Robbins Landon, *Haydn: A Documentary Study* (New York, 1981), p. 89.

7. G. A. von Griesinger, *Biographische Notizen über Joseph Haydn* (1810), ed. F. Grasberger (Vienna, 1954); quoted by Robbins Landon, *Haydn,* p. 75.

8. Haydn, letter to Roth; quoted in Robbins Landon, *Haydn,* p. 89.

9. Haydn's original contract as *Vice-Kapellmeister* to Prince Paul Anton Esterházy, dated May 1, 1761, is printed in English translation in Robbins Landon, *Haydn,* p. 41.

10. Quoted by Harold C. Schonberg, *The Lives of the Great Composers* (rev. ed., New York, 1981), p. 80.

11. A. C. Dies, *Biographische Nachrichten von Joseph Haydn* (Vienna, 1810); quoted in Robbins Landon, *Haydn,* p. 93.

12. Quoted in H. C. Robbins Landon, *Mozart: The Golden Years* (New York, 1989), p. 14.

13. Ibid., p. 15.

14. Charlotte Moscheles, *Life of Moscheles: With a Selection from His Correspondence* (1873); quoted in Norman Lebrecht, *The Book of Musical Anecdotes* (New York, 1985), p. 55.

15. Franz Xaver Niemetschek, *Life of Mozart,* trans. Helen Mautner, with an introduction by A. Hyatt King (London, 1956).

16. *Wiener Realzeitung,* July 11, 1786; quoted in Robbins Landon, *Mozart,* p. 163.

17. See *Reminiscences of Michael Kelly* (London, 1826), vol. 1, p. 257.

18. *Memoirs of Lorenzo Da Ponte,* trans. Elisabeth Abbott (New York, 1929, rpt. 1967), p. 174.

19. Robbins Landon, *Mozart,* pp. 170–71.

20. Niemetschek, *Life of Mozart.*

21. Georg Nikolaus Nissen, *Biographie W. A. Mozarts nach Originalbriefen* (Leipzig, 1828).

22. See *Memoirs of Lorenzo Da Ponte.*

23. For discussion of the Masonic aspects of *Die Zauberflöte,* see Robbins Landon, *Mozart,* chapter 12.

THE GOLDEN AGE OF ITALIAN OPERA

1. See *Lettere di G. Rossini,* ed. G. Mazzatinti with F. and G. Manis (Imola, 1902), pp. 325–27. The letter was later released to the press.

2. *Illustrated London News,* March 5, 1892.

3. See Richard Osborne, *Rossini* (1986; rpt. Boston, 1990), p. 124.

4. The greatest enterprise of the Fondazione Rossini is the ongoing preparation and publication of *Edizione critica delle opere di Giachino Rossini,* ed. Philip Gossett, Bruno Cagli, Alberto Zedda (Pesaro, 1979–).

5. Velluti created the role of Arsace, prince of Persia, in Rossini's opera *Aureliano in Palmira* (1813) at La Scala, Milan.

6. Edmond Michotte, *Souvenirs: Une soirée chez Rossini à Beau-Séjour (Passy), 1858* (1910), trans. Herbert Weinstock (New York, 1968, rev. 1982), p. 109.

7. See Osborne, *Rossini,* p. 154n.: "It may have been Wagner's sense of outrage at a medieval knight being given the music of a street-vendor which prompted him to parody 'Di tanti palpiti' in the Tailors' Song in Act 3 of *Die Meistersinger.*"

8. Ibid., p. 26.

9. Ibid., pp. 152, 232.

10. Translation by Henry Pleasants; quoted in William Weaver, *The Golden Century of Italian Opera: From Rossini to Puccini* (London and New York, 1980), p. 19.

11. *Lettere di G. Rossini,* p. 321.

12. Quoted by Weaver, *The Golden Century of Italian Opera,* p. 55. As with so much else in the story of nineteenth-century opera, I am indebted to Weaver's detailed narrative of this episode in chapter 5 of his book.

13. Ibid.

14. Ibid., p. 62.

15. Ibid., p. 94.

16. Ibid.

17. Ibid., p. 97.

18. Quoted in Charles Neilson Gattey, *Queens of Song* (London, 1979), p. 34. Velluti was singing the title role in Meyerbeer's *Il crociato in Egitto* (The Crusader in Egypt). In a letter to Francesco Pezzi dated July 10, 1825, Meyerbeer reported that the opposition of the first-night audience was not directed at Velluti's talent, "but rather at his person because a portion of the audience considered it improper and immoral to allow a *castrato* to appear on the stage. Velluti remained calm and did not let himself be shaken by the murmurs and whistles"; quoted in Heinz and Gudrun Becker, *Giacomo Meyerbeer: A Life in Letters,* trans. Mark Violette (Portland, Ore., 1989), p. 38.

19. See Henry Pleasants, "How High the G's in *Figaro,*" *Music and Musicians,* December 1969.

20. See H. Sutherland Edwards, *The Prima Donna* (1888; rpt. New York, 1978), vol. 1, pp. 158–60.

21. Michael Scott, *The Record of Singing* (Boston, 1993), vol. 1, p. 12.

22. Quoted in Weaver, *The Golden Century of Italian Opera,* p. 19.

23. Quoted in Edwards, *The Prima Donna,* vol. 1, p. 246.

24. See Michotte, *Souvenirs.*

25. Quoted in Gattey, *Queens of Song,* p. 63.

26. Quoted in Weaver, *The Golden Century of Italian Opera,* p. 83.

27. Giuseppe Verdi, autobiographical narrative related to Giulio Ricordi, October 19, 1879; printed in Arthur Pougin, *Giuseppe Verdi: An Anecdotic History of His Life and Works* (Milan, 1887).

28. Ibid.

29. Ibid.

30. Ibid.

31. C. V. Stanford, article in the *Daily Graphic* (London), January 14, 1893; quoted in Frederick J. Crowest, *Verdi, Man and Musician: His Biography, with Especial Reference to His English Experiences* (London, 1897). An almost

identical version of the story was related by Annie Vivanti, an English-born singer and poet, in her recollections of meetings with Verdi, published in 1892; see Jane Phillips-Matz, *Verdi: A Biography* (Oxford, 1993), p. 708.

32. Verdi used the phrase "years in the galleys" in a letter to Clara Maffei of May 12, 1858. In the context of the letter, Verdi would appear to be using the phrase to describe his entire career up to that time.

33. Quoted in Harold Rosenthal and John Warrack, *The Concise Oxford Dictionary of Opera* (Oxford, 1985, rpt. 1990), p. 288.

34. Giuseppe Verdi, letter to Antonio Somma, 1853, quoted in Andrew Porter, "Verdi," in *The New Grove Masters of Italian Opera* (New York, 1983), p. 218; the Porter essay was first published in Stanley Sadie, ed., *The New Grove Dictionary of Music and Musicians* (20 vols., London, 1980).

35. See Phillips-Matz, *Verdi*, p. 141.

36. Giuseppe Verdi, letter to Cesare de Sanctis, May 26, 1854; quoted in Phillips-Matz, *Verdi*, p. 329.

37. See Porter, "Verdi," p. 256.

38. Quoted in Phillips-Matz, *Verdi*, p. 586.

39. Boito wrote the line in *All'arte italiana*, a "sapphic ode, with glass in hand," which he improvised at a party to celebrate the success of Franco Facci's opera *I profughi fiamminghi* at La Scala; quoted in *The Verdi-Boito Correspondence*, ed. Marcello Conati and Mario Medici, trans. William Weaver (Chicago, 1994), p. xix.

40. "Verdi at the Time of Otello," *The Musical Times* 28 (1887).

41. See Howard Taubman, *Toscanini* (New York, 1951).

42. See Francis Toye, *Verdi: His Life and Works* (London, 1931, rpt. 1962), p. 187.

43. Ibid., p. 201.

44. Giuseppe Verdi, letter to Felice Varesi, January 7, 1847; quoted in Phillips-Matz, *Verdi*, p. 199.

45. Giuseppe Verdi, letter to Count Opprandino Arrivabene, December 27, 1877; quoted in Phillips-Matz, *Verdi*, p. 641.

46. See Giulio Gatti-Casazza, *Memories of the Opera* (2nd ed., New York, 1969).

GERMAN ROMANTIC OPERA

1. Otto Jahn, *W. A. Mozart* (Leipzig, 1905); quoted in George R. Marek, *Beethoven: Biography of a Genius* (London, 1969, rpt. 1974), p. 75.

2. Quoted in Marek, *Beethoven*, p. 362.

3. Anton Schindler, *The Life of Beethoven,* ed. Ignaz Moscheles (London, 1841). This was one of three letters from Beethoven published by Bettina Brentano (1785–1859) after the composer's death. She claimed that he had written them to her between 1810 and 1812. Brentano knew Goethe well (she was the recipient of his *Correspondence with a Child*), but she may be an unreliable witness where Beethoven is concerned. The autograph of this particular letter has never been found.

4. Lucy Poate Stebbins and Richard Poate Stebbins, *Enchanted Wanderer: The Life of Carl Maria von Weber* (New York, 1940), p. 162. Weber first had the idea for *Der Freischütz* in 1811, when he read the story in the newly published *Gespensterbuch* by Johann August Apel and Friedrich Laun. Caroline Brandt, who would eventually become his wife, was one of the singers Weber recruited in 1813 for the German Opera in Prague, of which he had been made conductor.

5. Carl Maria von Weber, review of Hoffmann's *Undine*, 1816; quoted in Harold Rosenthal and John Warrack, *The Concise Oxford Dictionary of Opera* (Oxford, 1985, rpt. 1990), p. 229.

6. Quoted in Rosenthal and Warrack, *The Concise Oxford Dictionary of Opera*, p. 470. Spohr's *Faust* was given its premiere in 1816 at the German Opera in Prague, where Weber was the conductor.

7. See John Chancellor, *Wagner* (London, 1978), p. 88.

8. Richard Wagner, *Mein Leben* (1911), reissued as *"My Life" by Richard Wagner*, "in an authorized translation from the German" (London, 1963), p. 276.

9. Ibid., p. 44.

10. Johanna Wagner (1826–1894) was the adopted daughter of Wagner's brother, Albert. She joined the Dresden Opera as a seventeen-year-old and had great success as Agathe in *Der Freischütz*. Soon after creating the *Tannhäuser* Elisabeth, she went to Paris to study with Pauline Viardot, sang briefly with the Hamburg Opera (1849), and then became a member of the court opera in Berlin (1850–61). Thereafter, married to a district judge, she became a well-known actress on the dramatic stage, but she returned to opera in 1876 to sing one of the Valkyries and one of the Norns in the first complete performances of the *Ring* at Bayreuth.

11. Richard Wagner, letter to Theodor Uhlig, 1851; quoted in Rudolph Sabor, *The Real Wagner*, with a foreword by Wolfgang Wagner (London, 1987), p. 265. Uhlig had been a violinist in Wagner's Dresden orchestra; he remained a devoted friend and correspondent.

12. See Chancellor, *Wagner*, p. 110.

13. Ibid., p. 154.

14. Quoted in Wilfrid Blunt, *The Dream King: Ludwig II of Bavaria* (London, 1970), p. 54.

15. See Kurt Wilhelm, *Richard Strauss: An Intimate Portrait*, trans. Mary Whittall (New York, 1989), pp. 24–26.

16. Richard Wagner, *Preface to the Poems of the Stage Festival Play "Der Ring des Nibelungen"*; quoted in Sabor, *The Real Wagner*, pp. 267–68.

17. Quoted in David Hamilton, ed., *The Metropolitan Opera Encyclopedia: A Comprehensive Guide to the World of Opera* (New York, 1987), p. 303.

18. Quoted in Sabor, *The Real Wagner*, p. 271.

19. Ludwig II, letter to Wagner, August 12, 1876; quoted in Chancellor, *Wagner*, p. 253.

20. *Die neue freie Presse* (Vienna), August 18, 1876.

21. Lilli Lehmann, *Mein Weg* (Leipzig, 1913); quoted in Sabor, *The Real Wagner*, p. 273.

22. Richard Wagner, "Das Judentum in der Musik," *Neue Zeitschrift für Musik* (Leipzig), August 1850. Wagner wrote the article under the pseudonym "K. Freigedank."

23. Quoted in Wilhelm, *Richard Strauss*, p. 52.

OPERA IN NINETEENTH-CENTURY PARIS

1. See William L. Crosten, *French Grand Opera: An Art and a Business* (New York, 1948), p. 87.

2. See Winton Dean, Denis Libby, and Ronald Crichton, "Romantic Opera, France," in Stanley Sadie, ed., *History of Opera*, The New

Grove Handbooks in Music series (London, 1989), p. 195.

3. Quoted in Crosten, *French Grand Opera*, p. 13.

4. For a discussion of Napoleon's (considerable) involvement in opera, see Patrick Barbier, *Opera in Paris, 1800–1850: A Lively History*, trans. Robert Luoma (Portland, Ore., 1995), pp. 6–15.

5. Ibid., p. 73.

6. Quoted in Crosten, *French Grand Opera*, p. 113.

7. Ibid., p. 13.

8. Théophile Gautier, Preface to *Mademoiselle de Maupin* (Paris, 1835).

9. Quoted in Crosten, *French Grand Opera*, p. 17.

10. Louis Véron, *Mémoires d'un bourgeois de Paris* (Paris, 1856–57).

11. Margot Fonteyn, *The Magic of Dance* (London, 1980), p. 213.

12. See Harold Rosenthal and John Warrack, *The Concise Oxford Dictionary of Opera* (Oxford, 1985, rpt. 1990), pp. 99–100.

13. Charles de Boigne, *Petits mémoires de l'Opéra* (Paris, 1865), p. 86.

14. Hector Berlioz, *Mémoires* (Paris, 1878), vol. 2, p. 91.

15. A comforting, but perhaps misplaced, hope. In her *Opera for Lovers* (Singapore, 1997, p. 44), written with Conrad Wilson, Kiri Te Kanawa recalls singing at La Scala in 1979: "I had this man coming to my dressing-room door, saying he was Signor So-and-So and asking what I was going to pay him, and I thought: 'I don't think I can deal with this.'. . . I knew that the claque was part and parcel of the Italian opera scene and most singers complied, but I had heard of some dreadful occasions when performers had refused to pay and were left standing at the curtain call without applause or—worse still—being booed. Naturally, I paid up. . . . So there I was with this man from the claque, wondering if I was paying him enough. In the end, they did applaud me. I got perfectly wonderful applause, but all I could think was: 'I paid for this.' "

16. Printed in Rosenthal and Warrack, *The Concise Oxford Dictionary of Opera*, p. 100.

17. See Crosten, *French Grand Opera*, p. 71.

18. Ibid., p. 56.

19. Gustav Kobbé, *Complete Opera Book* (1922), 10th edition, revised and edited by the Earl of Harewood (London, 1987), p. 579.

20. *La Revue musicale* 4 (1829), p. 332; quoted in Crosten, *French Grand Opera*, p. 41.

21. See Dale Harris, "A Composer by Moments," *Opera News* 55 (May 1991), p. 27.

22. *The Memoirs of Hector Berlioz*, trans. David Cairns (New York, 1956), chapter 59.

23. The remark was made by W. J. Henderson. First in the *New York Times* (1887–1902), then in the *New York Sun* (1902–37), Henderson was one of New York's most powerful, and conservative, music critics.

24. Quoted in Harold C. Schonberg, *The Lives of the Great Composers* (rev. ed., New York, 1981), p. 345.

25. Ibid.

26. Clara Leiser, *Jean de Reszke and the Great Days of Opera* (New York, 1934, rpt. 1970).

27. See Michael Scott, *The Record of Singing* (Boston, 1993), vol. 1, p. 63.

28. See Emma Eames, *Some Memories and Reflections* (New York, 1927).

29. Herman Klein, *Musicians and Mummers* (London, 1925), p. 111.

30. Eames, *Some Memories and Reflections*, p. 51.

31. During the early years of the century, Lionel Mapleson (nephew of the impresario, "Colonel" Mapleson) installed his cumbersome machine on the paint bridge of the Metropolitan stage and made live recordings of many of the greatest singers of the era, including Jean de Reszke and Emma Calvé—until one day the machine toppled off the bridge in the middle of a performance, just failing to end the distinguished career of the Wagnerian soprano Johanna Gadski.

32. W. J. Henderson, quoted in Scott, *The Record of Singing*, vol. 1, p. 34.

33. James Huneker, quoted in Scott, ibid.

34. Quoted in Schonberg, *Lives of the Great Composers*, p. 471.

OPERA OF THE PEOPLE

1. Quoted in Michael Beckerman, "Notes on Rusalka," *Stagebill* (The Metropolitan Opera, New York), November 1993.

2. Erik Chisholm, *The Operas of Leoš Janáček* (Oxford, 1971).

3. Karel Kovařovic (1862–1920) wrote a number of forgotten operas (of which the first, *The Bridegrooms*, was the one Janáček reviewed so ruthlessly); but he also wrote one, *The Dogheads* (1897), that had a considerable success in Prague.

4. See Boris A. Pokrovsky and Yuri N. Grigorovich, *The Bolshoi: Opera and Ballet at the Greatest Theater in Russia*, trans. Daryl Hislop (New York, 1979), p. 8.

5. See John Warrack, *Tchaikovsky* (London, 1973), p. 16.

6. Quoted by Harold C. Schonberg, *The Lives of the Great Composers* (rev. ed., New York, 1981), p. 357. Tchaikovsky described Glinka as: "A dilettante who played now on the violin, now on the piano, who composed colorless quadrilles and fantasies on stylish themes, who tried his hand at serious forms (quartet, sextet) and songs, but composed nothing but banalities in the taste of the '30s—who suddenly in the thirty-fourth year of his life produces an opera which by its genius, breadth, originality and flawless technique stands on a level with the greatest and most profound music!"

7. Ibid., p. 368.

8. Ibid., p. 364.

9. Ibid., p. 369.

10. Quoted by Gustav Kobbé, *Complete Opera Book* (1922), 10th edition, revised and edited by the Earl of Harewood (London, 1987), p. 710.

11. Tchaikovsky first saw *Carmen* at the Opéra-Comique, Paris, on March 15, 1876, just a year after the opera's premiere and nine months after Bizet's death. Célestine Galli-Marié was still playing the title role. According to Tchaikovsky's brother, Modest, it was Galli-Marié's performance that inspired in Tchaikovsky "an almost unwholesome passion for this opera."

12. The 1879 premiere of *Eugene Onegin* was given, at Tchaikovsky's own insistence, by students of the Moscow conservatory. The opera gained no real currency in Russia until the staging at the Imperial Opera in St.

Petersburg in 1884.

13. Quoted in Warrack, *Tchaikovsky*, p. 254.

14. N. A. Rimsky-Korsakov, *Autobiography: My Musical Life* (1909), trans. Judah A. Joffe (New York, 1942); quoted in David Brown, "Pyotr Il'yich Tchaikowsky," *The New Grove Russian Masters* (New York, London, 1980), p. 224. Rimsky-Korsakov wrote: "How odd that, though death was the result of cholera, there was free access to the requiems. I remember that Verzhbilovich . . . kissed the body on the face and head."

15. See A. A. Orlova, "Tchaikovsky: The Last Chapter," *Music and Letters* 62 (1981), p. 125.

16. See Ronald Harwood, *All the World's a Stage* (London, 1984), p. 236.

AN INTERLUDE WITH REALISM

1. The best and most substantial narrative of the Ricordi-Sonzogno rivalry is in William Weaver, *The Golden Century of Italian Opera: From Rossini to Puccini* (London and New York, 1980, pbk. 1988), chapters 10 and 11.

2. About the origins of *I pagliacci*, Gustav Kobbé wrote: "Although the *motif* [of the story] is an old one, this did not prevent Catulle Mendès (who himself had been charged with plagiarizing, in *La femme de Tabarin*, Paul Ferrier's earlier play, *Tabarin*) from accusing Leoncavallo of plagiarizing *Pagliacci* from *La femme de Tabarin*, and from instituting legal proceedings to enjoin the performance of the opera in Brussels. Thereupon Leoncavallo, in a letter to his publisher, stated "that during his childhood at Montalto a jealous player killed his wife after a performance, that his father was the judge at the criminal trial—circumstances which so impressed the occurrence on his mind that he was led to adapt the episode for his opera. Catulle Mendès accepted the explanation and withdrew his suit"; Gustav Kobbé, *Complete Opera Book* (1922), 10th edition, revised and edited by the Earl of Harewood (London, 1987), p. 554.

3. See Ethan Mordden, *Opera Anecdotes* (New York, 1985, pbk. 1988), p. 67.

4. Rosa Ponselle and James Drake, *Ponselle: A Singer's Life* (New York, 1982), p. 102.

5. See Weaver, *The Golden Century of Italian Opera*, p. 196.

6. Puccini had three close friends at the Milan conservatory: Mascagni, Buzzi-Peccia, and Tirandelli. In a description of a visit they made to Ghislanzoni, librettist of *Aida*, Tirandelli wrote: "Signor Ghislanzoni put us all in one big room with four beds. Mascagni was always up to some trick or other, so as soon as we were in bed and the light out, a shoe came flying through the air! Puccini, not to be outdone, threw two shoes, and Buzzi-Peccia followed suit with the candlestick, and I let fly pieces of the bedroom china until everything in the room nearly was in the air and the cry of all was 'Si salvi chi può' (save himself who can)! We were not out of our teens, you see!"; quoted in George Martin, *The Opera Companion* (London, 1962, pbk. 1984, rpt. 1990), p. 596.

7. See *Letters of Giacomo Puccini*, ed. Giuseppe Adami (New York, 1974), p. 67.

8. Mordden, *Opera Anecdotes*, p. 72. The conductor Giorgio Polacco (1874—1960) was the source of the story.

9. See Michael Scott, *The Record of Singing* (Boston, 1993), vol. 1, p. 187.

10. See Kobbé, *Complete Opera Book*, p. 979n.

11. See *Letters of Giacomo Puccini*, p. 140.

POPULAR MUSICAL THEATER

1. The patent had originally been granted by Charles II to the playwright and actor Sir William D'Avenant (1606—1668), rumored to be the natural son of Shakespeare. The patent specified that it could be passed on to D'Avenant's "heirs, exors, admors and assigns." Hence it came to John Rich's father, Christopher, a notoriously mean manager of the Drury Lane Theater. Christopher Rich built the Lincoln's Inn Theatre in 1714, but he died the same year, leaving both the new theater and the patent to his twenty-two-year-old son.

2. Jonathan Swift reported the facts: "The Duke of Bolton has run away with 'Polly Peachum,' having settled £400 a year on her during pleasure, and upon disagreement £200 more"; quoted in H. Sutherland Edwards, *The Prima Donna* (1888, rpt. New York, 1978), vol. 1, p. 31.

3. An alternative derivation sometimes cited for the word *vaudeville* is *voix de ville*, but the more likely derivation is *vaux* (valleys) *de Vire*. It appears to have been first used to describe songs composed by Olivier Basselin, a fifteenth-century cloth fuller who lived in Vire.

4. Offenbach later wrote: "I felt sure that something could be done for young composers like myself who were being kept waiting in idleness. In the Champs-Élysées, there was a little theater to let, built for the physicist Lazaca but closed for many years. I knew that the Exhibition of 1855 would bring many people into this locality. By May, I had found twenty supporters and on June 15th I secured the lease. Twenty days later, I gathered my librettists and I opened the 'Théâtre des Bouffes-Parisiens' "; quoted in Peter Gammond, *Offenbach: His Life and Times* (rev. ed., Neptune City, N.J., 1981), p. 37.

5. Rossini declined Offenbach's invitation to attend a rehearsal of *Il signor Bruschino*, which Offenbach had adapted, in French, as *Don Bruschino*. "I have let you do what you want to do, but I have no intention of being your accomplice," wrote Rossini. See Gammond, *Offenbach*, p. 140.

6. Ibid., p. 54.

7. Ibid, p. 91.

8. Ibid., p. 76.

9. The tragedy had a silver lining for *Die Fledermaus*. The role of Dr. Falke was promptly taken over by Alexander Girardi, who was well on the way to becoming the greatest star of the golden age of Viennese operetta.

10. See Richard Trauber, *Operetta: A Theatrical History* (New York, 1983, pbk. 1989), p. 120.

11. Ibid., p. 125.

12. *Die Czárdásfürstin*, renamed *The Riviera Girl*, was given an entirely new libretto by P. G. Wodehouse and Guy Bolton for its New York premiere in 1917. It flopped—but then, 1917 was not a good year to be playing a

German work in New York.

13. Quoted in Harold Rosenthal, *Opera at Covent Garden: A Short History* (London, 1967), p. 54.

14. Ibid., pp. 31–34.

15. See Diana Bell, *The Complete Gilbert and Sullivan* (Secaucus, N.J., 1989), p. 31.

16. The *Bab Ballads* first appeared in the magazine *Fun* between 1866 and 1871. Gilbert (whose parents had called him "Bab" as a child) illustrated them himself with line drawings.

17. See Bell, *The Complete Gilbert and Sullivan*, p. 102.

18. Ibid., p. 15.

19. See Trauber, *Operetta*, p. 324.

20. See Michael Scott, *The Record of Singing* (Boston, 1993), vol. 1, p. 151.

21. Quoted in Martin Mayer, *The Met: One Hundred Years of Grand Opera* (London, 1983), p. 102.

22. Ibid., p. 82.

23. Ibid., p. 151.

24. See Hollis Alpert, *The Life and Times of "Porgy and Bess": The Story of an American Classic* (New York, 1990), p. 45.

25. Ibid., p. 17.

ON THE TWENTIETH CENTURY

1. Quoted in Kurt Wilhelm, *Richard Strauss: An Intimate Portrait,* trans. Mary Whittall (New York, 1989), p. 100.

2. See Harold Rosenthal, *Opera at Covent Garden: A Short History* (London, 1967), p. 97: Covent Garden's representation of John the Baptist's head is described as "a dish of blood which, we are reliably told, looked like a dish of pink blancmange."

3. Quoted in Harold Rosenthal and John Warrack, *The Concise Oxford Dictionary of Opera* (Oxford, 1985, rpt. 1990), p. 71.

4. Quoted in Wilhelm, *Richard Strauss*, p. 100.

5. Quoted in M. Lawton, *Schumann-Heink: The Last of the Titans* (New York, 1928, rpt. 1977).

6. Quoted in Wilhelm, *Richard Strauss*, p. 121.

7. Covent Garden introduced electric lighting in 1892, the Metropolitan in 1893. Since about 1875, most theaters, using gas lighting, had been able partially to lower the house lights during a performance so that the audi-torium was half-darkened. Electric lighting enabled them to darken the auditorium completely.

8. See Adolphe Appia, *Die Musik und die Inszenierung* (1899); quoted in Rosenthal and Warrack, *The Concise Oxford Dictionary of Opera*, p. 14.

9. Quoted in John Percival, *The World of Diaghilev* (London, 1971, rev. 1979), p. 76.

10. See *Letters of Giacomo Puccini*, ed. Giuseppe Adami (New York, 1974), p. 140.

11. Quoted in Wilhelm, *Richard Strauss*, p. 143.

12. Ibid., p. 144.

13. Ibid., p. 142.

14. Ibid.

15. Quoted in Harold C. Schonberg, *The Lives of the Great Composers* (rev. ed., New York, 1981), p. 495.

16. Debussy amplified this thought: "The blossoming of the voice into true singing should occur only when required. A painting executed in grey would be the ideal"; see *Debussy on Music: The Critical Writings of the Great French Composer,* ed. Françoise Lesure and Richard L. Smith (New York, 1977); quoted in Schonberg, *The Lives of the Great Composers*, p. 471.

17. Both Debussy's commissions from the Metropolitan Opera were to be based on stories by Edgar Allan Poe: *Le diable dans le beffroi* (1902–11) and *Le chute de la maison Usher* (1908–17). Part of the latter was recon-structed by W. Harwood and performed in New Haven, February 1977.

18. Harlow Robinson, *Sergei Prokofiev: A Biography* (New York, 1987), p. 145.

19. Rosenthal and Warrack, *The Concise Oxford Dictionary of Opera*, p. 431.

20. *Pravda*, January 28, 1936.

21. These events were sparked off by the premiere, in November 1947, of an opera called *The Great Friendship* by an otherwise forgotten Georgian composer, Vano Muradeli. His opera was intended to be a tribute to his homeland, Georgia, which was also Stalin's native land. Stalin, looking for an excuse to stamp his authority on Soviet culture, announced that he was displeased by "historical inaccuracies" in the opera. He quickly ordered Andrei Zhdanov, the Politburo spokesman for cultural ideology, to prepare the central committee's resolution.

22. Quoted in Schonberg, *The Lives of the Great Composers*, p. 602.

23. Quoted in Wilhelm, *Richard Strauss*, p. 124.

24. Ibid., p. 81.

25. See John Piper, "Designing for Britten," in David Herbert, ed., *The Operas of Benjamin Britten* (London, 1979), p. 5.

26. Quoted in Eric Crozier, "Staging First Productions," in Herbert, ed., *The Operas of Benjamin Britten*, p. 28.

27. Benjamin Britten, acceptance speech at the first Aspen Award ceremony, July 31, 1964; quoted in George Martin, *The Companion to Twentieth-Century Opera* (New York, 1979, pbk. 1989), p. 95.

28. See Wilhelm, *Richard Strauss*, p. 129.

29. Charles Osborne, *The World Theater of Wagner: A Celebration of One Hundred Fifty Years of Wagner Productions* (Oxford, 1982), p. 152. The *Götterdämmerung* chorus in 1876 numbered twenty-nine.

30. See Geoffrey Skelton, *Wagner at Bayreuth: Experiment and Tradition*, foreword by Wieland Wagner (London, 1965), p. 151.

31. Ibid., p. 165.

32. Ibid., pp. 159–60.

33. Quoted in Rosenthal and Warrack, *The Concise Oxford Dictionary of Opera*, p. 538.

34. Quoted in Charles Neilson Gattey, *Queens of Song* (London, 1979), p. 151.

35. W. J. Henderson, writing in the New York Sun; quoted in Gattey, *Queens of Song*, p. 194.

36. See John Frederick Cone, *Oscar Hammerstein's Manhattan Opera Company* (Norman, Okla., 1966), p. 145.

37. Plácido Domingo, "Enrico Caruso," in David Hamilton, ed., *The Metropolitan Opera Encyclopedia: A Comprehensive Guide to the World of Opera* (New York, 1987), p. 78.

38. Michael Scott, *The Great Caruso* (Boston, 1989), pp. 47–48.

39. Michael Scott, *The Record of Singing* (Boston, 1993), vol. 1, p. 17.

40. Ibid., vol. 2, p. 248.

Suggestions for Further Reading

Histories of Opera

For many years, Donald J. Grout's *A Short History of Opera* (New York, 1947) dominated the field. Originally published in two volumes, it was revised in one volume in 1965, and was further revised by W. H. Williams in 1988. Leslie Orrey's *Opera: A Concise History* (London, 1972) is now available in a 1987 paperback edition, updated by Rodney Milnes, that is succinct and well illustrated.

Two more recent books, both of them scholarly and authoritative, contain extended essays by a number of leading authorities. *The Oxford Illustrated History of Opera* (Oxford and New York, 1994), edited by Roger Parker, is sumptuously illustrated. *History of Opera* (London, 1989), a publication in the New Grove Handbooks in Music series, is edited by the incomparable Stanley Sadie.

For opera's place in the much larger context of world drama, Ronald Harwood's *All the World's a Stage* (London, 1984) is recommended. It is the companion volume to his thirteen-part television series for the BBC.

Opera Synopses

Plots of individual operas, and commentaries on them, are contained in innumerable books, most of them concentrating on the most popular and frequently performed works. But there are two much more substantial publications that deserve to be in every operagoer's library, not just because of the synopses they contain, but because they tell the reader so much about the history of opera.

Gustav Kobbé's *Complete Opera Book* was first published shortly after Kobbé's untimely death in 1918. The work has been revised, extended, and updated several times, and is now available in its eleventh edition as *The New Kobbé's Opera Book*, edited by the Earl of Harewood and Antony Peattie (London and New York, 1997). It contains synopses, essential information, and some musical commentary for about five hundred operas.

The Viking Opera Guide (Harmondsworth, 1993) is larger and more recent. Edited by Amanda Holden with Nicholas Kenyon and Stephen Walsh, it contains synopses of more than fifteen hundred operas by some eight hundred composers. It claims to encompass the complete operatic works of every composer represented. More than one hundred experts have contributed to it, and it includes important information that is generally hard to find: running times, recommended recordings (audio and video), and available editions.

Reference Works

Dictionaries and encyclopedias of opera come in all sizes. One of the most compact, and authoritative, is *The Concise Oxford Dictionary of Opera* (Oxford, 1995), available in paperback. Originally compiled by Harold Rosenthal and John Warrack in 1964 and revised in 1985, it has since been further revised by Warrack and Ewan West. Warrack and West are also the authors of the more substantial *Oxford Dictionary of Opera* (Oxford, 1992). The most extensive reference in English is the four-volume *New Grove Dictionary of Opera* (London, 1992), edited by Stanley Sadie—a work that is unlikely to be superseded for many years to come.

In German, Italian, and French, there are encyclopedias of theater and opera conceived on even larger scales: *Die Musik in Geschichte und Gegenwart* (14 vols., Kassel and Basel, 1949–68); *Enciclopidia dello spettacolo* (10 vols., Rome, 1951–66); and *Histoire générale illustrée du théâtre* (5 vols., Paris, 1931–34), by Lucien Dubech.

Annals of Opera, 1597–1940, by Alfred Loewenberg, first published in 1947, is available in a version revised by Harold Rosenthal (London, 1978). Its information on local premieres of operas is invaluable.

Dictionaries of music and musicians are widely available; every reader has a favorite. For the present author, *The Concise Baker's Biographical Dictionary of Musicians* (7th rev. ed., New York, 1984), by Nicolas Slonimsky, is a bible.

General Reading

Some books have no peers. Patrick J. Smith's *The Tenth Muse: A Historical Study of the Opera Libretto* (London, 1971) is one such. So is Joseph Kerman's *Opera as Drama* (1952; rev. ed., Berkeley, 1988). So, from an earlier generation, are Ernest Newman's *Opera Nights* (London, 1943) and *More Opera Nights* (London, 1954).

The central characters in the story of opera are, quite properly, the composers. Harold C. Schonberg's *The Lives of the Great Composers* (rev. ed., New York, 1981) succeeds in bringing them to life in essays of barely a dozen pages each. Some of the most useful full-length biographies are noted below.

Historical Periods
Seventeenth Century

The origins and early years of opera are traced by Frederick W. Sternfield in *The Birth of Opera* (Oxford, 1993). An equally fascinating, and very scholarly, account is contained in *Divining the Powers of Music* (New York, 1986), by Ruth Katz. *Jacopo Peri: His Life and Works* (London and New York, 1989) is by Tim Carter, and there is now an English translation of Paolo Fabbri's 1985 biography *Monteverdi* (Cambridge, 1996). *The New Monteverdi Companion* (Oxford, 1985) is edited by Denis Arnold and Nigel Fortune. *Cavalli* (London, 1978), by Jane Glover, is the only full-length biography of that composer, but Thomas Walker's entry on Cavalli in *The New Grove Dictionary of Music and Musicians* (20 vols., London, 1980), reprinted in *The New Grove Italian Baroque Masters* (London, 1984), is, in itself, a major contribution. In her great study *Opera in Seventeenth-Century Venice: The Creation of a Genre* (Berkeley, 1991), Ellen Rosand has given a marvelously detailed description of the first golden age of opera. This may be read in conjunction with the briefer and very colorful account in *Five Centuries of Music in Venice* (London, 1991), by H. C. Robbins Landon and John Julius Norwich. For Lully and his French contemporaries, *The New Grove French Baroque Masters* (London, 1986) is an authoritative source, particularly the essay by J. R. Anthony on Lully himself. A fascinating account of French opera audiences in the age of Louis

XIV is given in an article by Georgia Cowart entitled "Of Women, Sex, and Folly: Opera Under the Old Régime" (*Cambridge Opera Journal*, November 1994). In 1995, the three-hundredth anniversary of Purcell's death generated a plethora of books and articles, none better than Robert King's *Henry Purcell* (London, 1995).

EIGHTEENTH CENTURY

There are two indispensable source documents for eighteenth-century opera: Charles Burney's *The Present State of Music in France and Italy* (London, 1773) and Charles de Brosses's *Lettres historiques et critiques sur l'Italie* (Paris, 1799). Of the many modern works that complement and add to these, Nicholas Anderson's *Baroque Music: From Monteverdi to Handel* (London, 1994) is particularly useful, and Marita McClymonds's article on *opera seria* in *The New Grove Dictionary of Opera* is invaluable. Edward Dent's biography *Alessandro Scarlatti* (London, 1905) was revised and brought up to date by Frank Walker in 1960. The dean of Handel studies is Winton Dean; of his many works, *The New Grove Handel* (London, 1980), with A. Hicks, is very accessible. So is Christopher Hogwood's *Handel* (London, 1984). French opera of this period is very well served by J. R. Anthony's *French Baroque Music* (London, 1978). Alfred Einstein's *Gluck* (London, 1936) was reprinted in a new edition in 1964.

Mozart's German and Italian contemporaries have a disappointingly small bibliography. *New Grove Dictionary of Opera* is generally the best and most convenient source for composers such as Hiller, Paisiello, Martín y Soler, Cimarosa, and Salieri. Haydn, on the other hand, has a literature of his own; *Haydn: His Life and Music* (London, 1988), by H. C. Robbins Landon and David Wyn Jones, and *Haydn: A Documentary Study* (New York, 1981), by Robbins Landon, are two of the most useful works. As for Mozart, books about him are practically an industry. Daniel Heartz is one of the most distinguished scholars; his *Mozart's Operas* (Berkeley, 1990) is a worthy alternative to Edward Dent's 1913 book with the same title. Here again, H. C. Robbins Landon has been a prolific contributor; his *Mozart: The Golden Years* (New York, 1989) is particularly recommended, for both its use of original

sources and its illustrations. Kurt Honolka's *Papageno: Emanuel Schikaneder, Man of the Theater in Mozart's Time* (1984; Portland, Ore., 1990), translated by Jane Mary Wilde, is an unusual and compelling work. The essential source documents for Mozart are, of course, his own letters, available in the three-volume *Letters of Mozart and His Family,* translated and edited by Emily Anderson (1938; 3rd ed., London, 1985). *The Memoirs of Lorenzo Da Ponte,* translated by Elizabeth Abbot (New York, 1929, rpt. 1967), may be unreliable as history, but they are great fun.

NINETEENTH CENTURY: ITALIAN

There is no better survey of nineteenth-century Italian opera than William Weaver's *The Golden Century of Italian Opera: From Rossini to Puccini* (London and New York, 1980; pbk. 1988). The biographies of the five principal composers of the period from *The New Grove Dictionary of Music and Musicians* are helpfully reproduced in a single paperback, *The New Grove Masters of Italian Opera* (London, 1983). Stendahl's *Life of Rossini,* translated and annotated by Richard N. Coe (Seattle, 1970), still makes good reading, but it needs to be studied alongside a more recent and more objective work, such as Richard Osborne's *Rossini* (London, 1986, rev. 1993). John Rosselli's *The Life of Bellini* (Cambridge, 1997) is a welcome, and highly readable, study, both complementing and supplementing Herbert Weinstock's more substantial *Vincenzo Bellini: His Life and Operas* (London, 1972). Donizetti's biographies include two useful English-language works: *Donizetti and the World of Opera in Italy, Paris and Vienna* (London, 1964), by Herbert Weinstock, and *Donizetti and His Operas* (Cambridge, 1982), by William Ashbrook.

Like Mozart and Wagner, Verdi has a huge literature of his own. The latest, longest, and best-informed account is Mary Jane Phillips-Matz's *Verdi: A Biography* (Oxford, 1993), but no serious student of nineteenth-century Italian opera should be without Julian Budden's three-volume *The Operas of Verdi* (1973; rev. ed., Oxford, 1992). Much light is thrown on the mature Verdi and his way of working by his correspondence with Boito, originally published as *Carteggio Verdi-Boito* (Parma, 1978), edited by Marcello Conati and

Mario Medici, and now translated as *The Verdi-Boito Correspondence* (Chicago, 1994) by William Weaver.

Puccini's correspondence is equally revealing. Much of it can be found in *Letters of Puccini* (New York, 1974), edited by Giuseppe Adami, translated by Eva Makin, revised and introduced by Mosco Carner. The letters are also put to good use by Vincent Seligman in *Puccini Among Friends* (New York, 1938). The standard biography is still Mosco Carner's *Puccini: A Critical Biography* (London, 1958; rev. 1974).

NINETEENTH CENTURY: GERMAN

German nineteenth-century opera is dominated by Wagner, but there are useful books about some of his predecessors. Beethoven may have written only one opera, yet his influence was enormous: George R. Marek tells the story well in *Beethoven: Biography of a Genius* (London, 1969, rpt. 1974). The standard work on Weber is John Warrack's *Carl Maria von Weber* (London, 1968, rev. 1976). Equally useful are Clive Brown's *Louis Spohr* (Cambridge, 1984) and Dean Palmer's *Heinrich August Marschner: His Life and Stage Works* (Ann Arbor, 1980).

Richard Wagner's autobiography, *Mein Leben,* breaks off in 1864, when he received Ludwig's summons to Munich. Privately printed for his friends, it was not made publicly available (and then only in an abridged edition) until 1911. The suppressed passages were made public in 1929–30, and a definitive edition based on the original manuscript was finally published in 1963. It is available in an authorized English translation (London, 1963). Books about Wagner proliferate, many of them written from an ideological point of view. The best of them (almost always the least ideological) must include Barry Millington's *Wagner* (2nd ed., London, 1992); John Chancellor's *Wagner* (London, 1978); and John Culshaw's brief and lively *Wagner: The Man and His Music* (New York, 1978). The greatest achievement in writing about Wagner, however, still belongs to Ernest Newman. His *Wagner Nights* (London, 1949) provides an intricate and detailed commentary on the music and drama of the operas, while his towering *Life of Richard Wagner* (4 vols., London, 1933–47) is the work of a great music critic who was also a fine scholar; it is available in paperback (Cambridge, 1976). A good deal of fascinating material is contained in *The Dream King: Ludwig II of Bavaria* (London, 1970), by Wilfred Blunt. There are many books about Bayreuth, but few better than Geoffrey Skelton's *Wagner at Bayreuth: Experiment and Tradition* (London, 1965) and the much more recent *Bayreuth: A History of the Wagner Festival* (New Haven, 1994), by Frederic Spotts.

Nineteenth Century: French

There can be no better account of the upheavals in the cultural life of France during the Revolution than in Simon Schama's *Citizens: A Chronicle of the French Revolution* (New York, 1989). Narrower in its compass, but more directly related to developments in opera, is Emmet Kennedy's *A Cultural History of the French Revolution* (New Haven, 1989). The scandals and glories of the half century that followed the Revolution are recounted in Patrick Barbier's *Opera in Paris, 1800–1850: A Lively History* (1987), translated by Robert Luoma (Portland, Ore., 1995). William L. Crosten's *French Grand Opera: An Art and a Business* (New York, 1948) is equally lively and full of interesting detail. Firsthand sources for this period include *Giacomo Meyerbeer: A Life in Letters* (1983; Portland, Ore., 1989), by Heinz and Gudrun Becker, translated by Mark Violette. *The Memoirs of Hector Berlioz* have been translated and edited by David Cairns (London, 1969). Cairns has also written a fine biography of the composer, *Berlioz: The Making of an Artist* (London, 1989). Other useful biographies of composers include *Bizet* (2nd ed., London, 1975), by Winton Dean, and *Jacques Offenbach* (London, 1980), by Alexander Faris. Much useful material about Gounod and his contemporaries may be found in *Second Empire Opera: The Théâtre Lyrique, Paris, 1851–1870* (London, 1981), by T. J. Walsh.

Nineteenth Century: Russian and Central European

Each of the national operas of Eastern and Central Europe has a growing literature of its own. *Czech Opera* (Cambridge, 1988) is by John Tyrrell; he has also written *Janáček's Operas: A Documentary Account* (London, 1992). John Clapham is the author of both *Smetana* (London, 1972), and *Antonín Dvořák, Musician and Craftsman* (London, 1966). Studies of Polish and Hungarian opera in the English language are hard to come by: "East Central Europe: The Struggle for National Identity," by Jim Samsom, in *The Late Romantic Era* (London, 1991), is one source; Gerald Abraham's *Essays on Russian and East European Music* (Oxford, 1985) is another. Russian opera has much better coverage. Short biographies of the principal composers have been adapted from *The New Grove Dictionary of Music and Musicians* and reprinted as *The New Grove Russian Masters* (2 vols., New York, 1986). Among several good biographies of Tchaikovsky is John Warrack's *Tchaikovsky* (London, 1973, rev. 1989).

Twentieth Century

Twentieth-century opera has accumulated an enormous literature of its own. The many different publications from *The New Grove* are almost always the most reliable and objective authorities. There are several good books about Richard Strauss, including Norman del Mar's biography *Richard Strauss* (3 vols., London, 1962–72) and William Mann's *Richard Strauss: A Critical Study of the Operas* (London, 1964). Works on Puccini and Janáček have been mentioned above. Arnold Schoenberg and his music are explored in *Schoenberg*, by Charles Rosen (1975; rpt., Chicago, 1996). Mosco Carner's *Alban Berg: The Man and the Work* (New York, 1975, rev. 1983) is an accessible one-volume account, as is Harlow Robinson's *Sergei Prokofiev* (New York, 1987). Stravinsky is well served by Stephen Walsh's *The Music of Stravinsky* (London, 1988) and Eric Walter White's *Stravinsky* (London, 1966, rev. 1979). Benjamin Britten has a lengthy bibliography of his own: Humphrey Carpenter's *Benjamin Britten: A Biography* (London, 1992) is the most recent and the most detailed book about him, and there is much useful material in *The Operas of Benjamin Britten* (London, 1979), edited by David Herbert, which includes contributions from many of Britten's closest collaborators.

Many, if not most, modern stage directors have written their own accounts of their work. Interesting, and generally more objective, accounts include *The Music Theatre of Walter Felsenstein* (London, 1991), edited by P. P. Fuchs, and *Wieland Wagner: The Positive Sceptic* (London, 1971), by Geoffrey Skelton. Tom Sutcliffe's *Believing in Opera* (London, 1997) is a fascinating, impassioned, and firsthand study of the staging of opera between 1972 and 1996; among many controversial but deeply held views, it includes the ultimate attack on the use of supertitles.

Singers

Henry Pleasants's *The Great Singers* (New York, 1966, rev. 1981) is a standard work. It may be complemented by J. B. Steane's *Singers of the Century* (Portland, Ore., 1996), which contains short profiles of fifty of the twentieth century's outstanding singers. An important and scholarly work, going all the way back to 1600, is John Rosselli's *Singers of Italian Opera: The History of a Profession* (Cambridge, 1992). One category of that profession is presented in *The Castrati in Opera*, by A. Heriot (London, 1956). Michael Scott's *The Record of Singing* (2 vols., London, 1977, 1979, rev. 1993), which will eventually extend to four volumes, is a critical review of recordings made by opera singers from the invention of the gramophone up to the end of the 78-RPM era, around 1951. In *The American Opera Singer* (New York, 1998), Peter G. Davis has written a wonderful account of American singers from the early nineteenth century to the present that is, in itself, a history of opera in America. As for individual singers, biographies abound (so do autobiographies, but they are generally less reliable and often less interesting). Particularly rewarding biographies include *Maria Malibran* (London, 1987), by April Fitzlyon; *The Great Caruso* (New York, 1988), by Michael Scott; *Callas* (London, 1974), by John Ardoin and Gerald Fitzgerald; *Mary Garden* (Portland, Ore., 1997), by Michael R.T. B. Turnbull; and *Rosa Ponselle: A Centenary Biography* (Portland, Ore., 1997), by James A. Drake. An unusual, and very moving, account of one of the greatest of nineteenth-century singers can be found in *The Great Tenor Tragedy: The Last Days of Adolphe Nourrit as Told (Mostly) by Himself* (Portland, Ore., 1997), edited by Henry Pleasants, translated by Henry Pleasants and Richard R. Pleasants. The cult of the prima donna has been extensively explored in print, nowhere more entertainingly than in Charles Neilson Gattey's *Queens of Song* (London, 1979).

Index

Note: Page numbers in *italics* refer to illustrations.

PHOTO CREDITS